The bust of John Clare by Henry Behnes Burlowe, 1828.

A RIGHT TO SONG

BY THE SAME AUTHOR:

North Bank Night (*Chatto & Windus*)
Portrait of the Fen Country (*Robert Hale*)
A Man in Winter (*Chatto & Windus*)
Four Seasons in Three Countries (*Robert Hale*)
The Solitary Landscape (*Gollancz*)
Call It a Summer Country (*Robert Hale*)
The Dark Music (*Annakin Fine Arts*)

A RIGHT TO SONG

The Life of John Clare

Edward Storey

Photographs by John Baguley

METHUEN

For
Marian, Hugh and Renate,
who had patience –
and
in memory of Leslie Tait,
who had faith

First published in Great Britain 1982 by
Methuen London Ltd
11 New Fetter Lane, London EC4P 4EE

British Library cataloguing in publication data:
Storey, Edward
A right to song.
1. Clare, John, *1793–1864*
2. Poets, English—19th century—Biography
I. Title
821′.7 PR4453.C6

ISBN 0-413-39940-0

Filmset in Monophoto Baskerville by
Northumberland Press Ltd, Gateshead
Printed and bound in Great Britain by
Richard Clay (The Chaucer Press) Ltd,
Bungay, Suffolk

I have always thought it to be of little consequence in the case of the creative artist, whether his natural surroundings are of great beauty or appalling ugliness . . . the real significance of an environment lies in its effect on the mind and imagination of the artist.

Charles Causley (from the Introduction
to *Twenty-five Poems* by Hamdija Demirović)

Contents

List of Illustrations

Acknowledgements

Any present-day biographer of John Clare must feel abundantly grateful to those earlier scholars who did so much pioneer work on the manuscripts and the facts of the poet's life. I think especially of the late Edmund Blunden and remember fondly the few occasions we sat and had 'Clare-talk'. I also express my debt to the late J. W. and Anne Tibble who encouraged me and whose own work on the subject has been of inestimable value, even though we differ on interpretation. Similarly I acknowledge my thanks to Eric Robinson and Geoffrey Summerfield whose editorship over the last twenty years has done so much to restore the original texts and give a deeper understanding of Clare's method of writing.

This book owes much to many people whose patience, enthusiasm, expertise and good sense helped me through the first difficult drafts. I thank especially Mr Bob Woodings who persuaded me to rethink my approach; Mrs Frances Shirley Bridger who cast a kind but critical eye over the early stages of the work; Miss Mary Liquorice of Peterborough City Central Library, whose eagerness to search for answers to my questions was often an inspiration; Mr George Dixon, Honorary Librarian of Peterborough Museum Society, who was always able to put his hand on any book I needed to consult; the Very Reverend Archdeacon of Oakham, Bernard Fernyhough, who made access to some parish records easier than it would have been; Mr Sidney Lawrence Young for first-hand information about the houses used as asylums at High Beach by Doctor Matthew Allen; and Mrs Jean Pemberton for the benefit of her study of Clare's personality and family background.

I am also indebted to the Curator of Peterborough Museum and Art Gallery for access to the collection of Clare manuscripts there (and for permission to reproduce one of them); to the Northampton Central Library and its catalogue – compiled by David Powell; to Miss Rosemary Dunhill and Miss Jacqueline Minchinton, archivists at Delapre Abbey

Records Office, for their replies to questions and for keeping an eye open for any relevant documents; Miss Margaret Grainger for her catalogue of the Peterborough Collection; to the staff of the British Museum Manuscript and Reading Rooms; the Rector of Helpston and the Vicar of Glinton for checking parish registers; the Headmaster and staff of Oundle School for discovering some previously unpublished Clare poems and for allowing me to quote from them; and I gratefully acknowledge assistance from the Arts Council of Great Britain during the first year of researching this work.

Acknowledgements to several works by other authors which I have quoted in this volume are recorded in the appropriate footnotes but I would single out *The Critical Heritage* by Mark Storey (no relation); *The Idea of Landscape and Sense of Place in the Poetry of John Clare* by John Barrell; and *The Making of the English Landscape* by W. G. Hoskins.

For the illustrations I would like to thank John Baguley – an indefatigable photographer who trod every step of the way; Peterborough City Museum and Oundle School for permission to reproduce manuscripts; Northampton Central Library for permission to photograph and reproduce the Behnes Burlowe bust of Clare; Mrs Dorothy Ward of Clare Cottage, Helpston, Mrs J. Waterworth, Woodcraft Castle, and Mr and Mrs Sutton of Northborough for allowing us to photograph their homes, and especially Mr Joseph Goddard for letting me know of his recently discovered portrait of Clare by G. B. Berry and for allowing me to be the first to use it in print for the purpose of this publication.

Finally, one needs tolerant friends as well as scholars and experts to see a task such as this through to the end, so I particularly extend my gratitude to Mrs Marian Edmunds, who shared my discovery of Clare thirty-five years ago; the late Mr Leslie Tait, who gave me my first opportunity to do something about it; and my wife, Angela, who read the final draft and prevented fewer errors than there might have been.

E.S.

Peterborough 1979–82

Textual Note

The texts of Clare's writings have always presented a problem and, until there is a definitive edition of the whole, will continue to do so. Although original manuscripts have been consulted wherever possible, some compromise is inevitable on the poetry and prose already in print. Earlier editors have frequently been known to change their minds – which is not surprising when one is faced with some of Clare's manuscripts, as they were often copied out several times and used for other poems. I have usually gone for the latest interpretation, using Clare's spelling and punctuation – or lack of it. Occasionally I have left a space in the prose where there should have been a fullstop and in a few instances have supplied an apostrophe in 'I'm', 'I'd', 'we'll' or 'she'll' where the meaning would otherwise have been temporarily confusing. If any words have been inserted to make sense of a phrase those words are in squared brackets.

Clare's own spelling was not always consistent and he was often careless in leaving out letters when he knew how the words should be spelt. Where he had several ways of spelling a certain word I have used the correct one. In the early days he usually missed out the letter 'l' from words like 'could' and 'would' but spelt them correctly later on. I have left them as he left them. Invariably he spelt the word 'rhyme' as 'ryhme'; 'recollections' as 'reccolections'; and persisted in putting the 'i' before the 'e' in words such as 'deceive' and 'receive'. Quite often he left out the letter 'h' from 'where' and if this was likely to lead to misunderstanding I have again put the letter in squared brackets.

But all these idiosyncrasies are soon overcome and acceptable, and ought not to spoil the appreciation of what he had to say. To amend all would take an age and also be unnecessary. Clare was usually able to make himself understood and the freshness of vision is what matters.

For the use of copyright material I offer my sincere thanks to Dr Eric Robinson and the late Mrs Anne Tibble.

Footnotes

In a work of this nature footnotes are inevitable and tend to pepper the page with their constant intrusions. I have, therefore, tried to keep them out of the way as much as possible by placing them at the end of the book where they can be used as reference, or ignored.

I would like to think that the narrative of the book is adequate and continual without them, and that their purpose is solely for those readers who wish to seek for more than what appears on the page and who need to know the source of each quotation and statement.

Introduction

1

For many years John Clare has been a tempting subject of curiosity to biographers, mainly because of the unfortunate – and sometimes peculiar – circumstances of his life. He might have suspected that in his own case this would have been so, for he expressed his distrust of biographers and considered that most of what they wrote was 'a parcel of lies'.

In recent years, however, a more serious attempt has been made to get his puzzling life into perspective by bringing a deeper understanding to the vast quantity of poetry which he produced.

It may still be confusing, especially to readers coming to him for the first time. On the one hand there has been the tendency to see Clare as nothing more than an unlettered, bemused nature-poet from the impoverished peasantry of the nineteenth century, not quite sure of what he was doing or where he was. On the other hand there has been the narrower view of him as an embittered social commentator who chose poetry in which to expose the appalling hardships of the peasant class from which he came.

There is a grain of truth in both arguments but he was certainly much more than either. He was, in many respects, a most remarkable man. In addition to being the finest nature-poet that this country has so far produced, he wrote also some of the best love poetry in the language, some superb narrative poems, and enough excellent prose to prove that he was a genuine, determined writer who believed he had been chosen to write about a landscape and its people as no one else could.

And what a success he made of it. He knew that he had something to say which had not been said before and he worked continually at his craft to perfect his way of saying it. He may not have had the profound thoughts of Wordsworth or the sophisticated skills of Byron, but he had a more observant eye, a fresher imagination, and a talent for the 'visualizing word' which gave his poetry a vitality it has not lost in a hundred and fifty years.

Clare had the most perceptive and original eye which enabled him to use words no other writer would have used. When he speaks of the cart-rut 'rippled with the burden of the rain' or the dandelions that 'closed like painters' brushes when even was', when he writes of the 'crampt horizon [that] now leans on the ground', or describes how 'the sheep unfolded with the rising sun', he involves the reader in each scene and emotion with the sureness of a painter. He makes us look at the familiar with new eyes.

Clare was not a literary freak unaware of what he was doing. He was born with an unusual poetic gift and he made a conscious effort to be the best poet of his time. In many ways he succeeded in that too.

Behind the naïve image – which he sometimes helped to create – was an ambitious man. He could be arrogant as well as humble, angry as well as timid, forthright as well as reserved. He was a very complex man, not an easy person to know during his lifetime and not an easy one to write about now. His life was, as he admitted, full of contradictions.

There are still many questions about his life that are unanswerable. The poems are the safest guide to understanding his personality and even they are full of contradictions. Yet the contradictions are what made the man, and poets frequently give themselves away in their writing more than they realize.

Clare's life was always a search – a search for his own identity, for the truth in nature, for the reality of love and for the existence of immortality. To gain a deeper understanding of his work we have to forget the romantic image of him as 'poor, sad John Clare'. We even have to forget that he was ever a peasant – real or unreal. We have to see him as the man be became – refined, independent of mind, a man out of his time and as solitary in his vision as Van Gogh or William Blake. There has been no other poet like him, nor can there be again.

2

The purpose of this new Life is to offer as complete a picture of the man as present knowledge will allow. It reassesses his marriage to Martha (Patty) Turner, questions his relationship with Mary Joyce, and considers his attitudes to both patronage and the opinions of his day. It also hopes to widen the appreciation of his work.

Clare was a realist as well as a romantic. The madness which eventually overtook him was only part of his life. The important years which led up to his isolation in a lunatic asylum belong to the villages of Helpston and Northborough on the edge of the Great Fen. Without those few years he spent in Northborough, for instance, there would not have been the great poems he produced in middle-age.

Although he was undoubtedly a 'poet of place', this biography aims to show that he was far less parochial than is frequently assumed and that he was a universal poet who speaks more vibrantly to our own times than he did to the nineteenth century. It supports his 'right to song' and his place among the immortals.

Not everyone will agree with that claim now any more than they have done in the past, but it is a considered one. Clare has always had his critics as well as his admirers. *The Nonconformist* of February 1873 declared, 'He is a sweet singer, but a singer of the second class only.' Some fifty years later, Edmund Gosse said of him in *The Sunday Times* of 23 January 1921, 'His poetry is like honey and water, the water is pure and the honey is Hymettan, but the brew is desperately thin. There is not one startling felicity, one concentrated ray in the whole body of his work. It is clean and delicate but tiresomely monotonous and, above all, the spirit is diluted.'

Gosse renewed his criticism three years later, again in *The Sunday Times* (5 October 1924), when he said, 'Clare had no thought . . . no intellectual basis. He was a camera, not a mind . . . let any unprejudiced lover of verse compare Clare's "Ode to the Skylark" with either Shelley's or Wordsworth's and he must confess that the Northamptonshire stanzas belong to a lower order of inspiration.'

Assuming that he meant 'The Skylark' (for there is no Ode as such) which appeared in *The Rural Muse* (1835) and was reprinted in *Poems Chiefly from Manuscript* (1920) – which were the poems under review – then he failed to see how much more accurate Clare's poem was than those of either Wordsworth or Shelley.

Larks were not just ethereal birds to Clare, rising out of some romantic landscape to sing to the poet alone. They were, in his wild heaths and open fields – especially at that time – as common as hedge-sparrows. Until the early years of this century there was a regular trade in lark-snaring, or *hingling*, as it was called in some parts of the fens. Larks were netted in their hundreds and sent to London for those select eating-houses where lark-pie was featured as a delicacy. Although Clare was appalled at any cruelty in nature, he would have seen the larks as belonging very much to earth as well as to heaven. They were only part of a much greater celebration, part of the countryman's daily experience. His poem is, far from belonging to a 'lower order of inspiration', a splendid piece of observation, of knowledge and reasoning:

> The rolls & harrows lie at rest beside
> The battered road & spreading far & wide

Above the russet clods the corn is seen
Sprouting its spirey points of tender green
Where squats the hare to terror wide awake
Like some brown clod the harrow failed to break
While neath the warm hedge boys stray far from home
To crop the early blossoms as they come
Where buttercups will make them eager run
Opening their golden caskets to the sun
To see who shall be first to pluck the prize
And from their hurry up the skylark flies
And oer her half formed nest with happy wings
Winnows the air – till in the clouds she sings
Then hangs a dust spot in the sunny skies
And drops & drops till in her nest she lies
Where boys unheeding past – neer dreaming then
That birds which flew so high would drop agen
To nest upon the ground where any thing
May come at to destroy had they the wing
Like such a bird themselves would be too proud
And build on nothing but a passing cloud
As free from danger as the heavens are free
From pain & toil – there would they build & be
And sail about the world to scenes unheard
Of & unseen – O were they but a bird . . .

These rhymed couplets are far from being monotonous. The lines run on so skilfully that the verse-form does not hinder the natural flow of the scene being described, but rather helps towards its continuous movement. Clare's images, too, come from an intimate knowledge of the bird's hovering and its relationship with the toils of man below as 'oer her half formed nest with happy wings' she 'winnows the air'. It is not a perfect poem – few of Clare's poems are – and it contains examples of one of his common weaknesses, that of repetition. But it is a poem of thought, of involvement and suspense, with a greater quality than just sweet charm. The bird's ethereal exaltation is there but only because of its existence with the rest of nature, with the rolls and harrows, the clods, hares, buttercups and schoolboys of the poet's daily world. It tells us something about Clare too. He needed not only distance but also a slow time-scale against which to place his own view of the agelessness of that living world in which Man, like everything else, is only a small but significant part, lasting no longer than the simple cowslip that 'shall come when Kings and empires fade and die/And in the closen as Time's partners lie/As fresh two thousand years as now.'[1]

Not all the critics have been as hard on Clare. There have been several, particularly in the twentieth century, who have recognized his talent and praised his genius for its true worth. H.J. Massingham was right when he said, 'He was unique because he solved his own special problem in his own way, and he solved it partly because of his peculiar advantages in inheriting a racial tradition in pastoral poetry and in possessing a native genius in close relationship with the soil.'[2]

Others who have appreciated this uniqueness include J. Middleton Murry, Edmund Blunden, Robert Graves and Geoffrey Grigson. Each has brought his own individual understanding to Clare's work, making it possible for others to continue a difficult and complex task. J.W. and Anne Tibble, Eric Robinson and Geoffrey Summerfield, James Reeves and Mark Storey, have also contributed greatly to establishing Clare as an important poet in English literature.

3

If Clare did not trust biographers – and he has had several since Frederick Martin published his *Life* in 1865 – why another? As a contradiction of his wish that no one should write a life of him, he did say:

> I would not that my being all should die
> & pass away with every common lot
> I would not that my humble dust should lie
> In quite a strange & unfrequented spot
> By all unheeded & by all forgot
> With nothing save the heedless winds to sigh
> & nothing but the dewy morn to weep
> About my grave far hid from the worlds eye
> I feign would have some friend to wander nigh
> & find a path to where my ashes sleep
> Not the cold heart that merely passes bye
> To read who lieth there but such that keep
> Past memories warm with deeds of other years
> & pay to friendship some few friendly tears[3]

To give him that remembrance, and to understand more of what he achieved, we shall have to go back to the beginning, to that place and that family out of which he came.

But, before doing so, the question 'Why another biography?' has to be more fully answered. There is, it is true, not a great amount of new material to present – though previously unknown poems have come to light during the last few years (see p. 111) and this volume draws on correspondence which has not been used before. There is also the fascinating portrait of Clare by G.B. Berry which appears in print for the first time – a portrait drawn by a fellow inmate at Northampton Lunatic Asylum (known there as George Duval Berry).

The biographies by Frederick Martin, J.W. and Anne Tibble, June Wilson, and the many long biographical essays on all aspects of Clare's work, have each in their way been an adequate account of the man's life as an introduction to his poetry. But, equally, in each of them there has been something missing. Clare the man has 'got off the hook', he has escaped the final interrogation, and may do so again. He was an elusive, many-sided man, and the temptation has been to present only one side of him. Some of the earlier portraits have shown him as a nice, innocent, unfortunate dreamer lost in the diminishing countryside of a forgotten England, a man who received unnecessarily hard blows from fate. Part of Clare's personality fits that kind of description, but he was (as already suggested) a proud, stubborn, blunt man always struggling to overcome fate; a man desperately trying to discover who he was; a man who wanted to achieve distinction almost at any price.

Contrary to some beliefs, Clare was, and remains a fine landscape poet who not only wrote of his world in miniature, but who also took in those vast sweeps of that fenland countryside which spread itself before him 'like a richly coloured map'.

As we shall see, no one has written of that land and its great skies with such variety or originality. In fact, Clare wrote about two landscapes – the gentle, wooded countryside of Northamptonshire and Rutland, and the flat, bleaker land of South Lincolnshire and the fens. Together they provided him with the two different worlds which mirrored his own dual personality and fortunes.

At last Clare has now reached the position where he can be considered primarily as a *poet*, without any excuses or concessions being made for him. The importance of any Life is to hasten the reader back to the work under discussion. The poems are what matter. Clare is his own best advocate.

Since I have spent the whole of my life in his own country, on the edge of the fens and within a stone's throw of his two villages – knowing them both long before expansion came to change them – perhaps he at least will forgive me if I attempt to 'keep past memories warm' and pry into *his* life for the sake of his poetry.

E.S.

Peterborough 1982

1
The Claim

1

John Clare was not an ordinary man and certainly not an ordinary poet. He came near to greatness and, but for an accident of birth, might have been thought of more often as a great poet. Equally, but for that accident, he might not have been heard of as a poet at all. The epitaph on his tomb – *A poet is born not made* – is only half the truth. Clare was born with a rare gift, but talent of itself is not enough. Its rewards have to be earned and his lifelong concern was to make himself a better poet.

With his natural, creative imagination – his painter's eye and musician's ear – he might have found expression in either of those arts. But words were what he loved above all, and the mastery of them was the only apprenticeship he chose to serve. Fortunately both art and music were able to serve his craft as a poet.

In some ways Clare was too gifted and never totally able to focus all his creative energy on the perfecting of his poetry. He was too prolific in his output and rarely had the critical help he needed to select the good from the mediocre at the source of inspiration. Few good poets have written so badly, or so well. Anyone looking for perfect poems in his work will be disappointed. But, because his poetry strangely transcends perfection, we have a record of human struggle and discovery, of awareness and achievement, which moves one to curiosity and admiration.

He was a solitary man. He lived in a land where the horizons were, and are, a long way off. He needed that space and distance for the journey he had to make. Slowly, from what he wrote, we can see that man emerge from obscurity into recognition; from raw peasantry into nobility of mind and presence.

The 'accident' which made his journey so difficult was the event which led to his being born to peasant parents in a simple cottage in the once undistinguished village of Helpston, Northamptonshire.[1] But, had he not been born under those conditions and in that place, we would not have had the poetry which isolates him from all other poets. Mystery surrounds Clare's ancestry and it is difficult to believe that Helpston could have produced this talent without the chance visit of the roving Scottish schoolmaster – John Donald Parker – the man who was, unknowingly, to be the grandfather of such an original poet.

As important as Helpston is in our appreciation of Clare's poetry, it is, nevertheless, necessary partly to forget that he was 'a Northamptonshire poet'. To think of him as such is to reduce his poetic stature to the parochial and to enclose his mind within county boundaries. He wrote surprisingly little about his native county, and most of what he did write came from his memories of the pre-enclosure years of his childhood. He took as much inspiration from Lincolnshire, parts of Cambridgeshire and especially Rutland. In fact, he created his own private world out of those neighbouring counties and made that world what he wanted it to be – *universal*. He peopled it with the characters, birds and flowers he needed for his poetry. The poetry came first. The fields, labourers and village life became his subjects.

Clare may have come in part from the peasant class but he was not a true peasant poet. The peasantry helped to make him the poet he was but it also shares in the responsibility for his destruction. The contradictions in his life begin with his ancestry. The elusive John Donald Parker, who was Clare's grandfather, must take some of the credit, or blame, for those contradictions. Without knowing more about him, we cannot know all we would like to know about the man who, a generation later, was to surprise the country with his unique gift.

We have only to look at the Henry Behnes Burlowe bust of the poet to see that Clare was no ordinary man. There is a nobleness and dignity about the features which defy the coarse, rustic image. Charles Lamb did not call him 'Princely Clare' for nothing, nor would the young ladies of London's society have thought him a nobleman in disguise if they had not been impressed by his physical bearing – short though he was. Clare uses the word *refined* about himself on several occasions and, from his writings, we can recognize as much pride as humility. He was humble only before Nature.

He has been seen too often as a misfit in English literature, a peasant versifier who did not really know what he was doing, a timid, melancholy man without wit or humour. His letters will deny this. So will those friends he was to know in London – Coleridge, Lamb, De Quincey, H.F. Cary and J.H. Reynolds, all of whom were to later pen their own descriptions of him.

On his first visit to London, to celebrate the publication of *Poems Descriptive of Rural Life and Scenery* (1820), he sat for the portrait-painter

William Hilton; had a setting of one of his poems sung at Drury Lane by Madame Vestris; and met some of his wealthy patrons. Helpston seemed a long way off and he understandably found it difficult to choose between the two. He needed, and enjoyed, both. This duality in his nature was to be repeated in several other ways. He was often a man of two minds.

Clare was neither freak nor *Wunderkind*. He was no one's protégé. All the recognition and success he achieved during his lifetime was earned and he deserved far more than the age would allow. He may have been underprivileged in some things but he was very fortunate in others. He did not get the degree of education from which he would have benefited so much – for he had a good mind – but he did receive a better education than any other boy of his social class in the village. He also inherited from his unlettered parents a tradition of folklore that would have been the envy of scholars from any class. While most village boys were scratching away on smelly slates, Clare was allowed the use of paper and to borrow books from the personal library of the village schoolmasters at Glinton. When he was not at school he turned the Helpston cottage into a classroom, or spent hours listening to the old sages and story-tellers of the village. If anyone was likely to write some of the best country poetry in the language then it was Clare. He had every opportunity, every encouragement and the necessary gifts from nature to articulate his feelings.

But it all went wrong, or appeared to during his lifetime and, in the end, the expectations were too great for him. He was finally unfortunate, misunderstood and too often alone in trying to realize his hopes. Because of the pressures upon him to meet those expectations, he sometimes became wasteful of his energies and his talent. He could be extravagant with his emotions and with what money he earned. His personality was self-destructive.

Yet, out of the turmoil of his life, came the poetry of serenity and quiet observation which speaks of a universal need.

2

Talent of itself may not always be enough but, even if it were, it is not always allowed to be itself. Often it is forced to please others, to pander to lesser visions, to satisfy duller minds. Clare came to realize that he was being exploited and fought over by his superiors, but he was unable to take matters into his own hands. Because of his frequent waywardness and unpredictability he failed to win their complete trust. When his poetry did earn money for him, little of it was allowed to find its way into his pockets. It was not poverty but success which made his life so miserable, even among his native woodlands where he sought to rediscover the self he had lost after the brief years of fame and fortune. Once the song had been heard beyond the boundaries of that secret world of his childhood, it was very difficult for the singer to remain untempted by those different horizons again. He knew that he had to prove himself beyond Helpston – not once, but several times.

The struggle between the poetry and the man – between the artist and his audience – did not come out of nothing or cost nothing. It was to cost him his health, his marriage and his happiness. Clare earned his place among the immortals. He knew he would. In 1844, at the age of fifty-one, alone and forgotten in a lunatic asylum, he was to write:

> In every language upon earth
> On every shore, o'er every sea,
> I gave my name immortal birth
> And kept my spirit with the free[2]

3

Clare was not the first English poet to emerge from the peasantry. Ann Yearsley, the Bristol milk-woman, had shown in the eighteenth century that poetry could come from very unexpected sources. Stephen Duck, the Wiltshire thresher (who sadly and ironically drowned in a duck-pond) had proved it by publishing his poem *The Thresher's Labour* in 1730. Robert Bloomfield, the Suffolk shoemaker, published *The Farmer's Boy* in 1800, and there were similar (though less successful) claims from Thomas Brown and Robert Millhouse, the Derbyshire and Nottinghamshire stocking-weavers, and James Woodhouse the cobbler. James Hogg, 'the Ettrick Shepherd', also came from the soil and, as the son of a poor farmer, taught himself to read and write.

There was also the very different talent of Robert Burns who certainly had a better start than Clare and a much wider acceptance. A 'peasant-poet' was a good item on any bookseller's list in the late eighteenth century. By 1831 enough working-class talent had come to light during the previous fifty years for Robert Southey to publish his *Lives and Works of the Uneducated Poets*.[3] The fashion was to last just long enough into the nineteenth century to give Clare his own chance to emerge from the rustic obscurity of Northamptonshire which might otherwise have stifled his voice forever.

He was, however, both fortunate and unfortunate to appear on the scene when he did. Had he not been published in 1820 he might not have been published at all in his lifetime but, because he was published then, his reputation was established for the wrong reason. As it happened his poetry was good enough to survive fashions, prejudices and curiosity value. It nevertheless remained a custom for a long time to think of him as just another unlettered rhymer who had accidentally stepped into the world of literature. Nothing could be further from the truth. He may have missed greatness by the skin of his teeth but he achieved a distinction few others have equalled. He became an important poet, even a distinguished poet. Not everyone has been able to accept his right to such a prominent place in poetry's history but the argument for such a claim is a strong one.

But already the reputation is coming before the man. What of Clare the unknown villager from Helpston? The early descriptions we have of him at the beginning of his writing career show him as a young man in a state of rawness, not too familiar with the customs and refinements of the world he was one day to encounter. A man reticent to speak among strangers, yet not slow to express his opinion when among friends. He admitted that he had a 'timidity that made me very awkward and silent in the presence of my superiors' but was quick to warn his publisher, John Taylor, that he was 'a blunt fellow'.[4]

Edward Drury, who was to become responsible for getting Clare's work published in the first place, wrote to his cousin – John Taylor – on 20 April 1819:

> Clare cannot reason: he writes & can give no reason for using a fine expression or a beautiful idea: if you read poetry to him, he'll exclaim at each delicate expression – 'beautiful!' 'fine!' but can give no reason. Yet he is *always* correct and just in his remarks. He is low in stature – long visage – light hair – coarse features – ungaitly – awkward – is a fiddler – loves ale – likes the girls – somewhat idle – hates work.[5]

Allowing for some exaggeration in Drury's description (and he was often guilty of that), there are aspects of Clare's nature there which are confirmed both by his own words and those of others. The distinguished features shown in the Behnes Burlowe bust may not have been apparent to Drury who, in those early years, was more accustomed to seeing the twenty-six-year-old Clare in his labourer's clothes, unkempt, frequently unshaven, clumsy in the presence of strangers, and certainly fond of a few pints as well as a few girls.

The portrait painted by William Hilton in 1820 shows something of Clare's timidity and apprehension but it cannot be accepted without question, especially given that the artist's friend, Benjamin Hayden, said of Hilton that there was an intellectual and physical feebleness in everything he did. Between the exaggerated coarseness of Drury's description and the romantic impression created by Hilton's portrait is a man whose character was slowly refined with that of his art. Clare and his poetry are inseparable.

Apart from his short stature (not so uncommon in the nineteenth century – and, at five feet high, he was no shorter than Keats), the most important and interesting feature about Clare's appearance was his eyes. Most of the descriptions we have of him make particular reference to his 'bright blue eyes and large head'. An unsigned review in the *Druid Monthly* (1835) recalls, 'the first glance of Clare would convince you that he was no common man, he has a head of highly intellectual character, the reflective faculties being exceedingly well-developed; but the most striking feature is his eye, light blue and flashing with the fire of genius.' The same reviewer also said of him that 'his conversation is animated, striking, and full of imagination'.

4

So much, for the time being, of Clare the man. What of the poet? Because the poetry outlived the man we can draw on opinions of it from over a hundred years and can still read it for ourselves. As we have seen, there was always to be conflict over the quality of Clare's work. But whatever the academic arguments might be, there is in his poetry a richness and an originality for anyone to enjoy. With Clare we can be surprised at the discovery of an unknown flower or the secret song of a bird heard only by those who tread quietly through the undergrowth. He instils into his reader a feeling of reverence. When he walked the meadows he tried to avoid treading on the flowers. When he went into the woods he tried not to disturb a brooding bird, such as the nightingale – 'Hush, let the wood gate softly clap – for fear/The noise might drive her from her home of love.'[6]

Gradually we become aware again of our own relationship with an unspoilt country – that Eden from which Clare makes us feel we have all travelled too far. It is poetry that will call us back repeatedly because it speaks about those values being sought today by sensitive people who do not want to see their world destroyed. There is an immediacy and freshness about his poetry that makes him more like a twentieth-century poet than an eighteenth- or nineteenth-century one. Some of those poems of stark realism, written in his middle years, portray a violence and a cruelty in nature which shocks even today. The hunting of the badger spares us nothing of the passion, noise, panic and, finally, death of that persecuted creature:

> He falls as dead and kicked by boys and men
> Then starts and grins and drives the crowd agen
> Till kicked and torn and beaten out he lies
> And leaves his hold and cackles groans and dies[7]

The fox fares no better when he too is discovered, chased and beaten by the ploughman. Again, the lines jab fiercely, uncompromisingly in their effort to make us feel the animal's pain:

> The ploughman laughed and would have ploughed him in
> But the old shepherd took him for the skin
> He lay upon the furrow stretched and dead
> The old dog lay and licked the wounds that bled
> The ploughman beat him till his ribs would crack
> And then the shepherd slung him at his back. . .[8]

That hard, staccato sound of the word *crack* echoes over the desolate plains of the fen country like a gun-shot. But the old fox was only feigning death. As soon as his pursuers took their eyes off him, 'he started from his dead disguise/And while the dog lay panting in the sedge/He up and snapt and bolted through the hedge.'

This is the precise, economic language that Robert Graves spoke of in *The Crowning Privilege* when writing of Clare's remarkable sense of language: 'He meant what he said, considered it well before he wrote it down and wrote with love . . . Clare never bores, being always precise and economical and relying on patient observation.'[9] It is a simplicity of language which must not be mistaken for naïvety. In many of the poems Clare uses a cinematic technique of cutting dramatically from one scene to another and then zooming in for a telling close-up. And, as always in such poems, he has suspense.

His use of language was not always conventional, but at least he established his own voice and had that natural instinct for what J. Middleton Murry described as 'the visualizing word'.[10] There is no mistaking who wrote:

> The crow goes flapping on from wood to wood
> The wild duck wherries to the distant flood
> The starnels hurry o'er in merry crowds
> And overhead whew by like hasty clouds
> The wild duck from the meadow-water plies
> And dashes up the water as he flies
> The pigeon suthers by on rapid wing
> The lark mounts upward at the call of Spring
> In easy flights above the hurricane
> With doubled neck high sails the noisy crane
> Whizz goes the peewits o'er the ploughman's team
> With many a whew and whirl and sudden scream
> And lightly fluttering to the tree just by
> In chattering journeys whirls the noisy pie

From bush to bush slow swees the screaming jay
With one harsh note of pleasure all the day[11]

That is Clare, with all his weaknesses and strengths, anticipating the shift that twentieth-century poetry was to make from the adjective to the verb in an attempt to convey something beyond the description. It is not a good poem, technically. We have the careless repetition of words like *whew* and *whirl*, the images are built up layer upon layer, and the rhymes are very predictable. But it is a picture of the countryside that no other poet of the age could have written with such authority. There are no nightingales or thrushes in that poem. It is about movement more than sound. There are crows, ducks, starlings, pigeons, cranes, peewits and the magpie, who *flop*, *dash*, *whizz*, *wherry*, *suther* and *swee* over the flat, watery landscape of the fens. There *are* sounds but not the song of the garden or grove. We are once again in the wild, open, untamed countryside where hungry birds *scream* and *chatter*, filling the whole day with their harsh notes. It is a poem that offers the smell of the earth and a breath of East Anglia to a degree that outweighs all flaws. It was this individualistic style of writing which gave Clare his strength and it is easy for us today to see why his vocabulary jarred on ears tuned to softer and more predictable word-music.

Clare's response to the world of nature may not have been the intellectual one that Edmund Gosse would have preferred but it was a physical one that had much more energy and truth. Clare was part of the earth and all that belonged there. He spoke for it as though that were his sole reason for being born. He became one with the flowers, insects, birds, animals, woods and rivers. He was a natural singer whose roots were firmly in the soil even when his wings 'winnowed the air'. He belonged with the daisy and with the sun. He was both rich man and poor man who could say – as he said of the nightingales – 'How curious is the nest no other bird/Uses such loose materials or weaves/Its dwellings in such spots.'[12]

5

Just as you cannot get to know the quiet, secretive lowlands of the fens in a weekend or a season, so you cannot get to know Clare's poetry after just a few readings. He asks that you see his world in his own way, throughout the changing months, customs, loves and experiences of a lifetime. There are few poets better at teaching us how to *see*, or for that matter how to *feel*. His enormous output shows that he was a man who did not timidly touch life, he wrestled with it for over seventy years.

Between his birth at Helpston in 1793 and his death at the Northampton General Lunatic Asylum in 1864 lay a journey few would have the strength to endure or the spirit to survive. It was a journey which, in some ways, knows no end, for out of that gifted, sensitive life comes a figure who is still being jostled by the crowd. It is reassuring to know that there is a growing interest in his work, especially among the young, but there is still a long way to go to make sure that his name is never forgotten or omitted from any list of major poets.

The 'land of shadows' which he eventually entered for those final lonely years must not cloud our appreciation of the whole life which was essentially one of celebration. In those last years he may have cried, 'I am – yet what I am none cares or knows/My friends forsake me like a memory lost',[13] but he was also the poet of 'Those sweet excesses [that] oft will start/When happy feelings cross the mind',[14] the man who could say 'I feel so calm I seem to find/A world I never felt before'.[15]

In his autobiographical poem, 'The Progress of Rhyme', he tells us that his first ambition was to praise poetry and the world out of which poetry comes. For many years he kept that ambition a secret from his neighbours and friends. He feared the 'gibes and vulgar tongue/The curse of the unfeeling throng'.[16] But so sure was he of his calling that he was also able to say 'I felt that I'd a right to song/And sung ...'.

The villagers, indeed, would have thought it a strange claim from one who appeared frail, lazy and aloof from their daily drab existence. To see how they and Clare lived together in that changing landscape around Helpston we now have to go back to days before the name of the poet was ever heard on their lips.

2
The Place

1

Helpston is not a particularly attractive village of ancient charm or fossilized history where the only people to be seen walking about are tourists. It has its visitors, it is true, but for a different reason. It is a pleasant enough place, a mixture of the old and the new, and no doubt much more comfortable now than it would have been in the nineteenth century.

Since the county boundary reorganization of 1974 it has been a village in Cambridgeshire rather than a Cambridgeshire village. Until then it always was – and in some ways always will be – in Northamptonshire, especially when it is spoken of as the birthplace of the poet John Clare.

But, as the preceding pages claim, Clare was more than just a Northamptonshire poet. In more than one sense he stood at the crossroads of the four counties surrounding his village and these have to be kept in mind when discussing the poet's landscape. To the east, and within earshot of the fourteenth-century village cross, can be heard the frequent metallic swish of high-speed trains on their way from London to the north of England and Scotland. Beyond the railway lines and the slender spire of Glinton church the eye can see over thirty miles of the Lincolnshire and Cambridgeshire fens – though 'fens' is a misnomer in these days of efficient drainage and rich black farmlands. To the north the lowlands slowly give way to the wolds, to fields still patterned with dry-stone walls and a brooding suggestion of an earlier Scandinavian dourness. To the west the even more intrusive noise of jet-fighters at a nearby RAF base regularly destroys the sound of bird-song that once helped to make this village a place worth visiting. Between the distractions of railways and flight-paths is the distant throb of heavy traffic on the A1. On the surrounding skyline are the steeples of industry, the cumulus clouds of smoke from sugar-beet factories or cement works. The city of Peterborough is now within easy reach and the busy town of Stamford only minutes away by car. Helpston, sandwiched between the two, is far from being isolated, forgotten, or quiet. And yet it is remembered mainly because of that lover of quietness – John Clare – a poet who made this mixed landscape his own and who remains, as Edmund Blunden said of him, 'the best poet of nature that this country and for all I know any other country ever produced'.[1]

It is important, then, that we try to remap, as well as we can, the world that Clare would have known, to rediscover something of that mixed countryside which inspired more than three thousand poems. Surprisingly, after some skin-deep adjustments, it is still possible to find much of his world. Forget the noise, blot out the rows of pylons from the mind's eye, and the poems will take over. Clare's world has retained many quiet retreats where the wildflowers and birds' nests he wrote about can still be found, where the solitary walks can be retrod, and where the local names have the evocative ring they gained when he first gave his voice to their syllables more than one hundred and fifty years ago – Langley Bush, Emmonsail's Heath, Lolham Brigs, Royce Woods, Cowper Green, Barnack, Maxey, Glinton and Northborough.

The village cross is the most suitable point on which to balance all these places. Helpston itself is not a fen village but built on that ridge between limestone and peat – having the best of both worlds – where wooded uplands dissolve into immense flat, open spaces. Within an eight-mile radius of that cross can be found virtually the whole of Clare's kingdom – the fields where he sat alone, or the lanes where he walked as a boy with Mary Joyce, the places where he lived and worked, and the roads that always brought him back home. Between these landmarks are the streams, spinneys and hedgerows out of which came the imagery and syntax of the poet's private world. When we have seen a heron rise out of the grey, silent mist we can appreciate even more the accuracy of Clare's description of the heron who, from the lake on Emmonsail's Heath, 'Starts slow and flaps his melancholly wing'. When we read of the cart-rut 'rippled with the burden of the rain' or of the sheep that 'unfolded with the rising sun' we are getting the reactions of a man who watched, listened, and recorded intimately the ordinary moments of his life and in doing so made them – and the landscape to which they belonged – extraordinary. For us such moments are still there but made vivid by his poetic vision.

It is not necessary to see for oneself all the remnants of that world in order to appreciate the poetry it produced, though it is not easy to agree with Geoffrey Grigson who said, 'No one will find it very rewarding to visit "John Clare country" instead of visiting and revisiting John Clare's poetry.'[2] The poetry must, of course, come first, but, because of its particular nature, a knowledge of the countryside does help. Such poetry could have come from nowhere else. One of the problems Clare had in gaining an understanding readership (once the initial sensation of his origins had died a predictable death) was that of getting his readers to accept an unfamiliar, even unknown, landscape. It was not the kind of 'nature' with which many of them would have been acquainted and Clare was not the usual kind of topographical poet. The Romantic English landscape of Wordsworth was one which his readers would have known about – if only through paintings. Clare's landscape was unvisited and unsung. Octavius Gilchrist, the Stamford businessman and scholar, who was to befriend and encourage Clare, said of it, 'Fancy, surely can scarcely suggest scenery less fitted for the excitement of picturesque and vivid description than the dank copses and sedgy margins of the fens.'[3]

East of that village cross Clare would have walked slowly down into fen country, much of it at sea-level, some even below sea-level. It was a landscape made up of six hundred thousand acres of mostly wild country, only half-drained for seven or eight months of the year. It was an area known for dangerous floods, penetrating mists, boggy marshes, long dykes, and a race of surly people who preferred outsiders to stay away. For generations it had been a land of wild-fowling, eel-netting, lark-snaring and hunting; a world of snakes, frogs, bitterns and marsh-harriers. The sports and the livelihoods have changed but some things never do. The great skies are still there, the extremes of weather, and the dark soil that hides more mystery than any other. There are times when it is a silent, haunting world where neither the land nor the water will give in to each other. Beyond the fens is the Wash where the grey sea lurks like some ancient beast about to pounce back. In Clare's day a wet winter could isolate villages for weeks:

So moping flat and low our valleys lie
So dull and muggy is our winter sky
Drizzling from day to day with threats of rain
And when that falls still threatening on again
From one wet week so great an ocean flows
That every village to an island grows
And every road for even weeks to come
Is stopt and none but horsemen go from home[4]

The land was won only slowly and often with great bitterness. When Cornelius Vermuyden was appointed by the Gentleman Adventurers in 1630 to drain the fens the local people were so hostile to his plans that they refused to work for him. For twenty years he fought to tame the waters and, to some extent, succeeded; but he never tamed the men. His labour-force was eventually provided by one thousand Scottish prisoners-of-war taken at the battle of Dunbar and five hundred Dutch prisoners captured by Admiral Blake.[5] But draining the fens did not begin or end with Vermuyden. The problem remained and the work has gone on ever since. The annual cost of maintaining the dykes, sluices and relief channels is now measured in millions of pounds. But for that constant protection the land would soon be lost. Clare was to know and love one of the last great undrained stretches of water in the fens – Whittlesea Mere, which he was to declare far more impressive than the River Thames.

Because of the damp climate nearly everyone in Clare's day suffered at some time with the ague – a type of malaria for which brandy and opium were considered the only reliable palliatives until sixty or seventy years ago. As the fens gradually became more effectively drained so the ague died out. The fens can be kept dry now for most of the year because of sophisticated machinery and skilled engineers, and the rich soil is still the most fertile in Europe. The vast fields of potatoes, sugar-beet and cereal crops exist because of the labours of men. Clare knew more of their struggles than their achievements, more of that wildness than its cultivation. The dampness crept up to Helpston, bringing both its complaints and its doubtful remedies.

It was a world to which Clare responded with the same excitement as he did to the more intimate world of a spinney or hedgerow. To the south and west of Helpston he had the gentler landscapes of Rutland and Northamptonshire – modest, uneventful counties with a reputation for squires and spires but, for Clare, interesting mainly because of the wealth of wildflowers, woodlands, heaths and gentle valleys. There the uplands were high enough to be considered locally as hills. The birds were songbirds rather than the coarse-voiced creatures of marsh and flood. And yet, with all its differences, it was a world still near enough to the fens to share many of the same qualities – the sky, light, space, climate and even the stubbornness of its people. It was an ideal compromise for a man whose imagination needed to stretch from the sun's rising to its setting. He could have expanse and hidden seclusion, both offering their own kind of freedom.

From Langley Bush we can still look back over the valley in which Helpston hides itself. Northwards lie those uplands where the distant fields of corn often shine white with ripeness under a summer moon. Nearer are the woods and fields where Clare spent his childhood, places defaced now by quarries and pylons. The heaths and paths around the village created then a world remarkably profuse in wildflowers – which is why Clare became the botanists' poet. The air's stillness then was disturbed only by such sounds as came from thrush, wren, woodlark and nightingale – which is why Clare also became the ornithologists' poet. But it was not only a world of birds, insects and flowers. It was a world of people, history and ancient customs. It was a world to inspire the imagination and the heart – which is why Clare is a universal poet.

Until the poetry of that ever-watching man came to attract the outside world, the village would go on in the sure belief that nothing unusual was ever going to happen there. Change would be imperceptible; events hardly noticed. Days would continue to be a repetition of days. The world would pass it by and few strangers would stay long enough to disturb the placid pattern of its ways. Poetry and enclosure seemed not to threaten a community whose life had remained virtually unaltered since the Middle Ages.

2

Whatever their tasks, for most people in Helpston the day began at four o'clock in the morning. Yawning boys, still rubbing sleep from their eyes, set off to feed the stock or fetch the horses from the common. Young girls added the clank of milk-pails to the sound of men sharpening their scythes. Cocks crew. Cows puffed their misty breath into the air, and geese chattered noisily into the street already patched with cattle-dung. The 'loud-tongued village clock' of St Botolph's church chimed its early hour and suddenly the place was awake with all its smells and noise. The day, like any other, had begun and for that the villagers were grateful. Ploughmen went 'whistling to their toils' and the milkmaid came 'singing from her bed'. Clare was to mention several times the singing that could be heard in the fields, the songs keeping alive the stories and traditions of three hundred years or more. Few of the local people on any such morning in the second half of the eighteenth century could have foreseen the dramatic changes that were to come to their countryside and way of life, particularly with the enforcement of the Enclosure Act of 1809.

Changes had, of course, been happening in its history for a long time. Men had built huts and made fires there nearly three thousand years ago. The Romans too had lived nearby in some splendour. Their armies had marched up over the heath from Durobrivae,[6] along King Street into West Deeping and northwards to Sleaford and Lincoln. A Roman villa, which stood to the east of Heath Road, was occupied up to the second century and was only discovered as late as 1827 by Edmund Artis, the amateur archaeologist and gentleman steward to the Earl Fitzwilliam at Milton Hall. The Saxons also made the village a place of habitation. Legends of their courts at Langley Bush survived to inspire verses by a Helpston inhabitant twelve hundred years later.[7] The Danes too had developed their winter quarters on the edge of the fens into permanent settlements, remembered now in several nearby place-names such as Thurlby, Langtoft and the Deepings.

Helpston, as such, was still without its present name. It was not until after the Norman Conquest, when a stipendiary knight called Sir Helpo was given the rights of the village that the place became known as 'Helpo's Towne'.[8] With a few variations it was an identity it has kept to the present day, the only difference being that in modern spelling the final 'e' has disappeared. From Saxon times a church had been established and soon the village had claimed its feast-days and markets. Half a mile to the west of Helpston once stood the ancient castle and manor of Torpel, a favourite royal retreat during the time of Richard I's crusades, and later of Edward I. His wife, Queen Eleanor, loved the manor and its countryside so much that the king gave it to her. For a time Torpel was known locally as the Queen's Manor and her rides became popular footpaths over the fields for the next two hundred years.[9] By the end of the seventeenth century the great house was in ruins and much of its stone went to build new cottages in Helpston. From that time onwards if kings or queens came to the district they usually stayed with the Exeters at Burghley House near Stamford. During the Civil War a few skirmishes were fought around the village – at Woodcroft Castle and on Cowper Green – but the memory of such events faded and passed into legend as the village went on with its ordinary daily life.

The market cross – an unusual one with a heart-shaped base – was built in the fourteenth century. For generations it became the place where labourers were hired out to farmers, where women sold their eggs and butter, and where children played their games. The shape of the base underlines the power of the religious principles held then. All contracts, agreements, sales, hirings or dealings done there had the unwritten guarantee of being 'sworn by the holy heart of Christ'[10] and no bargain thus made could be lightly broken.

When John Donald Parker – the itinerant Scottish schoolmaster – arrived in Helpston sometime between 1761 and 1764, he would have found a village that had known little change for over three hundred years. Its two streets contained less than a hundred dwellings. Its population of 270 consisted of families who belonged to the soil – ploughmen, threshers, shepherds and labourers, a mostly uneducated people who worked on land owned by Earl Fitzwilliam, the Trollope family of Torpel, or Christ's College, Cambridge.[11] Those who did not work in the fields relied for their livelihood on those who did. Work was seasonal. Corn was an important crop but only marginally more so than turnips, which were then the most popular root crop needed for both cattle and humans. Winter or summer, the villagers' existence depended on the success of their crops. It was not efficient farming. Some of the landowners could see the need for change. The village was surrounded by open fields and heaths on which the people enjoyed their common rights. But the ways of three hundred years ago were not necessarily those needed now to keep the village alive. Harvest failure concerned everyone. The blacksmith, wheelwright, carpenter, stone-mason, shoemaker, butcher and publican knew when harvests were good or when times were bad. They too were only tenants and had their rents to pay. If the crops were poor the villagers were poorer. There was nothing in reserve. It made a long winter hard to endure. Starvation and the workhouse were menacing threats over the cottage hearth. It was not, of course, all gloom. A successful harvest brought its annual rejoicings to the whole village. The ancient rituals were celebrated. The social differences were relaxed in relief and gratitude.

In addition to its houses the village had two or three shops, the forge, two alehouses, the village green with its trees, pond, stocks and market cross, and the church. Most of the houses were built of the local grey stone and roofed with either Collyweston tiles or reed thatch. Apart from the occasional vagabond or journeyman, the villagers saw few people whose history was not already common knowledge in the parish. Tradesmen came from neighbouring villages; people came from other parishes to share in Helpston's feasts and fairs; a few families of gipsies were tolerated on their traditional camping sites at Swordy Well, Langley Bush or Cowper Green; otherwise it was not a place to attract many strangers. If Helpston people wanted a day out they went to Market Deeping or Stamford, rather than Peterborough. The Old Great North Road then passed through the lovely stone town of Stamford and news from London was not long in reaching the provinces. At the inns or markets the villagers would have heard of the century's history being made – the battle of Quebec, the discovery of New South Wales, the expansion of the colonies and the need for more troops to serve in these new countries. They would have heard of the wars in America and the unrest on the Continent. They would have heard too of the effects in England of the many private enclosure acts being introduced on behalf of landowners, of the threats to the common land in their own parish, of rising corn prices and fears of rebellion.

In those pre-enclosure days at Helpston most families – whatever their station – had an understanding relationship with the rest of the community. There was trust and respect, in both directions. The social structure of the village was, on the surface, clear and accepted by all from the lord of the manor down through the local squire, tenant farmer, tradesman and cottager to the labourer. It had always been so. Father's son inherited from father's son the position he was expected to have and, as it was not easy for families to move from one part of the country to another, local loyalties, customs and traditions, remained very strong. The distribution of wealth went a long way towards keeping that pattern of society intact. Landowners could receive up to £2,000 a year in rents alone; a squire £800; farming freeholders £70; and industrious cottagers £35.[12] The land determined the prosperity. It is little wonder that much of the village conversation Clare heard as a boy was about work in the fields, market prices and grazing rights. The most significant threat to life then was the weather. The latter half of the eighteenth century experienced several wet summers. Consequently corn prices rose and labourers' wages fell. The poorer sections of the community suffered most and survival became the major concern. To make sure that destitution would be kept as far from their doors as possible every member of the family worked when they could. While the men and boys laboured in field and barn, the women took to spinning, weaving, or making beer for the local ale-houses, as well as doing the usual household tasks of washing, baking and preserving food for the winter. Farmers' wives then were not exempt from this dual economy. At harvest time women and children were also busy in the fields, especially when carting-time was over and they were allowed to go gleaning. It was not easy work. The sharp stubble would tear the skin on their arms and legs. Even so, if children tired or ran off to play, their mothers would soon threaten a good hiding with a cane hastily made from the twigs of a nearby grey-willow. This cane, Clare was to tell us later, was usually no more than a gesture to underline the words of warning that 'they who in the harvest lye/Shall well deserving in the winter pine'.[13]

John Donald Parker would, then, have found a reasonably settled community when he arrived in Helpston and, as a much-travelled man, would have seen the poverty there as no worse than that which he had seen elsewhere. In many ways it was not as bad. The village had mainly good landlords, good grazing, good markets, and even a compassionate vicar. Helpston provided Clare with the scenes of his greatest childhood happiness.

3
The Family

1

Very little is known about Mr Parker. He was said to have been a Scot by birth, a schoolmaster by profession, and a good fiddle-player by way of an entertainer.[1] He told the villagers that he had travelled on the Continent, that he had seen places they would never even read about. If they could find him lodgings he would educate their children, provide them with music for their merrymakings and offer them advice when it was needed. It all sounds a good bargain but his words would have been received in silence, or with suspicion, at least to begin with. The people were like that, cautious, wary of strangers, slow to make up their minds. Clare was himself to write some years later that Helpston was 'a rum place'. John Donald Parker would have needed all his eloquence and subtle persuasion to convince them that such benefits were necessary to their lives. Maybe he had such a tongue. Perhaps the villagers were, after all, looking for a man like him. Whichever way, he won the day and stayed long enough to run a school in the church vestry, enchant the natives with his fiddle and leave at least one young woman in the village carrying his child.

John Cue of Ufford,[2] who was head-gardener for Lord Manners of Ufford Hall, three miles away, had been Parker's trusted companion in their younger days and was to recall how his friend had been attracted to the girls, particularly the parish clerk's daughter. But when she gave him the news that she was pregnant by him he disappeared and was never seen or heard of again. The parish clerk's daughter's name was Alice Clare. She was about twenty-eight when she started going out with Parker and must have resigned herself to being a spinster until he came along. She may have given herself willingly to Parker, believing that pregnancy would ensure marriage. It was not uncommon in the eighteenth century for couples to have sexual relationships before getting married. Marriage came only when the woman was already far advanced in pregnancy and had proved she could bear children. In England at that time the average age of marriage was twenty-seven.[3] So Alice Clare, at twenty-eight or nine, would have still been hoping to be wife as well as mother. She realized only one of those ambitions.

Unlike some of the local girls, she did not throw herself into the nearest pond or river when her lover abandoned her and she knew the consequences. Indeed, she must have had a genuine love for the man who was father of her child because she gave her son Parker's surname as a first name. Thus, Parker Clare enters the story and with him the unsolvable mystery of his runaway father.

There is also something of a mystery about Alice Clare's age because the parish registers are exceptionally confusing up to 1800 and not in chronological order. Their dates do not always agree with the few facts we have and a margin of two or three years sometimes has to be allowed. When the poet Clare came to write the *Sketches in the Life of John Clare* for his publisher in 1820–21,[4] he said his grandmother, who did not marry, lived 'to the age of 86 and left this world of troubles Jan. 1. 1820'. This is confirmed by an entry in the burial register. She should, therefore, have been born in 1734. But the only Clare child baptized in that year was a girl called Mary, born to John and Alice Clare who had married in 1725. There was a daughter called Alice baptized in the previous year on 22 July 1733 but she died a week later. It was customary then to keep Christian names in a family and so a later child would often receive the same name of an earlier child who had died. The Clares clearly wanted to keep 'Alice' in the family and gave it to their fourth daughter who was born in 1737. She survived and, if she was the Alice who died in January 1820, she was of course 83 and not 86 as claimed – a not uncommon error then among the old. To make matters more complicated there were at least two other families of Clares in the village, including a different Alice who had three illegitimate children. As the Alice Clare who conceived Parker Clare also did not marry, it is easy to see how mistakes can be made. We have to assume that the poet Clare, writing at the age of twenty-seven, knew when his grandmother died and, as the burial register gives only one entry for a deceased Clare in 1820 – that of Alice, we have to accept her as the mother of the bastard child who was to become John Clare's father. Her name was never mentioned by Clare but it was not usual for grandchildren to refer to their grandparents by first names. She may well have been called by some other name to avoid confusion with the other woman. She was undoubtedly a person of stubborn character, of independent pride and single-minded strength, who lived long enough to see the early achievements of her grandson, whose first volume of poetry was published just three weeks after her death. The vanished Scottish schoolmaster had contributed more to the village than he would ever know.

Whether Parker Clare himself was actually born in Helpston is also difficult to establish. He does not appear in the register of births or baptisms even though it was usual for 'base-born' infants to be baptized. As Alice's father was the parish clerk, and a man of some standing in the village, she might have gone to a relative in a neighbouring parish to have her child, returning to Helpston when the tongues had stopped wagging. She certainly returned to the village fairly soon and brought up the boy in her own home with her parents.

2

Parker Clare – who was to be described by his son fifty-five years later as 'one of fate's chancelings who drop into this world without the honour of matrimony'[5] – was born in 1765. Although he was not a particularly robust child at birth, he grew to be a strong young man fond of wrestling, ballad-singing and his horn of ale. He proudly displayed his scars as he spoke of his fighting victories. It was a hard sport then: the wrestlers wore spiked boots and were allowed to kick as well as pull, punch and throw. Parker Clare always liked an audience and also knew how to tell a story. He was popular at feasts and, when the ale loosened his tongue, would boast that he could recite over a hundred ballads and sing as many songs, all learnt by heart for he could read but little and write not at all.

He was twenty-six when he started courting Ann Stimson of Castor, a village three miles away over the heath. Ann was the second daughter of John Stimson, the town shepherd. John had married Elizabeth Dawes on 5 November 1750 in the parish church. They were to have six children – four daughters and two sons. Ann, who was the fourth child and born on 17 April 1757, may well have been the last one still at home by the time she wanted to marry Parker Clare at the age of thirty-five. Her father was against the marriage. As town shepherd he saw himself as a man of some position, a man who had the responsibility of all his neighbours' flocks, the tending, grazing and marketing. He hoped that his daughter would still find someone better than a rough thresher from Helpston and no doubt told her so. But Ann loved Parker and felt she had been single long enough. Not many more chances would come her way. It was not an easy decision for her to take. She was eight years older than her husband-to-be and such an age difference was considered to be a very poor match. But, like Parker's own mother, she could be stubborn and independent. She could also be sharp-tongued and was, according to Edward Drury who was to meet her later, 'gipsy-like in her appearance'.[6] It was perhaps her pregnancy that forced her father to give in.

Ann too had conceived out of wedlock and was two months pregnant when she was married in December 1792. It is not known where the marriage took place. They were not married in the parish church at Castor, or Ufford, or by licence anywhere in the Peterborough diocese.[7] When the time came for her to give birth she bore twins – a boy and a girl. They were born on 13 July 1793 when Ann was already thirty-six years old. (Her father died just three months earlier, on 16 April, and was to know nothing of his grandson's achievements.)

After their marriage the Clares moved to a cottage in Helpston but, again, whether the children were born there is not certain. For some years there was a generally held belief in the village that John Clare was not born in the cottage in Woodgate but in the house of his grandfather, the parish clerk. But no more than a few days, if any, separated the birthplace from the cottage which was always to mean home.

When Mrs Clare gave birth to her twins, the girl – 'a fine lively bonny wench' – was looked upon as the only survivor of that difficult time, whilst the boy – a pint-sized creature 'of waukley constitution'[8] – uttered not a whimper and was pushed to one side as one of birth's casualties. Fortunately, the midwife took another look at him, saw there was some life there after all and reunited him with his mother. Within four weeks the bonny, strong female child was dead and Mrs Clare was left with her weakling son who had so nearly been discarded. He was baptized on 11 August 1793. The poet's name 'John Clare' was written for the first time in the parish registers where several other John Clares had already been entered, but only his was destined to give the name 'immortal birth'.

It is worth considering that had John Donald Parker married Alice Clare the poet's name would have been John Parker, which might not have had the same ring to our ears as the maternal name he inherited. Clare was always interested in names and part of his complex search for identity must be attributed to this broken link in the family's history.

His twin-sister was not baptized, nor is she mentioned in the register of burials. It is possible that she was baptized in the cottage and she might have received a Christian burial anonymously. In those days a poor family, unable to afford a burial service, would have a word with the local undertaker who, for a small consideration, would hide the infant corpse in the coffin of some better-off deceased and so the two bodies went down into the same grave with the same reassuring words uttered over their remains.

Clare was to mourn the loss of his twin-sister on more than one occasion and he always seemed to be searching for her. She was the first person he was to lose from life. Because of this, and his physical weakness as a child, he was over-mothered. His life was to be one of several dualities. He was to be a man always in love with two women. He was to be accepted and rejected by two very different societies – those of Helpston and London. His experience was to be a mixture of reality and unreality, of doubt and belief. He could see himself but never find himself. His search for a lost childhood, for the distant horizons, for his twin-sister, for the perfect woman, all became part of that quest which led, ultimately, to the asylum. The uncertainty and loneliness of those first few years made an indelible impression on his creative imagination. In those early years his company was mainly that of middle-aged women – his mother, his grandmother and Granny Bains, a local herdswoman with whom Clare often liked to spend a day.

Nor was it a favourable start to life in the material sense. Most families were going through a period of depression. A succession of bad harvests between 1793 and 1814 meant that yields were well below expectations and for the first seven years fears of starvation were very real. Children grew up on a diet of thin gruel and turnips. The poor were made increasingly poorer. The fight to avoid debt and destitution became harder. Clare's early years were lived against this constant struggle and want. He was to record several years later the gratitude his parents felt at only having two children to feed instead of the four to which they gave birth. The workhouse or the graveyard claimed several of Clare's neighbours before they reached their middle forties. And yet, despite these oppressive conditions, the quality which emerges from his own account of childhood is one of complete happiness. Each day was new, each experience was something to add to his growing awareness of belonging to a place. In what he received – and was to know – he was more fortunate than any of his neighbours' children. If nothing else he had a bright imagination and his books to lift him out of their drudgery. The Clares certainly had their share of poverty and were to know the humiliation of being listed as paupers. At the same time it must be said that they often fared better than many of the villagers and were to receive many unexpected bonuses.

Parker Clare, although suffering from acute rheumatism by the age of forty, was still regarded as one of the best workers in the village and frequently accepted benefits from the Fitzwilliam family at Milton. A few years later, when Parker was becoming too disabled to work, Lord Milton – the son of the fourth Earl Fitzwilliam – paid for him to go to Scarborough Sea Infirmary to have what was then the most fashionable treatment for rheumatism; a degree of benevolence that does not appear to have reached many of the other villagers, though they too had few complaints against their landlord. Parker Clare felt so much better after the five-week treatment that he unwisely decided to save on the return fare by walking part of the way home, thereby making his condition worse than it had been before he went. Later still, when John Clare wanted to ask a favour of his lordship, he told the steward at Milton to impress upon his master that he was the son of the lame man of Helpston. Parker Clare, then, was not just a nobody and seems to have had some pull on attention in high places. Whatever may have brought about that special relationship, it was going to help the Clare family for many years to come.

3

In 1793, however, the Clares could not have imagined what was in store for them, nor could they have known what a significant decade it was in the literary world to which they had made their uncertain contribution. Shelley was born in 1792; Keats in 1795; and Thomas Hood in 1799. It was an era which saw the publication of Blake's *Songs of Experience*, Wordsworth's *Lyrical Ballads*, and Robert Bloomfield's *The Farmer's Boy*, as well as the emerging talents of Jane Austen, Coleridge, Lamb, Hazlitt, Cobbett and Landor. It was also a decade which saw the death of Robert Burns in 1796 and William Cowper in 1800 – two poets for whom Clare was to have a special affection. Books were popular and writers were popular. Advanced royalties of several thousand pounds were frequently paid to popular authors before a line was written.

Parker Clare, not having the wildest dream that his own small son would ever be named with such men, went about his daily tasks of threshing, hoeing and gardening. His main concern was to provide food and shelter for his family.

Ann Clare had two more children – Elizabeth (perpetuating a family name on both sides) was born in July 1796, and Sophia (mostly referred to as Sophy) was born in April 1798. Elizabeth died in childhood, leaving John with his youngest sister for company, with his mother now forty-one and his paternal grandmother sixty-one. Sophy was also a bright, intelligent child and received some formal education and read almost as avidly as her brother.

When the Clares first rented their cottage, which was 'as roomy & comfortable as any of our neighbours',[8] their old landlord, Edward Gee, charged them £2 a year rent and allowed them the whole of a large garden. The garden included a Golden Russet apple tree and its annual crop generally made enough money for them to pay their rent. Gee, who was a retired farmer, lived in two rooms at the end of the house and was a good friend to his tenants. He had 'had a good bringing up & was a decent scholar' who loaned books to John Clare even before the boy had learnt to read. They included the usual fairy stories, some *Robin Hood Tales* and the more substantial *Robinson Crusoe*. But when Edward Gee died in August 1804 the new young farmer who took possession of the cottage not only raised the rent to three guineas a year but also divided the building into four tenements. The Clares were left with only one room downstairs and one bedroom, which they divided so that the family could have some privacy. So, from what could be seen as a comparatively spacious home, they were reduced to very cramped quarters for which they had to pay considerably more. The garden was similarly divided into four strips but, as Parker Clare was the oldest tenant, he was allowed to choose that strip which had the apple tree. Fortunately the old Russet's yield continued to make up the greater part of their rent.

But even those years of hardship did not mar Clare's sensitive enjoyment of his childhood and he was able to look back and say:

> There is nothing but poetry about the existence of childhood real simple soul moving poetry the laughter and joy of poetry and not its philosophy and there is nothing of poetry about manhood but the reflection and the remembrance of what has been nothing more Thus it is that our play-prolonging moon on Spring evenings shed a richer lustre than the midday sun that surrounds us now in manhood for its poeticl sunshine hath left us it is the same identical sun and we have learned to know that – for in boyhood every new day brought a new sun – we knew no better and we was happy in our ignorance . . . where we laughed in childhood at the reality of the enjoyment felt we only smile in manhood at the reccolections of those enjoyments . . . we see the daisy and love it because it was our first favourite in childhood when we sat upon the doorstep and cropt its smiling blossoms by the threshold[9]

Clare's world was always at his door. From the moment he stepped outside he was in his timeless kingdom. The daisy was not just a simple flower carelessly trodden on by other people. It became a gift from Eden, something that had been handed down from the beginning of creation, something that would last until all else was destroyed. It also became a symbol of the ability of the down-trodden to survive, just as the weeds – those 'gifts too choice to throw away' – represented those ordinary people who daily toiled in the fields for other men's gain, the labourers who made harvest possible. Life was to become poetry and poetry was to become his life. Time present and the time past were brought together in those waiting poems:

> . . . . trampled underfoot
> The daisy lives & strikes its little root
> Into the lap of time – centurys may come
> And pass away into the silent tomb
> And still the child hid in the womb of time
> Shall smile & pluck them when this simple rhyme
> Shall be forgotten . . .[10]

John Donald Parker may have arrived in Helpston as a stranger and must have left with a poor reputation when he deserted the parish clerk's daughter bearing his child. But, through her, he gave something to the village it would not otherwise have had – a son who was to become the father of the country's truest nature poet.

Clare's inheritance, however, was more than the gift of that stranger's blood. He also received the traditions of that village community and the qualities of the countryside in which he was born. The events and the place went into his making. The beginning had already marked him out as someone different, a boy with a poet's eye, a child with a gift no one could explain and a future no one could predict.

At the same time it needed several people and quite a few more accidents to make the fulfilment of his life possible. A poet is made, as well as born.

4
Childhood

1

If the early years of a person's life are the most important years in the development of personality and response, they are particularly so to a writer. What follows into adulthood is a variation of the patterns, rhythms and sensations woven into the first experiences and revelations. The vibrations begin then. The echoes which come later may sometimes be no more than whispers of what was expected but the thread is unbroken. Those first five or six years feed the writer's imagination and begin the collection of memories that will be drawn on for the rest of life.

The importance of childhood in Clare's life cannot be overstressed. He was always writing about it, even in his late years in the asylum. Yet he was seldom sentimental. When he came to write of childhood it was because it had meaning for him as a poet. It fed his mind with daily wonders and, as a solitary child, it left a deep impression upon him. 'Childhood,' he wrote, had 'a strong spell over my feelings.'[1] The important word there is *spell*. Nature, in all her moods, cast a spell over him and made him part of her secrets.

From infancy it was noticeable that he was an unusually bright child. Some of the neighbours were saying just *unusual*. There was something strange and different about him. With his staring blue eyes and his uncommonly high brow he did not conform to the pattern of features found amongst the labouring class of Helpston. He was a dreamy boy who preferred his own company and had a habit of talking to himself. When he was five years old he set off one morning on a walk to find what mysteries existed beyond the horizon. He wanted to discover for himself where the world ended and what you would see when you reached the edge and looked down into some eternal space from which the sun, stars, moon and clouds all emerged in their correct time. It is a temptation hard to resist in a landscape where the distant rim is a very real boundary between earth and sky. He was not being stupid or disobedient. He was being curious – as he always was – and he wanted an answer to those childish questions. Beyond his own country there might be other countries with valleys and mountains. But not around Helpston. The clouds were his mountains:

> The sun those mornings used to find
> Its clouds were other-country mountains
> And heaven looked downward on the mind[2]

It was no coincidence that throughout his work he was to mention the sky and the sun some three hundred times each; and the adjectives do more than describe, they say something about the particular character and mood of the day – 'a tender watching sky'; a 'bickering sky'; a 'laughing sky'; an 'unfrequented sky' and an 'eternal sky'. The sun, too, is important because of the vastness of that sky. It shared Clare's loneliness and isolation, his glory and his despair. He was its child. On a cloudless day he could watch its whole journey from sunrise to sunset. It rose over Glinton – the village that was to mean so much to him. It paused at noon over Helpston – the mid-day of his happiness, and at evening it set beyond Barnack and the secretive trees of Rutland where he became both man and poet. He knew he was lost that morning when he went in search of the horizon because 'the very sun seemed to be a new one & shining in a different quarter of the sky'.[3] Oblivious of time and distance, he had walked on hoping to reach that edge of the world where all his questions would be answered. In different ways it was a journey he was to make several times during the years to come. That day, tired and disappointed, he returned home and could not understand his mother's anxiety when he found her and half the village women out looking for him.

No doubt as much for safety as for improvement, Mrs Clare decided that it was time for her son to go to school. Although she 'knew not a single letter' herself, and went so far as to believe 'the highest parts of learning the blackest parts of witchcraft', she nevertheless had hopes of getting her two children educated. Clare's young sister, Sophy, was to follow him to school and had as much appetite for her lessons as her brother. She also became a good reader and eventually possessed several books, including one (when she was only ten years old) called *Essays on Elocution*, a volume which contained rules of correct speech and lengthy extracts from the works of Shakespeare, Dryden, Milton, Pope and Collins. She marked some of her favourite passages and prized the book enough to pass it down to her own children. She also owned *The Female Shipwright*, an anonymous autobiography which her brother frequently borrowed. It was, he said, a 'winter evening favourite in my first book-days'.[4]

Whatever their situation might have become it is clear that, from the beginning, the family strived for betterment, as if to regain a status they had lost. For Mrs Clare education may have seemed as mysterious as witchcraft, but for her children it was the only way to escape from the drudgery being endured by that peasant class to which they belonged. As her son was not as strong as other village boys she was particularly anxious to find an alternative life for him. At the age of five he started attending a local dame-school run by a Mrs Bullimore.[5] Her teaching was elementary in the extreme. The only moment that Clare remembered was the day when she explained to him how the whitethorn tree in the schoolyard came to be there. She told him that, as a very young girl, she had dug the root from the fields, carried it home and planted it in her own backyard, where it had grown ever since. To Clare this was little short of a miracle. That tree, like the daisy near his doorstep, had come down from the beginnings of creation and was part of his daily world. Perhaps that simple lesson did more to awaken his creative imagination than Mrs Bullimore or anyone else ever realized. Beyond that the dame-school had little to offer apart from the alphabet, some elementary numbers and playground games. Within two years Mrs Clare arranged for her son to join Mr Seaton's day-class held in the church vestry at Glinton, just over two miles away. What was the vestry is now the Lady Chapel, and when Clare was a boy there was a small porch on the east wall of the church through which the pupils went into their classroom. It was there where he was to carve 'J.C. 1808 Mary' to record his love for Mary Joyce, the girl with whom he went to school.

It cost Mrs Clare a few pence each week out of her own purse to keep her son at school and, although there were often many difficulties she never lost an opportunity of sending him off for his lessons, whatever the weather. Parker Clare supported her in her ambitions until 'downright necessity from poverty forced him to check her kind intentions'. Her independence and determination nevertheless meant that seldom a year passed without Clare getting ten or eleven weeks' schooling each year until he was nearly twelve. Nor did his education end there.

2

Before the Enclosure Act there was no straight road from the village cross to Glinton as there is today. Clare took the path beyond the church, round by Eastwell Spring and on to Etton. The small boy, with his bundle of books, became a familiar sight to the country people between the two villages. Some may have admired him, others may have already thought him mad. Most of those journeys would have been made during the winter weeks of the year when there was no demand for extra hands on the land or any work left in the barns. Winter was always to be a favourite time for Clare. It meant he could spend those weeks studying algebra, geography, history and religion, as well as reading. His desire to improve himself was undiminished even when he 'could not muster three farthings for a sheet of writing paper' and was reduced to writing on 'every morsel of blue or brown paper' from his mother's wrapped groceries.[6] Sometimes he amused himself by writing on the whitewashed walls of barns or tracing his arithmetical symbols on the dusty floors. He improved his skills at every opportunity and the copperplate handwriting he was able to display on his exercise book at the age of ten proves what a confident hand he had already acquired.[7] His 'taste and passion for reading became furious' and he received every encouragement from his teacher, including from time to time a sixpence as a special reward. He was soon envied at school for his prodigious memory, especially when it came to reciting the Bible. He knew an abundance of passages by heart and could repeat most of that 'fine Hebrew Poem of Job' – a task which did not lessen for him, as it did for the other boys, the majesty of the language found in the Authorized Version.[8] 'Fine poem' he may have thought it then but, like most of his Christian teaching, it left him with an impression of personal guilt and fear of retribution which caused him much distress in manhood. As a boy, however, he loved the Bible as much for its language as its message and was quite certain that it should not have been used in school in the way that it was:

> a dull boy never turns with pleasure to his schooldays when he has often been beaten 4 times for bad reading in 5 verses of Scripture ... The Bible loses its relish the painful task of learning wearied the memory irksome inconvenience never prompts recollection ... The Bible is laid by on its shelf and by 9 cottages out of 10 is never disturb'd or turn'd to further than the minute's reference for reciting the text on Sunday[9]

His own knowledge of the scriptures was always deeper than any meagre acquaintance that would have come from it being an 'irksome inconvenience'. He brought the same enthusiasm to them as he did to all his lessons, as his later journal entries show.

Whatever the subject, learning became an obsession that was to stay with him for the whole of his life. He had a 'restless curiosity that was ever on the enquiry & never satisfied ... a thirst after knowledge in everything & by that restless desire'[10] still felt that he had only acquired a very superficial knowledge of many things.

It was, all the same, a knowledge for which many boys in more privileged circumstances would have willingly paid extra. His education naturally had its limitations but he did receive more instruction and help than most working-class boys at that time. It is a mistake ever to think of Clare as an unlettered poet, a natural but illiterate singer, just because his spelling is not always accurate and his grammar less than perfect. He became very well read and his knowledge of books was to surprise his London acquaintances when he later joined their company. Long before he had any idea of becoming a poet, it was decided that he should be a scholar. His hopes then were that he might one day become a schoolmaster.

To appreciate his achievement it has to be remembered that elementary education in the early nineteenth century was for the prime purpose of teaching children to read, mainly so that they should study the Bible and other moral works which were considered necessary instruction in their daily duties towards their superiors. As most of the working-class children who did go to school were expected to go into domestic service of some kind, good manners and correct speech were almost as essential as reading. To go beyond those basic requirements was thought unwise, not so much by the landowners – who often encouraged and subsidized education – but by the trades-people and tenant-farmers who were worried about the position of their own children. How could they set up their offspring in life if the children of labourers were to be educated to the same level and prepared to do the work 'hitherto performed by their immediate betters'?[11] A poor child met resentment on both sides. Its own people often ridiculed it for trying to be better than it was, and the middle class resented it for trying to get out of that class into which it was born. For every word of encouragement that Clare received he would have had a hundred criticisms to bear. They were attitudes which made him sensitive to criticism for the rest of his life, and he frequently found it impossible to separate literary criticism from criticism of his social inadequacies.

When lessons were finished at school Clare continued with his studies at home, returning to give that cramped livingroom in Helpston the dignity of a study. Although the cottage, with its whitewashed walls and sanded floors, was undoubtedly a 'humble home' as Clare called it, it was hardly the 'narrow, wretched hut, low and dark, more like a prison than a human dwelling' described by Frederick Martin. Martin would not have seen it until thirty-two years after the Clares had lived there, when it had been allowed to deteriorate. In the years between it had been used as the local school when education became compulsory and it is still standing today. Farm-labourers' cottages never were renowned for being over-scrupulously clean or well-ordered. It was not easy to keep a 'working cottage' spotless when it was in use from four o'clock in the morning until sunset. Many of them continued to have a healthy untidiness about them even when conditions improved, and if Mrs Clare was 'gipsy-like' in appearance, she may well have been a carefree, untidy housekeeper.

Not that Clare minded. He objected more than once when a broom went too near his books and, as a young man, was not too particular about his own dress. His home did, no doubt, look a mess to sophisticated eyes and was far from being comfortable as we understand the word today. But it was not a 'wretched hut' or a 'low and dark prison' about to fall down. Many of Clare's descriptions of it leave us with adequate proof of what it meant to him. It was a place of love, security, understanding, amusement and care; a place of story-telling and mirth, where the old customs were celebrated each year and many pleasures enjoyed; a place to which he returned again and again, both in reality and in the poetry. The family had their pet dog and cat, their bird in a cage, and even a robin which hopped in from time to time to perch on a chair-back or gather crumbs from their table.

After their evening meal and some recounting of the day's events, the bare table was spread with books, pens and ink, so that Clare could continue with the exercises he had been wrestling with earlier in school. His mother watched with affection. Looking up from her spinning-wheel she more than once expressed the hope that one day he would reward them all for the trouble they had taken over his education. It was not a hit-and-miss affair but a deliberate effort to gain that success he wanted. It would not have been possible without the support of home. Nor would such trouble have been taken had he not shown more than average promise of 'reward'. To deny him the credit for hard work in his early studies is to devalue the inspiration that appeared to come to him so easily later on. Inspiration only comes to the mind that is prepared for it and most of Clare's life was a preparation, whether he was studying algebra, flowers, birds, literature, or listening to the songs and ballads he heard from his father.

During the spring and summer months he was not able to spend as much time with his books as he would have liked. He was needed for crow-scaring, weeding, sheep-tending and, at those times of extreme poverty, for helping in the barn with the threshing. He was no older than ten when his father first made him a small flail and taught him the rural skills he might still need to know when he grew up – cutting, stooking, gathering, binding, threshing and winnowing the corn; planting, weeding and lifting of turnips; and how to look after animals. Clare's contact with the land was a physical one. He was to write from firsthand experience of the hard work as well as the joys of the countryside. He was involved in it all the year round, working under a fierce sun or in frost and snow. Unlike George Crabbe, or William Cowper, Clare knew what it felt like to be a farm-labourer with cracked hands and an aching back. He wrote about the soil with the eye of a realist, not a romantic. His voice came from the heavy furrows of a muddy field, not the velvet sofa of a parsonage. When his tired body returned to school he was relieved to find that he had managed to keep up with the rest of the boys who had been able to continue with their lessons uninterrupted. Their success was always a challenge and helped to develop that determination which drove him on all his life. However much he was to appear surprised at his achievements, there was always (beneath his modesty and doubts) an unswerving ambition to surprise everyone else. But his claims had to be justified and the ridicule silenced. As he was to write in 'The Village Minstrel', 'Ambition's prospects fired his little soul/And fancy soared and sung 'bove poverty's control.' Not knowing which way his gifts would take him, he could only continue in those early years to prepare.

3

By the summer of 1803 the old, white-haired Mr Seaton had retired and Mr James Merrishaw had been appointed as the schoolmaster at Glinton. Clare set out to impress, and succeeded. Merrishaw was unable to conceal his delight at the progress made by his part-time pupil. His work improved beyond his years and Merrishaw, like his predecessor, never failed to give Clare 'tokens of encouragement'. In addition to extra tuition the schoolmaster also gave his pupil the use of his own private library. Clare was overwhelmed. It opened up more new worlds, fired more ambitions. Often he walked home in a state of such excitement at the prospect of what books could do for him that he walked right past his cottage gate. He now wanted to possess books, even began to dream that one day he might write them. Money was more important now, not only to keep him at school but to buy those volumes he needed for his own library.

He made few friends at school but two were to be particularly dear to him. One was Richard Turnill, who was about Clare's age; the other was Mary Joyce, who was four years younger. Mary was by far the greater of those two affections and was to be the inspiration of many of Clare's finest love poems. Richard was a quiet, refined boy from a well-off family of farmers. Unlike Clare, he did not have to work in the fields to earn the money he needed to attend school. He was receiving a full-time education and hoping soon to go on to boarding-school, like his elder brother John.

Clare and Turnill shared interests, exchanged books and played together. Mrs Clare was happy to think that her son had found someone his own age and no longer wanted to spend all his time alone. But the friendship was suddenly and sadly broken when Richard died of typhus fever. Once again Clare had lost someone who had become very close, even necessary, to him. Later he became friendly with Richard's elder brother John, who continued to lend books and help with his studies, but the relationship could not be the same. John was a cooler, more superior mortal and within two years he was offered a post in Excise and left the district.

One of the interests John Turnill was able to share with Clare during that time was astronomy. He had a good telescope with which he explored the night sky. He invited Clare to look through it and its revelations sent him home puzzled and excited at all the undiscovered mysteries of nature. Already he began to question the complete accuracy of the story of the Creation as he had found it in Genesis. (He was to express the same doubts years later in his journal entry for 12 September 1824: 'the sacred historian took a great deal upon credit for this world when he imagines that God created the sun moon & stars those mysterious hosts of heaven for no other purpose than its use "the great light to rule the day & the lesser light to rule the night" . . .'[12]).

Clare remained on good terms with the Turnill family and was to work on their farm on several occasions when they needed extra hands at haymaking or harvest. It was on their farm that he was to witness a dramatic death, the suddenness of which caused him to faint and be haunted by its memory for many years. Thomas Drake, a loader, fell from his wagon and broke his neck. Although serious accidents were common on farms even in those pre-mechanized days, this incident was so alien to Clare's world of creation and joy that he could never forget the shock. More than ever he wanted to retreat into the realm of the scholar and so he returned once more to his studies with greater determination and purpose.

His only close friend in Glinton now was Mary Joyce. But, in many ways, Mary was unattainable, unreal and beyond his reach. She was the daughter of a prosperous farmer who did not encourage her friendship with the poor boy from Helpston. Their affection was separated by more than the distance between the two villages or the weeks spent working in the fields. Her very existence intensified Clare's loneliness. She became one of those childhood memories which in later life never leave the mind.

4

Away from school he continued to spend most of his time alone. He wrote that he 'never had much relish for the pastimes of youth'[13] and grew so fond of being on his own that his mother sometimes forced him into company. When he did agree to join in the games on the village green, however, he appears to have become as wild and boisterous as all the other boys, perhaps even more so as his release was less regular than theirs. Frequently he became the laughing-stock and on a number of occasions got himself into trouble. Once, when wading in the meadow-pits with some young cow-tenders he joined in a game of 'dares' near the deep water. It was his turn to go again when he slipped and sank to the bottom of the pit. He felt the water choking him, the thunder in his ears. He was not a good swimmer and thought he was going to drown. But then the boys stopped laughing and came to his rescue. On another occasion they were swimming on a bundle of bulrushes when Clare's raft suddenly bounced from under him and he was left clinging to the overhanging branches of a sallow bush. Again he had to be helped out of trouble. Once more he had to survive the jibes of being a coward. He was a little more successful at hop-scotch and whip-and-top, and also tried to live up to his father's reputation for strength by attempting to throw a stone over the church's weather-cock, for 'he who pelted oer/Was reckoned on a mighty man'.[14]

In 1803 the war with France had been renewed and the boys could then imagine that they were Wellington defeating Bonaparte, or Nelson attacking the Spanish Fleet. Or they could stalk on their home-made stilts like giants chasing the neighbours' cats, or:

On summer eves with wild delight
We bawled the bat to sky
Who in the 'I spy' dusky light
Shrieked loud & flickered bye
And up we tossed our shuttlecocks
And tried to hit the moon
And wondered bats should fly so long
And they come down so soon.[15]

Or they would go fishing near Lolham Brigs, the pastime that Clare enjoyed most. It met all his needs – sport, solitude, time for reflection. He would rise before the sun came up over Glinton, dig for worms in the back garden, then make his way over the dew-wet meadows to some shaded spot on the river-bank or reeded stream. One of his favourite books became Izaak Walton's *The Compleat Angler* which he bought for two shillings in Stamford. He admitted that it did not help him to catch fish any easier but the quality of the writing gave him immeasurable pleasure while waiting for the fish to get themselves caught. The book remained for him 'the best English pastoral that can be written' and he considered 'the descriptions are nature unsullied by fashionable tastes of the times'.[16] It was through Walton's writings that he was later introduced to the poetry of John Donne, George Herbert, Henry Wotton and Charles Cotton.

When he was not playing games or fishing he would resort again to his solitary habits of wandering off for days through the woods or over the heath, studying the behaviour of birds, looking for rare wildflowers, or collecting snail-shells. Sometimes he would walk as far as the small lake on the southern side of Emmonsail's Heath and there watch the heron with its 'melancholly wing' flap off into the mist. He noticed the busy, ordered lives of ants, followed the paths of beetles and bees, always observing the minute and seemingly insignificant things as well as the mighty and dramatic. In those early years he had little idea that he was already a poet, looking with a poet's eye, recording the daily sensations of his world for later years. With all the other subjects he had to study, he had not been able to give much time to reading poetry, or trying to write it. But that did not matter. The words are often written down later and worked into poems. The experiences were happening then. He made notes, stuck them in the brim of his hat and frequently forgot they were there. Without always knowing why, he was preparing himself for the poetry he had to write.

5

If childhood is important to the imagination so too is it to the growth of memory. Together they are the source of genius. Memory preserves an impression and gives new birth to the buried experience in wiser moments of perception. Imagination, by the quality of its originality, gives the re-collected moment a new dimension. Clare possessed these two necessary gifts and only needed to acquire the skills that would allow them to be fulfilled. His outstanding quality as a boy was this patience in watching. He saw wonder in the ordinary things, as he did in the ant: 'Thou little insect infinitely small/What curious texture marks thy minute frame.'[17] In his mind the ant, so easily trodden on like the daisy, is given the dignity, awe and 'fearful symmetry' of Blake's tiger. We also have in that one phrase two vital words in Clare's vocabulary – 'little' and 'curious'.

The insect world fascinated him. Grasshoppers, midges, mayflies, moths, bees, all were treated with the same respect and wonder as oak trees, harvest fields, sunsets and floods. Those 'insects of mysterious birth/Sudden struck my wondering sight'.[18] They were not separate, dispensable things from the greater world of skies and forests, but part of it. His close-focus attention to them is intensified because of that vast, wilder drama round them. He was finding new wonders every minute and 'walking in a new world'. It was this hourly amazement as a child which gave him his personal vision. When he measured the pace of a snail travelling over a stone, or counted the times a bluecap fed its young in one day, he surrendered himself completely to the laws of that world.

His memory and imagination were enriched too by the local folk stories he heard. If he wanted company on those excursions over the heath he would rather talk with the gipsies at Langley Bush or seek out old Granny Bains tending the cattle or sheep. She was a character with a reputation for being as rough or as calm as the weather, a woman with an unceasing flow of strange stories, songs, gossip and folklore which filled the boy's mind with fantasies. The tradition of story-telling was not a lost art then among the people. Clare heard good story-telling every day, either in the fields or round the cottage hearth; stories that were narrated with excitement and poetry. The narrators' skills never failed. They could keep the tales going for hours, becoming so involved in the plot themselves that they frequently acted some of the parts or burst into improvized song.

Clare may not have come from such a strong folk-song tradition as Robert Burns but he did inherit a love of folk melodies and often wrote words to go with them. When he eventually came to play the fiddle he collected more than 280 tunes.[19] He copied out the words of 'My Love is Like a Red Red Rose' and prefaced the verses with the comment, 'This is an old ballad which my father says he learnt when a child off his mother who knew it when a lass therefore it cannot be less than 100 years old.'[20] Clare's grandmother, Alice, may have heard the song from John Donald Parker in their courting days and Clare's affinity with the Scots, and with Burns in particular, might have something to do with his part-Scottish ancestry. He would have heard the Scottish dialect, too, in Helpston when the Scottish drovers arrived with their cattle on the way to London. They would stay a night or two in the village to let their herds get a good feed of sweet Northamptonshire grass, before driving them down to Huntingdon, where they were then handed over to the London drovers. The village children came out of their houses to stare at these kilted men 'so oddly clad/In petticoats of bonded plad/Wi blankets oer their shoulders slung',[21] and no doubt they found the strange accent hard on the ear. But, for Clare, the sounds might have stirred old, forgotten yearnings for a land which he himself had never known but from which part of his inheritance had come.

6

When the family's increasing poverty meant that he could no longer keep up his day-school he continued the remainder of his formal education by attending evening classes run by Mr Merrishaw, also in the church vestry at Glinton. Clare felt his knowledge and confidence growing. He now wished 'to gain notice and rise above' his fellows. The more he read the more he realized that he was different from all the other boys for whom study held little joy.

When he saw some of those acquaintances out walking on Sundays he would test their reaction to some 'striking beauty in a wildflower or an object of surrounding scenery'[22] but they did not respond and could seldom make an answer. If they did it was only to say that they could see nothing worth looking at and walked away, laughing at Clare's 'droll fancies' until he thought he surely had a taste peculiar to himself and that no one else thought or saw as he did. He was now aware of how they saw him: 'How half a ninney he was like to be/To go so soodling up and down the street.'[23] But he persevered and learnt to close his ears to their ridicule, even though it drove him into deeper isolation.

During those last years of childhood he must have wondered at the dual roles he was expected to perform. Why could he not be one thing or the other? Why not leave him with his books instead of sending him to tend sheep or scare crows? Life was already a compromise.

If he had to work then he preferred those jobs where he could spend some moments of each hour reading. On Sundays, too, when people were forbidden to read anything but the Bible or prayer book, he would steal off into the woods with his latest adventure-story to read in hiding until the distant church-bells, and fear of retribution, were completely forgotten. Sometimes the vicar inquired about his absence from the services and Clare made the excuse of having to work on the sabbath to help his family. The vicar, like the villagers, raised his eyebrows and put the boy's behaviour down to some rebellious blood in the Clares.

Clare did not mind. He had won his freedom. He went on reading those stories that mostly appeared in the cheap chap-books sold by hawkers at local fairs, markets, or at cottage doors – *Little Red Riding Hood*, *Valentine and Orson*, *Jack the Giant-Killer*, *Long Tom the Carrier*, *The King and the Cobbler*, *Tawny Bear*, *The Seven Sleepers*, *Tom Hickathrift*, and *Old Mother Shipton's Prophecies*. There was still no real poetry yet, though Clare considered those popular stories 'real poetry in all its simplicity'.[24]

His infancy and childhood were, then, vitally important years to his silent growth as a poet. When he eventually came to write about the world of a vanishing England his mind was already well-stored with images and memories. In many ways, of course, he always remained a child. Whatever burden his growing into manhood might place upon him, in his private moments he never lost that innocence.

> Our childhood soon a trifle gets
> Yet like a broken toy
> Grown out of date it reccolects
> Our memorys into joy
> The simple catalogue of things
> That reason would despise
> Starts in the heart a thousand springs
> Of half forgotten joys[25]

5
Starting Work

1

At the age of twelve and with his schooldays over Clare's parents now had the problem of finding a suitable job for him, if only to prove that the privileges he had received could be put to good use. It was no easy matter. There was little work around Helpston that could make use of his education. A man called Mowbray, who lived at Glinton, offered him an apprenticeship (though at what Clare does not say)[1] but his parents could not afford the required premium. Will Farrow, 'a village wit and very droll fellow', would have taken him out of kindness to Parker Clare but the small bond he needed could not be found. Mr Stimson, a local shoemaker, also offered to take him but Clare did not like the idea of becoming a cobbler. He thought it a complete waste of the knowledge he had so painstakingly acquired. The next suggestion was that he should become apprenticed to Mr George Shelton, a stone-mason. This time Clare made the excuse that he did not like climbing and had no head for heights – conveniently forgetting the number of trees he had climbed in search of birds' nests. People began to say he was born idle. Clare said it was because he was 'timid & fearful of undertaking the first trial in everything'.[2]

One of the things that made him fearful was the thought of leaving home. It was customary then for apprentices to live in with their employer and the prospect of taking any job away from the village filled him with dread. He admits that he was 'such a silly shanny boy' and did not like the idea of being taken away from that safe home where he had been 'coddled up so tenderly & long'.[3] His mother, no more eager than her son for a separation, was determined not to commit him to a trade he would not enjoy. So the days of waiting continued and each postponement meant that more time could be spent out on the heath.

Clare, understandably, was never to like hard manual work, even though there were times when he had to do plenty of it to earn some sort of living. Long before his poems were published he expressed hopes that they would one day release him from working on the land. In a letter to the Reverend Isaiah Knowles Holland, written sometime in the autumn of 1817, he wrote, 'All that hurts me is the Nessesity of taking to hard Labour again after all my hopes to the Contrary.'[4] He was, by his nature, lazy and found any excuse to avoid doing a job when he wanted to be alone with his thoughts. He regretted those long hours of toil that deprived him of the time he needed for his reading, and later his poetry. But few people could understand that. He lived in a society where a man's worth was judged by the amount of sweat he lost. He would have received little sympathy from men unacquainted with the demands of thought. The isolation he had felt at school was now experienced in the adult world he was too quickly entering.

During that spring and summer of 1805 he went weeding in the fields or haymaking. He listened to the women singing their ancient songs or telling stories, all of which helped to shorten the hours of work. When he could not find employment in the fields he went to the woods to collect rotten sticks, or gather dried cow-dung for the fires at home. More and more his thoughts were turning to becoming a writer. He listened not only to the stories of his neighbours but to the rhythms and cadences of their speech. Language had a local tongue and dialect words were always a natural part of his vocabulary. Later this matter of vocabulary caused friction between Clare and his publishers. Although he refined his speech over the years he always pronounced 'cross' to rhyme with 'horse', 'voice' to rhyme with 'mice', and 'smile' to rhyme with 'toil'. He usually kept 'childern' for 'children' and stubbornly refused to change some dialect words which he felt expressed his sentiments better than any other word in the language. When John Taylor crossed out the word *gulsh'd* from a poem because it was too 'provincial' Clare defended it by saying that he thought the word 'expressive' – it means 'tearing or thrusting up with great force'.[5] The labouring people with whom he worked had their own poetry. It was for them he wanted to write and their language he wanted to use.

But his main problem then was not in finding the right way to express his feelings in the most suitable language but of finding work that would help him to stay at home where that language stood most chance of survival. After a while he was offered a job as a ploughboy by Mrs Bellairs who lived at Woodcroft Castle, half-way between Helpston and Glinton, on the way to Marholm. In those pre-enclosure days there was a trackway from Helpston to Woodcroft.

Woodcroft Castle was a small, fortified, moated manor-house which had been attacked by Cromwell's troops during the Civil War. There is a story (which Clare certainly knew) of the king's chaplain, Dr Michael Hudson, trying to escape by climbing over the battlements but, as he hung there, the soldiers chopped off his hands and he fell into the moat where he was killed by one of the Stamford soldiers fighting for Cromwell.

It is a shadowy manor which still half-hides itself in a ring of trees made noisy by rooks. On a summer's day the walls are reflected in the still water of the moat and the lawns are embroidered with flowers. But in winter the greyness and the silence must be as Clare knew it. The sight of the house always made him tremble. Although the owners were to show kindness to him then, and later, it was not the happiest place to be and he did not stay too long.

One of the more disagreeable things about it was having to get up before the first light of dawn and another was getting wet feet every morning and night. In wet weather the moat would overflow the path which led to the porch. This meant that Clare had to wade up to his knees in icy water to get in and out. After a month he decided that he had had enough. Nothing his parents could say would persuade him to return.

2

Their next attempt at finding a job for him was both fortuitous and ambitious. Clare's maternal uncle, Morris Stimson, had, in the eyes of the family, done rather well for himself by becoming a footman to a Mr Bellamy, a wealthy lawyer, benefactor and councillor of Wisbech, a small, attractive town which considered itself the capital of the fens.

One day Morris decided to visit his poor relations in Helpston and Mrs Clare spoke to him about the problems they were having in getting employment for their son. Morris agreed that the boy's education fitted him more for a clerical job than some menial work on the land and told them that his own master was looking for a new junior clerk in his Wisbech office. Was it possible that the important man would consider his nephew? He might. Could he arrange an interview? Yes, he could do that. The excitement grew. Clare was at last going to be somebody. He was going to be a clerk in a country lawyer's office.

But he would need new clothes. He could not go to Wisbech dressed like a ploughboy. He would need money for the fare. He could not walk all that distance. Wisbech was twenty-one miles away and the cheapest method of getting there was by barge on the River Nene. They had no money for such immediate demands. Morris told them to wait until they heard from him again. Meanwhile, Mrs Clare, convinced that the answer would be yes, went to work with her needles and thread. She lengthened John's coat and sleeves, pressed and brushed his trousers which 'betrayed too old an acquaintance', found a white neck-cloth for him to wear, an old pair of gloves to hide his already rough hands, and generally made him look 'as genteel' as possible.

Word came and, with little more than his barge fare and his parents' blessing, Clare set off for a new world. For someone who had not yet been beyond eight miles of his village it was an adventure. It meant first of all walking eight miles from Helpston to Peterborough, getting the canal boat at the town bridge, and finally moving away from the quayside, down that long narrow stretch of water that had been cut less than a hundred years before by the drainage engineers. It was a slow journey. The Dutch canal boat was drawn by one horse on the towpath. There was a large saloon in front for common passengers and a little room at the stern for any select company. The boat only went once a week, leaving Peterborough on Friday and returning on Sunday. The fare was eighteen pence.

Clare spent most of the journey thinking up answers to imaginary questions rather than taking in the flat countryside through which he travelled. He saw himself as Mr Bellamy cross-examining the prospective junior clerk. He composed and shaped the correct replies he would make to all the questions that would be asked. A few hours later the barge tied up at the town bridge in Wisbech and the passengers disembarked. Clare stood on the quay and realized he had been so engrossed in rehearsing his interview that he had completely forgotten his uncle's directions to Mr Bellamy's house. It meant asking strangers the way. He was soon to experience in that small town something he was to be more aware of later when he went to London – people staring at him, amused, disbelieving, doubting his right to be there, wondering what this wide-eyed youth was doing away from home. Their attitude did nothing to restore his confidence. By the time he found the big house all his eloquent replies had evaporated. He rang the bell and was relieved when his uncle, the footman, opened the door. He told him, 'You must not hang your head but look up boldly & tell him what you can do.'[6]

Clare waited in the kitchen, ate some food which had been provided for him, and tried to retrieve some of the thoughts he had planned on the barge. At length the lawyer appeared with his footman and looked down at Clare. 'So this is your nephew!' Morris Stimson agreed. 'Well, I shall see him again,' said Bellamy, and walked away. He never saw Clare again and the young boy felt another of the many rejections he was to experience in his life.

Once that humiliation passed, however, he sighed with relief that the ordeal was over. He thought now that he would have cut a poor figure for a lawyer's clerk. The office would have been awful for him. It would have suffocated his love of the open air. Its files and pink-taped documents would have shut him away from the light of the sky and the woods' bird-song. Its calculated, legal language might have stifled his own love of words. He was not sorry. He had escaped again.

He now had to wait until Sunday morning before he could get the boat back to Peterborough. Mrs Bellamy offered him bed and food in the servants' quarters and he was free to spend the rest of his time looking about the town after amusements. It would not have been easy to find too many distractions there in the early nineteenth century. But one of his pleasures was shop-window gazing and there were certainly more shops in Wisbech than in Helpston:

> I was fond of peeping into booksellers windows & I found one full of paintings of a painter who was taking portraits & teaching drawing in the town ... I remember one of them was the village ale-house another was the pencil sketch of the Letter-Carrier of the Town whose face seemd familiar with everyone who pass'd by ... I little thought when I was looking at these things that I should be a poet & become a familiar acquaintance with that painter who had blinded the windows with his attempts into fame[7]

The painter was Edward Rippingille, a self-taught artist who was born in King's Lynn some twenty years earlier. He specialized in scenes of rural and domestic life, and painted a series of six pictures entitled 'The Progress of Intemperance' – a subject he knew something about for he was, as Clare found out when they became acquainted, 'a pleasant fellow over the bottle'.[8] They were to spend many all-night drinking sessions together in London and he was a man for whom Clare had a great affection.

Clare had a natural affinity with artists. He was to admire and also become friendly with Peter de Wint, a man nine years older than himself but one who shared the poet's love of the lowlands. Throughout his work Clare refers to nature's brush or pencil, to the artist's palette, the hues and tints of his craft. The artist's brush, laid aside at the end of a day's work, became a metaphor for the closed dandelion in the evening, and the fields and woods were seen as nature's studio in which colours were mixed and related with a painter's skill. Had he not become a poet Clare's creative skill might well have led him to become an artist. He had a good eye for detail and perspective, and a love of colour. He went so far as to buy himself a box of paints when he wanted to make sketches of some of the butterflies, moths and wildflowers he found on his walks. The paintings he saw in Wisbech that day would have held a fascination for him without knowing anything of his own future, or the artist's.

On Sunday the narrow boat returned to Peterborough and Clare had plenty of time to reflect on his failure to impress Mr Bellamy. He still had no regrets. As he walked the last few miles from Glinton to Helpston he felt light-hearted enough to sing and was glad to reach home 'and its snug fireside' again.

After all their efforts to secure the post for him his parents were naturally despondent. The boy would come to nothing, as many had warned. He was now thirteen and most boys of his age had already spent two full years at work, either on the land or at a trade. Fortunately their neighbour, Mr Francis Gregory, who was the landlord of the Blue Bell Inn next-door to the Clares, came to the rescue. He wanted a day-servant, someone to do odd jobs and run errands. He offered to take Clare for a year. Clare agreed with his parents to work for Gregory. It meant he could stay at home, be near his woods, do work that was not too heavy, and work for a man who was fond of singing and country amusements. Travellers called at the inn with their wares and their tales. It would at least be better than field-work, for a time.

3

It was, of course, a solution which fell far short of all those earlier expectations but at last he was to be employed for the next twelve months. It turned out to be a good place where he was treated more like a son than a servant. Gregory's mother was still alive and the real master of the house, but she was often ill and confined to her room so she left Francis to run the inn and look after the boy. Gregory himself did not enjoy good health either and seldom wanted to leave the house so Clare was left alone for much of the time. He was to recall that it was his year at the Blue Bell which became the 'nursery for that lowly and solitary musing which ended in rhyme'.[9]

His daily tasks were not demanding. He looked after the horses, tended a few cows, ran errands and, as usual, made up for company by talking to himself. It was a habit that came in useful when he went once or twice a week to Maxey flour mill for Mrs Gregory, who was always anxious to save a penny. She was able to get her flour ground at Maxey cheaper than anywhere else and it was Clare's job to collect it from that neighbouring village a mile away. The road to the mill was lonely and narrow. It passed over low land with a reputation for ghosts and supernatural happenings. His highly-sensitive nature responded quickly to any strange sights or sounds. After all, the stories he had heard from Granny Bains had acquainted him with every haunted spot in the area. He knew where the murders had been committed, where suicides had taken place, where men had been seen hanging from trees, or the bodies of young girls found in ponds, and where the spirits of the long-ago dead rose from their ancient burial grounds. A quaking thistle was enough to make him swoon with terror. He was always afraid of passing a churchyard where 'Dread monsters fancy moulded on his sight/Soft would he step lest they his tread should hear.'[10]

The walk to Maxey always made him sweat with fear and not without cause. It meant passing through the hamlet of Nunton and over an old stone bridge where frequently he saw the mysterious Jack-o'-lanterns or, as the local people called them, Jinny Burnt-arses. They were the tiny self-igniting flames of marsh-gas also known as lantern-men, or hob-o-lanterns, sights and terms that were common throughout the low marshy lands of the fens before drainage became as efficient as it is today. There was a tradition that these Jack-o'-lanterns always meant trouble for a traveller at dusk for they could lure a man from his chosen path and into the fens inhabited by evil spirits. And the traveller dared not whistle to keep his own spirit up, for it was believed that the lantern-men always ran towards the whistle and from that moment the traveller was lost. The conditions for those marsh-gases occurred when a hot summer and autumn followed a long wet winter. Then the dykes and ditches dried out creating cracks in the baked mud from which the marsh-gas escaped. The gas exploded in small globes and became flickering flames in the approaching darkness. Many square miles of fen could be illumined by those weird, dancing lights and, to the superstitious fenmen, no amount of explanation could disperse the dread caused by their appearance.

Certainly as Clare walked home from the flour mill in the evenings he would have gone between fields that would usually be flooded in winter and dry in summer, leaving the cracks in the soil from which the marsh-gas escaped. The Jack-o'-lanterns were very real to him and were mentioned several times in the poems he wrote later:

> Ive seen the midnight morris dance of hell
> On the black moors while thicker darkness fell
> Like dancing lamps or bounding balls of fire
> Now in and out now up and down now higher
> As though an unseen horseman in his flight
> Flew swinging up and down on lamp alight[11]

Nor was it only these Jack-o'-lanterns that made the journey so full of spirits. Recent excavations have shown that sites of ancient tribes and pagan burial mounds also had to be passed on the way to the mill. Understandably the young Clare talked to himself, telling stories in which he always made himself the hero. Often he became so engrossed in these impromptu fantasies that he was still narrating aloud as he arrived back in the darkening streets of Helpston, where 'I have often felt ashamed at being overheard by people that overtook me it made my thoughts so active that they became troublesome to me in company.'[12]

Solitude became not always a choice but imposed upon him by his growing eccentricities and he became 'the sport of all the village'. This did not worry him on too many occasions or make him unhappy. The reverse is true. He preferred to be alone to hear the black-brown beetles sing their evening song and to see 'the black snail steal out upon some dewy bank'. But he was to become more than just a microscope looking into the secrets of a little known world. He was to become an interpreting eye, knowing himself to be part of that creation's plan. At the age of thirteen he had already begun to channel his curiosity into a deeper knowledge of his world. He watched, listened and remembered the exciting discoveries of his intimate explorations into nature, believing it all had a purpose – 'Twas thus his fond inquiry us'd to trace/Through nature's secrets with unwearied eye.'[13]

4

That first year working for Francis Gregory not only allowed Clare to live at home but also to observe more critically the life of his village, its daily toils and seasonal celebrations, its hardships and feast-days, scenes repeated year after year and eventually recorded with Chaucerian vigour in *The Village Minstrel* and *The Shepherd's Calendar*.

Some of the annual feasts had been held on the village green since the reign of Edward III and were a continuance of the revels and rituals enjoyed for generations. They gave the villagers an opportunity to put on their brand new clothes, to leave the milk-pails unscoured and the house unswept. They also provided a good excuse for flirting, love-making, gambling, dancing and drinking. There were fortune-tellers, Punch-and-Judy shows and, by the end of the day, a few brawls going on in the streets over some bragging deed or inflamed jealousy.

There were other festivals too when most of the merry-making went on inside the cottages. There 'beside the fire large apples lay to roast/And in a huge brown pitcher creaming ale/Was warming seasoned with a nutmeg toast . . .'.[14] When everyone had shared in these refreshments traditional games were played, and jokes made at the expense of those who were not too bright.

Many of these party games, like most of the village sports, were not without their degree of cruelty. In 'St Martin's Eve' Clare recalls how a fool is told to 'open your mouth and shut your eyes/And see what gifts are sent you'. He obeyed, only to receive a mouthful of warm ashes from the fire. Then they played the game of the three knives which were hidden somewhere in the room while someone, who was blindfolded, had to say where they were:

> Hodge hiding two did for the third enquire
> All tittered round & bade him hold it fast

But ah he shook it from his hands in ire
For while he hid the two they warmed it in the fire[15]

While he nursed his burnt hand the rest of the company 'laughed and laughed again until their ribs did ache'.

Only one person in the room failed to join in the fun. She was the latest girl in the village who had made 'one slip in love' and found herself 'condemned to live without a mate'. It was a situation Clare was to refer to often in his poems about village life and he may have been particularly sympathetic to the victim's plight because of his own grandmother's story. Sometimes there was cause for bitterness, as he was to relate in his long satire 'The Parish', which will be discussed later. The rich farmers' sons were quite prepared to forget their social superiority when they fancied one of the village girls. The dandy would then 'venture to bemean his pride' and take the girl of his choice by force – 'thus maids are ruin'd and mothers made/As if bewitched without a father's aid'.[16] Paltry bribes were usually enough to silence any gossip. The heartaches were endured, the suffering paid for in ways that brought misery instead of marriage.

Clare continued as an observer of the people's customs. Each season, event, feast and experience grew in fascination and meaning: Plough Witch Monday and the celebration of a new year on the land; spring and the resurrection of nature; St Valentine's Day and the secret confessions of love; April Fool's Day and the pranks on the village green; May Day and the May Feast with dancing round the maypole and singing in the streets; lambing-time and sheep-shearing; haymaking and harvest; the July Feast 'when the Cross was thronged round with stalls of toys & many colored sugar-plums & sweets'.[17]

Martinmas and Christmas; the gipsies and the Scottish cattle-drovers' arrival; the suppers, dances, games, brawls and skittles of a nineteenth-century rural England; all these experiences found their way into hundreds of poems, such as 'The Village Minstrel', 'Village Tales', 'The Village Doctress', 'The Cellar Door', 'The Parish', 'The Lout', 'Tit-for-Tat', 'Farm Breakfast', 'The Mole-Catcher' and many more – poems which unroll like a documentary film of a village on the edge of the fens, a social and historical record of fifty years that has not been surpassed in English poetry. The surprise is not that Clare wrote about these things; indeed one would have been surprised had a man of his talent not written about them.

5

During that year with Francis Gregory two brief but important encounters took place for Clare. He saw again the young girl he had fallen in love with at school, Mary Joyce, and he discovered the book of poetry that was to help direct the course of his own life as a poet, James Thomson's *Seasons*. This was a revelation which excited him to impulsive action, even though he was to be vague about the precise moment when it happened:

> I think I was 13 years of age now but trifling things are never punctually remembered as their occurrence is never strikingly impressed on the memory ... I met with a fragment of Thomson's Seasons ... I knew nothing of blank verse nor rhyme either otherwise than by the Ballad Singers but I still remember my sensations in reading the opening lines of Spring ...[18]

Those lines which made his heart 'twitter with joy' were clearly not trifling things never strikingly impressed on the memory. He was sufficiently impressed to 'greedily read over all' and long to possess a copy for himself. The copy he had borrowed belonged to a young man in the village who was a weaver by trade. Most of the section on 'Winter' had gone and, when asked about it, the weaver only shrugged his shoulders and said that it was reckoned nothing of by himself or his friends and that, as Methodists, they considered Wesley's hymns far superior. Even so, he wanted his copy of Thomson back and Clare then asked how he could obtain a complete edition for himself. It could be bought quite easily in Stamford, he was told, for one-and-sixpence.

His mind was made up. He badgered his father for the eighteen pence, which was almost a fifth of his father's weekly wage, and set off for Stamford. In his eagerness to possess the book he had forgotten which day of the week it was and found all the shops closed. He stopped a boy in the street (who was reading Collins's *Odes and Poems*) and asked when the shops would open. Tomorrow. Shops did not open on Sundays. Disappointed and agitated as to what he could do now, Clare walked home and sulked all day until he managed to bribe one of his fellow workers to look after his horses the following morning while he went on his errand. Once again the walk to Stamford. But it was only half-past six when he arrived and it was far too early for the bookshop to be open. He sat on the stone step and waited patiently for the town's business hours to begin. The clocks of the six churches ticked and chimed the hours away. As each new set of footsteps approached along the cobbled street Clare looked to see if it was the shopkeeper arriving for work. The footsteps passed. The bookseller lived above the shop. When he came down to open his door he was surprised at the eagerness of his first customer. When he also saw the excitement in those staring blue eyes he let Clare have the volume for sixpence less than the asking price. Could he have known that his shop would one day be stocked with the poems of that strange boy he might have thought it a good investment.

Clare could not wait until he reached home to read his book, nor did he want anyone to see him 'reading on the road of a working day', so he climbed over the stone wall into Burghley Park and sat down beneath a lime tree. Time stopped. The horses in Helpston, and the boy caring for them, were forgotten. The sun halted in its journey. The young, rough hands became tender with their prize. It was the most perfect, innocent conversion. An awakening to a truth that had slowly been unfolding. He knew then that he was to become a poet. There were no alternatives. It was beyond his reason to argue. The scenery around him was so beautiful, Thomson's poetry was so intoxicating, that he forgot all about the job he was supposed to be doing. Nothing could ever be more real than this unreal moment.

When he eventually climbed back over the wall and walked on to Helpston he had already started composing 'The Morning Walk' – 'the first thing I committed to paper'.[19] During the next few days he added to it 'Evening Walk' and several other verses about the world of nature to be found in his own favourite fields. He felt that Eden had been recreated, even bigger and better, just for him:

> I worshipped yet could hardly dare
> To show I knew the goddess there
> Lest my presumptuous stare should gain
> But frowns ill humour & disdain
> My first ambition was its praise[20]

Like all good conversions Clare's realization had conviction, immediacy, strength, resolution, and modesty:

> I felt that I'd a right to song
> And sung – but in a timid strain –
> Of fondness for my native plain
> For everything I felt a love
> The weeds below the birds above[21]

But then a circumstance occurred which nearly stopped him writing, even for his own pleasure. He borrowed from a friend he had known at school an anthology of poetry and prose. In the introduction the compiler had set down the rules for correct composition of English, stating that a person who knew nothing of grammar was not capable of writing a letter or even a bill of parcels. Clare admits that he was 'quite in the suds' seeing that he had gone this far 'without learning the first rudiments of doing it properly'.[22] But he was nothing if not tenacious and determined. He had an itch for trying everything and so bought himself a spelling book. It confused him more than it encouraged. The jumble of words classified under one heading or another made him turn 'from further notice of it in an instant disgust'.[23] He decided that as he could speak to be understood so by the same method he would commit his thoughts to paper. So, in the teeth of grammar, he pursued his literary journey.

Whatever he may not have known about the correct composition of English he did know that poetry was made of other things. He knew he had a right to song and if only he wrote as he felt then he would be understood. This is not to say that he took no trouble over revision or improvement; we shall see later that he did. The expression of those feelings became a consuming passion. Within weeks of discovering Thomson he had read some of Robert Bloomfield, some Pope and Collins, and was asking his father to recite again some of the old ballads. The more he read the more he realized that his own early verses had to be worked over and polished. He burnt many of his first compositions. Others he corrected 'perhaps 20 times over till their original form was lost'.[24]

To perfect their poems poets need an audience, however small, and a critic, however biased or inadequate. Clare's first audience was his parents. His first critic his father. Like most young poets he was working at his craft alone, finding out by trial and error how a poem worked. His instruction came from as many of the more established writers as he could find. He copied ballads and songs. He imitated favourite poets. His small library began to grow. As well as Thomson's *Seasons* and Pomfret's *Love Triumphant Over Reason* (which had been in the house for some time), his books now included *Pilgrim's Progress, Paradise Lost*, a volume of hymns by Isaac Watts, some poems of George Crabbe and William Cowper. Having been inspired by these poets he would read out his own efforts at night to his parents as they sat round the fire, passing his own verses off as those of some well-known writer. 'Aye boy,' said his father, 'if you could write so you would do so.'[25] Clare was quietly encouraged and continued the deception. Sometimes his parents would laugh and so he learned how to 'distinguish affectation and conceit from nature'.[26] Sometimes his father would ask him to read the verses over again and so he learned how to distinguish obscurity from commonsense. Clare was fortunate that poetry meant so much to his family. It was taken seriously. It belonged to an ancient tradition and privilege. It was a gift beyond price.

Some of those early successful poems he hid away in a hole in the wall near the fire-place, but his mother – who could not read – found them and unconsciously took them for kettle-holders and fire-lighters whenever she wanted paper, thinking them no more than finished exercises her son had forgotten to throw away. Clare was reluctant to confess that the pieces of paper contained *his* poems – the poems they had praised, that had been born in their house. He stood by in silent shame and anguish to see them slowly disappear into ashes. Then he left the room and went out again to the heath and the fields to look for other verses to take their place. Few heads have been more filled with words rushing towards the light. Fewer have fought so resolutely for the right to sing their words. Whatever happened now, at home or at work, he had a purpose to which all else took second place.

6

Not even the easy-going, generous Francis Gregory could keep Clare for ever and he, too, was getting tired of doing those many menial tasks from emptying the morning slops to scrubbing the floors of the inn. He now had 'the restless hope of being something better than a ploughman' and, by the end of 1806, his ambitions 'kept burning about me to make a better figure in the world'.[27]

For a moment it looked as if he might become a sign-writer or stone-mason. A man named Manton from Market Deeping came into the bar one day and talked so enthusiastically about his craft that Clare was anxious to become a sign-writer and stone-mason too. At least he would be making letters, words and names. He might even be given the task of cutting the 'mortuary poetry' that was engraved on those morbid, brief biographies of a churchyard's library. But again it meant becoming an apprentice and paying the mason to be taught the mysteries of his art, rather than receiving payment for his labour. Disappointedly Clare left the inn realizing how hopeless it was to learn a trade from anyone when such knowledge had to be bought. When, at the end of that year, he left the Blue Bell, he had no idea when or where he would find work. What hopes he had still rested in the knowledge he had bought from the schoolmasters in Glinton. He felt sure a chance would come one day. So he returned to his books and waited. Often he would stay away from the cottage all day so that his parents did not have to provide him with food. He pulled a turnip from the field, picked berries from the hedgerow and drank water from a stream. To forget his hunger he concentrated even more on the natural life around him. It survived. So too would he.

6
Leaving Home

1

During the months of unemployment Clare walked over each week to the hamlet of Ashton, near Barnack, to see Tom Porter who had been a friend since early childhood. Their tastes were parallel in everything except poetry. Porter was, nevertheless, a lover of books. He often went into Stamford with Clare to browse among the second-hand bookshops, or along the bookstalls which were once a common feature at local fairs and markets. He knew how desperate Clare was to find work and one day had news for him. He had heard that the master of the kitchen gardens at Burghley House wanted an apprentice. Clare knew the estate well. He had trespassed in its woodlands and, not so long ago, had sat under its lime trees to read his first real book of poems. It was a good house, one of the great Elizabethan houses of England and the seat of the Marquis of Exeter. The thought of working there appealed to him and he asked his father if he would go with him the following Sunday morning to apply for the job. Parker did not relish the long walk but was so anxious to find a place for his son that he agreed to go. Clare also thought that his father's reputation in the area would be to his benefit.

When they saw the head gardener dressed in white stockings they thought it must be the Marquis himself and quickly took off their hats in an embarrassing act of obeisance. This mistake may have gone some way towards persuading the vain gardener to offer Clare an apprenticeship for three years, living in with the other servants and earning his keep.

His tasks included taking fruit and vegetables up to the hall kitchens twice a day and running errands into nearby Stamford whenever the head gardener wanted something. This usually meant more supplies of liquor and he was a man of such a harsh temper that neither Clare nor anyone else liked him. There were times when he disappeared altogether and his wife would send Clare to look for him. Clare knew where he would be but, rather than disturb his master angry with drink, he would lie down under the trees and go to sleep himself. He slept so soundly that on late autumn nights he would wake to discover his clothes white with rime and his limbs numb from cold. It was a numbness he was to feel every spring and autumn for the rest of his life, though it never stopped him sleeping out of doors when there was nowhere else. During those teenage years he grew used to sleeping in the open, especially when he had been merrymaking in Stamford and had 'taken too much of Sir John Barleycorn'.[1]

It was during his time at Burghley that he first acquired his 'irregular habits'. All the under-gardeners were locked up at night in a garden-house to prevent them from robbing the fruit trees, but they had fixed a window through which they could climb and so escape to Stamford where they could enjoy some midnight revels. Clare liked to think he was as good as the men and went with them. When he had no money his companions would treat him for the sake of his company and to keep him from giving the game away. His liking for ale certainly began when he was only a boy and his wish not to be thought inferior in anything pushed him to drink more than he could hold.

Their favourite drinking place was the Hole in the Wall, a cramped, smoky inn tucked away in Chain Lane (now Cheyne Lane); a place renowned for its strong ale, its amusements and its loose women. The landlord was a hearty sort of fellow called Tant Baker who had himself worked as a servant at Burghley and he was only too willing to help the present servants drink their cares away. The drinking and singing went on until the early hours of the morning. Some of the men then went to a local brothel and the others made their unsteady way home. When the head gardener realized that young Clare had been party to these escapades he threatened to dismiss him and send him back to Helpston. Rather than have this happen Clare decided he would dismiss himself.

Towards the end of his first year – and after another rowdy night in Stamford – he agreed with one of the gardener's foremen that the time had come to leave Burghley and look for work elsewhere. They left early one morning and walked twenty-one miles to Grantham. But there was no work there. They spent the night at the Crown and Anchor and the following morning set off for Newark-on-Trent, fifteen miles further north. Suddenly Clare became very homesick:

> I felt quite lost when I was here though it was a very lively town but I had never been from home before scarcely further than out of sight of the steeples I became so ignorant in this land that I could not tell

which quarter the wind blew from & I was even foolish enough to think the sun's course was alterd & that it rose in the west & set in the east[2]

After making many enquiries in the town he and his companion found work in Newark with a Mr Withers, a nurseryman. To begin with it looked as if they had been lucky in their choice of employer but, in those days of surplus labour, Withers turned out to be no better than most and would only pay his new gardeners a small wage until they proved themselves by further trial. Clare was now very weak and found the long hours of work too heavy both for his strength and liking. Once again he and his companion decided they could find something better and left by the first light of morning. Both men were now depressed and wondered if their adventure was such a good idea after all. Later in the day they agreed that when they came to the next village they would spend their last few pence on drink and forget their troubles. Clare became so drunk that he made up his mind to end all his worries by accepting the King's bounty and joining the Nottinghamshire Militia. Fortunately for him, the recruiting officer did not think the boy was tall enough or fit enough to wear the colours and rejected him at the swearing-in. Looking at some of the ruffians who were accepted, Clare felt this rejection was final. After months of living rough, and now with no hope of employment, there was only one thing to do – return to Helpston. At least he would be with his family and could hopefully find solace in his native fields again. And perhaps the poetry, which had been neglected for over a year, would return with him.

2

The need to find work once more became a priority. Parker Clare was now so crippled with rheumatism that he could hardly stand. When he did walk it was with the aid of two sticks. But his spirit was, as Clare said of him, 'strongly knitted with independence and the thought of being forced to bend before the frowns of a Parish to him was the greatest despair'.[3] So Parker Clare stubbornly strove with his infirmities and 'pottered about the roads putting stones in the ruts for his 5 shillings a week'.[4]

The family was now heavily in debt. Two years' rent was due, there were bills from the grocer, baker and cobbler, and mounting debts at the bookshop in Stamford. Clare himself became ill for a year with 'a severe disposition' and his mother was now suffering from the dropsy. His own 'indisposition' came from a recurrence of fainting fits which he imagined owed their origin to the accident he had seen a few years earlier on

Turnill's farm when Thomas Drake was killed. In these fits he swooned away without a struggle and felt as if he had been through nothing more than a dreamless sleep. He always knew when an attack was on its way. A chilliness and trembling crept through his body, from his toes to his head, and then he fell. 'Sparks as of fire often flashed from my eyes,' he was to recall, 'or seemed to do so.'[5] Then he knew no more until he came round some minutes later. (Although there is no medical evidence to prove that these fits were epileptic, their symptoms are very similar to those described by Margiad Evans in *A Ray of Darkness*, her own story of coming to terms with epilepsy.[6]) Clare's attacks were serious enough for him to consult Dr Arnold of Stamford who was able to give some relief, but the fear of them always returned in spring and autumn, bringing back his dread of death and a terror of open graves.

Indisposed or not, Clare now had to earn some money for his family to help keep them out of the workhouse. But employment prospects had not improved, certainly not for him. With the country still at war, and the threats of an invasion by Napoleon's army growing, he decided again that there was nothing else for him to do but join the Militia, this time for his own county. A national campaign had been launched to raise a raw army of volunteers and Helpston was expected to make its contribution. Rumour even went round the streets that the French had already reached Northampton. By the end of the week who knew what would happen. The village suddenly had something else to talk about. It certainly had a few idle young men it could spare.

Clare was not a militant but felt he had a 'cross-grained sort of choice . . . which was to be forced to be drawn & go for nothing or take on as a volunteer for a bounty of two guineas.'[7] He accepted the latter and went with a neighbour's son – W. Clark – to Peterborough where they were to be sworn in before joining the county regiment at Oundle. The morning they left home their mothers parted with them as if they were going to Botany Bay. The villagers came to their doors to wave a mixed farewell. By the time they reached Oundle Clare was regretting his mercenary patriotism. When he saw all the other young men lined up in the field which served as a parade-ground he had to confess that he had never seen a 'more motley multitude of lawless fellows'.[8] Thirteen hundred men had responded to the call. They were sorted into companies and kitted out in whatever uniforms were thrown at them. Clare, as one of the shortest recruits, received a uniform for a Goliath. Because of his size he was put into a battalion nicknamed 'bum-tools' but he did not know for what reason. Other companies were called 'light-bobs' and 'bacon-bolters', and the enmity between them was at times greater than any hatred felt for Napoleon.

Most of the men had to find their own camp or lodgings, but lodgings in Oundle were hard to come by and, human nature thriving in adversity, personal profits came before patriotism. People who could provide accommodation 'took advantage of the tide' and charged high prices. Clare went to the Rose and Crown, a small inn kept by a widow and her two daughters, who were modestly good-natured and may have momentarily brightened Clare's despair. The inn is still there and outwardly has probably changed little since he was a guest.

The captain commanding the regiment was a quiet, understanding man who spoke civilly to his troops and advised the men more as a friend than an officer on how they should put wrongs right. But the corporal in charge of drilling them was ignorant and uncouth, a 'little louse looking man' who took delight in finding fault with everything Clare tried to do, particularly making fun of his size and awkwardness as a soldier.[9] Clare admits that he was never 'wonderful clean in my dress' and that when he was given a gun he handled it most clumsily. At the same time he was not going to be the object of this upstart's malice and so decided that the next time he criticized him he would fall out of ranks and politely address him. But, when the corporal's jests and jeerings started again, a madness flushed to Clare's cheeks and politeness was immediately forgotten. He could stand it no longer. Throwing his gun aside he seized the corporal by the throat, hurled him to the ground and kicked him. To Clare's surprise this suddenly 'got the fellow fame for those that had been against him before lifted him up & calld him a good fellow & me a coward.'[10] Clare was threatened with a few days in the 'Black Hole' but his captain came to his aid, heard his account of the incident as well as the corporal's and punished his young recruit with just one extra guard duty. Clare realized he had been let off lightly.

A very different episode, however, nearly landed him in trouble with the officers. They had decided that the recruits needed more discipline and ordered them to be on parade at six o'clock in the morning instead of eight. But, as most of the men had been used to starting work at four o'clock, this was a hardship only to the officers. The wife of one of the captains was very concerned about her husband being up this early and felt sure he would catch cold. So she sent her serving-maid off to the camp with a substantial breakfast. As an officer and a gentleman he knew he could not accept the meal or his wife's anxieties. He told the girl to go home and teach her mistress to know better. His fellow officers applauded his action but the recruits thought it all ridiculous and made great fun of it. Clare thought the story too good to lose and wrote a satirical ballad about it which he proposed to publish and sell among the ranks – an early example of his practical attitude to making some money out of his talent. But when the printer read through the manuscript he considered it too personal, even libellous, and warned Clare that it would get him into trouble if he was ever discovered as the author. So as he went back to his lodgings Clare tore his ballad into little pieces and the matter was forgotten. He then accepted two guineas to enlist for overseas duty should he ever be needed – five shillings to be paid on signature and the rest when the time for call-up came. But, with the fears of invasion receding and his presence at Oundle no longer required, he returned to Helpston to see what he could make of life there again. There was no hero's welcome.

3

To begin with the thought of going home made him happy. He felt he was going back to the scenes of his childhood which had once given him so much joy. But those times were past. 'Though all my scenes are in my sight/Sad manhood marks me an intruder now.'[11] He realized he had to go beyond childhood, deeper into those old allegiances that he was beginning to recognize, back to the forgotten music and the mysteries within birds-eggs or flower-root. Nature needed interpretation as well as description. Already some of those wild places were disappearing like half-remembered dreams. Enclosure was coming to Helpston. His world was changing. He had to preserve what he could of Eden.

His moods of despondency, though often fathomless, were never without hope. He fluctuated between despair and rapture. He knew that the discovery of Self was something that had to be earned and the journey towards finding his own voice as a poet was going to be a lonely, frustrating one. It would mean recognizing and then discarding some of those dreams. It would mean being misunderstood, even by those whom he loved and trusted. But, in coming home, he had already confirmed one growing belief – that he was going to be a poet and that his native landscape already held most of his poetry. He would absorb every mood and moment of this land until he became a mirror of each day and until the earth, in turn, became a mirror of himself.

No one's roots had ever gone deeper into their native soil. If nature rejected him then there was nothing. If his roots were ever severed from that ancient supply then he would die. He knew how important it was for a man like himself to have a physical contact with the soil. This contact increased his awareness of the long tradition between man and the earth. His returning was, once more, an affirmation of his belonging to a place, of feeling a child of that place, of making that place his private, personal world.

Laurens van der Post recalls how Carl Jung told him repeatedly 'That the nature of the earth itself had a profound influence on the character of the people born and raised on it. He could not define it. Nor was there any scientific means by which he could prove it' and yet he maintained that a character was an expression of the soil.[12]

Clare certainly belonged to the soil and all it meant. He loved to handle it, loved to sit on a molehill or grassy bank and feel himself being absorbed back into the mysterious darkness of the roots. He smelt it and breathed it. He did not praise nature from *outside*, as a pastoral poet, but from deep *inside*, where the relationship is binding. He could not have broken faith with that tradition and his poems are better understood when they are seen as expressions of that faith. He was oversimplifying it when he said that he 'found his poems in the field/And only wrote them down'.[13] He took his apprenticeship years very seriously and saw the importance of learning his craft. But the craft stood a better chance when the natural flow of inspiration came from a familiar source.

The pressures upon him to meet the demands of his mind, and the growing need to earn enough money to keep himself and his parents out of the workhouse, drove him deeper into nature for consolation and frequently into riotous evenings for release. During the day he discussed his secret life with the fields, flowers, birds, insects and everything that he saw struggling to survive. When darkness came he went to see his friends the Billings brothers at 'Bachelors Hall' where they drank home-brewed ale until the early hours of the morning. There he could be as rowdy, bawdy and coarse as the rest:

> It was a sort of meeting-house for the young fellows of the town where they usd to join for ale & tobacco & drink the night away the occupiers were two bachelors & the cottage was calld 'Bachelors Hall' it is an old ruinous hut & has needed repairs ever since I knew it for they neither mend up the walls nor thatch the roof being negligent men but quiet & inoffensive neighbours[14]

Clare was a popular visitor, often taking his fiddle with him to provide some music, or writing a song specially for them on the spot. On one occasion he wrote some doggerel verses which caused some amusement. The song was called 'Billings Sorrows in Being Sober for Want of Money to Get Drunk' and had to be sung to the tune of 'Doleful Dumps'.

Clare was never such a serious and dreamy poet that he could not turn his skills into entertainment for his friends. The Billings brothers were a regular audience for his impromptu songs, especially the bawdy ones which he never wrote down, or if he did, destroyed fairly soon afterwards. Explicit words for male and female organs often gave him outrageous rhymes which earned applause and laughter from his friends. He tried using such language more seriously years later in his poem 'Don Juan' and frequently strived for a robustness which shocked his editors.

John Billings, the older of the brothers, had a 'very haunted mind, for any supernatural event and kept his company enthralled with ghost stories or shadowy mysteries. The younger brother, James, was keen on shooting and the two would sometimes take Clare with them on Sundays when they went out for a kill. Clare had no eye for the sport though in those days his will 'was as good as the rest'.[15] One day, however, when James Billings raised his old gun to shoot a hare, the barrel exploded and blew into fragments, an alarm that cured Clare of ever going with them again.

He began to feel that his life was charmed, that he had been spared too many times for it always to be a coincidence. He had been close to death so often, whether it was at birth, or when he feel into deep water as a boy, whether it was sleeping in collapsing barns after a night's drinking in Stamford, or standing near exploding guns. Perhaps he was after all different from all the other men of the village and had a claim to something greater than any of them would know.

4

When he was not with the Billings brothers he was most likely to be found with the gipsies, that race of law-defying people with whom he felt more than a sentimental sympathy. He had joined them at their camps in the evenings on many occasions to improve his fiddle-playing and to learn more of their customs. The first family he became acquainted with was the Boswells, a 'popular tribe well known about here & famous for fiddlers & fortune tellers'.[16] The more he got to know them, the more he believed them to be an unfairly persecuted race:

> everything that is bad is thrown upon the gipsies their name is grown into ill omen & when any of the tribe are guilty of petty theft the odium is thrown upon the whole tribe An ignorant iron-hearted Justice of the Peace at ——— Sessions whose name may perish with his cruelty... mixed up this malicious sentence in his condemnation of 2 gipsies for horse-stealing – 'This atrocious tribe of wandering vagabonds ought to be made outlaws in every civilised kingdom & exterminated from the face of the earth!' & this persecuting, unfeeling man was a clergyman![17]

Clare had several reasons for being anti-cleric and thought those clergymen who served as magistrates were particularly lacking in the compassion recommended by Christ. He felt their interpretation of the civil laws, the poor laws and the holy laws usually went in the opposite direction – at least for the poor, who generally believed that there was one law for the rich and one law for themselves, and that law had little charity and no mercy. After reading George Fox's *Book of Martyrs* Clare wrote in his journal that 'the sum of my opinion is Tyranny & Cruelty appear to be the inseperable companions of Religious Power'.[18]

He had avoided attending church too often as a boy and now felt his Sundays were more wisely spent with the gipsies than with the men who used the pulpit for condemning the meek and blessing the privileged. He enjoyed the vagabonds' earthier company enough to think seriously of joining them. But although he enjoyed their music and dancing, although he envied them their freedom under the stars and escape from convention, he found that they were very loose in their morals, which, considering some of his own excesses, sounds more like a public statement than a private conviction. A more persuasive reason for not joining them was their food, which he did not find very agreeable to his delicate stomach. They ate the flesh of badgers and hedgehogs – which he did not mind because he had eaten of them in his evenings of merrymaking with them – but 'they never eat dead meat but in times of scarcity which they cut into thin slices & throw on to a brisk fire till it is scorched black when it loses its putrid smell.'[19] He also thought they smoked to excess. Both the men and the women were seldom without their pipes. At his first acquaintance with them he was puzzled to find that all the young men had a crooked finger on one hand. When he asked about this they refused to give him an explanation. Later, however, when he had gained their confidence, they told him the reason – a finger of every male child was disabled by his parents to keep him from being drawn or press-ganged into the army when the country was at war, or from being sent as soldiers for any petty theft they might commit during the peace.

The hours he spent with the gipsies, like many other experiences of those years, were to find their way into the poems waiting to be written, poems which would be brought into existence by a similar experience – the impression preserved by memory being given new life in a wiser moment of perception. The gipsies were remembered in 'The Gipsies' Evening Blaze', 'The Gipsy's Camp', 'Gipsies' and the many references to them in the longer poems. They emerge unmistakably as the characters they were – 'With tawny smoked flesh and tatter'd rags/Uncouth-brimm'd hat and weather-beaten cloak' crouched round their ancient fires.[20]

Not all the hours back at Helpston were so carefree. He still had hopes that he might yet win Mary Joyce when his fortunes changed. He did not go to Glinton regularly now but he did walk those field-paths where he knew he stood a good chance of seeing her. How often they met we do not know. Perhaps no more than half a dozen times during the next two years. But her very existence was enough. Inconsistent, unfaithful, Clare was to remain faithful to Mary Joyce in spirit if nothing else. The more distant their relationship became the more passionately he sought her. Could the man succeed where the boy had failed?

7
Mary Joyce

1

It is not easy to place Mary Joyce precisely in the chronological order of Clare's life because although the time they spent together could be measured in days she was, for a number of reasons, to become his recurring passion for fifty years.

But there is a difference between the Mary Joyce of reality and the Mary Joyce of the poems. Most of the poems about her were written long after they had parted, and certainly after he had married Martha (Patty) Turner. Had that early separation not occurred there would not have been the intense poetry which later came out of his torment and dream world.

Like other aspects of his life, Clare's Mary remains a mystery. The love may have been real, or it may have been unreal – spiritual rather than physical. But Mary Joyce did exist and, as a young girl, did know John Clare. She may, indeed, have had a deep affection for him. She was born in January 1797 and was four years younger than Clare. She came from a prosperous farming family, highly respected in the neighbourhood. Her father, James Joyce, served as churchwarden until 1817 and the whole family went regularly to church. They lived in a good, large stone house in Glinton and employed servants and labourers.

Nearly everything else that can be learnt about Mary is to be found in the poems that Clare wrote for her, including 'A Daydream in Summer', 'The Progress of Rhyme', 'First Love's Reccolections' and many other love ballads. From them we know that she had blue eyes that 'once did steal their sapphire blue from even',[1] that when Clare was seventeen the only recognition he wanted then was a look from her eyes in which 'the blue of thirteen summers' could be seen,[2] and that she had a 'sweet voice' which was always remembered as 'the self-same voice as soft and dear/As that which met his youthful ear'.[3] She liked solitude and shared Clare's reverence for nature, even to the point of telling him off for disturbing a linnet from its nest. They went blackberrying or nut-gathering together and he was to record that 'the shells her auburn hair did show/A semblance faint yet beautiful'.[4]

As a girl Mary had preferred his company at school. He was different from the other boys. He knew the names of all the plants and liked picking wildflowers. He could recognize the songs of birds and could identify butterflies and moths. He, in return, worshipped her and was never happier than when they were alone. Once, he hurt her by accidentally hitting her in the eye with a green walnut and, because he did not want to be thought a cissy, he laughed with the other boys who thought it funny. But he brooded over the incident all night and the following morning waited anxiously at the churchyard gate until she arrived. There was no need to explain or apologize. She understood. He was forgiven.

When the busy weeks of land-work kept him away from school he used to walk over to her village in the evenings in the hope of seeing her. Sometimes they might meet by a stile near the hawthorn bushes, or by an old stone bridge near a Roman dyke, along a lane which is now known as North Fen Road, between Glinton and Northborough. If he could not find her waiting for him near the bridge he would go to her house and stand outside while she practised the piano. Her parents did not encourage their friendship even when he was a young man. He was harmless enough but not of their class. It would pass. As their daughter grew older she would see for herself that she should find someone better.

There could be no one better for Clare, or so he thought. Mary was gentle, sensitive and understanding. As experience never came to challenge those ideals she was to remain the goddess of his poetry. The love which grew out of their innocence has sometimes been seen as a story that could take its place beside those of Dante and Beatrice, Petrarch and Laura, Abelard and Heloise. But should it? Clare was not to remain faithful or changeless in his affections. There were to be several loves in his life, though none more ultimately significant than his fictitious love for Mary. So what went wrong? Was it more than the difference in their social position which prevented them from marrying, or was Clare again afraid and uncertain, 'fearful of undertaking the first trial in everything'?

Some of the earlier biographers[5] have suggested that it was Mary's father who put a stop to his daughter seeing the Helpston farm-labourer. It is possible that he did, or that he at least expressed strong objections to their relationship. In those days of fluctuating fortunes in agriculture anyone with a chance in life wanted to better themselves, and their families. It would have been natural for James Joyce to want his daughter to marry above rather than below her station. She was an attractive girl (as most of Clare's girls were) and could have been courted by any of the eligible young farmers in the area. But Mary, it appears, did not want their wealth and doubtful manners, for she never married. Clare, on the other hand, was only an ill-dressed son of an out-of-work thresher, a shy, weak boy with no prospects, 'a clownish, silent aguish boy/Who even felt ashamed of joy'.[6] The social differences of the nineteenth century were both distinct and unbridgeable. Marriage might not have been impossible for two people like Mary Joyce and John Clare but it was extremely difficult, and frequently accompanied by bitterness and shame. Even though Clare was to hope that one day literary success might justify his claims to the hand of a farmer's daughter it is unlikely that the traditions of that class-ordered society would have been altered by a successful book of poems. Literature did not have the same value as land. Because of this distinction in class there was a deep-rooted inferiority in Clare which made it agonizing for him to hope beyond dreams. Any hint from Mary of their differences (even when kindly meant) would have been taken by him as a personal insult.

Mr Joyce may have told his young daughter to stop seeing John Clare but it is a little unfair to blame him entirely for their parting. What had she said, for instance, that made Clare write 'when she grew to womanhood she felt her station was above mine at least I felt that she thought so...'?[7] He was not sure. Had she simply told him to pull himself together and do something positive with the intelligence he possessed? He half-admits that he probably misunderstood her remarks. He could be idle. He was over-sensitive about his humble origins. The wish to escape from his background was to motivate his work and recharge his ambitions more than once, especially when he came to taste that better life which existed beyond his village street. At the same time he was equally conscious of his limitations and worried about his lack of formal education. It made him feel insecure and, however great his natural talent, the absence of any academic training put him at a disadvantage in any company outside that of his neighbours. He was to despise even that at times and it, in turn, was to fail him. The effort to belong anywhere always demanded a high price, emotionally and intellectually.

When Edward Drury came to write to John Taylor on 5 May 1819 about his new young poet he made particular reference to Clare's 'envy and anguish at other people's education and opportunities'.[8] They were so deep that Clare made himself 'really sick and ill' worrying about them. He remained equally worried all his life about the lack of money which deprived him of improvement. These injustices gnawed away at his personality, made him at times short-tempered, and wounded his natural pride. They helped to make him his own worst enemy. He was constantly torn between what he might *expect* and what he had to *accept*.

He saw himself in an impossible position 'where toil and slavery bear each fancy down/That fain would soar'.[9] Although he felt he had a 'right to song' he could not easily dismiss the fact that there was a world which did not share his belief. 'I dreaded laughter more than blame/I dared not sing aloud for shame.'[10] He even thought in those days that it would be wrong 'for one so lowly to be heard so long'.[11] Nothing had, in those days, given him cause to believe better. If Mary tried to inspire some confidence into him it is a pity that he misunderstood her criticism. Maybe she tried too hard and lost patience. They argued about it. She was becoming a sophisticated young woman. Clare could not match her. Being unable to meet her on her level did him as much harm as the remembered love did good. Perfection and virtue are dangerous ideals.

But what did Clare have to say about their relationship outside the love poems? The prose accounts are at variance with what we find in those poems. It is likely that he was too self-conscious in the prose to reveal all, whereas in the poems he told more than he realized. In the *Sketches* of his life he wrote:

> It was a platonic affection, nothing else but love in idea for she knew nothing of my fondness for her no more than I did of her inclinations to forbid or encourage me had I disclosed afterwards. But other Marys &c excited my admiration and the first creator of my warm passions was lost in a perplexed multitude of names that would fill a volume[12]

Among his manuscripts and notebooks there are multitudes of names and we are left in no doubt that throughout his life Clare had a constant sexual hunger, that he was sensuous and did admire attractive women. His frankness in writing about the subject often offended his patrons. Those poems in which he mentions love-making, rape, incest and the amorous conquests at feasts were to be heavily censored by his editors. He was to have more than one affair after his marriage to Patty Turner and his guilt frequently led him to believe he had caught a venereal infection. He was, he says, 'a lover very early in life' but then tempers his love for Mary Joyce with some caution:

> if I coud but gaze on her face or fancy a smile on her countenance it was sufficient I went away satisfyed we played with each other but named nothing of love yet I fancyed her eyes told me her affection . . . but when she grew to womanhood she felt her station above mine at least I felt she thought so for her parents were farmers & farmers had great pretensions to something then so my passion coold with my reason & contented itself with another tho I felt a hopeful tenderness that I might one day renew the acquaintance & disclose the smotherd passion she was a beautiful girl & as the dream never awoke into reality her beauty was always fresh in my memory[13]

So although there were to be other girls Mary was the first and the most desired – 'Thou wert the first my heart to win/Thou art the last to wear it.'[14] But still doubts persist. If the dream never awoke into reality how far can we go in accepting anything he wrote about her? Was she nothing more than a dream, an illusion? The poems are so convincing, so explicit, they surely must contain some truth:

> When honied tokens from each tongue
> Told with what truth we loved
> How rapturous to thy lips I clung
> Whilst nought but smiles reproved[15]
>
> *
>
> For by this bridge my Mary sat
> And praised the screaming plover
> As first to hail the day when I
> Confessed myself her lover[16]

If we are to believe the poems we have to accept for a moment that she meant more to him than the two prose accounts will admit. We also have to believe that there was a time when she was more than a dream for if 'nought but smiles reproved' his passionate kisses then Mary must have felt some love for Clare in return. But years passed between those early expressions of love and Clare's writing about them, so the figure who haunted his imagination in later life was probably more than just Mary. She was mother, sister, goddess, all things that filled his need of beauty, identity and perfection – part of that innocent world lost before enclosure and his own bitter experiences. As a human relationship it could not last. And it was something very human which separated them. They quarrelled. Mary's father may have objected to her seeing Clare but he could not stop her. Something else happened between them with, it would appear, an equal share of impatience and misunderstanding. They had an argument. It must have been a long and heated one in which Mary threatened to go off with someone else. The memory of that day filled Clare with remorse for years to come. Thinking of a daisy he had once plucked for her, he wrote:

> [I] little thought an evil hour
> Was bringing clouds around me
> & least of all that little flower
> Would turn a thorn to wound me
> She showed me after many days
> Though withered how she prized it
> Then she inclined to wealthy praise
> And my poor love – despised it
>
> . . .

When lovers part the longest mile
Leaves hope of some returning
Though mine's close by no hopes the while
Within my heart are burning
One hour would bring me to her door
Yet sad and lonely hearted
If seas between us both should roar
We were not further parted[17]

If Clare ever really *loved* Mary Joyce at all it was not until he moved to Northborough in 1832 and was living within a mile of her house in Glinton. But then it was too late. He was forty, married, with six children, and losing his reputation as a poet. There has been much speculation about when he saw Mary last and whether he ever saw her while living in Northborough. It is almost certain he did. The favourite lane between the two villages became one of his daily walks. The references in the poems written during those important years, as we shall see in the chapter about Northborough, suggest that the lovers did meet and share their regrets together. By that time Mary would have known of the fame Clare had enjoyed. She could read and must have possessed his published work. It is natural to assume that Clare himself would have made sure that copies reached her. With the impetuous moments of youth behind them they must have both felt that their lives had been separated by the narrowest of threads. Had she remained a spinster because no one else could ever replace that first innocent love of Clare's? As it turned out the parting may have prolonged that love and given us the most moving poems of its loss. Mary died in July 1838, at the age of forty-one unmarried and unaware of the poetry she was still to inspire.

2

With the wild years over it was easy for Clare to see his mistakes but, as a young man, he was to need (as he found) his Martha as well as his Mary, and he was to love that simpler, more down-to-earth girl from Walkherd Lodge – Martha Turner – with a genuine but totally different kind of affection. Mary inspired in him moments of supreme poetry. Her love never became tarnished with the mundane, domestic realities that his other life was to know. Had it been it could not have survived at such a level of perfection. His love for Mary was as unreal as Eden. No matter how often Clare tried to bring it back to life he could not alter the fact that his separation from Mary came at a very disturbing period of his own development. His months away in Grantham and Newark had given him other things to think about and other girls to admire. For a time he himself put Mary beyond his reach. Out of sight, out of mind. He 'lost that lonely feeling & grew dissipated'; he 'drank to stifle unpleasant feelings' which his follies often brought on. These follies, he explained, were 'love follys that made the heart ache a pain well known to lovers caused by rejected addresses to someone whom I felt a sudden affection for & who on my disclosing it woud affect to sneer & despise me.'[18] Could this really have been Mary, the guiltless, virtuous woman of the later poem, or someone else? If it is Mary then the poems have to be seen as fiction, as Clare's own imagined love-story. Indeed, he forgot so much about Mary that in the notes for his autobiography he says, 'my first love really was with a girl of Ashton whose name was Elizabeth Newbon She was no beauty but I fancyd she was everything & our courtship was a long one.'[19]

Clare was allowed to meet Elizabeth at her home, the lodge-house on Ashton Green, where her father was the wheelwright. He was an old man who professed to be very knowledgeable about the Bible. He was always trying out Clare's knowledge of it too. Clare, often intimidated into silence by the old man's fanaticism, frequently failed to answer. Elizabeth's father took this to mean that her young man was ignorant of the scriptures and had no religion. He believed that religion consisted of learning long paragraphs of the scriptures off by heart, of knowing on which mountain top Noah's Ark came to rest, and other 'Bible curiosities'. But he never went to church himself and thought it did not matter. Clare agreed with him there and generally felt that the old man was harmless enough and tried to humour him with his own knowledge of other books. But no sooner had he won the approval of Mr Newbon than he ran into trouble with Elizabeth. They argued over many things but mostly 'petty jealousys' and she charged Clare with having an affair with another girl. Probably with very good reason. He resented her criticism. He never liked admitting he was in the wrong. The relationship came to an end. Although he continued to visit his friend Tom Porter who lived in the village he had no more to do with Elizabeth Newbon. Despite their 'long courtship' she does not appear to have inspired any poetry in him either.

Soon Clare was seeking the company of other girls and enjoying himself again in Stamford or Market Deeping with his fellow drinkers. For a time it seemed as if his life was to be spent wastefully and without purpose. No woman was ever going to take the place of Mary Joyce in Clare's mind but it was a fortunate day for him when, a couple of years later, he met Patty Turner. She was real. She, more than Mary, must be given some credit for making Clare into a poet.

But he had more than love's uncertainties to worry about between the years that led up to his marriage in 1820. For ten years his world had been changing – 'Inclosure like a Buonoparte [sic] let not a thing remain.'[20]

8
Enclosure

1

Clare had seen something of enclosure from the private agreements on the Earl Fitzwilliam's estates. He had heard of the Parliamentary Enclosure Acts in other parts of the country and knew how they were changing the face of the landscape. By 1800 nearly fifteen hundred Acts had been passed affecting two and a half million acres. By 1844 a further one thousand Acts were to bring the total of open fields brought under enclosure to more than four million acres. Add to this some two million acres of wild land – heaths, moors and commons – and we get some idea of the extent of the changes that Clare was to live through during his development as a poet. Virtually the whole of rural England was being transformed and nearly three thousand parishes found themselves involved in this transformation.

These changes had been given an added dimension by the recent wars with France. They had come at a critical moment in the country's social development. They had threatened the economic life of the land and had helped to distract the government's attention from some of the serious problems at home. They had also had the effect of cutting off vital supplies of corn from the Continent, supplies much needed in an island whose population was rapidly increasing. Between the census of 1801 and the census of 1831 the population of England, Wales and Scotland was to rise from eleven million to sixteen and a half million. Between 1810 and 1820 Helpston's own population rose from 276 to 372. Several families had arrived to help with the enclosing – planting hawthorn hedges and fencing – and had stayed in the village when the work was finished. Clare himself was forced to help in the work of enclosing his native fields, even though he was bitterly opposed to the policy.

But the country's population was not the only thing rising. Between 1792 and 1812 the price of wheat rose from forty-three shillings to one hundred and twenty-six shillings a quarter. Nor did it stop there. The meeting at Speenhamland of the Berkshire magistrates in May 1795 led, not to an agreement for fixing and enforcing a minimum wage in relation to the price of bread (as it intended), but to an iniquitous system whereby the poor should receive from the parish rates a certain sum each week to supplement their wages as the price of flour and bread rose.[1] The farmers could only gain. They could make more profit but did not have to worry about paying higher wages. The decision taken by the magistrates not only meant that the rich grew richer and the poor grew poorer, it also hardened relationships between employer and employees – or, more often, the unemployed. The understanding and respect which had existed in former days between the landowner and his workers, even between the tenant-farmer and his men, was suddenly broken. No more were men and master to share the same supper table at harvest time, or talk over the problems of the land round a jug of ale. Enclosure brought into existence a new breed of farmers who paid little respect to the traditions of the past. The days of which Clare was once able to write, when 'To close the ranting night the master's health/Went round in bumping horns to every swain' had gone.[2] In their place had come the age where 'Every village owns it tyrants now/And parish-slaves must live as parish-kings allow.'[3]

Clare did not use the word 'slave' carelessly or with any sense of melodrama. It was still the age of Wilberforce. Slavery was a condition not very far removed from English life. Its meaning was clear in Clare's mind. As he saw it slavery was not even abolished in this country despite the Acts of Parliament. Poverty and slavery were the same. The parish officers were to show about as much humanity and mercy as the new farmers. The hardships of Helpston could be multiplied a thousand times. The Midland counties were caught up in these changes more than most and Northamptonshire suffered worse than any. Half of its open fields were dealt with by Parliamentary Acts and three per cent of its wild lands was enclosed.[4] The spacious, wandering countryside was being sliced up and criss-crossed with new roads. Hedgerows of hawthorn, miles of fencing, new gates and sign-posts were destroying the countryman's knowledge of his own world. The old familiar lanes, footpaths and meadows were disappearing and with them much of the countryman's freedom.

> Inclosure came and every path was stopt
> Each tyrant fix'd his sign where paths were found
> To hint a trespass now who cross'd the ground[5]

Clare's response to the world around him was no longer solely personal or secretive. He was expressing the thoughts and fears of his neighbours. They did not want the changes either. Enclosure meant not only new boundaries and new ownership, but also new ways of farming. Restrictions on the movement of cattle became a major issue. Some smallholders now found it difficult, if not impossible, to graze their stock. For some it meant giving up their cow – a status symbol then – and using their allotment of land for growing vegetables or corn. Clare wrote of their 'anguish of mind' and of the 'formidable foes' when 'civil wars 'gainst nature's peace combin'd/And desolation struck her deadly blows.'[6]

In many parts of the fen-country peasants were taking matters into their own hands. By 1816 Clare would have read in the newspapers of the Hunger Riots of Littleport and the consequent trials in Ely, when more than eighty of the rioters came before the magistrates. When the trials ended in June some twenty-four prisoners, including one woman, were sentenced to death and the rest to transportation. But such was the outcry and threat of revolt that nineteen of the prisoners had their death sentences reduced to transportation for life and only five were hanged.[7] There had never been greater unrest in the east of England and the troubles spread to within twelve miles of Helpston.

Apart from forced transportation there was a constant exodus of working-class families to the colonies – Canada, Australia and New Zealand. There was also a steady drift from the rural areas of Britain into the new industrialized centres where men were promised a better life. Many soon found that they had exchanged one kind of slavery for another and the smoky towns soon deprived them of what health they had enjoyed in the country. The conflicts that Clare found in the world outside his diminishing Eden drove his imagination deeper into the memories of childhood, especially when he wanted to escape the realities of that new world. His childhood was to be then, as it was to be much later, a life-line to all that he believed to be sane.

Whatever the economic or technological arguments in favour of enclosure were, and there were some, the Act was another blow to that innocent world already distanced by Clare's own approach to manhood. He was lamenting two passings. Each axe-ring, each fence-post driven into the soil was like a personal wound. He saw everyone involved in this destruction of his native fields as enemies and tyrant knaves. The wildlife that he had reverenced for so long was victim too. The 'birds and beasts of fate's despited birth' were 'Forced from the wilds which nature left [their] home/By vile invasions of encroaching men.'[8]

Not everyone saw enclosure as such a terrible disaster. For many it had been clear for some time that with such a rapidly growing population, and the changes being brought about by the industrial revolution, that there would also have to be changes in the way the country's land was farmed. More food was needed. The methods of the thirteenth century were now long out of date, wasteful of land and manpower. Agriculture need reorganizing. Irrespective of political motives some farmers saw the wisdom of making a better, more efficient use of their farms. Robert Bakewell was a Leicestershire farmer who had experimented with enclosed fields in the 1750s and he was convinced that 'fifty acres of pasture ground divided into five enclosures will go as far in grazing cattle as sixty acres all in one piece.'[9] Each ten-acre field was grazed in turn until 'you could whip a mouse across it' and the cattle moved round from one field to another so that they were always eating fresh, springing grass. The cattle were also easier to manage and the farm could be more economically controlled. Similarly, if crops were rotated they would give better results. Quality would improve, profits would rise. The arguments were persuasive, but Clare was not a farmer or an economist. He was a labourer and a poet. More and more he saw the need to protest as well as preserve. His poems about the past are not poems of nostalgia but of loss and regret for a way of life he thought better. He did not want to see any advantages in enclosure.

John Barrell, in his book *The Idea of Landscape and Sense of Place . . .*,[10] suggests, with reservations, that 'had it not been for the enclosure, the demand for labour would have diminished considerably, and the problem of poverty would have been much more severe . . . the actual work of enclosing – the making of new roads, the planting of hedges – could not have been put off until better days; and in this way the enclosure must to some extent have protected the labourer of Helpston from the effects of depression.'

It is true that enclosure brought work for some and benefits for a privileged few but it also brought hardship and loss of dignity to a great many more. Property and holdings were reduced while rents and demands were increased. Land in Helpston owned by Christ's College, Cambridge, had its rent raised from twelve shillings an acre in 1808 to twenty-nine shillings by 1816. By 1820 it was to rise to as much as £3 while the standard weekly wage in the area was still no more than six or seven shillings a week. A four-pound loaf was then costing at least one shilling and the price of milk went up as the number of cows grew less. These conditions did not change greatly during Clare's lifetime. Ebeneezer Elliott's *Corn Law Rhymes* of 1831 were to tell their own sad story, when there were 'ten dogs to one bone' and the poor knew only varying degrees of poverty. Many labourers never knew the colour of money and received bread or flour in lieu of wages. Families survived on a diet on thin gruel, swedes or turnips. The village mole-catcher was so hungry that Clare was to write of him:

> Want often makes him on the folded land
> Stoop down a turnip from the sheep to steal

> Borrowing the shepherd's knife with palsied hand
> To clean & peel it for a morning meal.[11]

Tea and coal were comforts seldom enjoyed by working-class people. Herbs often made the one and turf or cow-dung substituted for the other. When young men married they were entitled to an extra one-and-sixpence a week. If they had a good master they married quickly to get the increased wage. If they had a bad master they were afraid to tell him in case they lost their jobs. A man found smoking the last fragments of tobacco in his pipe because he had no food for his dinner-break was suspended for three days without pay; labourers were not allowed to smoke at work – a necessary rule but harshly applied. When conditions grew worse there was always the parish with its threat of the workhouse – the final dreaded indignity in the hearts of the poor.

Although Clare was to have opportunities and favours never known to his neighbours, he also shared their hardships and, for a time, experienced their despair. This struggle to rise above such poverty was an added burden on someone trying to make sense of the gift he had inherited. The two did not seem to go together, even though that gift was to use that community's impoverishment as one of its major themes. Frederick Martin perceptively remarked in his life of Clare that the poet 'had an innate consciousness of being born to a freer and loftier existence, and thus deeply found the burthen of being condemned to the fiercest struggle with poverty and misery.'[12]

Clare's own grandson was to write many years later, in a letter to the *Leicester Mercury*, dated 26 October 1920, that his grandparents were:

> no worse off than many of their class at a time when the lot of the agricultural labourer was little removed from serfdom. It is not surprising that the position of Clare's parents was no sinecure, with one advantage only, their small family. Yet it is to their lasting credit that they managed to give their son a fairly good education... and it is certain that Clare's childhood was not the round of drudgery that it has been made out to appear.[13]

It is, nevertheless, understandable that Clare sometimes gave up hope, that there were times when 'poetry for a season was thrown by'. Once again this man of 'too refined clay' found himself thrown into rough company, working with gangs of labourers, many of them from outside the area, putting fences up on land he wanted to leave open. And again, he found himself being taken along on the tide of 'loose habits':

> these habits were gotten when the fields were enclosed mixing among a motley set of labourers that always follow the news of such employment I used to work at setting down fencing & planting quick-lines[14]

> with partners whose whole study was continual striving how to get beer & the bottle was the general theme from weekend to weekend such as had got drunk the oftenest fancied themselves the best fellows & made boast of it as a fame but I was not such a drinker as to make boast of it though I joined my sixpence towards the bottle as often as the rest I often missed the tot that was handed round for my constitution would not have borne it Saturday nights used to be what they calld randy nights which was all meeting together at the public house to drink & sing & every new beginner had to spend a larger portion than the rest which they calld 'colting' a thing common in all sorts of labour[15]

It was after one of these randy nights that Clare 'escaped a great danger very narrowly'. A fight had broken out at the dance, where the beer had been flowing liberally. One of the men ran off with a supply of ale and Clare joined him. They hid in an old barn which had been open to the weather for years. There they hugged themselves over their bottle until it was finished and fell asleep. When they woke in the morning the gable end of the barn had collapsed and lay in a heap of ruins about them. They brushed themselves down and with no thought of breakfast returned to their work.

2

The 1809 Act for 'enclosing lands in the parishes of Maxey with Deepingate, Northborough, Glinton with Peakirk, Elton and Helpstone' meant that it was not only the village but the whole of his native landscape that was to disappear under the plough. A landscape whose 'only bondage was the circling sky' was now being fenced and staked out for someone else's gain. His regret and anger were to be expressed time and time again, in poems such as 'The Mores', 'The Fens', 'The Fallen Elm', 'The Lamentations of Round Oak Waters', 'On A Lost Greyhound', 'A Favourite Nook Destroyed', parts of 'The Village Minstrel' and 'The Parish'. In condemning enclosure he also looked back and preserved in his poetry the landscape that was being lost:

> Far spread the moorey ground a level scene
> Bespread with rush and one eternal green
> That never felt the rage of blundering plough
> Though centurys wreathed springs blossoms on its brow
> Still meeting plains that stretched them far away
> In uncheckt shadows of green brown and grey
> Unbounded freedom ruled the wandering scene
> Nor fence of ownership crept in between

To hide the prospect of the following eye
Its only bondage was the circling sky
One mighty flat undwarfed by bush and tree
Spread its faint shadow of immensity
And lost itself which seemed to eke its bounds
In the blue mist the orisons edge surrounds

Now this sweet vision of my boyish hours
Free as spring clouds and wild as summer flowers
Is faded all – a hope that blossomed free
And hath been once no more shall ever be
Inclosure came and trampled on the grave
Of labours rights and left the poor a slave

. . .

Fence now meets fence in owners little bounds
Of field and meadow large as garden grounds
In little parcels little minds to please
With men and flocks imprisoned ill at ease[16]

W.G. Hoskins points out in *The Making of the English Landscape* that Clare is the only poet to describe the ragged, solitary heaths of England before enclosure:

> Perhaps it is not remarkable, after all, that no poet should have described this world to us before it expired, described it in language that would bring home to us what kind of world it actually was and how its inhabitants looked upon it, for it was above all a peasant world and the peasant was inarticulate. Clare was the great exception, an articulate peasant, and he might have described that world for us in all its natural beauty and its deep associations for the human race – twelve or thirteen centuries of unbroken continuity – but he came too late for this kind of England. By the time he began writing, about the time of Waterloo, the open fields had nearly disappeared.[17]

Clare was, in fact, writing some time before Waterloo and the enclosure of land around Helpston took at least four years. He also talked with older people who knew what that earlier world was like and was, therefore, able to give one of the best accounts possible of that diminished world and what it meant to the individual. Although the final Enclosure Award for Helpston was not published until 1820, when Clare was twenty-seven, the new geography of his world was mapped out by 1816. The public roads were established by the summer of 1811 (seven years after Clare had finished his school journeys to Glinton), and the new allotments of land had been agreed by early in 1812. These were the years when Clare was struggling to become a poet 'with none to help and none to hear'.[18] The events and the experiences of those years leading up to 1820 – which was also the year of Clare's first publication – continued to influence his work long after most people had accepted their new way of life and the land's orderly pattern.

3

During that period of enclosure in Helpston important events had been taking place in the literary world. George Crabbe had published *The Borough*; Jane Austen's *Sense and Sensibility* appeared; Byron's *Childe Harold* (which was to appeal so much to Clare a few years later) was eagerly received by the thousands of readers he regularly attracted; H.F. Cary had completed his translations of Dante's *Divina Commedia*; new volumes of poetry had been published by Shelley and Keats, as well as Coleridge's *Biographia Literaria*. They were years which also saw the births of Robert Browning and Charles Dickens. Literature flourished.

Clare's own reading and book-buying at this stage still lacked direction and he acquired whatever could be had for a few pence from the bookshops of Stamford, Market Deeping and Oundle. They were, he recalled, 'old books of motley merits' and included Boneycastle's *Mensuration*, Ward's *Mathematics*, Cocker's *Land Surveying*, Ray's *History of Rebellion*, Ball's *Astrology*, Harvey's *Meditations*, Lee's *Botany*, Culpeper's *Herbal – A Comprehensive Description of Nearly All Herbs with their Medical Properties*, a volume of Aesop's *Fables*, and an assortment of ballads and poems by anonymous or little-known authors. These, together with those few volumes mentioned in an earlier chapter, made up an odd collection of subjects for a young man preparing for a life of poetry. But, such was Clare's enthusiasm for knowledge that any reading-matter was worth having, even the local newspapers. He took most of these subjects seriously, whether his immediate interest was botany, algebra, herbal remedies, or fossil-hunting. He was interested in the new sciences as well as the buried past. At the same time he began to realize that his intellectual energies were being used haphazardly and to no definite purpose. His 'habits of study grew anxious and restless' and he had little ambition to write anything down but his rhymes.[19] The frustration which accompanies ambition or eagerness in the self-educated both motivates a greater effort to learn and yet blurs the mind to knowledge that the more disciplined student takes for granted. Clare was always aware of this and continued to fret about his inadequate education. It meant that he was never to be truly a 'literary man' when he went to London to share the company of Coleridge, Lamb, De Quincey and others. He could talk with them but not speak from their classical background. They were from a different world and, equally, were never to fully appreciate his own language and achievements. Whatever London had to offer Clare, he was to remain a countryman even when his education isolated him amongst his own kind. Each situation was another thread in the pattern of loneliness he was always to know. Though far removed from that romantic image of a peasant poet he could never forget that he had received little from the village school at Glinton to prepare him for all he wanted to know. What he learnt alone gave him an independence of opinion but he still longed for the confidence of an academic mind.

Enclosure emphasized his loneliness because it deprived him also of a world that had given him the only knowledge in which he excelled, in which he was superior to all his cleverer acquaintances. If he lost the smallest memory of that world his own survival was threatened. He knew he must use his poetry to both preserve and celebrate. But, as yet, 'The Harp imagination strung/Had neer been dreamed of'[20] and although the vision left him 'itching after ryhme'[21] he still could not call himself a poet. It was:

> A title that I dare not claim
> & hid it like a private shame
> I whispered aye & felt a fear
> To speak aloud though none was near
> I dreaded laughter more than blame[22]

4

Enclosure not only changed the shape of this world, it also changed the nature of its society. In his long satirical poem 'The Parish' he was to write:

> That good old fame the farmers earnd of yore
> That made as equals not as slaves the poor ...
> At whose oak table that was plainly spread
> Each guest was welcomd and the poor was fed
> Where master son and serving man and clown
> Without distinction daily sat them down
> Where the bright rows of pewter by the wall
> Served all the pomp of kitchen or of hall
> These all have vanished ...[23]

Things that had had a useful and traditional value for generations were suddenly thrown out by a new breed of prospering farmers who wanted to ape the county squire, and whose wives especially wanted to be seen as equal to the latest high fashion. The old oak table was replaced by the more elegant walnut or mahogany, as much for show as use; the pewter was considered vulgar and gave way to china and glass; the servants had to wear the same style of clothes as in the great houses, and the farmers' daughters no longer took their place in the barn or field, but stayed at home to pamper their pale skins and colour their cheeks with the latest cosmetics:

> They sit before their glasses hour by hour
> Or paint unnatural daubs of fruit or flower ...
> All the profits pigs and poultry made
> Were gave to Miss for dressing and parade[24]

Clare never made a final draft of 'The Parish' but from the thousand and more lines that exist in manuscript, we have a picture of village life during a social revolution that is unequalled in verse. The poem was written, he says, 'under the pressure of heavy distress, with embittered feelings under a state of anxiety and oppression almost amounting to slavery, when the propensity of one class was founded on the adversity and distress of the other. The haughty demand by the master to his labourer "Work for the little I choose to allow you and go to the parish for the rest – or starve".'[25] His bitterness was personal. He wrote with anger and contempt. Although the poem was never to be published in his lifetime, he stood by what he had written and made similar attacks in other poems. The characters he was to expose included all the local upstarts and charlatans who had come to replace the old order. Common daughters became imitation society ladies overnight and foppish sons were lifted from the toils of field labour into wealthy idleness and arrogance. 'The Parish' also included the prejudiced magistrates and the new sport-loving clergy; it ridiculed the coxcomb, lecher, profiteer, oppressor and persecutor. It became a rogues' gallery of men like Squire Dandy, who had just returned from France ready to woo every girl in the district; Young Farmer Bigg, who was wise among fools but with the wise an ass; Young Headlong Rackett, who dealt more openly in sin and aped forged love with less mysterious guile; and there was Dandy Flint, whose dirty name had grown into a proverb for bad deeds; Proud Farmer Cheethum, whose prosperous times had ripened into wealth; Old Saveall, Dr Urine, Justice Terror, the constables and Overseer, and, above all, Bumtagg the Bailiff, who had visited Clare's home when the family were threatened with the workhouse, a man:

> Who fattens best where sorrow worst appears
> And feeds on sad misfortunes bitterest tears
> Such is Bumtagg the bailiff to a hair
> The worshipper and Demon of despair

Who wants and hopes and wishes for success
At every nod and signal of distress[26]

Religion too was changed. It became 'little more than cant/A cloak to hide what goodliness may want.' The new congregation now preferred mild sermons and fewer threats. As soon as the service was over the men went back to talking business. The Ranter priests declaimed damnation in the streets to all who did not confess their sins and go down on their knees for mercy. The new Church of England vicar encouraged class distinction by visiting only the rich and riding most weekdays with the hounds instead of caring for the pastoral needs of his parish.

The changes that came into village life can best be seen in the two portraits Clare gives of the clergy. The new man was a hunting parson who had wealth to spare and no charity. The old vicar was as 'plain as the flock dependent on his cares':

He'd nought to waste while hunger sought his shed
And while he had it they ne'er wanted bread
His chiefest pleasure charity possest
In having means to make another blest ...
Oh sure it was a melancholly day
That calld the good man from his charge away[27]

For the rest, most of the characters who earn a place in 'The Parish' are base, crooked scoundrels. The poverty of the agricultural labourers in the nineteenth century, which was to shock William Cobbett, was made appreciably worse by the class of compassionless rogues who did not escape Clare's pen. It is not difficult to see why the poem was never published during his lifetime. It was, however, not the only poem in which he spoke of the miseries of the under-privileged. His early poem 'On A Lost Greyhound' speaks of the discarded labourer as of no more worth than an animal that has served its day:

Though thou'rt a dog with grief I say't
  Poor man thy fate partakes
Like thee lost whelp the poor man's help
  Erewhile so much desir'd
Now harvest's got is wanted not
  Or little is requir'd[28]

Clare may not have been a disciplined political thinker but his political convictions were born out of a personal experience and he could never see it being otherwise. Although he could often be annoyed by his neighbours' narrow-mindedness and ignorance, he rarely lost sympathy for them. He was fortunate. He was the one who was to get off the treadmill and claim some human dignity. Even though he was seldom to be a stranger to poverty, he was spared the drudgery and dull monotony that their existence was to know for the whole of their lives.

It is his daily involvement in and concern for such people that gives Clare's poetry its warmth and authority. He was to write about men and women in a way that gave them their own little share of immortality. They were ordinary, at times as insignificant as daisies in their own backyards, but he had the same respect for them as he had for the rest of his world. It was the world in which he was to feel most 'at home' and in harmony with himself. Although his London friends were to urge him away from such common themes, from such uninspiring subjects,[29] he remained loyal to his own kind. As soon as he recognized what he had to do as a poet he moved quickly away from the faded conventions and traditional concepts of pastoral poetry and closer to reality. Against the advice of his literary acquaintances he persisted in using his own vocabulary, bringing to his poetry a freshness of language in which to express his own truths about nature, love and life as he saw it. It is true that he did not use dialect words so freely as he matured as a poet but his imagery and vocabulary remained individual and authentic, coming from the same springs which had fed his mind since childhood.

5

If his relationship with people was never entirely easy, his relationship with poetry was to be, at times, equally difficult. There were moments when he was to regret that life had placed upon him the burden of being a poet; times when he was to express his belief that he would have been happier left to work in those fields with his dull neighbours, and certainly times when he felt hopelessly inadequate to meet the demands of poetry:

> Muse of the fields oft have I said farewell
> To thee my boon companion loved so long
> And hung thy sweet harp in the bushy dell
> For abler hands to wake an abler song
> Much did I fear my homage did thee wrong[30]

But his Muse was to be never less than alluring and even when full of doubt he found himself surrendering to her call 'To win by new attempts another smile from thee'.[31]

His ordinary world and the world of poetry had to become one. Only then could it answer all his needs. He could no longer listen to the voice of Collins, or Bloomfield, of Thomson or Cowper. He had to appear as himself and respond to poetry in his own way. He used to sit down under a bush and scribble his fresh thoughts on the crown of his hat and, as he found nature then so he made her, with all her unpleasantness as well as her beauties. What he felt about much of the 'nature poetry' he had read is clear from a fragment of prose:

> Pastoral poems are full of nothing but the old threadbare epithets of 'sweet singing cuckoo' 'love lorn nightingale' 'fond turtles' 'sparkling brooks' 'green meadows' 'leafy woods' etc etc these make up the creation of Pastoral and descriptive poesy and every thing else is reckond low and vulgar in fact they are to rustic for the fashionable or prevailing system of ryhme till some bold inovating genius rises with a real love for nature and then they will no doubt be considered as great beautys which they really are[32]

Clare must have secretly believed that he was a candidate for that role for he spent the rest of his life fighting to justify the claim. The parish had found its village minstrel if it did not always appreciate the song. The title of 'poet' was slowly being earned.

9
Expectations

1

By the time he was twenty-one Clare was writing six and seven poems a day, mostly in response to some village or domestic scene, or from an unusual moment on his walks. They were not always good poems. Clare was not yet able to distinguish between inspiration and enthusiasm. He was still trying to find his own voice, struggling with a language and style already out of date. He adopted many of the poetic affectations he found in the mediocre poets he read and often used a vocabulary that was unnatural to him. In those early poems he could write of the glow-worm as a 'Tasteful illumination of the night/Bright scatter'd twinkling star of spangled earth'. Or he could address the evening with a phrase like 'Hail, lovely Eve! whose hours so lovely prove'. When we read in his poem 'Solitude' of the blossom 'Which the dews of eve bedeck/Fair as pearls on woman's neck', we are not getting genuine Clare, not the Clare of *The Shepherd's Calendar*. He was, after all, more acquainted with village girls and their working mothers in coarse aprons, with half-naked breasts in harvest-fields and necks adorned with the smudges of manual labour rather than pearls. In the early poems the ear was not always in tune with the eye. The sounds were alien, the rhythm of the lines ungainly:

> Where the wild weed dips its head
> Murmuring – dribbling drop by drop
> When dead leaves their progress stop[1]

He still wrote of the 'brook's sweet dimples' and of the 'zephyr's breath'. There were more things to write about than there were words to praise them – joys which could not yet be named, raptures which could be held in the hand no easier than he could hold a flame of fire; the daily celebrations of things 'For which his language can no utterance find'.[2]

The dating of Clare's poems has always posed problems because on several occasions his own dates are not reliable. There are frequently different manuscripts of the same poem where the handwriting varies as much as the text. Sometimes the date given by Clare belongs to a much earlier version of a poem he later revised. 'Helpstone', he says, was written in 1809 when he was only sixteen. But, as a large part of that poem is about the effects of enclosure on the village, he must have added to it over the next few years. Only these long periods of reworking can explain the contradictions in lines 35–6 and 39–40:

> Dear native spot! which length of time endears,
> The sweet retreat of twenty lingering years ...
>
> Those golden days long-vanish'd from the plain,
> Those spots, those pastimes, now belov'd in vain ...

At the age of sixteen he could not have been writing about the retreat of twenty lingering years or of those golden days 'long vanish'd from the plain'. By the time the poem was published in 1820 it had undergone several changes and had been extended.[3]

The importance of those early writing years is in the growth of his imagination and its application to the poetry being written. This growth can be followed in his descriptions of snails, flowers, birds, weeds and insects. In 'Summer Evening' he was to describe how 'the moth with snowy wing/Circles round the winding whirls'. In 'Pastime in Summer' there is a scene 'Where small black moths dip their fluttering wings' and in 'River Gwash' we read how 'The light-winged moths steal out again to play/Crossing with hasty wing thy rippling tide'. Bees 'with their legs stroke slumber from their eyes'[4] and grasshoppers 'in every mood still wear/The short night weary with their fretful song'.[5]

The more Clare trusted his own vocabulary, the more exciting became his poetry; the more competent he became as a poet, the more his own intimate knowledge of nature was revealed. This applies not only to insects, birds and flowers but also to the seasons. Writing in 1809, he was limited to a twelve-lined and predictable description of autumn:

> Now autumn's come, adieu the pleasing greens
> The charming landscape and the flow'ry plain
> All have deserted from these motley scenes
> With blighted yellow ting'd and russet stain ...[6]

But sixteen years later, after considerable practice of his craft, he was able to sustain his poetic impulse and thought over one hundred and sixty lines, including:

> Come bleak November in thy wildness come
> Thy mornings clothed in rime thy evenings chill

E'en these have power to tempt me from my home
E'en these have beauty to delight me still ...
Though naked fields hang lonely on the view
Long lost to harvest and its busy scenes
Yet in the distance shines the painted bough
Leaves changed to every colour ere they die ...
A wild confusion hangs upon the ear
And something half romantic meets the view
Arches half-fill'd with wither'd leaves appear
Where white foam stills the billows boiling through ...[7]

In the same poem we read how in autumn we are left with a 'pleasure that's unspeakable' even 'amidst the wreck of perishable leaves'.

The development of his poetic skill was to be both deliberate and more distinguished than one would have expected of a peasant poet. In his first twenty years he refined his talent to a degree unappreciated in his own time. The variety of verse-forms he experimented with exceeded those of most of his contemporaries. He was to try all the conventional patterns and to invent several of his own. He was to write in syllabic verse, unrhymed verse, employ internal rhymes and assonance, and write a few prose poems as well. He could be both imitator and innovator.[8]

That he found the time, energy and determination during those apprenticeship years is itself amazing. Conditions in Helpston had not in any way improved. He was often away from home looking for work. His parents were again threatened with spending their last years in the workhouse. Still no one knew of his ambitions to become a poet. Some of his neighbours, knowing of his reading and learning, thought it a waste of his talents to do hard manual labour and persuaded him to ask Lord Milton if there was an opening for him as a clerk on the estate. The parish clerk, who also taught at the local Sunday school, offered to go over to Milton with him. By nightfall they had to admit that their journey had been a waste of time. His lordship had not been able to see them. But the clerk, knowing which farms Lord Milton would be visiting the following day, suggested that they should conveniently put themselves on the same road where he could not fail to see them:

> as soon as we came up to his Lordship my companion began to descant on my merits in a way that made me hang my head & begd his Lordship to do something for me but I found he had a double errand for before he had finished his tale of my [learning] he pulled an antique box out of his pocket... which contained several farthings of King Charles the first or seconds reign his Lordship reachd & took it & gave him a good exchange for his curiosity which raisd the clerks voice in the conclusion of his story of me when his Lordship heard to

whom I belongd he promisd to do something for me but such trifling things are soon shovd out of the memory of such people who have plenty of other things to think of[9]

Clare heard no more and went on with his usual labouring. He wanted to be more than the village scholar or clerk on the Milton estate. The poems were now beginning to take shape and fill his mind with other ambitions. He believed that one day he might 'sing as well as greater men' and surprise everyone by his achievements. By the time he was twenty-one there was no doubt in his mind that he had to be, and was, a poet. He had that vision which left him 'itching after rhyme'.

2

In the summer of 1814 he decided that it was time to start preserving the best of those poems in a book, ready for that day when someone might show an interest. He knew exactly what he wanted – a stoutly-bound volume of blank pages with a special title page. One day he walked over to Market Deeping to see the printer and bookseller, J.B. Henson. He had met Henson before, both in Deeping and in Helpston, for the printer belonged to the growing number of 'congregational dissenters or Independents' who had a chapel in the village. Clare had attended some of their meetings in his search for an alternative, more acceptable religion than that of the Church of England which, in his view, had never found much time for the meek and the poor. It was a search that lasted many years and was never fully met. On the one hand he was to tell Octavius Gilchrist of Stamford (who did not approve of Clare's nonconformist friends) that 'my father was brought up in the communion of the Church of England and I have found no cause to withdraw myself from it'[10] and, on the other hand, he was to scorn the hypocrisy and humbug he found in the established church which failed to practise Christ's example of humility and love. True Christianity was acceptable but, in the end, neither the Anglicans nor the 'Ranters', the Methodists, Congregationalists or Unitarians, had found a way of putting God's love into the lives of ordinary men and women. Where one succeeded the other failed. For a time the Unitarians held his interest as much as any. Their liberal-mindedness and belief in an impartial God appealed to his own concept of divine goodness and justice. They were not bound by tradition but used all wisdom as they found it, in whatever creed or literature. But Clare did not become a Unitarian, even though several of his poems were eventually at one time selected to take their place in the Unitarian hymn-book.[11] His nearest commitment to another sect was to the Quakers. In a later prose-fragment he wrote:

> give me for humility & meekness the quakers the primitive quakers not the hard featured phisio[g]nomy of worldly cunning which we often encounter peeping under a colourless coat & creeping from under a large broad brimmed hat[12]

In other prose-fragments he also expressed his view that any religion that 'teaches us to act justly to speak truth & love mercy ought to be held sacred in every country' and he made his own belief clear by saying:

> My creed may be different from other creeds but the difference is nothing when the end is the same – if I did not expect & hope for eternal happiness I should ever be miserable[13]

It was a faith which added a new dimension to his poetry and even makes the phrase 'a religious poet' worth more consideration. In those poems which have an expressly religious theme his orthodoxy is paramount – the Trinity, the Incarnation and the Resurrection are seldom far from his thoughts:

> Is there another world for this frail dust
> To warm with life & be itself again
> Something about me daily speaks there must
> & why should instinct nourish hopes in vain
>
> Een the small violet feels a future power
> & waits each year renewing blooms to bring
> & surely man is no inferior flower
> To die unworthy of a second spring[14]

It was a faith which not only brought hope, or consolation, but also serenity. In his poem 'The Stranger' he was to achieve the intimate, sure style of George Herbert:

> And who could such a stranger be?
> The God, the Saviour from on high
> That aids the feeble. Need I sigh?[15]

Similar evidence can be found in 'The Moon', 'To Religion', 'Sunday', 'To An Early Butterfly', 'The Calm', 'Sunday Evening', 'Nature's Hymn to the Deity' and 'The Fountain of Hope'.

Mr Henson might have known something of Clare's religious quest but he knew nothing of his literary ambitions that morning when the shy young poet walked into his shop and asked for the volume of blank pages. Puzzled as to why the untidy-looking labourer should want such a book, Henson said that he had nothing like it in stock but could make one up for about eight shillings. That was something like a week's wages then, but the impetuous Clare would not let such considerations hamper his dreams. With them he could, as usual, afford to be extravagant. He told the printer to bind such a book for him and promised to pay for it by regular instalments. Henson agreed and said it would be ready by the time of the next Deeping fair – an event of great local gatherings both for trade and amusement. Before letting his customer leave, however, he again made 'many side-wind inquiries' as to why the book was needed. But the secret had been kept too long for it to be easily surrendered and the title of 'poet' was still one that Clare 'dared not name before the world'. So he returned home to write secretly of those native fields and the village scenes that might one day justify his extravagance. As he walked back over the fields the excitement of that dream gave him new confidence.

> No matter how the world approved
> Twas nature listened I that loved
> No matter how the lyre was strung
> From my own heart the music sprung.[16]

When, some weeks later – and 'flusht with ale' – Clare called to collect his blank volume, he found Mr Henson even more eager to know why he was making his purchase. Released from his 'timid embarrassment of reserve' by the amount of free beer he had received at the fair, Clare 'dropt some loose hints' about writing poetry. The printer's curiosity turned to surprise, even disbelief, and he asked if he might see some of the poems that were to be preserved in the pages he had just bound. Clare, in his liberated state, promised that he would bring a few verses with him when he next came to Market Deeping.

As the effects of the alcohol wore off on the way back to Helpston he soon began to regret that he had let the secret of his dreams be so cheaply gained. It was certainly with less courage that he eventually delivered his first small collection of poems to Henson, who found them better than he expected. The poet knew something after all about the craft. The verses were not sentimental doggerel but skilfully worked sonnets of some originality. Clare was asked to produce more. Encouraged by this interest, he wrote and copied several poems which were then taken over to Market Deeping. Early in 1817 he gave Henson a group of poems which included the sonnets 'To the Setting Sun' and 'To a Primrose', both of which he 'approvd of very much', as well as a longer poem on the death of Chatterton.

Henson was now sufficiently impressed to offer Clare the hope of getting some of the work published. They 'entered into proposals about the manner most beneficial to get them out' and Henson assured Clare that, from his experience, this was best done by subscription. The printer's experience was in fact limited and Clare was not very impressed when shown some of the pamphlets that had already been published. But elegance of binding or style of printing were not major considerations, yet. Publication was all that mattered and Henson had the answer. If poems were best published by subscription then Clare would agree to accept Henson's advice. To get subscribers, however, the public had to be informed of the proposed publication. Then, when sufficient orders had been received, the book could be printed. Henson said he could print 300 copies of a prospectus and order-form for one pound. This silenced Clare for a moment. He was already in debt. Could he afford nearly three weeks' wages, with his parents living on the parish, to promote such an ambitious and even selfish plan? He did not relish parting with his money so quickly, especially as it still had to be earned. Nor, when he thought about it, did he like the idea of begging for customers either. Again, the thought of what people would say made him 'decline coming to an immediate agreement'. But, he had to admit, 'force puts us to no choice' and if he wanted to get his poems published he had to be prepared for publicity, good or bad. Having then agreed to publish he assumed that Henson would write the prospectus. This was not, said the printer, his responsibility. The poet must write the prospectus. By this time Clare's ambition was such that he gave in to every demand made upon him. It was to be the beginning of a familiar pattern for the next eighteen years. Printers, publishers, editors, critics, all wanted him to give in to them.

This time as he walked away from Henson's office the fens suddenly had mountains. Clare had promised to compose his *Address to the Public* and find the money to get it printed. Such a decision meant that regular work was now more urgent than ever. Without a job there would be no wages. Without wages, no prospectus. Fortunately he had found work. Not the work he once thought his education would ensure for him, nor the work he expected as a poet. It was harder than field-work or gardening. It put him in lower company. But the money was good. And he had an incentive.

3

With no chance of getting a job in Helpston he had set out, in the spring of 1817, with Stephen Gordon to become a lime-burner at Bridge Casterton, seven miles away. Gordon, an itinerant labourer from Kingsthorpe near Northampton, had persuaded Clare to go with the promise of many advantages from working with him, which he never intended or at least was never able to perform. It was, nevertheless, a move which was to determine the course of Clare's life in more than one aspect.

Their employer was Mr Wilders, who owned two or three kilns in the area and who expected his men to work from daybreak to dark and, in emergencies, all through the night. It was tiring work with many of the days lasting fourteen and fifteen hours. Their lodging-house also provided them with little rest and less comfort. It was 'a house of scant fame' run by a man named Cole and his wife. They thought nothing of packing three men into one bed – a deprivation Clare had never known, not even in his cottage at home when their rooms had been divided. His fellow lodgers were of all descriptions, few of them clean, and many of them looking like 'an assemblage of robbers in the rude hut dimly & mysteriously lighted by the domestic savings of a farthing taper'.[17]

During his first six weeks as a lime-burner Clare earned and saved fifty shillings. As well as having enough money to pay Henson he also had enough now to order a new olive green coat, a garment and colour he had wanted for some time. He had already been measured for it before leaving Helpston but 'an accident happened in the way which prevented'[18] it ever passing into his possession. Exactly what that accident was we do not know. Clare had one or two accidents at that time, especially when he started going out with one of the local girls. He may have been referring to some trouble after a drinking bout, or pressure from a creditor, or some kind of blackmail. Whatever it was it cost him his olive green coat.

To escape the dingy lodging-house, and no doubt to celebrate after a hard week's work, Clare and his friends used to go on Sundays to the neighbouring village of Tickencote where there was an inn called the Flower Pot. Although the inn itself no longer exists the house does, in a village little changed. It was a place of Saxon origin – 'a place where goats and kids were herded' – a quiet settlement on the banks of one of Clare's favourite rivers, the River Gwash. Its church is popular with visitors for its extraordinary quintuple arch. H.V. Morton, in *In Search of England*, thought 'this solid little building, planted in the lovely soil soon after the Conquest, one of the fairest things I have ever seen. The interior lives up to it. The vaulted chancel is a marvel, but the most remarkable feature is the quintuple Norman arch. There is nothing that I am aware of like it in all England.'

Clare may have gone inside but never mentions it. There were other attractions, and not only those of the village inn. It was on one of his visits to the Flower Pot that he first saw Martha (Patty) Turner as she made her way home across the fields to Walkherd Lodge, between Casterton and Pickworth. He fell in love at first sight and was 'very ill at rest' until he found out who she was and from where she came. He climbed to the top of a pollard-tree to see which way she went. He watched until she was out of sight and made up his mind to look for her again. The chance came a few weeks later when he was going to play his fiddle at an inn in Stamford. This time he walked over to her and started a conversation. He was seldom shy with women. He lost no time in asking if he could walk home with her. Martha did not mind. She lived four miles away. It would be good to have company. Immediately Clare forgot about his promise to provide his drinking friends with some music during the evening. He was now close to the girl whose beauty had so bewitched him just a few Saturdays ago. 'It became,' he said, 'the introduction to some of the happiest & unhappiest days my life has met with.'[19]

The young girl who was to share his life from that evening would later, no doubt, have expressed similar sentiments had she been able to commit her feelings to the printed page in the same way. Unlike her lover, she could neither read nor write at the time and learned very little of the arts when she became Clare's wife.

10
Martha (Patty) Turner

1

Martha Turner was born on 3 March 1799. When she met Clare she was, according to Frederick Martin – who was to meet her much later at Northborough – a 'fair girl of eighteen, slender, with regular features, and pretty blue eyes'.[1] Spencer T. Hall, who was also to visit the Northborough cottage in 1865, said that she was 'still a fine, matronly, blooming woman who must have been a very comely girl in her day'.[2] Someone who did meet her at her comeliest was John Taylor, who wrote of her as a woman having 'the virtues of industry, frugality, neatness, good-temper and a sincere love for her husband'.[3]

Clare took to calling Martha 'Patty' about a year after their first meeting. In the earliest poems he wrote to her she is still Martha, as in this previously uncollected 'Ballad':

> Now that the evening is hanging so glooming
> & the grey mist is shrouding the hurn
> & the streakt woodbine nights bosom perfuming
> Closes its blossoms for mornings return
> Martha till then be thy milking delaying
> Hints are loves language thou kens what they mean
> Then wi thy swain thru the welcome gloom straying
> To breath[e] on thy lips his fond rapture unseen
>
> Now the night bird at his singing is seated
> While the pale moon seems delighted to hear
> While they swain roams wi one wish uncompleated
> The pleasure of meeting his lassy so dear
> Martha be thou neath thy brinded cow seated
> Chanting thy love ballads over in glee

Sweet tho the nightingales songs the wood ringing
Sweeter will thine be while I listen thee

Now the bent flower neath eves burthen is laden
& the ripe rose on its stem doth recline
Just as Ive seen the flusht cheek of the maiden
Bowing unwilling a kiss to resign
Down in the valley do thou me be meeting
Thy first broken promises let me never see
Still let thy fond heart in sincerity beating
Be free from all sighs but whats breathed for me[4]

He need not have worried about broken promises from Martha and she was certainly to breathe many sighs for him in the years to come. Despite his unfaithfulness, despite his later pining for Mary Joyce, despite the unhappiness and arguments that were to come, Clare grew to love Martha with a love that was real, warm and lasting. It was at least as real as it could be, with all their differences, and more real than the fantasy love he nourished in his poems for Mary Joyce. Those childhood sweethearts were never to know how their love would have survived beyond their youthful dreams. Martha was to become his wife and bear him eight children. She was to care for him and eventually do all that she could to save him. Accusations that she did not bother or understand are unfair. Her task was by no means easy and Mary Joyce would not necessarily have been a greater success. Indeed, she might have been a greater failure. Her importance in the poet's life was in being so unattainable, so unproven. He needed Martha as well as Mary and the second would not have survived without the first. Martha Patty Turner made the poetry possible. She did not read or understand it, but she understood its author. She must have been a woman of infinite patience to put up with his moods, his selfish nature and frequent outbursts of temper. He was to admit, 'I have one fault which had ought to be noticed – a heated spirit that instantly kindles in too hasty bursts of praise or sensure . . . when I fancy myself injur'd I cannot brook it no more than stifle my gratitude when I am under obligations.'[5]

In those early days at Tickencote and Walkherd Lodge his poems came as freely for Patty as they did for Mary. They prove that there was true love there as well as infatuation. 'My only repentance,' he was to write, 'was that I did not become acquainted with her sooner than I did.'[6] Were these idle words, or was he, in fact, saying that if only he could have met Patty earlier he would have been spared much of the longing, hurt, even guilt, that came with the recollections of his other amorous affairs? The poems to Patty have a tenderness and affection that ring true. When he wrote, 'There is a day I love the best/When Patty first was found' he meant it.[7] Poem after poem was to confirm that belief:

When first I look'd upon her eye
And all her charms I met
There's many a day gone heedless by
But that I'll ne'er forget . . .
And all the days the year can bring
As sweet as they may prove
There'll ne'er be one like that I sing
Which found the maid I love.[8]

*

O thou wert once a wilding flower
All garden flowers excelling
And still I bless the happy hour
That led me to thy dwelling
Though nursed by field & brook & wood
And wild in every feature
Spring neer unsealed a fairer bud
Nor formed a blossom sweeter
And of all flowers the spring hath met
And it hath met with many
Thou art to me the fairest yet
And loveliest of any.[9]

As lyrical as he could always be in love, these poems to Patty reveal a genuine expression of his love for her. She is shown as something lovely to *hold* – a flower, an unblemished bud that could be easily bruised, something of flesh and blood, wild and loving; whereas Mary Joyce is more often seen as a shaft of sunlight, or a bird moving swiftly over the landscape, present only in spirit, impossible to catch. The ethereal beauty of Mary hardly needed a mortal's inadequate protection but, when the neighbours were to say hurtful things about Patty, her husband had words of comfort for her in verse:

Thou lovely bud with many weeds surrounded
I once again address thee with a song
To cheer thee up 'gainst envy's adder-tongue
That deeply oft thy reputation wounded.[10]

Nor was such love contrived or forced upon him by a necessary marriage. Clare continued to express his affectionate feelings for his wife in those poems which were to be written at Northborough, and in the asylum, twenty years later. It was not love of Mary Joyce that came between them, it was poetry. The Muse was always Clare's goddess and mistress. Mary would have taken second place had she been in Patty's.

So exciting and immediate was his love for the milkmaid of Walkherd that he sometimes lost his way home from her cottage and he would then sit down under a tree to write another poem. Patty restored his faith in himself. She became the new image of his Muse. On one occasion he was about to step on to a path, which he thought must have been beaten shiny-bare by the sheep or cattle, when he discovered, just in time, that it was not earth at all but water. In his ecstasy he was one step from drowning.

The undulating countryside around Walkherd, with its quiet northern air, became (like the native fields of his childhood) a paradise. He was to write there some of the best poems that were eventually published in his first volume. The landscape is still open and unspoilt, the small areas of woodlands still have some of the wildflowers he picked with Patty.

He was now in the habit of going over to her house each weekend, not always, he admits, 'on love-errands' but just to get away from his dreary lodgings and uncouth workmates. He loved the feeling of tranquillity about those fields and woods. Their ancient quietness appealed to his sense of antiquity and timelessness. All joy or sorrow, all problems and blessings, had to be seen against the eternal power of nature:

> there were places where the foot of man had not printed for years... I usd to wander about them with my artless & interesting companion in more than happiness A large wood in summer usd to be coverd with Lillys-of-the-Valley of which she usd to gather handfuls for her flower-pots & I helped her[11]

Even though Patty was never able to share Clare's love of books and writing, there were some things in which they had a common interest. In a poem to her, written as late as 1848, he remembered that 'we both looked on the self-same thing/Till both became as one'.[12] She was a true country girl 'wild in every feature', but one who liked the daintiness of flowers in her room, a taste she kept all her life. There was a natural harmony in her relationship with Clare when they shared these simple pleasures. It only became discordant with his growing ambitions and success.

2

During that summer of 1817, however, Clare realized that he was not the only suitor on the scene. An eligible shoemaker of Stamford was also paying regular visits to Patty's home. He had the advantage in being seen by her parents as a far more favourable candidate than the lime-burner. They encouraged him to win their daughter away from the less acceptable, lower-class labourer who was claiming too much of her attention. The Turners were, after all, cottage-farmers renting six acres of land. They were not in the same class as the Joyce family of Glinton but they did have their own pigs and a cow, and they also hoped that their daughter would move up the social scale rather than down. She was too good for John Clare. The shoemaker, on the other hand, had his own shop, was always expensively dressed and handsome. Patty wanted her head examined if she preferred the untidy labourer of no fixed address. But Clare had a persuasive tongue and was a good lover. Beneath the coarse exterior there was a romantic, a very different man from the one her parents could see or understand. He had a tenderness and dignity that the shoemaker could never match. Her father warned her that she would rue the day she decided to walk out with Clare. It made no difference. The two lovers continued their excursions into the woods where Eden was regained and where their passions grew intimate. They gave themselves to each other without a care. Soon Patty was pregnant.

Her importance in these early years of the poet's development is once more confirmed in a letter Clare was to write to his publisher a year later, in March 1821:

> Patt & myself now begin to know each other & live happily & I deem it a fortunate era in my life that I met her . . . the cut of her face always delighted me more than any other & had I never seen her my attempts at poetry woud never have been resumed after my removal to Casterton.[13]

Because he was to say, on hearing of her pregnancy, that he 'held out as long as [he] coud & then married her' does not contradict the feelings he had already expressed for her. Even with working fourteen hours a day, and getting reasonably good pay, his prospects were nothing to boast about and marriage was not uppermost in his mind then. He still had his parents to think of, his debts to settle and his poetry to publish. Love, as much as he wanted it, was an added responsibility when his own life was full of doubts and promises.

By the autumn of that year Clare and his lime-burning friend had been moved from Casterton to another kiln at Pickworth, between Casterton and Castle Bytham. It was a place with its own antiquity. The kiln was near a site that was full of bones and the old foundations of a buried church, the site in fact of an earlier settlement where forgotten cottages and the inn once stood. It was a subject which had to be written about. Clare felt the words coming to him and the lines taking shape. Usually there was no time to write anything down. The lines had to be memorized until the end of the day when manual toil was over. This was never a problem to Clare. One of his virtues was that he could compose in his head (an advantage that poetry has over prose) and this gift was now benefiting from the early training his memory had at school, where he had learnt those long passages of scripture off by heart. When he spoke of finding his poems in the fields and only writing them down, he was saying that the poems were *made in*, as well as inspired by, those fields. At Pickworth, however, he could not even wait until the end of the day. His 'Elegy on the Ruins of Pickworth' was 'Hastily Composed and Written with a Pencil on the Spot'. The buried past is reborn. The village rises again, with its inn and labourers' cottages, with its stately hall and remnants of unfair wealth.

Not only are those ruins no more but the kilns where Clare worked have also disappeared. Only a solitary chimney stack and a few grass-covered mounds show where he once laboured all day and pondered on his future as a poet. The ale-house has gone, the church is redundant, locked and chained. The Methodist Chapel is vandalized and the hall no more. Only the fields with their sheep and stone walls retain some echo of that world he knew, the world where he had to decide whether to be a professional poet for the world's gaze or whether he should keep his verses to himself.

> Like yours, awaits for me the common lot,
> 'Tis mine to be of every hope bereft.
> A few more years and I shall be forgot
> And not a vestige of my memory left.[14]

The sense of loss, the frailty of life, the thought that his own contribution might be so utterly insignificant, recur throughout his work. In 'The Fallen Elm' he was to write, 'I see a picture which thy fate displays/And learn a lesson from thy destiny.'

In most things in nature Clare saw an image of himself, in the dying cowslip, the death of a butterfly, the destruction of Langley Bush, a meadow under the plough, the fading song of a bird or its broken nest, all would be changed. Life would become no more than a worn-out coat – 'Fame will grow old like garments'[15] – and the ambitions be fruitless.

At Pickworth, and before a line of his poetry had been published, Clare sensed the conflict between obscurity and recognition, between rejection and fame. The chance of success was fragile and yet his mind was always fashioning the possibilities of becoming something other than a labouring man. He quietly strengthened his belief that he had a claim to some immortality. But how to justify that claim was still an anxiety and a mystery. He had to admit that fame's hopes were, indeed, faint to look upon.

Beyond the ruins of the past, and even the past of his own family, he had to build a world for himself that would make his secret ambition become a reality. Despite the improbability of success, he was able to say 'Yet do I follow with unwearied eyes/The shadowy recompense for real toils.'[16]

3

The task of composing his prospectus could not have come at a worse time. He was being asked to work longer hours at the kilns, he had Patty on his mind, and there was hardly time to scribble down his verses, let alone plead for their survival or recognition. He could not make up prose in his head as he could poems. It could not be done in a hurry or with other people around, so he kept putting it off until Henson wondered whether it would ever be written at all.

Clare's employer, Mr Wilders, also had a kiln at Ryhall, three miles from Pickworth, and he frequently sent Clare there to work on his own. The walk from his lodging-house each morning, and back again at night, at last gave him time to reflect on what he should say in his *Address to the Public*. He would sit down on the grass verge five or six times on each journey to 'plan this troublesome task'.

It was during one of these moments that he thought again upon the futility of such ambitions. He thought of his parents' distress at home, of his own miserable working life to keep out of debt, and now the 'added perplexities of ill-timed love'. What chance did his poetry have? 'Striving to remedy all,' he wrote in his *Sketches*, 'and all to no purpose, I burst out in an exclamation of distress':

> And what is Life? an hour-glass on the run
> A mist retreating from the morning sun
> A busy bustling still repeated dream
> Its length? A moment's pause, a moment's thought.
> And happiness? A bubble on the stream
> That in the act of seizing shrinks to nought . . .[17]

In such despair it was the *poet* who stood up to face life's hopelessness, as it was to do throughout most of his career. Even though everything seemed against him he recognized that his thoughts could be best expressed in poetry.

The elation he felt at writing the first two verses of 'What is Life?' restored his confidence. He could no longer keep his mind on his day's work and decided there and then to draft a prospectus for Henson. He sat down on a lime-scuttle, took out his notebook and pencil, and determined to finish something before the end of the day, good or bad. When he had finished he set off for Stamford three miles away. The distance was long enough for him to have several doubts about what had been written. But, if his poems failed, he could only benefit from his disappointment, so he walked on. Their downfall would free his mind from all foolish hopes and let him know that he had nothing to trust but work.

The *Address* was composed of such modest, even negative phrases, that it was hardly likely to rouse the neighbourhood into rapturous support:

> The Public are requested to observe that the Trifles humbly offered for their perusal can lay no claim to eloquence of poetical composition, (whoever thinks so will be deceived), the greater part of them being *Juvenile* productions ... It is hoped that the humble situation which distinguishes their author will be some excuse for their favour, and serve to make an atonement for the many inaccuracies and imperfections found in them ...[18]

From this it would appear that Clare was the first to trade on his 'humble situation' and, recognizing the politics of the class structure, probably thought it both prudent and appealing to present himself as a 'peasant-poet'. It would be a way of drawing attention to his verses, even if the outcome was rejection.

With the *Address* finished and Stamford in sight, the future of the poet still hung on a very fine thread. When the Post Office wanted a penny for forwarding the letter Clare's frail hopes almost withered completely. Only a lie could save him. He told the clerk that as the letter was nothing to do with him he saw no reason why he should be expected to pay for other people's mail. The clerk looked suspiciously at Clare in his dirty working-clothes, then at the crumpled sheet of paper, folded and sealed with shoemaker's wax and addressed in pencil. After several moments of deliberation he agreed to forward the letter without charge.

A relieved, if uneasy, Clare returned to his lodgings and then went over to find Patty. All he could do now was wait. It was all Patty could do too. She was still not sure whether she would become Mrs Clare. She was certainly not aware of her part in those crucial weeks of the poet's life. But her love sustained him then, as it was to on many occasions during the next twenty-five years when the demands of poetry took him more and more away from her. But it took Clare some time to find out just how good Patty had been for him.

11

Towards Publication

1

Few literary careers have started so naively or so modestly. Clare's *Address to the Public* reached Market Deeping where Henson, anxious to get the poems into print, produced three hundred copies of the prospectus within a week. He sent one hundred to Clare at Pickworth and suggested that they should meet at the Dolphin Inn on Stamford Market, on 1 December 1817, to compare progress.

The first thing Clare learned at that meeting was that the cost of printing the prospectus had gone up by five shillings. The path to fame looked like being an expensive one. For a few moments the two men sat silently over their ale until some dull fellow brushed passed them. Henson handed him a prospectus. It could have been an unwanted religious tract or an out-of-date notice of an auction sale for all the interest shown in it by the receiver. Clare's embarrassment increased. He was ready to rush out of the inn and forget all about publishing. Another customer arrived; again Henson offered him a prospectus. He stopped, read it, praised the quality of the sonnet and invited the poet to have a drink. He also told Henson to put his name down as a subscriber, saying that he felt sure the publication would be a great success. Suddenly the colour of the world changed. This unexpected encouragement gave Clare heart and did him more good than all he 'ever met with before or after'.[1] What pleased him especially was that the stranger had been impressed, not so much by his 'humble situation' as by the quality of his poetry. His remarks had confirmed for Clare that he could write.

That first subscriber was the Reverend Thomas Mounsey, a master of the Stamford Free Grammar School, and Clare never forgot his name. At the same time he was reminded that there were still another two hundred and ninety-eight prospectuses in need of the same response before Henson could print. Clare knew that few people would be as enthusiastic as his first customer. The *Address* was distributed throughout the villages around Stamford and Market Deeping. Clare waited. Customers were hard to find but he did have more success than Henson. In a note to his printer some weeks later he wrote:

> I send you some of the principal subscribers which I have procured lately, the first of which is a Baronet!!! who speaks very highly of my sonnet in the prospectus – good God, how great are my Expectations, What hopes do I cherish! as great as the unfortunate Chattetons were on his first entrance in London which is now pictured in my Mind – & undoubtedly like him I may be building 'Castles in the Air' but Time will prove it.[2]

Time did prove it. After three months only seven subscribers had been found and only one of them had paid. Henson now had the unpleasant task of telling Clare that he needed an advance of £15 before he could begin printing. Clare said he did not have so much as fifteen *pence* to call his own. Henson's demand was out of the question. He could see now that his *Address to the Public* had been a waste of time and energy. Not only would there be no volume of poems published to justify all his earlier hopes but he now had the agonizing worry that he had also revealed to the world what his secret ambitions were – a Helpston peasant wanted to be a poet! He felt open to ridicule every time he went out of the house. He wished that he had never engaged in the matter – 'I went down the street scarcely daring to look anybody in the face for the prospectus had filled everybody's mouth with my name & prospects most of which was Job's comforters & the cry was against me.'[3]

Only Patty could again console him and help him to forget his embarrassment. They continued their walks over that gentle landscape around her home, with its woodlands and sloping fields, and talked of other ways in which he could become acceptable to her parents. But there was nothing he could do. On two occasions he went into Stamford to enlist in the artillery but his love for Patty prevented him from finally putting his signature to the papers. Once, when he had tried to drown his misery by getting drunk, he got as far as taking the money for a recruit but the following morning the sergeant, realizing Clare's plight, said he would not take advantage of such a slight fellow who had been the worse for ale the night before. Again Clare's weakness and stature had saved him from becoming a soldier, but they did not solve his problems about Patty, work, home, money or poetry.

2

Clare had always been extravagant in spending what money he earned, especially on books and magazines he could not afford. Mr Thompson, a bookseller of Stamford and proprietor of the New Public Library, was just one of the trades-people now pushing Clare for payment of outstanding debts. He was owed fifteen shillings and wanted immediate settlement as he was selling his business and leaving town. Clare wrote to say that he could not possibly pay that amount all at once but would do so by instalments, enclosing at the same time some copies of the prospectus in the hope that Thompson would be sufficiently impressed to grant him more time. Clare could not, or perhaps was too proud to, deliver the letter himself and asked his friend Thomas Porter of Ashton to take it for him. When Thompson read the letter he poured contempt on both the poet and his emissary. The Helpston peasant was a dishonest, conceited rogue. His claims to poetry were preposterous. Porter defended Clare's reputation but it did not lessen the threats of the Stamford bookseller.

It was then that one of those lucky accidents (necessary in most careers) happened to the frustrated Clare. Edward Drury, who had just arrived to take up business in Stamford, was not one of the most unselfish and benevolent of men but he was a most welcome saviour at that time. He was the son of John Drury, a Lincoln printer, and proud to belong to a family of Elizabethan descent which had given its name to one of London's famous thoroughfares – Drury Lane. Edward Drury was ambitious and before the age of twenty had decided to buy his own business, preferably in the book trade. Thompson's shop and library in Stamford's High Street appealed to him. The mellow stone town was pleasant and conveniently placed on the Great North Road to attract travellers. He could both sell books and continue as an agent for Twinings Tea. He was browsing round the shop on the day that Thomas Porter delivered Clare's letter. He listened to the argument and, out of curiosity, read one of the prospectuses which the irate bookseller had thrown aside. Like the Reverend Thomas Mounsey, Drury was impressed. It might not be a bad thing to encourage this unusual local poet. If he did buy Thompson's business this was one bad debt he was prepared to accept. He paid Thompson the fifteen shillings to settle Clare's account and decided that as soon as he had the time he would find out more about the farm-labourer with such an unfavourable, or remarkable, reputation.

Clare, in the meantime, had, on his return to Helpston from the lime kilns, taken up his old drinking habits with the Billings brothers. He was at Bachelors Hall one Sunday when his young sister, Sophy, arrived to say that two gentlemen were waiting at home to see him. He left his friends and hurried back to the cottage where he found Mr Drury and Mr Newcomb (who was the publisher of the *Stamford Mercury*) already talking about his poetry with his parents. Drury said little to Clare at their first meeting and left it to Newcomb to ask most of the questions. Newcomb wanted to know how many poems Clare had written, where were they, how were they to be published and what agreement he had made with Henson. When Clare told them, the two men expressed their surprise and said that instead of wanting payment for printing, they would let Clare have money for his necessities. He quickly saw the difference of advantage a good one and decided he would get his manuscripts back from Market Deeping.

By the summer of 1818 the battle for Clare's talents was on. Anyone connected with publishing then knew that such an unusual talent could still be something of a sensation if handled properly. By the end of their first visit both Drury and Newcomb felt that Clare was good property. As they left the cottage Mr Newcomb invited him to have lunch with him the following Monday, adding on reflection that the invitation stood only if he had his manuscripts to deliver, otherwise he was not to come. Clare saw through these remarks and was deeply insulted. Nevertheless it was a chance he could not miss and he had to bite his tongue.

When the excitement at home had died down Clare asked his mother if she would go over to Market Deeping the following day to get his poems back from Henson. Again, whether he could not go because of work or was afraid to go because of what Henson might say, we cannot be sure. Frederick Martin suggests that it may have been the latter, that Clare feared that Henson would 'put obstacles in his way'[4] and so persuaded his mother to argue for him. If Martin's account is true (and it is always worth remembering that his biography was written within a year of the poet's death in 1864) Clare was not at work but waiting 'halfway between Deeping and Helpston, near the village of Maxey'.[5] Here both mother and son sat down in a field to examine the contents of the parcel. All the poems he had given to Henson were there, so too was the crumpled, pencil-written original of the *Address to the Public*. Henson may have been relieved to get rid of the poems in view of the poor response to the prospectus.

Equally relieved to have all his work back, and to be free of the responsibility of having to pay towards its publication, Clare wasted no time in taking his poems over to Edward Drury at Stamford, deliberately ignoring Mr Newcomb's invitation to lunch. Drury, delighted to have the manuscripts in his possession so soon, gave the poet a guinea and told him to bring all the remaining pieces he might have so that a suitable collection could be made.

Clare's reaction to this first practical sign of encouragement was to work with all the determination he could command. He stopped visiting Bachelors Hall and spent each night revising old verses or composing new. If Drury continued paying him like this for all the poems he wrote then he need never labour in the fields again. He might even grow rich enough to rent a better house for his parents. Certainly Patty's parents would view him differently then. He would no longer be penniless, no longer inferior to the shoemaker. He would be an author, a poet whose name would appear on title-pages and covers. Just as his despair could take him to the lowest depths of depression so too could his expectations take him to the highest realms of excitement. But when he visited Drury again with some more poems he found the new bookseller of Stamford had grown very cool about the publication of his work. Seeking another opinion, Drury had shown the earlier poems to the Reverend Mr Twopenny of Little Casterton. The Reverend gentleman saw no harm in raising the poor man a small subscription but said the poems appeared to possess 'no merit to be worthy of publication'.[6] Drury read the whole of Mr Twopenny's letter to Clare, thinking that he should know of what kind of reception his poems might receive if they were ever published. At the same time he told his poet that this letter was but the opinion of one man and he would seek others.

Even constructive criticism is not always easy to accept when you are so anxious to prove yourself, and Clare returned to Helpston utterly dejected. The more optimistic his hopes, the deeper his sense of rejection. Once again he felt that he had been spurned. This time it was worse. The matter now not only affected him but also his family. His parents were beginning to share in his dreams. They too held the hope that their son's fame would alleviate their poverty. But they could not help him in his mood of hopelessness. He would have to do what Drury had suggested, go back to working on the land until a better opportunity presented itself for the publication of his poems. That was the final admission of defeat.

3

But work was not easy to find now that the summer was over, and he returned to his old habits of late-night drinking sessions with his friends at Bachelors Hall. For a time he even lost interest in Patty. With his hopes of success shattered he could not face her again. Instead he started an affair with Betty Sell, of Southorpe, a village near Barnack. She was an attractive girl with black hair, hazel eyes and, at sixteen, a reputation for her sexual generosity. In a letter dated August 1819 Edward Drury wrote to his cousin, John Taylor, saying 'she appears to be a cyprian',[7] a local whore whose name was well-known in the district. Clare met her at Stamford Fair and went out with her several times during the next few months. Apart from her physical attractions it is interesting that he should have chosen another Elizabeth – a name which always meant much to him. Their relationship grew into an affection that made his heart 'ache to think it must be broken for Patty was then in a situation that marriage only coud remedy'.[8] Clare was in a dilemma:

> I had a variety of minds about me & all of them unsettled my long-smotherd affections for Mary revivd with my hopes & as I expected to be on a level with her bye & by I thought I might have a chance of success in reviving my former affections[9]

But now such optimism was mixed with despair. He was still some way from being Mary's social equal, still unpublished and unknown. Patty Turner was also pregnant with his child and now he had this growing passion for Betty Sell. He was, he admitted, 'never all my life anything else but a fool, committing rashly and repenting too late'.[10] Like many another romantic he deceived himself into thinking he was in love with a girl whenever his ego – and poetic inspiration – were flattered by her attention and admiration:

> When a face pleased me I scribbled a song or so in her praise, try'd to get in her company for the sake of pastime merely . . . then left off for new allurements in fresh faces that took my fancy as superiors . . . Temptations were things that I rarely resisted, when the partiality of the moment gave no time for reflection I was sure to seize it whatever might be the consequence. Still, I have been no-one's enemy but my own My easy nature either in drinking or anything else was always ready to submit to persuasions of profligate companions who often led me into snares and laughed at me when they had done so[11]

Nowhere is the contradictory nature of Clare's life more apparent. Often torn between opposites he found himself stranded in long periods of guilt. He could be very strong-willed and definite about his writing, but could be equally weak and influenced by others in his emotions and social behaviour. He could take a censuring view of his friends' failings but did not always want to recognize his own. He held certain moral values which he could not always maintain, and this disturbed him. But when he went to the local fairs and was 'coaxed about to bad houses, those painted pills of poison by whom many unguarded youths are hurried to destruction like the ox to the slaughterhouse'[12] he could be as loose in his morals as anyone else. Intense guilt followed. 'Here not only my health but my life has often been on the eve of its sacrifice by an illness too well-known and too disgusting to mention.'[13] He may have considered suicide on more than one occasion but his stubborn faith in his true nature and purpose in life always brought him back from that edge of destruction. Whether he ever had a venereal infection is difficult to say. The fear of it was certainly real enough to Clare and, as a hypochrondriac, he would have interpreted any unnatural symptom as a sure sign that he had caught the disease as a punishment. The fears always came after he felt he had debased himself in some sexual affair either in Stamford or later in London. We know from his letters that he was for several years taking 'the blue pills' which might have been the *Pilula Hydrargyric* drug prescribed then for gonorrhoea and, in some cases, syphilis. This was a mild dose of mercury which, although known to be harmful to the brain, was considered by the physicians as the lesser of two evils. Clare was, however, frequently examined by different doctors and there is no specific reference to his being treated for either gonorrhoea or syphilis. The doctors' reassurance, nevertheless, would do little to ease Clare's conscience. A moment's pleasure was followed by days of remorse.

Whilst Clare was rueing 'Th' expense of spirit in a waste of shame', Edward Drury, true to his word, had been getting other opinions on the Helpston poet's talents, this time with better results. He had sent the poems first to Sir John English Dolben of Finedon Place, in Northamptonshire and then to his cousin, John Taylor of Fleet Street, London. Sir John wrote back to say that he was impressed and would gladly subscribe to the publication. Drury passed this good news on to Clare and urged him to start writing again. But one cannot just pick up a pen and move immediately into a new period of creativity, so Clare spent the next few weeks busily revising, or completing, many of those earlier poems he had left in rough draft. Night after night the Helpston cottage was again littered with poems in various stages of completion. New poems eventually began to get written too, and when the scenes of nature failed to inspire he turned to the local newspapers to see which items of interest could be made into verse. 'Crazy Nell', for instance, was taken from a narrative Clare read in the *Stamford Mercury* and many of his verses were written round the margins of newspapers.

John Taylor's opinion had an even greater impact on Clare. Taylor was already publishing the works of William Hazlitt, Charles Lamb, Thomas De Quincey, Henry Francis Cary and John Keats. Drury knew that having gone this far for an opinion he would have to accept whatever verdict his cousin gave. He knew that Taylor was an unpredictable man. It could be the end or the beginning of a curious enterprise. Drury had no intention of handing Clare over to Taylor without protecting his own interests, for he believed that there could be profit in these poems as much for himself as for anyone else, but he needed Taylor's backing. He could do nothing now until he heard from London. Clare became impatient. He was once more heavily in debt and feeling ill. He did not even know the name of this 'other person' from whom Edward Drury waited to hear.

4

John Taylor was the son of a bookseller, James Taylor, who had married Elizabeth Drury at Newark in September 1778. They later moved to Repton and it was there, on 31 July 1781, that their third son was born. At the age of twelve he was sent to Lincoln Grammar School where he met William Hilton and Peter de Wint, who were to become artists and close friends of Taylor and Clare years later in London.

As a boy Taylor earned himself the nickname 'Old Associate' because he preferred the company of people several years his senior. He was always keen to help his father in the bookshop and studied all aspects of the publishing industry from production to sales. He became ambitious and wanted to make his own way in the world as soon as possible. At the age of twenty-two he moved to London, the centre of the world's book trade, and went to work for James Lackington, who ran the well-known Temple of the Muses house at that time. Lackington prided himself on having over half a million books in stock and also on making an annual profit of £4,000.[14] His flair for selling was what Taylor had been hoping to find. Books could be big business if only you knew how to sell them. One of Lackington's principles was that a big turn-over with smaller profits would build up a wider, more loyal public. Taylor worked thirteen hours a day for 7/6d a week. It was at Lackington's that he first met James Augustus Hessey, a man four years younger than himself and the person with whom he was to go into partnership.

After his apprenticeship with Lackington, Taylor joined the firm of Vernor and Hood – the latter being the father of the poet Thomas Hood. It was there that Taylor had what was perhaps his first experience of publishing rural verse. He had accepted Robert Bloomfield's *The Farmer's Boy* for which he paid the poet the amazing sum of £4,000 for the copyright. Such payments were not unusual then. In 1810 Sir Walter Scott received £4,000 for *The Lady of the Lake*; in 1816 Lord Byron received £2,200 for the Third Canto of *Childe Harold*; and Thomas Moore was offered £3,000 for a poem of which he had not written a line. Sales, of course, matched these advanced royalties. In 1814, on the day of its publication, Byron's *The Corsair* sold over 10,000 copies.

Seeing what high profits could be made out of publishing, Taylor and Hessey decided in 1806 to set up their own business at 93 Fleet Street.

Ten years later they were publishing most of the books they handled as booksellers. Taylor, always a great talker, held dinner parties to which he invited authors and patrons alike. They were occasions of prestige as well as celebration.

In 1817 he discovered John Keats and said of him, 'I cannot think he will fail to become a great poet.'[15] He was, for once, more of a prophet than a good judge of the poetry market. Keats did not take London by storm as Byron had done, and his work received very sparse notice or enthusiasm. His first volume, published before Taylor knew him, had been criticized as immature. Taylor believed he could improve matters and agreed to take all the new poems Keats might write. Their relationship became a very special one and the publisher never lost faith in his new poet even though sales remained depressingly poor.

It was early in 1819 that he received from his cousin in Stamford the package of poems from another new poet. This time the verses were written by a true 'labouring man in this neighbourhood who seems to have a strange taste for poetry'.[16] Taylor was very impressed. He liked their freshness and peculiarity. He thought that, when edited, the poems would find a sympathetic readership, especially if the poet's situation was made known, even exploited. A 'peasant poet' would be a different proposition. He was not another John Keats but his verses would sell. Drury was delighted. He could now give Clare the encouragement he needed. But he would still not tell him from whom this latest opinion came. He would only say that the poems were in good hands and that he must be patient. There was much work to be done on the manuscripts – editing, copying, deciding what to do about the many dialect words, preparing the poems for the discerning public. Clare was only half satisfied with his explanations. He insisted on knowing more about the person who was deciding the future of his poetry. Some weeks later Drury had to let him know about John Taylor of London. Clare could hardly believe his good fortune. The battle for possession of his work, which was to go on between those two gentlemen, had little significance for him then. The only thing that mattered was that he was going to be published, not in Market Deeping at his own expense, but by the respectable firm of Taylor and Hessey, with Drury's help.

Taylor's interest in Clare grew and he asked to see more poems. Drury was cautious. He had no intention of parting with the poems, or Clare, without safeguarding his own position. Writing to Taylor in April 1819 he said, 'I acknowledge, dear cousin, that I desire to secure to myself some merit in bringing this rustic genius into notice, but I am far from caging a lion when I have caught one and will take care that the poet shall have every justice done him by me.'[17]

Everything that Taylor knew of Clare at that time came from Drury.

He learned from him that the poet lived 'in the worst hut in the meanest village I ever saw' and that when he called to see Clare at home his mother – 'the gypsy-looking woman' – just sat there and shouted, 'Jack!' Then, 'lumping down the steps came the poet from the upper room . . . shy and clownish in his manner'.

Clare's shyness did not last long enough for Drury who was soon saying, 'I have been obliged to make all securely my own from the man's conceit, for now that he has made it known that he has received some money for his works it is astonishing what various proposals he has received from different quarters . . . if he is removed from his humble occupation of gardening his talent will be ruined.'[18] There could have been some truth in that statement if we did not know that Drury's intentions were not to protect Clare or the poetry. A month later, in a letter dated 5 May 1819, he was telling Taylor that the poet 'must be kept in his station and the notice he receives should tend to improve his condition further as a gardener than as a poet'. Clare was, for Drury, simply another commodity to sell for his own profit. In June of that year he made his position ruthlessly clear. 'My view of these poems is to consider them as wares that I have bought which will find a market in the great city. I want a broker or a partner to whom I can consign or share the articles I receive from the manufacturer . . . His talents will not be hid in a napkin.'[19]

Taylor, equally, was to protect his own interest in Clare's future but never so cold-bloodedly as Edward Drury. Taylor at least saw Clare's gift for what it was and came to enjoy an intellectual dialogue with him on the writing of poetry that would never have concerned Drury. The two men were, nevertheless, to quarrel over the possession of this 'maker of wares' for many years to come, at Clare's cost.

Clare, meanwhile, went on writing poems and in his enthusiasm handed them over to Drury for forwarding to London. His ambition concerned itself more in those days with the problem of choosing someone to whom he could dedicate his first volume. There was only one obvious choice – Lord Milton. Clare wrote to him, asking if he would accept the dedication, but his Lordship was preparing for a visit to Italy and did not answer the letter.

Throughout the autumn of 1819 Taylor worked on the poems and wrote a long introduction which he thought the collection needed. He also compiled a glossary of the dialect words he had retained and began placing advertisements in the press. The original title of the volume was *Pastoral Sketches in Songs, Ballads and Sonnets*, by John Clare, a Northamptonshire Peasant. But, by publication day, it had been changed to *Poems Descriptive of Rural Life and Scenery*. The 'peasant' remained unchanged.

In December Clare wrote to his friend, the Reverend Isaiah Knowles

Holland, to say that he had heard Lord Milton was home again and could he be informed of the publication. As in the past, he referred to the influence his father Parker Clare might have on his Lordship: 'Inform him that I am the son of the Lame Man at Helpstone please to hint likewise the Intention of Sending me to the National School to act in the Capacity of a School master.'[20] His hopes and ambitions were now clearly two-fold. The years at Glinton and the nights spent over his books at home might yet give him a profession and the publication of his poems might also bring fame.

He was now even more determined that he should not have to return to 'the Necessity of taking to hard Labour again – after all my hopes to the contrary'.[21] But, as was often the case, there were as many dark threats as there were bright prospects. Once more he was in debt, his parents owed two years' rent and were faced with eviction. Hard labour still seemed the only answer. No more was heard of the idea to send him to a National School to become a teacher. He became depressed and felt his poetry had dried up in the bleakness of that winter. Edward Drury became concerned. He did not want anything to happen to his poet, or the family, so he paid off all the arrears and thereby made it possible for Clare and his parents to stay in their cottage for at least another Christmas. He also gave Clare the freedom of his shop, to read the latest books which arrived from London, or to copy out new tunes for his fiddle. He then invited him over to Stamford on Sunday mornings to have breakfast with him and, both men being fond of music and literature, their conversation lasted most of the morning. Sometimes Clare arrived before Drury was awake and coaxed him out of bed with some new jig on the fiddle. It was on one of these visits that he was to meet a Dr Bell, a 'man of odd taste but a pleasant acquaintance' who was also a lover of books. Bell had compiled an anthology of jests called *The Banisher of the Blue Devils*. He had been a doctor in the Army and had served in the colonies. He took to Clare and, concerned about his future as a poet and his present poverty, wrote to Earl Spencer, who agreed to give the poet a salary of £10 a year.

It was also at Drury's shop that Clare was eventually to meet his publisher, John Taylor, who was staying with Octavius Gilchrist. Taylor told Clare how long he had worked on editing the poems, that they were now in the press and would definitely be published early in the new year. The two men had a lengthy discussion, though Clare's initial shyness in the presence of strangers made him grateful when it came to an end. Later that day a servant arrived from the Gilchrists with an invitation to dine that evening with John Taylor and his hosts. Clare was petrified. He had never dined anywhere grander than servants' kitchens. He did not have the right clothes to wear. He had working boots, but no shoes.

Townspeople, he had heard, had carpets on their floors, not sand as the village-folk did. It was impossible, he could not go. But, with a little persuasion from Drury and a borrowed shirt, Clare made his first step into a society which he had seen only from a distance.

5

Octavius Gilchrist, born at Twickenham in 1779, was, to all outward appearances, no more than a prosperous grocer. His father had been a lieutenant and surgeon in the third regiment of Dragoon Guards and it had been his hope that his son would enter the church. Octavius went to Magdalen College, Oxford, but before he could take his degree, or enter holy orders, his allowance came to an end and he was sent to help his uncle in the Stamford grocery business. The weighing and serving of provisions left him plenty of time to continue his academic interests and he occasionally contributed to the literary periodicals. In 1803 the uncle died, leaving the Stamford property and the business to his nephew. Octavius was suddenly a wealthy young man who could employ assistants and so devote even more of his energies to study. In 1804 he married Miss Nolan of London and, through her, was introduced to much of London's literary society. He became friendly with William Gifford and began contributing articles to the *Quarterly Review*. He became recognized as an authority on Elizabethan drama and in 1805 published a volume of poems and helped Gifford edit the works of Ben Jonson. Later, when he was established in Stamford, he edited *Drakard's Stamford News* for several years.

Had Clare known this much about Gilchrist that evening he would have trembled even more as he sat at table with him. But he need not have worried. Gilchrist was a very kind and understanding person who was to become one of Clare's closest friends and allies. At Taylor's suggestion Gilchrist wrote an account of that evening for the January number of the *London Magazine* (1820). The publisher thought that a sympathetic portrait of the 'peasant poet' he was about to launch on to the literary scene would not do the sales any harm at all. After describing how the three men came to be together, Gilchrist continued:

> Clare announced his arrival by a hesitating knock at the door – 'between a single and double rap' – and immediately upon his introduction he dropped into a chair. Nothing could exceed the meekness, and simplicity, and diffidence with which he answered the various inquiries concerning his life and habits, which we mingled with subjects calculated or designed to put him much at ease. Nothing certainly could less resemble splendour than the room in which Clare was

shown; but there was a carpet upon which it is likely he never previously set foot; and wine, of which assuredly, he had never tasted before. Of music he expressed himself passionately fond, and had learned to play a little on the violin... His account of his birth is melancholly enough. Nothing can be conceived much humbler than the origin of John Clare, poetry herself does not supply a more lowly descent ...[22]

Gilchrist's article included a brief biography of Clare and how he came to poetry. He also took the opportunity of unfairly chastising him in public for fraternizing with the Reverend Isaiah Knowles Holland (whom he referred to as 'a Calvinistic preacher') and finally praised the poet for his modest demeanour and decent habits which were a credit to the faith of the established church – comments which would have caused some of Clare's friends a wry smile. Clare's shyness was, perhaps, a convenient mask that night for, during the two-hour long interview, Gilchrist saw only one aspect of his complex nature – and one no doubt that Clare wanted him to see. When it was time to leave he was, as Gilchrist observed, 'not sorry at being released from restraint'.

6

Back in London John Taylor finished his long introduction to *Poems Descriptive of Rural Life and Scenery*, in which he established the image of the 'peasant poet' which was to outlast Clare's lifetime:

> The following Poems will probably attract some notice by their intrinsic merit; but they are also entitled to attention from the circumstances under which they were written. They are the genuine productions of a young Peasant, a day-labourer in husbandry, who has had no advantages of education beyond others of his class; and though Poets in this country have seldom been fortunate men, yet he is, perhaps, the least favoured by circumstances, and the most destitute of friends, of any that ever existed.[23]

Taylor was clouding the truth in saying that Clare had received no advantages of education beyond others of his class. Although his education had obvious limitations, it was considerably more liberal than the average working-class child received in Helpston, or anywhere else, and continued throughout his teenage years to a stage where he was considered worthy of better things. Edward Drury had told Taylor earlier in May that 'He has tried at almost all studies – Music, Mathematics, Drawing... but having only 1/- old books from the meanest bookstall to instruct him, his laboured progress was, as he states, accompanied with the most heartfelt anguish.'[24] There is a difference between 'going to school' and 'being educated', as Clare knew. Nevertheless, Taylor had set the pattern. His new poet was a poor, uneducated peasant who had, through some freak genius, written a volume of poems which now made its plea to the world for sympathy if not recognition. It was this patronizing tone which, as Frederick Martin observed, unwisely drew the public's attention more to Clare's poverty than it did to his poetry.

Something else, however, emerges from Taylor's introduction which is equally important – an assessment of Clare the man:

> In the real troubles of life, when they are not brought on by the misconduct of the individual, a strong mind acquires the power of righting itself after each attack, and this philosophy, not to call it by a better name, Clare possesses.[25]

Poems Descriptive of Rural Life and Scenery was published on 16 January 1820. The next twelve months were to give Clare a year of acclaim he had neither dreamt of nor could believe.

12
'Wearing into the Sunshine'

1

Clare was at home and out of work at the time that his first volume was published. He received the news from the Reverend Holland who had galloped over from Market Deeping to congratulate him. For a moment Clare failed to understand his friend's enthusiasm. 'But have you not heard from your publishers?' asked Holland. 'Then let me be the first herald of good news; I can assure you that your utmost expectations have been realized. I have had a letter from a friend in London this morning telling me that your poems are talked of by everybody; in fact, are a great success.'[1]

Taylor had, however, written to Clare on 13 January 1820, saying, 'I hope you like the work now it is finished, and if you can make presents or otherwise dispose of 12 copies they are yours.' It may have taken a week or more for that parcel to reach Helpston and the Reverend Holland may have been the first to tell Clare of the impact that his poems had made in London. But it seems clear that Clare was a success even before he realized his poems were published.

Within days of publication the volume was in great demand. Drury wrote to Taylor, 'I shall want more of Clare's Poems before you can send them ... send another 25 p. Coach ... about fifty more by Waggon will satisfy the town & neighbourhood which seem disposed to buy freely.'[2] Even Drury underestimated the sudden interest in the Helpston poet. A few days later he was sending an urgent request to Taylor for 'another one hundred copies'.[3]

The first edition of a thousand was quickly sold out and a second edition soon in the shops. By May a third edition was necessary and a fourth in preparation by the end of the year. The critics, too, were mostly enthusiastic. 'We have seldom an opportunity of learning the unmixed and unadulterated impression of the loveliness of nature on a man of vivid perception and strong feeling, equally unacquainted with the arts and reserve of the world, and with the riches, rules, and prejudices of literature. Such a man is Clare.' So said the *New Times* in January 1820. The reviewer, admittedly, had reservations about Clare's vocabulary and use of provincialisms but believed these were weaknesses which experience would help to remedy. The *London Magazine*, of March 1820, declared that Clare had an

> intense feeling for the scenery of the country, a heart susceptible to the quietest and least glaring beauties of nature, a fine discrimination and close observation of the distinguishing features of particular rural seasons and situations ... Nothing in these pieces has touched us more than the indications they afford of the author's ardent attachment to places, that can have witnessed little but his labour, his hardships and his necessities ...

A month later, the *Eclectic Review* went further: 'Genius such as characterises these productions of John Clare, is not common in any rank ... Clare is hardly likely to produce anything much more beautiful than some of the descriptive passages in the present volume ... Society owes it to itself, to prevent the Author of these poems from adding another name to the annals of unbefriended genius.'[4] Again, such praise was not without criticism of Clare's provincialisms and frequent 'grammatical blemish', nor did it miss the opportunity of suggesting that some of the more vulgar pieces should be omitted from future editions. 'My Mary', 'Dolly's Mistake', and 'The Country Girl' were three of the poems recommended for displacement, and perhaps Clare's patrons had not been inactive in making their views known on this subject. This question of Clare's vocabulary and the 'vulgarity' of some of the poems will be considered more fully in the following chapter.

The praise Clare received during those early weeks of January 1820 was enough to lift the poet out of his depressions and doubt. In the excitement of publishing a successful book of poems he began to think more positively about his future. The days of hard manual labour were over. He was recognized. And this was only a beginning. Already he had more than enough poems for another collection. The news of his fame in London was the talk of most people in the neighbourhood. But not all of it was friendly or admiring. Many of the natives had known Clare when he was a nobody, a scrounger, an idler, a rebel at heart and a morose man. He had mixed with gipsies, had wasted his nights and money at Bachelors Hall. He would disappear for days at a time or walk the streets talking to himself. And he was a woman's man.

> Envy was up at my success with all the lyes it coud muster some said that I never wrote the poems & that Drury gave me money to father

> them with my name Others said that I had stole them out of books & that Parson this & Squire t'other knew the books from which they were stolen Pretending scholars said that I had never been to a grammar school & therefore it was impossible for me to write anything our Parson industriously found out the wonderful discovery that I coud not spell & of course his opinion was busily distributed in all companies which he visited that I was but a middling promise of success[5]

When the parson realized that Clare was being applauded by men of much greater learning, he excused himself by saying that he did not read poetry and subsequently knew little about the subject – a confession gleefully endorsed by Clare.

His success, then, had its drawbacks and the poet still needed all the encouragement he could get to offset the local criticism and jealousy. His neighbours were certainly going to have plenty of events to talk about during the months to come.

2

As soon as the poems were published Clare asked his mother to take a copy over to Milton for him. She returned with the exciting news that his Lordship wanted ten more copies and that the poet himself was to visit the house the following Sunday. Edward Drury advised Clare not to wear the new clothes he had just bought 'which are more suitable to a Squire of high degree than humble John Clare',[6] and again loaned him one of his own shirts.

If Clare had thoughts above his station who can blame him, and he may have done better to ignore Drury's advice. All his life he had struggled to rise above the insignificance into which his talent had been born. Now, out of nothing, he had achieved something that not even money could buy. Although he could be untidy and careless about his dress he could also be flamboyant. He had ideas about how a poet should look. He may have lost the green coat he had ordered from the tailor a year ago but now his prospects warranted some extravagance and, with his fine looks, he could certainly carry expensive clothes with dignity.

Drury had always been afraid that success would go to Clare's head. As early as 3 June 1819 he had written to Taylor about Clare's expectations: 'Though his daydreams picture the most exaggerated success & though his hopes are preposterous to excess, I do not fear with careful management his pride and ambition will be checked.' Drury, with his usual insensitive bluntness, had hit the nail on the head even though he was unable to see at that moment just how much 'careful management' was going to check Clare's hopes. In January 1820 it was enough to warn Clare from dressing too much like a gentleman and keeping to his true station.

Dutifully, Clare went to Milton Hall dressed as a farm labourer and could eat or drink nothing as he sat in the servants' hall waiting for his Lordship to send for him. Lord Milton tried to put Clare at his ease straightaway by explaining in a quiet unaffected manner why he had not answered the poet's letter about the dedication. He then spoke about the poems and showed great interest in them. Lady Milton also asked several questions and invited Clare to name any book that was a favourite, expressing at the same time her wish to give him one. But Clare was confounded and could think of nothing on the spur of the moment, so lost the gift – 'I did not like to pick out a book for fear of over-reaching on her kindness or else Shakespeare lay at my tongue's end.'[7]

Lord and Lady Fitzwilliam were also there and talked freely with Clare – 'His Lordship gave me some advice which I had done well perhaps to have noticd better than I have he bade me beware of booksellers & warnd me not to be fed with promises.'[8]

On his departure they gave Clare a handful of money which he dared not look at until well away from the house. It was more than he had ever possessed in his life up to that moment and he felt sure he would be poor no more. There was seventeen pounds. He could not make enough haste back to Helpston to show his parents.

He was also invited to visit Burghley House on the following Sunday but when the day came it began to snow 'too unmercifully for a traveller ever to venture thus far', so he declined to go, though, he admits, it was not the weather which prevented him from making the journey but the fear that his shoes would get too dirty to be seen in such a fine place. When he did go, a day later, the porter asked him why he had not come when expected. Clare blamed the weather and was told 'you should stand for no weathers tho it rained knives & forks with the tynes downward'.[9]

After a while the Marquis of Exeter sent for him. Clare was taken upstairs and through winding passages as fast as he could hobble and 'almost fit to quarrel with my hard-nailed shoes at the noise they made on the marble & boarded floors & cursing them to myself as I set my feet down in the lightest steps I was able to utter'.[10] Even so, it was a far cry from the days when Clare had gone there to work as a gardening boy.

When the Honourable Mr Henry Pierrepont, who was brother-in-law to the Marquis of Exeter, had delivered the invitation to Clare he had also told him to bring his manuscript of the poems with him to Burghley House. This his Lordship now asked to see, expressing at the same time the regret that his sister, Lady Sophia, could not be with them – she had sat up so long the day before waiting for Mr Clare to arrive that she had become very ill. Clare apologized. She had, however, left him a gift of Campbell's *Pleasures of Hope*. After a brief audience Clare was told that a meal was waiting for him in the servants' hall and he turned to go. The Marquis, sensing that his visitor was completely lost, offered to show him the way. As they walked together down the corridors he explained to Clare that although he could not offer any work in his gardens he would allow him fifteen guineas a year for the rest of his life.

Clare was so relieved and overjoyed at this news that he let the servants make him drunk on strong brown ale before sending him home. Back at Helpston he told his parents that they were now all well-off and secure. Even so, he did not want his good fortune to change his style of life. Or so he thought:

> I never attempted to alter my old ways & manners I arboured no proud notions nor felt a pride above my station I was courted to keep company with the 'betters' in the village but I never noticd the fancied kindness the old friends & neighbours in my youth are my friends & neighbours now ... I keep on in the same house that we always occupied & have never felt a desire to have a better[11]

Not all of this is entirely true. He was not always to feel as warm and charitable about his neighbours. Soon he was to tell his publisher that he lived 'among the ignorant like a lost man', that his neighbours dare not talk in his company for fear that he 'should mention them in my writings', and that they were 'insensible to everything but toiling, and that to no purpose'.[12] Nor was he to be always content with the same house. Soon he was to write a poem called 'Proposals for Building a Cottage', one which would stand beside a stream; a cottage with room for his books and fit to live in. He was to have a much roomier house a few years later when he moved to Northborough and his 'ways & manners' could not remain unaltered after his experiences in London. But, in the euphoria of early 1820, he was prepared to see paradise regained in the simplest things he had ever known in life. He may have been selfish in many matters but his success was something he wanted to share with his parents, his sister and the best of his friends. In this moment of acclaim he even looked longingly once more towards Glinton and wondered what Mary Joyce might be thinking of him now.

3

But it was not Mary Joyce who mattered. Exactly two months after the publication of *Poems Descriptive of Rural Life and Scenery*, Clare married Martha (Patty) Turner on 16 March 1820 at the church of Saints Peter and Paul, Casterton Magna (now Great Casterton). The entry in the parish register is both moving and significant in its simplicity. Under the flowing signature of John Clare is the crude, shaky cross made by Martha as 'her mark'. The marriage was solemnized by the Reverend Richard Lewis and the couple's signatures witnessed by Patty's uncle, John Turner, and Clare's sister, Sophia. Clare was then twenty-seven and Patty twenty-one – and seven months pregnant. After the ceremony the wedding-party went over to the Crown Inn for a short celebration. Clare then walked his wife home to Walkherd Lodge, where she was to continue living with her parents, even though they remained unforgiving. Clare went back to Helpston. There was no honeymoon, not even the chance of living together. The Clares had no room and John could not afford to rent any other property. Patty, nevertheless, had a 'bride cake' for, on 29 March, Edward Drury wrote to Clare: 'Thank you for the piece of cake you sent me, and I heartily wish you every joy & happiness that your changing station can bring you.'

When Clare's change of fortune was known in the district some of his wife's friends – who had been very cool before – now wanted to know him, but he remembered their former slights and refused to have anything to do with them. Patty's parents had already told her that 'as she had made her bed hard she should lie on it'. Similarly they wanted to hear nothing more about their son-in-law. Clare had given Patty money towards the wedding and had also helped with buying things for the expected baby. But he could not yet provide her with the home they both so urgently needed. He could only hope that his success, and his patrons, would soon remedy this frustration.

Just how much his publishers and patrons knew about Patty at this stage of his career we cannot say for sure. Taylor and Hessey certainly knew of the marriage but when Clare's first child, Anna Maria, was born on 2 June, he did not hurry to tell them. It was not until 29 June, whilst writing to James Hessey about a variety of other subjects, that he mentioned as an afterthought that he was now also a father: 'I forgot to say I fetch home "Patty of the Vale" next Sunday & that she has got a daughter – but for credits sake to all but our particular friends this is a secret.'

The reason why Clare was able to 'fetch home Patty' was because the occupiers of the small tenement next-door to his parents had decided to move out. Parker Clare immediately applied to the landlord for the tenancy on his son's behalf. Clare, happy at last to have his wife and daughter living with him, was also aware of his responsibility to keep them and so he wrote with even greater fervour. Drury was already worried that the poet was overworking and had written to Taylor earlier in the year to say:

> It is to be greatly feared that the man will be afflicted with insanity if his talent continues to be forced as it has been these 4 months past; he has no other mode of easing the fever that oppresses him after a tremendous fit of rhyming except by getting tipsy. A simple pint of ale very often does this, and next morning a stupor with headache and pains across the chest afflicts him very severely. Then he is melancholy and completely hypochondriac – you will easily suppose how true is my account when I assure you he has rhymed and written for 3 days and 3 nights without hardly eating or sleeping . . .[13]

If Taylor needed any confirmation of this fact he had it from Clare himself who, in April, had written: 'I have been terribly plagued with the muses since I saw you I think I have wrote 50 sonnets' and, in May, he had confessed that 'when I am in the fit I write as much in one week as would knock ye up a fair size vol'.[14] Writing to James Hessey in July he again boasted that he had found the knack of writing eight ballads a day.[15] When he wrote in 'The Rural Muse' that 'True poesy owns a haunted mind/A thirst enduring flame', he was speaking from experience.

What Patty thought of her obsessed husband during these early months of living with him at Helpston can only be surmised. If the child gave them sleepless nights it does not appear to have decreased Clare's output. One of the poems he wrote during those prolific nights was 'To An Infant Daughter'. It was a strange, revealing and, in some ways, prophetic poem, especially in its last four verses:

> And much I wish, whate'er may be
> The lot my child that falls to thee
> Nature may never let thee see
> Her glass betimes
> But keep thee from my failings free –
> Nor itch at ryhmes
>
> Lord help thee in thy coming years
> If thy mad father's picture 'pears
> Predominant! His feeling fears
> And jingling starts
> I'd freely now gi' vent to tears
> To ease my heart
>
> May thou unknown to ryhming bother
> Be ignorant as is thy mother
> And in thy manners such another
> Save sin's nigh quest
> And then with 'scaping this and t'other
> Thou mayst be blest

Lord knows my heart it loves thee much
And may my feelings aches & such
The pains I meet in folly's clutch
Be never thine
Child it's a tender string to touch
That sounds 'Thou'rt mine'.[16]

The poem is not only one of praise, it is also a prayer for protection. He did not want her to carry the burden of too great an intellect nor be as ignorant as her mother. He would rather she acquire those virtues remembered in someone like Mary Joyce. The fear of his own madness would not let him promise her that such blessings would be hers. He could only be grateful for the birth of his first child.

He read, and gave a copy of, the poem to Patty, who was sufficiently proud of it always to keep it by her, even though she could not read. He also sent a copy to James Hessey. Hessey praised the poem highly but said it would be indiscreet to publish it for a while as the revelation that Clare was a father within three months of marriage would upset his London patrons: 'None of your friends here but Taylor and myself are acquainted with the addition to your family – keep your counsel and we shall not betray you.'[17]

Taylor objected to the verse referring to the mother's ignorance and Clare mentioned this to Patty. But she did not mind. She 'thought it a compliment so little does she know of poetry'.[18] When the poem was first published in 1821 that verse was, however, omitted and Clare was pleased, 'for I have found out by experience which is a good adviser that I possess a more valuable article in her than I at first expected & believe her from my soul an honest woman'.[19]

All the doubts had been on Clare's side. Patty was determined to make the marriage a success and had no second thoughts at that stage about her love for her husband. She did everything to make a comfortable home for him. It was not always easy and they frequently quarrelled. Often Patty got the better of Clare for, on 30 August 1820, he wrote to Taylor, 'I fancy my W—— "you know you do" will turn out to be a termagant she is one of the most ignorant & I fear will turn out the most obstinate woman in creation.' Harsh and unfair words, which were to mellow within the year.

It could not have been easy for her to adjust to the life-style at Helpston, which was not foreseen when she was being courted by the hopeless young lime-burner of Ryhall and Pickworth. Not only did she have to learn to live with Clare's infirm parents, she also had the quite unexpected task of receiving all the visitors to the house; people of all ranks and attitudes who arrived to see her husband, the poet. Parsons by the score, fashionable ladies, scholars, country squires, a bishop and his wife, all knocking at the cottage door from early morning until dark, asking for Mr Clare. Patty must have found it an utterly bewildering change of fortune for the man she had known only as a labourer. Both she, and Clare's mother, were often thrown into bad tempers over the arrival of visitors, especially those who came before they had had time to clean the house. Patty's annoyance had little balm, nor could she escape in the way her husband did. Anna Maria, who was not a strong baby, needed much attention. Parker Clare was house-bound. Clare, on the other hand, left early for the fields and his irritation must have been calmed, or flattered, when he reflected on some of life's ironies.

4

During the remainder of that year letters and tributes arrived from near and far. Hardly a day went by without some visitor turning up in Helpston. A few were helpful, but most were just curious. One of the first important people was Dr Herbert Marsh, who had been appointed as Bishop of Peterborough in 1819, after serving as Bishop of Llandaff for three years. He was the author of several controversial theological works and was persuaded by his German wife to take an interest in the Helpston poet. Mrs Marianne Marsh had read of Clare's success and struggles and, according to Martin, 'induced her husband to drive over to the obscure village and give Clare his episcopal blessing, together with half a dozen bottles of port wine'.[20]

That seems a well-balanced approach to Christian charity, with consideration for both the spiritual and the temporal needs of man. But, in view of Clare's liking for a drink, it was, perhaps, not the wisest choice. He only records that he had a visit from the Bishop who gave him a 'beautifully bound copy of *The Memoirs of the Court of Queen Elizabeth*' by Lucy Aiken, which was published in 1818.

The Bishop himself was not too impressed with either Helpston or its poet, but this did not prevent his determined wife from continuing her support, nor did he object when she invited Clare to be a guest at the Palace, which he was on a number of occasions. Mrs Marsh also visited Helpston several times, always taking with her parcels of food and clothing. Her eldest son suffered from bouts of insanity and she was to understand Clare's temperament better than most, and more quickly than many of his friends. She certainly showed great patience and lack of condescension when in his company. She was tolerant and forgiving, even when Clare deserved censure. For the most part he was grateful for her good intentions, but, as we shall see, the relationship was not to be without its embarrassing moments.

Another early visitor was Chauncy Hare Townshend, who was then a student at Trinity Hall, Cambridge. He was to take holy orders but illness prevented him from accepting a living. He travelled extensively, became a friend of Charles Dickens – who dedicated *Great Expectations* to him – and was to publish some religious meditations and three volumes of verse. Despite the great social differences between them, he and Clare were to become good friends. Not that their friendship started too well. Clare recalls that he was on his way home, looking 'shabby and dirty', when the stranger stopped him and asked if he could direct him to the poet Clare's cottage. Clare was not sure what to say. He saw Townshend then as another inquisitive dandy who had a lisp in his speech 'which he owd to affectation rather than habit'.[21] For a few moments the two men were tense in one another's company. But, as they talked, Clare sensed that this young visitor was different:

> He was a feeling & sensible young man he talked about Poets & Poetry & the fine scenery of the lakes & other matters for a good while & when he left me he put a folded paper in my hand which I found after he had gone was a sonnet & a pound bill[22]

Townshend also promised, and sent, a copy of James Beattie's *The Minstrel*. Clare wrote and thanked him for the gift, and they exchanged several letters during the next few months. Inviting Townshend to visit him again, Clare said:

> your first visit found me in a glowering desponding condition that often gets the sway but when I have been inspired with a pint of 'John Barleycorn' & in one of my sunshiny moments you would not know me I am a new man & have too many tongues, tho your visit did not find it, still I can be cheery but in my sullen fits I am defiled with the old silence of rusticity that always characterized me among my neighbours before I was known to the world[23]

Clare was learning quickly what it was like to be a personality – a piece of public property that was allowed no privacy and little respect. Some of the poet-hunters asked him if he kept a visitors' book in which they could write their names and were disappointed when he said he did not. Others, when they found that he spoke like any other 'vulgar fellow', shrugged their shoulders and, with a superior air, walked away. Some were insulting. Among the many that came:

> there was a dandified gentleman of unconscious odditys of character that not only bordered on the ridiculous but was absurdly smothered in it he made pretensions to great learning & knew nothing . . . he then begd my walking stick & after he had got it he wanted me to write my

> name on the crook I really thought the fellow was mad he then askd me insulting liberties respecting my first acquaintances with Patty & said he understood that in the country the lower orders made their courtship in barns & pigsties & askd me whether I did I felt very vexd & said it might be the custom of the higher orders for aught I knew as experience made fools wise in most matters but I assurd him he was very wrong respecting that custom among the lower orders here His wife said he was fond of a joke & hoped I should not be offended but I saw nought of a joke in it & found out afterward that he was a scant removed from the lower order himself as his wife was a grocer's daughter after he had gossiped an hour he said 'Well I promised to give you a book but after examining your library I don't see that you want anything as you have a great many more than I expected to find Still I should make you an offer of something have you got a Bible?' I said nothing but it was exactly what my father had long wanted & he instantly spoke for me & said 'We have a Bible Sir but I cannot read it the print is so small so I should thank you for one'[24]

Parker Clare, who could read very little whether the print was large or small, was not going to let the dandy get away without giving something in return for his son's time and walking-stick. With rural shrewdness he knew that the visitor had slyly suggested the very book he knew every cottage possessed to 'escape giving it'.

But, for all these annoyances, Clare admits that he 'was now wearing into the sunshine'.[25] The village continued to see carriages coming and going and the cottage often filled with gossiping gentry. From many of his visitors he received invitations to their homes. He was 'swarmed with promises of books till my mother was troubled & fancied the house would not hold them'.[26] She need not have worried. The books never came. He had the works of Lord Byron promised by six different people but never heard from one of them again.

In addition to the callers there were the letters which needed answering and the tributes in the national journals which he often felt needed acknowledgement. One, in verse, published in the *Morning Post* on 8 February 1820, had been from a Mrs Eliza Louisa Emmerson, the wife of a London picture importer and a friend of Lord Radstock. Both were to become important influences in Clare's life – often to his advantage, but frequently not. With the conflict growing between Drury and Taylor over the copyright of the poems, Clare certainly did not want patrons who were going to squabble with his publishers over what he could, or could not write.

But it was to be so. Soon he was to find that the natural joy of writing had to take into consideration the literary tastes of other people, people who had never seen or knew nothing of his world. For a time he was able to listen to their advice and write on in the amazement of his good fortune. But as their demands increased he was to see that his ideas of poetry and theirs differed greatly. There was London and Helpston. Often he was torn between the two.

13
Fame

1

With so much excitement over the publication of *Poems Descriptive of Rural Life and Scenery*, it was inevitable that Taylor and Hessey should want Clare to visit London as soon as possible. Octavius Gilchrist was asked to find out how willing Clare would be to leave Helpston for the capital. He wanted to go but was filled with anxiety. London, he believed, held terrors he could not face. Gilchrist promised him he would not be expected to make the first journey alone. The Stamford grocer was needing to go to London himself and told Clare that they could travel together. Clare needed little further persuasion. London was, in fact, to become a great attraction to him during the next few years and he was to stay there on four occasions.

The first visit was arranged for early March 1820, just before Clare was married and while he was still the talk of the literary circles. Taylor immediately organized meetings, put advertisements in the press to say that the manuscripts of the peasant poet could be seen at his offices, and arranged dinner parties. At these Clare would be introduced to London society, meet his patrons, have his portrait painted and be displayed to the public as the amazing rustic man he was.

On the morning of their departure he and Gilchrist joined the 'Regent Coach' at the George Inn, Stamford. At six o'clock the stage rumbled out from the cobbled yard and on to the Great North Road. Clare felt awkward and uncomfortable in his dress as he tried to settle down amongst the staring passengers. For mile after mile his mind was full of expectations and the wonders of the town which he had heard his parents talk about on winter nights by the fireside. London was a wicked place, with robbers, body-snatchers and loose women. Whenever there was a threat of doom or fear of trouble in the village his neighbours would say, 'Well, let's hope the devil stays in London.'[1]

As the coach made its way along the boundary wall of Burghley Park Clare could not help reflecting on his change of fortune since that day when he had climbed over the park wall to read Thomson's *Seasons*. And when he saw the farm-labourers toiling in the fields at his old occupations of ploughing and ditching while he was 'lolling in a coach' on his way to London, the thoughts created such feelings in him that he fancied he had changed his identity as well as his occupation, that he was not the same John Clare but some strange soul that had jumped into his skin.

Later, when they passed through Huntingdon, Gilchrist pointed out the house where Oliver Cromwell was born and the house where William Cowper had once lived. Clare found the second by far the more interesting. He had always admired Cowper's poetry and now felt over-awed to see the grand, melancholy parsonage where the poet had brooded alone over his verses.

When the stage finally arrived in London the streets were already lamp-lit and Clare noticed that the bill-boards carried his name. One of his poems, 'The Meeting' had been set to music by Haydn Corri and was to be sung that night at Drury Lane by Madame Vestris. Clare did not hear the performance because, by the time he and Gilchrist had refreshed themselves after their long journey, it was too late to get to the theatre. Even so, the poet was 'uncommonly pleased at the circumstance'.[2] It was a typical, pleasant enough setting of the poem and the first of many that were to be composed to Clare's verses. Frederick Martin says that Rossini also set one of the poems but there is now no trace of the score and it is unlikely that one ever existed.[3]

Although the two travellers could not go to the theatre Taylor did take Clare down to Westminster Bridge to see the River Thames by moonlight. Clare was unmoved. It was less impressive in his eyes than Whittlesea Mere, which was, at that time, still undrained and provided the fens with an attractive piece of inland water about the size of Derwentwater. In winter time the Mere covered up to 3,000 acres and seldom fell below 1,800 acres in summer. It appealed to naturalists from all over England and was a popular resort for regattas, water-picnics, lavish parties, sailing and skating. It had been sailed on by King Cnut and described most vividly in Lord Orford's account of his *Voyage Round the Fens* in 1774. When it was drained in 1851 its mud revealed the skulls of wild boar and a wolf, as well as a silver censer and incense-ship from Ramsey Abbey. Clare preferred to visit it when it was quieter, when he could study its rare ferns and bird-life alone. He was particularly interested in the 'Lady Fern' and the dwarf willows which seldom grew more than a foot high. It was also a place where the cranberry trailed itself by the water's edge and where several 'beautiful or peculiar flowers that have not been honoured with christenings from modern botany' shone among the grass.[4] The muddy Thames had to be an anticlimax after such a paradise under those sparkling summer skies of the fens and Clare's London friends were disappointed that their famous river had failed to excite him.

What did excite him was the number of young women. He was 'uncommonly astonished to see so many ladys as I thought them about the streets I expressed my surprise & was told they were girls of the town'.[5] There were at that time an estimated 80,000 prostitutes in London and, although Clare probably saw no more than fifty that night, it must have seemed a multitude of gaudy temptations for someone used to no more than two hundred respectable country people enjoying themselves at a village feast.

On that first visit to London Clare stayed for a week with Gilchrist's German brother-in-law, John Christian Burkhardt, who kept a jeweller's and watchmaker's shop in the Strand. He was then entertained at Taylor's dinner-parties, where he met two of his important patrons, Lord Radstock and Mrs Emmerson. He also met Charles Lamb, Allan Cunningham. H.F. Cary, T.G. Wainewright, J.H. Reynolds and William Hazlitt. He was taken to the theatre to see Kean and Macready, and went to Westminster Abbey to see Poets' Corner. Taylor also introduced him to William Hilton, who was to paint his portrait. All the problems back in Helpston must have seemed as far away as a half-forgotten dream. This was a new life and for a time he wanted to enjoy every moment of it.

2

Clare found himself uncommonly at ease with his patrons. Lord Radstock – formerly Admiral the Honourable William Waldergrave – was the second son of the third Earl Waldergrave, and had received his title after an active and distinguished career in the Navy. He was Vice-Admiral of the Blue in the victory over the Spanish Fleet off Cape Lagos in February 1797; could boast of having been a friend of Lord Nelson's; of having quelled a mutiny on board HMS *Latona*; and he was the author of two books, *The Cottager's Friend* (which went into twenty editions) and *The British Flag Triumphant*. He was also zealously religious. Clare wrote of him:

> Lord Radstock at first sight appears to be of a stern & haughty character but the moment he speaks his countenance kindles up into a free blunt good-hearted man – one whom you may expect to hear speak exactly as he thinks He has no notion of either offending or pleasing by his talk & cares as little for the consequencies of either

> there is a good deal of the bluntness & open-heartedness of the sailor about him & there is nothing of pride or fashion he is plain in manner & dress as the old country squire[6]

Clare did not like people to be mealy-mouthed or evasive in their talk. He was usually forthright himself and wanted others to be so. In his letter to Taylor of 2 April 1820 he was to tell Taylor, 'I am a blunt fellow' and it is noticeable in all his relationships that he began as he meant to go on, offend or please. By the summer of that year he felt himself to be on sufficiently familiar terms with his publishers to say to James Hessey, in a letter of 16 July, 'give my love to old Chuckey Taylor'.

Mrs Eliza Louisa Emmerson was less straightforward than Lord Radstock. She lived then at 4 Berners Street, London, but later moved to 20 Stratford Place where Clare was eventually to be her guest. Although her many kindnesses to the poet and his family were well meant – and Clare was to value her friendship for some twenty years – she could at times be both interferring and almost insufferable. She was sentimental, theatrical and considered herself something of a poet. She became a persistent correspondent, sending Clare well over three hundred letters. Her attentions grew increasingly possessive and, within the year, she was to tell him 'I have one wish nearer and dearer to me than another, it is to promote your fame, your welfare, your happiness! Though not the *child* of my adoption, you are *the poet* in my mind and heart.'[7] Many of her advances were flirtatious and, considering his recent marriage to Patty, embarrassing: 'Your "dear Patty" must not be jealous that I write thus to you; I do it for her sake in part, for in comforting and cheering your drooping spirits with the warm language of true friendship, I am at the same time, securing her future happiness in you.' Or, again, 'I've ever addressed you in your own very affectionate language – for we unblushingly acknowledge ourselves lovers in poetry.' If Clare did not reply to her letters immediately she would gently chastise him: 'I have felt piqued at your silence', or 'I will own to you my dear friend that I have several times within this week said to myself "I will renounce all further care or friendship for this ungracious, ungrateful Clare".' Very soon she was signing herself 'Yours affectionately, Emma', the name by which she liked Clare to know her. Certainly, to begin with, he enjoyed being the focus of her flattery and it would have been fascinating to see how much he had played her at her own game – if only his letters to her had survived. Nothing of them has so far been traced and they were either lost, accidentally, or destroyed by the Emmerson family. In the notes for his autobiography he left an adequate account of their relationship for us to see how it was, at one time, something of a dilemma to him:

> she has been & is a warm kind friend of tastes feelings & manners almost romantic she has been a very pretty woman & is not amiss still & a womans pretty face is often very dangerous to her common sense for the notice she received in her young days threw affectations about her feelings which she has not got shut of yet for she fancies that her friends are admirers of her person as a matter of course & acts accordingly which appears in the eyes of a stranger ridiculous enough but the grotesque wears off on becoming acquainted with her better qualities & better qualities she certainly has to counter-balance them she at one word is the best friend I found & my expectations are looking no further her correspondence with me began early in my public life & grew pretty thick as it went on I fancied it a fine thing to correspond with a lady & by degrees grew up into an admirer sometimes writing as I felt sometimes as I fancied & sometimes foolishly when I could not account for why I did it[8]

The last sentence is the tantalizing one and its confessional tone proof enough that the advances were not all in one direction. But, without those letters, a complete and accurate picture of their actual relationship cannot be established. Some of the sentiments expressed were teasing or light-hearted, but others were clearly more serious.

Mrs Emmerson, knowing that Patty could hardly read a word, once asked Clare if he ever read her letters to his wife as she read his to her husband. The extravagance of her feelings towards him and her censuring tone in the frequent criticism of his 'indelicacies' puzzled him, but he was still to use her as his confessor and she, in turn, was mostly tolerant of his behaviour, especially when he admitted he had had too much to drink. After those first few years, however, he was not sorry when her ardour cooled and she returned to being more 'sisterly' and another young man took his place.

Nevertheless, it must be emphasized that in the beginning Mrs Emmerson was genuinely moved by Taylor's account of the poet in the introduction to *Poems Descriptive of Rural Life and Scenery* and wanted to help. She had sent a copy to Lord Radstock and had written to the editor of the *Morning Post*, asking him to reprint some of Clare's poems to persuade 'the liberal encouragers of genius to snatch from impending misery this wonderful Child of Nature! so that by degrees, he might be raised from the lowly and lost situation in which he now stands; not only for himself, but indeed, I may almost say, still more so for the world.'[9]

3

For Clare, who was never to be anything less than a true child of the countryside, those few days in London were a stimulating experience of intellectual companionship and good conversation. But, at the end of the week, he was longing once more for home, for the quiet fields and green lanes of Helpston. London would see him again, but enough was enough, he travelled home a tired and bewildered man.

On his return he wrote to his publisher:

> Dear Taylor – Excuse the warm expression – according to promise I send you a note to tell you of my safe arrival home & glad enough I am for I was weary of noise & bustle . . . as soon as I got home I found the tables in the hut coverd with Letters . . .[10]

Among those letters was one from Captain Markham E. Sherwill, a young man who admired Clare's work and, as a friend of Sir Walter Scott, had hoped to get some gift of recognition out of the great man. After much persuasion he succeeded in getting two guineas and a copy of *The Lady of the Lake*, which the author refused to inscribe. As Captain Sherwill explained, 'All my endeavours, all my efforts of persuasion, proved fruitless in the anxious desire I had expressed to Him, that He would address a few lines to you in the blank leaf. Sir W. seemed bound hand and head, not from any disapprobation of your talent or taste, but occasioned by the high path in which He strides in the literary field of the present day.'[11]

It was perhaps significant that Sherwill used a capital letter each time he referred to the novelist by a pronoun. Clare's reply, however, was not without its wryness: 'There was a day when as a poet he shone little above his humble servant.'[12] But he accepted the two guineas and spent them on Currie's *Life and Works*.

Soon after his return from London Clare received from Lord Radstock a copy of Hugh Blair's *Sermons*, and from Mrs Emmerson a copy of Edward Young's *Night Thoughts*. He also received a number of invitations to some of the more important country houses in the area. One came from General Birch Reynardson (a descendant of the Lord Mayor of London of 1649) who lived at Holywell Hall, just beyond Pickworth. Clare was in Drury's bookshop one day in April when the General came in and made some enquiries about him. Drury was delighted to have the poet there and the two men were introduced. By the end of their conversation it was agreed that Clare should visit Holywell and stay for dinner. He knew the house well. It stood in some of the loveliest countryside on the northern boundary of Rutland and was not far from where he had often walked with Patty.

As soon as he arrived Clare was shown into the General's library, which was, he says, the largest he had ever seen, but whether it was larger than those he had seen at Milton Hall or Burghley House is hard to believe. The General then took down from the shelves a thin quarto beautifully bound in red morocco which, he explained, 'were Love Elegies written by his father & of course in his mind they were beautiful . . .'.[13] Clare 'just glanced over them & fancied they were imitations of Drummond' and handed them back.[14]

He then walked through the gardens and parklands where he met a young lady whom he took to be the General's wife. They talked amicably for some time before he discovered she was the governess to the children. He was embarrassed, she was impressed. After his dinner (in the servants' hall) they met again in the housekeeper's room. The governess gave Clare her address and asked him to write to her. She was, he recalled, 'a pretty impertinent girl & mischievously familiar to a mind less romantic than my own'.[15] Later in the evening when he was setting out on his homeward journey he was even more surprised to find the young lady waiting for him outside the park. She asked if she could walk part of the way with him, and did not wait for an answer:

> I felt evil apprehension as to her meaning but I was clownish & slow in smiles & advantages to interpret it she chatted about my poems & resumed her discourse of asking me to correspond with her which I promisd I woud when we came to the break of the heath that stands in view of Patty's cottage I made step to get rid of her but she lingered & chatterd on till it grew very late[16]

The seduction continued until it 'grew between the late & early' and Clare hastily bid her goodnight. It was, he said, 'One of the oddest adventures my poetical life met with and it made me rather conceited as I fancied the young lady had fallen in love with me.'[17] He never mentioned her by name. We only know she came from Birmingham and must have found Clare a very attractive man, certainly not clownish even if slow.

Another attempted seduction was not very far away when he received a note from the reverend Mr Hopkinson, a clergyman and magistrate who lived at Morton, near Bourne. The note said that a horse would be at Clare's door at a certain time on a certain day, leaving him no option whether he chose to go or not. It was harvest time and Clare was busy reaping corn with his neighbours. All hands were needed at this season of the year and he was already getting a bad name as a poor worker, always dashing off to meet some stranger, rather than get the crops in.

Once again he had to tell his master about the order to visit one of the gentry, knowing that he may well have lost his job by the time he got back.

When he arrived at Hopkinson's house the reverend gentleman was away at a court sitting. He had left his wife to look after the poet. She took him on a tour of the parish, introducing him to everyone they met. In the end Clare had to tell her that he did not like being on show, so she took him home.

> she was one of the oddest & most teasing fancied kindnesses that I ever met with – as soon as I got in she took me upstairs to show me a writing desk which she told me to consider as my own & showd me Papers Pens Ink saying that she expected I woud make use of it & hoped I woud write something everyday[18]

She hastened to tell him that such gifts were only his to use whenever he came to visit her, not ones to be taken away. Clare knew then that he had lost the gifts. She then introduced him to her two daughters who were amiable enough and well-read, but they quarrelled with their mother so much they preferred to keep out of her way. Mrs Hopkinson continued to flatter Clare and told him that since his position had improved so greatly following his success he should now correct the image by printing in the next edition of his poems a list of all his new friends and patrons. Clare smiled and thought he had never met such a scheming woman.

Eventually the Reverend Hopkinson returned and rushed the poet off for a day to show him the jail at Folkingham (on the road to Sleaford) and then to Belvoir Castle to see the gardens. With those visits over Clare then returned to Helpston, to the fields and to his fellow labourers who either snubbed him or made fun of him. He was none the richer for having lost two days' work and less popular at home than he was among strangers. It was certainly not easy being a celebrity in Helpston.

4

Such popularity was not even without its price among the new friends and patrons in London. By the time the third and fourth editions of *Poems Descriptive of Rural Life & Scenery* appeared there had been several changes in the contents. As his readers became more intimately acquainted with the poems they began to question their initial enthusiasm. All was not as lyrical and in praise of nature as they had been led to believe. There were vulgarities, indelicacies, accusations of injustice against the rich and sentiments of ingratitude which offended the minds of people like Lord Radstock and Mrs Emmerson.

As early as 12 February 1820 Taylor was forced to write to Clare to say that Lord Radstock and others were objecting to poems such as 'The Country Gril', 'My Mary' (his clever parody on Cowper's gentle poem), 'Dolly's Mistake', 'Friend Lubin', 'Dawnings of Genius' and 'Helpstone'. Not only were they objecting, they were also insisting that these poems should be omitted from all future editions. Lord Radstock wrote to Mrs Emmerson on 11 May:

> You must *do your duty!* You must tell him – to expunge certainly highly objectionable passages in his first volume... passages, wherein, his then depressed state hurried him not only into error, but into the most flagrant acts of injustice; by accusing those of pride, cruelty, vices, and ill-directed passions – who, are the very persons, by whose truly generous and noble exertions, he has been raised from misery... tell Clare if he has still a recollection of what I have done, and am still doing for him, he must give me unquestionable *proofs* of being that man I would have him be – he *must expunge*![19]

That was an ultimatum rather than a piece of advice and, for someone of Clare's social sensitivity, a provocative and pompous condemnation. The criticisms were not so much of the poems but of the comments within them that Clare was making on the class system where, as in the 'Dawnings of Genius', the peasant was shown as 'That necessary tool of wealth and pride' and where, as in 'Helpstone', wealth was seen as the evil responsible for poor men's misery:

> Accursed wealth! o'er-bounding human laws
> Of every evil thou remainst the cause:
> Victims of want, those wretches such as me
> Too truly lay their wretchedness to thee.
> Thou art the bar that keeps from being fed
> And thine our loss of labour and of bread,
> Thou art the cause that levels every tree
> And woods bow down to clear a way for thee[20]

Once again his bitter resentment over enclosure becomes part of his general anger over those who, because of their position, believe they have the right to take whatever they want. He did not want to recant.

Mrs Emmerson obediently took up the matter and wrote to Clare:

> Let me entreat you, as a true friend – as a sister – to write immediately to Mr Taylor and desire him *from yourself* to expunge the objectionable lines – you have them *marked* in the volume I sent you – for alas! they were named to me too soon after your poems were published – as conveying *Radical* and *Ungrateful* sentiments.[21]

Six months later she was still reminding him of his early indiscretions. In a letter of 25 November 1820 she told him of the reaction to his poetry by readers in Bristol: 'They all lamented that yr publishers introduced in your volume *"Mary"*; *"Dolly's Mistake"*; *"Lubin"*; and *"The Country Girl"*.' But even then they were getting a slightly expurgated edition because Taylor had already softened the shock by taking out, or substituting, some words which he knew would offend. Some readers were upset over his parody of William Cowper's poem 'Mary' and did not like the 'unpoetic language' in verses such as:

Who lives where noises never cease
And what with hogs & ducks & geese
Can never have a minute's peace?
My Mary.

Who nearly battled to her chin,
Bangs down the yard thro thick & thin
Nor picks her road nor cares a pin?
My Mary.

Who, save in Sunday's bib & tuck
Goes daily waddling like a duck
O'er head & ears in grease & muck?
My Mary.

Who prates & runs o'er silly stuff
And 'mong the boys makes sport enough,
So ugly, silly, droll & rough?
My Mary.

Who, low in stature, thick & fat
Turns brown from going without a hat
Though not a pin the worse for that?
My Mary.

Who's laugh'd at too by every whelp
For failings which she cannot help?
But silly fools will laugh & chelp,
My Mary.

For though in stature mighty small
And near as thick as thou art tall
The hand that made thee made us all,
My Mary.[22]

Clare did not set out to shock, or offend, only to be honest. Usually he was doing no more than employ words which were in common, daily usage among the people with whom he worked; words which were natural to their vocabulary, too. In rural areas words considered indelicate, or 'bad language' are more often used as words of endearment, or are of such ancient tradition as to be acceptable. Certainly to Clare's ear the word 'arse' was more tuneful than all its alternatives. Nevertheless, he was to lose it, and others, from the early editions of his work. He had already pleaded his case to Taylor when he said, 'The language of nature... can never be disgusting.' He had also told him, 'I heartily desire no word of mine to be altered.'[23]

A poet's vocabulary is important to him. It holds the key words to a true understanding and determines the images he will use. It is only when the poet finds his own language – his 'own voice' – that his work becomes original and alive. Clare was fully aware of this and strove towards clarifying his identity. He did not want to be an imitator, or dilute the richness of his vocabulary to please others. Taylor tried to understand this and Clare, in return, tried to trust his judgement. But both were under pressure and, Mrs Emmerson, for one, obviously could not appreciate Clare's argument, especially when she wanted to rewrite some of his lines for him, as she suggested in her letter of 11 May 1820: 'I venture to write a line in the margin to substitute this' – referring to 'That necessary tool of wealth' – and added that she thought it 'connected the subject very well – if you will indulge me by adopting this line, no person can ever know, or indeed any other alteration I presume to suggest.'[24] She requested alterations on many occasions and was always urging Clare away from his natural style to 'loftier regions of poetry'. On 23 August she wrote: 'Your subject will afford you good scope for simple and sweet description, also matter and opportunity for much reflection – 'tis in *these* you *excel* . . . ' Two weeks later, on 4 September, she sent a flattering note in which she said, 'Your "Peasant Boy" is uniformly sweet and simple . . . your Sonnets – ah! there my dear friend – you stand alone, you are yourself – all simplicity – all feeling and soul.'[25]

Clare could write sonnets as naturally as breathing, and many of the five hundred or more are fine, but Mrs Emmerson was seeing her poet as a miniaturist. And if it wasn't 'simplicity' then it was 'gratitude' should be his theme. He was always being reminded of his position, still being kept in his place. His sensitive nature was aware of these attitudes even if he could not always see the manipulators at work. He half-expected them. Whatever he achieved as a poet, he was still an intruder in their privileged world and would never be accepted as an equal. He was as much alone in the success of 1820–22 as he was in the asylum years of 1840–60. He did not forget. He was grateful for their good intentions but the sweet taste of recognition had a sour kernel. He was always to be a poor man, a man whose gift increased rather than released his bondage. All he was ever to get from that gift was a charitable hand-out for his 'simple verses'. Most of the money he received was because he was an unusual peasant rather than an extraordinary poet. He did not want charity. He wanted true recognition. The occasional payments made from his publishers and patrons became not much better than being kept by the parish. Clare was a proud man. His mind suffered greatly because of it. Even when Lord Radstock established a subscription fund for him he was not, as we shall see, able to draw any substantial amounts from it, and certainly not when most needed. All these frustrations, inferiority complexes and resentments were to sap his emotional strength and aggravate his fears of madness.

Clare had hoped for a more positive lead from Taylor over the question of the offending passages in *Poems Descriptive of Rural Life and Scenery*, but the publisher was to show how negative and contradictory he could be in this and other matters. Taylor found Lord Radstock an abrasive personality and was prepared to play Clare off against him. He thought the over-zealous man was being too fussy. At the same time he recognized his considerable influence in town, especially in the world of books, and he could not afford to lose him. Lord Radstock's complaints were reaching a good many ears in London and Taylor wrote to ask Clare if he had heard any adverse comments in and around Helpston. The only news Clare had received was through Mrs Emmerson's chiding letters. But she had persuaded him to listen to her advice and on 16 May Clare was forced to write to Taylor:

> Being very much bothered lately I must trouble you to leave out 8 lines in 'Helpstone' beginning 'Accursed wealth' & two under 'When ease and plenty' – and one in 'Dawnings of Genius' – 'That necessary tool' leave it out and put ***** to fill up the blank this will let em see I do it as negligent as possible D-n that canting way of being forced to please I say – I cant abide it and one day or other I will show my Independence more strongly than ever[26]

Taylor had already admitted earlier in the year that he 'was not so fastidious' over some of the lines objected to and also praised Clare for his independent spirit: 'Take your own Course, write what you like; if you feel obliged, say so, if it suits you; if not, scorn to utter Falsehood in Rhyme.'[27]

Clare would have welcomed such support had it meant anything, but he was not yet in a strong enough position to hold out alone. He conceded and asked Taylor to make the amendments. He had to remember too that all this fuss was over his first book and its success was due as much to Lord Radstock as to John Taylor. His second volume was already in preparation and he wanted its reception to be even better than that of the first. He could only appeal again to his publisher for guidance and ask that a line should not be given up without a fight. But the patrons won. 'The Country Girl' was omitted from the second edition; 'My Mary' and 'Dolly's Mistake' were left out of the third; 'Friend Lubin' and the offending lines of 'Helpstone' and 'Dawnings of Genius' disappeared by the fourth. Their omission had, Clare told Taylor, 'cut my muses wings cursedly this you know well & I doubt not you will remedy it.' It was wishful thinking.

Usually Clare had little idea of what was happening to his work until it was too late. Taylor had always taken it upon himself to edit, punctuate and correct the spelling of all the poems Clare sent, and he only selected from the mass of material at his disposal. When Clare received his copy of the third edition of *Poems Descriptive*... he wrote to James Hessey:

> I am cursd mad about it the judgement of T. is a button-hole lower in my opinion – it is good – but too subject to be tainted by medlars *false delicasy* damn it I hate it beyond everything... I have long felt enough for poor T. I assure you I know his taste and I know his embarrassments I often picture him in the midst of a circle of 'blue-stockings' offering this and that opinion for improvement or omission I think to please all and offend all we should find out 215 pages of blank leaves and call it 'Clare in fashion'[28]

Hessey replied immediately:

> I am not at all surprised at your being vexed at the omission of any part of your volume of Poems, and you may be assured that it was not resolved upon without the most mature deliberation... If we are satisfied that in the Society which we frequent certain subjects must not even be alluded to, we must either conform to the rules of that Society or quit it. An author in like manner is expected to concede something to the tone of moral feelings of the Age in which he lives... There is plenty of room for a man of Genius, of Delicacy, of Taste, to exercise himself in, without touching upon such things as are of common consent now avoided in all good Society as repugnant to good Taste & real Delicacy. We make allowances for Shakespeare's little touches of indelicacy & double-meaning, because such conversation was common in Society in his Day – but it would not be tolerated now, or if admitted at all, must be much more delicately wrapped up[29]

In an age of such double standards and hypocrisy – which Clare was beginning to learn all about – he found it incomprehensible that a good honest, down-to-earth ballad about seduction could not be accepted and that Shakespeare himself would have been similarly chastised for his indelicacies.

One thing in Edward Drury's favour was that he supported Clare in his choice of vocabulary and was frequently a better judge than the firm of Taylor and Hessey in the matter. Writing to Clare on 9 May 1820, he told him, 'You always excel when you write as you would have spoken and acted in reality... You have a talent within you of which you are scarcely aware.'[30] This was far different from the advice Clare was to receive from Charles Lamb two years later when he was urged to turn away from natural speech and provincial phrases: 'I think you are too profuse with them. There is a rustick Cockneyism as little pleasing as ours of London. Transplant Arcadia to Helpstone...'[31]

Had Clare tried to do that we would have lost his descriptions of the primrose's 'curdled leaf', the 'brazen magpies', the 'bickering sky', the 'squirting rabbit' and the 'wherry, suther, or swee' of sounds over that vast landscape. If fame meant losing the right to sing his own song in his own language, he began to wish that he had kept his poems for those who would understand:

> 'tis not the thought of being rich
> That makes my wishing spirit itch
> 'tis just an independent fate
> Betwixt the little and the great[32]

14
Agreements and Disagreements

1

Between his first and second visits to London Clare tried to get used to being a celebrity, both in the city and at Helpston. It was not easy for him to reconcile the advantages with the disadvantages, or the benefits with the penalties. He gained friends and lost friends. He was promised riches but very little money found its way into his pocket. He had won a measure of independence but had forfeited much of his freedom. He had obligations and duties to perform because he had stepped out of his private world into a public one. Success had its price. But, unlike Lord Byron, George Crabbe and Thomas Hood, who had received such generous advanced royalties from their publishers, Clare was less fortunate. This was not because his work sold badly. He had done much better than some of his contemporaries. Keats and Shelley were lucky if their poetry achieved five hundred sales. Wordsworth's *Excursion*, published in 1814, took six years to sell five hundred copies, whereas Clare's *Poems Descriptive of Rural Life and Scenery* sold nearly four thousand in the first year of publication and *The Village Minstrel* was to sell eight hundred copies a year later. But his popularity was brief. Interest, and sales, declined rapidly. It took another eight years to sell a further six hundred copies of *The Village Minstrel* and when *The Shepherd's Calendar* appeared in 1827, it sold even more slowly and went almost unnoticed. But, in 1820, Clare was justified in being hopeful of a much better income from his work than he ever received.

Immediately after the appearance of his first volume Lord Radstock had started a subscription fund for him, inviting several eminent noblemen to contribute. They included the Dukes of Bedford, Devonshire and Northumberland; the Earls of Cardigan, Winchelsea and Egremont; Lord Kenyon and Lord John Russell; Sir Thomas Baring and Sir Thomas Plummer; and Prince Leopold, who later became King of the

Belgians. Their gifts amounted to nearly £200. To this was added £100 from Earl Fitzwilliam and an advance from Taylor and Hessey of a further £100. By the end of the summer Taylor had appointed Richard Woodhouse, a young lawyer and friend of Keats, to act as a trustee.[1] The money was then invested in Navy Five Per Cents with the intention of providing Clare with a regular, and safe, half-yearly dividend – to be paid through his publishers. To begin with this realized for him £18. 15. 0d. a year, which, together with the annuity of £10 from Earl Spencer and the £15 from the Marquis of Exeter, gave Clare an annual income of £43. 15. 0d. – an achievement that Taylor was prepared to boast about in his introduction to *The Village Minstrel* a year later. During the first few months of success the poet also received gifts of money from visitors and correspondents. In one good week he was given £11 and felt he was now one of the wealthiest men in the district.

It was a false sense of good fortune and security. Most of his wealth was no more than figures on paper. It was not ready cash on which he could draw to meet his growing needs. He still had to go out to work each day and take what jobs he could find. Six months was a long time to wait for money when so many bills needed paying. He was always having to remind Taylor of when payments were due. And, to make matters worse, the value of the Navy Five Per Cents began to decline. The Literary Fund was threatened and certainly not giving the returns it had promised. By 1823 Clare's annual dividends were down to £15. 15. 0d. With all his influential friends and success he realized he was still only getting little more than a farm-labourer. In many ways he saw the farm-labourer better off. He did not have to worry about appearances, or buy expensive clothes, or books, or lose a day's work when some stranger called. Clare's money was often spent before he received it. He wrote to Taylor in June 1820 saying, 'You are to receive Earl Spencers half annuity due now or nearly – £5 Send it down in the fund money in a check on Eaton & Cayleys Bank, Stamford. Send it as soon as you can too as I am quite out don't think me extravagant for I feel myself to the contrary.'[2]

Taylor was negligent about financial matters and always believed that Clare would be incapable of handling too much money. He seldom saw, until it was too late, how necessary it was for Clare to have that sense of material success to support his literary achievements. It would have given him greater independence. Instead, the frustration at not being able to benefit from the money his poetry had earned added to his anxieties and often made him angry.

Another person fighting for a share of Clare's money was Edward Drury. He knew that he had virtually lost control of the poetry he believed he had discovered and now feared he would also lose some of

William Hilton's portrait of Clare, painted during his first visit to London (1820).

The Helpston cottage where Clare was born.

The village cross (with heart-shaped base) and St Botolph's Church, Helpston.

The Lady Chapel, Glinton Church, which was the vestry where Clare went to school.

The site of Langley Bush, near Helpston.

The lake on Emmonsail's Heath, Castor Hanglands.

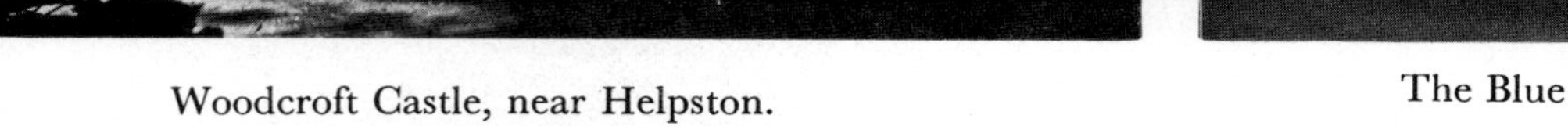

Woodcroft Castle, near Helpston.

The Blue Bell Inn, Helpston where Clare worked.

Bachelors Hall, Helpston, the home of Clare's friends, the Billings brothers.

The remains of the limekiln at Pickworth.

Ballad

Now that the even is hanging its glooming
& the grey mistes shrouding the Green
& the streakt woodbine nights bosom perfuming
Closes its blossoms for mornings return.
Martha [illegible]
till then be thy milking dellaying
Hints are lovers language thou kens what they mean
Then wi thy swain thro the welcome gloom straying
To breath on thy lips his fond rapture unseen

Now the night bird at his singing is seated
While the pale moon seems delighted to hear
While thy swain roams wi one wish uncompleated
The pleasure of meeting his lassey so dear
Martha be thou neath thy brinded cow seated
Chanting thy love ballads over wi glee
Sweet tho the nightingales songs the wood ringing
Sweeter will thine be while listen thee

Now the bent flower neath eves burthen is laden
& the ripe rose on its stem doth recline
Just as I've seen the flusht cheek of the maiden
Bowing unwilling a kiss to resign
Down in the valley do thou me be meeting
Thy first broken promise let me never see
Still let thy fond heart in sincerely beating
Be free from all sighs but whats breathed for me

A facsimile of a previously unpublished ballad, written *c.* 1819.

The cottage at Northborough where Clare lived 1832–7 and his family remained until 1871.

ples like a child
becomes a man
oughts like weedlings wild
blossom where they can
ies known so long
ng was dwelling there
pleasures fills the song
es in [illegible] joys to [illegible]

Pastoral affections

s were shadows seem to me
[illegible]ifying things
y old home to be
ds of gravel springs
bbles clear as smooth
nd by gentle floods
doth my spirits sooth
n into mossy woods
k upon a tree
er a leaning stile

[illegible] [illegible] stolen [illegible]
[illegible] old [illegible] way
In thronged streets flowers
never grew there but
And many a flower hath
died away

Where moss did mantle
gather round
Where maybe moss [illegible] seat
Green springing in its velvet
cushion [illegible]
Where moss might [illegible]
Green spreading in its velvet
A little [illegible] unnoticed by
[illegible]
By all but heavens [illegible]
[illegible]
Davids crown hath [illegible] away
His poesy breathes his shepherd [illegible]
His hallowed cost [illegible]

A facsimile of 'The Flitting'.

The road and bridge between Northborough and Glinton, where Clare and Mary Joyce met.

The graves of Martha Clare and members of the family, Northborough churchyard.

Pen and ink portrait of
John Clare. sketched about
six months before his death by
a Maniac an inmate of the
Asylum
G. B. Berry of Bristol. Artist

the profit he hoped to make out of his protégé. He felt that Clare's total commitment to Taylor showed ingratitude and lost no opportunity of displaying his grievances. Hints of the rift came as early as February 1820 when Clare wrote to his publisher, 'Drury and I are not very good friends...'[3] And, less than a month later, after he had discussed the matter further in correspondence with Taylor, he wrote:

> as to Drury I think we are under no obligations to him for anything I shoud always wisht him to have been a partner in the things I publish but as he cannot speak well of me when he has no longer hopes of interest in my concerns I think I have done with him altogether... I was mentioned by somebody in Stamford Town Hall this week (it is from good authority) & Drury I suppose answered him strictly 'no more Clare for me' you know that's enough I think he is paid very well for his journeys to Helpstone & I think to pay myself with resentment is to wipe out his name at the bottom of the next book[4]

Clare, so resilient and strong in some things, was touchy and easily wounded in others. He could nurse a grievance for a long time, as he did over Patty's family and friends. Drury's understandable peevishness played on his mind. He continued to hear reports of what the Stamford bookseller was saying about him and told Taylor that he was now enjoying the reputation as a 'deep shifty designing scoundrel'[5] who could not be trusted. He was more out of favour than ever before and Drury should be dropped as soon as possible.

Looked at from Drury's point of view, he had some reason to feel slighted, if not by Clare then at least by his cousin John Taylor. It was Drury who had, after all, been the first person to promote Clare and pay him something for his poems, even though he may have had his own selfish motives. He had also helped Clare out of debt on a number of occasions, to the point of keeping the family out of the workhouse when their rent was two years in arrears. Drury had both recognized and believed in Clare's talent, and the two men had initially enjoyed each other's company. The least he expected was to be an equal partner in all the publications of the poet's work, especially as he held what he believed to be the sole copyright on most of the poems Taylor had used, or was planning to use. But Taylor had taken over completely. Clare was his poet. Drury was to be mentioned only as a courtesy. A poet of such talent could not be handled properly by a provincial bookseller. Drury was becoming something of a nuisance. The less said to him the better.

To protect his own interests against being excluded from any financial gains, Drury had persuaded Clare to put in writing that he had sold to him the first collection of poems for £20. This was, he assured Clare, no more than a safeguard, a sum of money to be set against the poet's accounts as a check against Taylor and Hessey. Clare, puzzled by such complex book-keeping, signed one evening when he admits he was the worse for drink.

The squabbling and confusion of Clare's financial position were to get worse and he had to believe that errors, if not deliberate mistakes, were being made. When Taylor came to write the introduction to *The Village Minstrel*, he claimed that 'the present publishers gave Clare twenty pounds for his poems'. But Clare had not received that twenty pounds from Taylor nor was the amount ever satisfactorily accounted for with Drury. Clare wrote to Taylor and asked, 'How can this be? I never sold the Poems for any price. What money I had of Drury was given to me on account of profits to be received but here it seems I have got nothing and brought in minus twenty pounds of which I never received a sixpence.'[6]

It was to be a familiar cry during the next twenty years of his career and he was never to understand what he believed to be the devious ways of publishers. As the accusations cross-fired between London and Stamford, he reflected deeply on the words of Earl Fitzwilliam who had once bade him 'beware of booksellers [and] not be fed with promises'.[7]

After months of bitterness Taylor was able to explain to Clare, 'We have settled to give E.D. on condition that he sends us the agreement for us to destroy it, one half of whatever profit we may derive from the present or future Poems, retaining in our own Hands the sole management, and perfectly uncontrolled in what we think proper to give the Author.'[8] Taylor then made the point that he was not making any money out of the poetry and had charged nothing for his trouble as editor.

Without understanding all that this meant, Clare wrote to say he was pleased the affair had been made straight with Drury for he felt sorry that their relationships had become as sour as they were. So, for a time, a reconciliation was established and he resumed his visits to the Stamford bookshop. Drury, for his part, was still sufficiently interested in his poet to offer him this advice: 'Do not force your mind to produce anything it is disinclined to; and disregard all kinds of recommendation to any particular subject... Sonnets are beautiful but everybody can write a Sonnet if they bestow labour and time, and have any idea of poetry – they may even produce Sonnets of tolerable merit, but none but a real poet can produce a song like "The Meeting".'[9] At that point Drury's business interest affected his literary judgement.

He continued, nevertheless, to copy out Clare's songs which he still wanted to use for musical settings, thinking they could both make money from them. But the trust of 1819 could never be truly restored and Clare was already a very different poet from the one discovered by Edward Drury. From all the arguments that had gone on he now realized that if his poetry made any money at all he would see very little of it. Drury claimed half and Taylor said he reserved the right to pay the author what he 'thought proper'.

To aggravate matters Clare also found himself unwillingly involved in the conflict developing between Lord Radstock and Taylor. Taylor had expressed his dislike of 'Patronage for its Selfishness' in February 1820, and now felt game enough to take on his most influential patron. Lord Radstock had been just as blunt in suggesting that Taylor should be watched very carefully. He wanted Clare to have a legal agreement (similar to the one which he knew existed between Robert Southey and his publisher), in which the profits arising from all future sales should be equally divided between Clare and Taylor, once the cost of publication had been met. Taylor did not like that idea and told the Admiral that they were at that time 'benefitting the author more than your proposals would have bound us to do'.[10] This statement would have surprised Clare, who was getting far less than fifty per cent of the profits from *Poems Descriptive of Rural Life and Scenery*. He found it almost impossible to get any information out of Taylor about the sale of his books and could not get any kind of statement about his financial position.

Lord Radstock and Taylor were now prepared to mount their horses and making threatening charges:

Taylor: My Lord, if you think your arbitration will be advantageous to Clare I as a Publisher can have no objections to it; in the meantime I shall suspend those labours which are not within the province of a publisher – for I have many other subjects on which I ought to bestow my time.[11]

Radstock: I still apprehend in matters of real business no man's word (however well established his integrity) would be sufficiently binding, unless accompanied by a written document . . . You talk of suspending your 'present labours, as not coming within the province of a publisher' – In this I shall only observe that had Clare's poems appeared without an 'Introduction' and no Lord Radstock had stepped forth in support of the work, my own opinion is, that a second edition of the poems would not have showed itself – That your labours were great respecting the little Vol. in question, I most willingly allow – but that you were amply remunerated I am equally convinced.[12]

Taylor: My Lord, the observations contained in your Lordship's last letter, have materially altered the complexion of your correspondence – I will write to Clare to know whether we are to treat with him, or your Lordship, for the copyright of his next volume . . .[13]

Clare duly received a long, detailed account of what had been happening and Taylor made himself quite clear: 'Unless you commission Lord Radstock to interfere in this Matter I know of no Right that he has to write to me on the subject.'[14]

Mrs Emmerson also wrote to Clare about the quarrels going on in London: 'I regret to learn that Mr. T does not act so respectfully to Lord R. as he deserves from him, and equally regret his keeping you in such total ignorance of your affairs. It is most unpardonable of him.'[15]

Letters between Lord Radstock and Taylor, Radstock and Drury, Drury, Taylor and Clare, Mrs Emmerson and James Hessey, continued to volley over the poems that sat waiting to be edited and published. Clare had no contract, was still to go on fighting for what money he thought he should have, and tried bravely to be 'his own man'.

2

With all this arguing going on he was still expected to meet visitors to Helpston, accept more invitations, answer letters from admirers, write songs for Drury, keep working in the fields to earn the money he needed for his family, and write the new poems for his next volume.

During the summer his mother was taken ill and had to go to a hospital in Stamford to have an operation on a poisoned finger, which meant she had to stay in lodgings for a short time. Clare visited her every other day, with Sophy and Patty going on the intermediate days. She returned home by the middle of August and the family tried once more to settle down to a normal existence. But by this time Clare himself was feeling exhausted and ill. He had already told Taylor that he was 'worse in health than you can conjecture or than myself am aware of . . .'.[16] He had consulted a number of local doctors in Market Deeping, Peterborough and Stamford, but the one who was to play a vital role in his life was Dr Fenwick Skrimshire of Peterborough Infirmary. He was an author of books on medicine, chemistry and natural history. At Lord Milton's request he attended to Clare's illness on several occasions and provided him with medicine. (He was also the doctor who was to certify the poet in 1841 as insane and have him removed to the Northamptonshire General Lunatic Asylum.)

Health was a constant worry to Clare. He had hardly survived birth, had lived a charmed life and showed remarkable stamina. Physically, for his size, he was a strong person, hardened by weather and heavy work. But his letters and journals are full of references to his illnesses, fears of death, or of having some undiagnosed, incurable disease, frequently brought on by his sense of guilt or remorse. In his darkest moments of depression he would often think of his twin sister who died in infancy and wish to be with her. The death of children moved him deeply: 'On An Infant Killed By Lightning', 'Stanzas on a Child', 'To An Infant Sister', and 'The Dying Child':

> He could not die when trees were green
> For he loved the time too well
> His little hands when flowers were seen
> Were held for the bluebell
> As he was carried o'er the green.
>
> His eye glanced at the white-nosed bee
> He knew those children of the spring
> When he was well & on the lea
> He held one in his hands to sing
> Which filled his heart with glee.
>
> Infants, the children of the spring,
> How can an infant die
> When butterflies are on the wing
> Green grass and such a sky
> How can they die at spring?[17]

He wrote as if each child's death reminded him of the death of his own childhood and all its innocence. Disappointment, bitterness, sin and shame, rejection and failure, were all destroyers of that state of grace. He longed always for the Eden he knew he had once seen. Eden, spring and childhood were essential elements in his quest for happiness. He felt them more removed from him than ever.

Once again he poured out his despair to John Taylor, in a letter dated 31 August 1820:

> its no use making resolutions to work you see now – they will not let me keep quiet as I used to be – they send for me twice or 3 times a day out of the fields & I am still the strangers Poppet Show what can their fancys create to be so anxious & so obstinate of being satisfied I am but a man (& a little one too) like others still they come I will sit still in my corner in readiness for them & ryhme & jingle in the teeth of trouble & scrat away at my 'Cremona' striving to make the best use of the world while I am in it[18]

The Cremona violin had been given to him by James Hessey and he valued it much more than the last phrase would suggest, for he certainly tried to improve his playing beyond the 'scratting' stage. He was also aware of the value and quality of the instrument. But he still kept his old fiddle for scratching jigs at pubs or feasts, and was too fond of it ever to sell it. The Cremona he reserved for his own pleasure. He told his publishers that he did not play one tune in twenty by notes but was considered a first-rate scraper among his companions. The violin, he said, 'makes a rare noise & thats plenty – a professional at Stamford tells me shes a valuable instrument & her equal is not to be met with in our parts.'[19]

3

Clare's moods, like his fortunes, fluctuated rapidly. He could be depressed one day and full of song the next. Sometimes he spoke of his neighbours as rural companions and at other times they were sullen, ignorant men who despised him. Some days he considered himself rich and yet within hours could be complaining of his poverty. He said he hated Stamford but still went to its inns and to see Drury. He resented the public prying into his private life but would have felt neglected if no one came to see him. His only constancy was in the love he had for his countryside and his poetry. He was, as John Taylor told him, when writing to him in the August of that year about Keats, 'a richer Man than poor K. and how much more fortunate'.[20] Fortunate, maybe, in some things, but hardly richer. Keats was never as financially poor as Clare. The four Keats children had inherited £1,000 between them and had other money in trust. When the London poet wanted to go on a walking tour of the Lake District and Scotland he was able to draw £140 from an account left by his brother George before he sailed for America. True, Keats did not get all the money he was entitled to, but he was never reduced to Clare's poverty.

Clare had been hoping that he could arrange another visit to London during the summer so that he could meet his fellow poet and discuss with Taylor the publication of *The Village Minstrel*. It would have been an interesting meeting because they were two very different poets and each had reservations about the other. As it was, the nearest they ever came to meeting was when Keats used the back of one of Clare's letters he found on Taylor's desk to revise one of his own couplets in 'Lamia' – a poem Clare admired less than 'Endymion'. Clare had received his copy of 'Lamia' from James Hessey in the June and had also learned of Keats's illness. A blood vessel in his lungs had broken and the young poet was now under the care of Dr Darling – to whom Clare himself would go for treatment so soon after.

Keats had been much more severely mauled by the critics than Clare and his sales were but a fraction of the Helpston poet's. Taylor admitted that they were £130 out of pocket over 'Endymion' and 'Lamia' did not cover the cost of printing. Despite this, he believed Keats to be a great poet and advanced him £150 to make the trip to Italy for the winter in the hope of prolonging his life. On 27 August 1820 Taylor wrote to tell Clare that Keats was now on his way to Rome and when he felt better he would write to him from there: 'I think he wishes to say to you that your images from Nature are too much introduced without being called for by a particular Sentiment... his remark is only applicable now and then when he feels as if the Description overlaid and stifled that which ought to be the prevailing idea...'.[21] Clare's view of Keats is equally absorbing and perceptive:

> He keeps up a constant alusion or illusion to the grecian mythology & there I cannot follow – yet when he speaks of woods Dryads & Fauns are sure to follow & the brook looks alone without her naiads to his mind yet the frequency of such classical accompaniment make it wearisome to the reader where behind every rosebush he looks for a Venus & under every Laurel a thrumming Apollo – In spite of all this his descriptions of scenery are often very fine but as it is the case with other inhabitants of great cities he often described nature as she appeared to his fancies & not as he would have described her had he witnessed the things he describes – Thus it is he has often undergone the stigma of Cockneyism & what appears as beautys in the eyes of a pent up citizen are looked upon as consciets by those who live in the country – these are merely errors but even here they are merely the errors of poetry – he is often mystical but such poetical liscences have been looked on as beautys in Wordsworth & Shelley & in Keats they may be forgiven[22]

Keats's country was a country of the mind. Clare's was one of the heart. He had a physical contact with the fields. He belonged *with* nature. He witnessed the things he described. It was an emotional and an intellectual response born of the earth. Keats had admitted in 'Endymion' that he could not draw from such native depths: 'Where soil is men grow/Whether to weeds or flowers; but for me/There is no depth to strike in....' His early reading of Homer, Virgil, and the English classics had considerably influenced his imagery and literary references so that he naturally used a language which Clare found difficult to understand. For Keats the legends of Pan, dryads, fauns, Narcissus and Zephyr were, with his poetic fancy, easily transformed into the world of his own poetry. He, on the other hand, was never able to understand the down-to-earth imagery of field-labour and peasants to be found in the poetry of Clare. Nor had he seen the profusion of wildflowers in the Northamptonshire landscape which was part of Clare's everyday existence. He was right in his opinion of the early poems he had seen from Helpston. Many of them were full of images from nature which had been introduced 'without being called for by a particular Sentiment' and the descriptions were sometimes 'overlaid and stifled', but these were the faults of an apprentice. The two poets were writing about totally different worlds and their response was different. The world of Keats belonged to the past and was already immortal. When he longed for the countryside he saw himself as someone who:

> . . . . sinks into some pleasant lair
> Of wavy grass, and reads a debonair
> And gentle tale of love and languishment.
> Returning home at evening, with one ear
> Catching the notes of Philomel – an eye
> Watching the sailing cloudlet's bright career,
> He mourns that day so soon has glided by:
> E'en like the passage of an angel's tear
> That falls through the clear ether silently.[23]

When Clare wrote of his countryside at the end of the day it was a more immediate and living world:

> The sunshines gone & now an April evening
> Commences with a dim & mackerel sky
> Gold light & woolpacks in the west are leaving
> And leaden streaks their splendid place supply
> Sheep ointment seems to daub the dead-hued sky
> And night shuts up the lightsomeness of day
> All dark & absent as a corpse's eye.
> Flower tree & bush like all the shadows grey
> In leaden hues of desolation fade away[24]

Those lines reveal again the weaknesses to be found in his verse of repetition – 'sky/sky', 'hued/hues' – but the excitement of his description excuses his minor blemishes. Again, he makes us see, makes us experience something we have never known before.

During the brief time that the two poets were aware of each other's existence each nevertheless had respect for what the other was trying to do, and Clare was genuinely upset when he heard from Taylor in March 1821 that Keats had died in Rome on 23 February. He wrote a sonnet which he sent to Taylor a few days later:

> I send you my sorrows for poor Keats while his memory is warmly felt – they are just a few beats of the heart – the head has nothing to do with them – therefore they will stand no criticism[25]

4

The first few weeks of 1821 did not give Clare the happiest start to the new year. His family had not been well. His wife, child and parents had all shared with him some of winter's illnesses. The bad weather had also kept him indoors for longer periods than he could bear. After a couple of days in the cottage he became depressed and suffered from claustrophobia. The fields, which so often gave him comfort, now seemed faraway and remote. He worried too about the new volume of poems which was about to appear. He had wanted to call this collection *Ways In A Village*, but had been persuaded by his publishers to call it *The Village Minstrel*, despite its echoes of James Beattie. His patrons, too, were annoying him again. Lord Radstock had written to Lord Milton suggesting that the poet's illness had been caused by over-indulgence in Stamford's ale-houses. Clare feared this would seriously harm his reputation locally and lose him the support of the Fiztwilliam family. He did get drunk on several occasions as he frequently admitted in his letters, but not necessarily from the amount of alcohol he consumed. One pint could make him ill. If he went drinking on an empty stomach, which he often did to leave more food for his family, the ale was not long in having its effect. He was certainly not as riotous as some rumours had it, and he wrote to Taylor and Mrs Emmerson to assure them that he was taking as much solace from the Book of Job as he was from John Barleycorn.

He was also concerned at this time about making his will. In a letter of 23 January 1821, he said to Taylor, 'When you write me again I want some instructions respecting making a will as life is uncertain.'[26] He wished to leave five shillings a week to his parents from the literary fund and the rest to Patty with an equal share of whatever came from his publications, and after her death the money was to go to his children. His feelings towards Patty at that time were strained. He was anxious to make a will because, if he did not, he knew all his money would go to her and 'I shall be d—d mad at that I assure you'. It was clearly an attitude of the moment for, a month later, he was telling Taylor of his concern over Patty's illness, saying, 'I coud not have thought I shoud have felt so anxious for her safety.'[27]

Another anxiety of that winter was over the two elm trees at the back of his cottage. The owner was threatening to chop them down. To Clare this was akin to murder. Again he poured out his troubles to his publisher. Taylor was so moved by Clare's letter that he not only offered to buy the trees to protect them but he also considered the matter important enough to mention in his introduction to *The Village Minstrel*. To impress the reader he quoted Clare's letter:

> My two favourite elm trees at the back of the hut are condemned to die – it shocks me to relate it, but 'tis true. The savage who owns them thinks they have done their best and now he wants to make use of the benefits he can get from selling them. O, was this country Egypt, and I was but a Caliph, the owner should lose his ears for his arrogant presumption, and the first wretch that buried his axe in their roots should hang on their branches as a terror to the rest. I have been several mornings to bid them farewell. Had I one hundred pounds to spare I would buy them reprieves – but they must die. Yet this mourning over trees is all foolishness – they feel no pains – they are but wood, cut up or not. A second thought tells me I am a fool; were people all to feel as I do, the world could not be carried on – a green would not be ploughed up – a tree or bush would not be cut for firing or furniture, and every thing they found when boys would remain in that state till they died. This is my indisposition and you will laugh at it.[28]

The making public of Clare's feelings could not have endeared him, or his cause, to the owner. Taylor had also replied to Clare saying that he was not the best person to put so high a value on the trees. Instead he would ask Octavius Gilchrist to have a look at them and make a more realistic offer. But Clare felt he had made his protest and there was nothing more that anyone else could do to alter the fate of the two elms. He thanked Taylor for his generosity and said, 'let them dye like the rest of us'.[29]

The gloomy depression of winter did not lift with the late arrival of spring. Once again, and against his will, Clare found himself seeking an escape in bouts of drinking, both at Bachelors Hall and in Stamford. Drury warned him to restrain himself, to think more of his future, of getting a better house for his wife and family. Taylor, hearing of Clare's mood, also wrote urging him to take himself more seriously. In a letter dated 7 April, he said that he was 'full of Concern at your late unfortunate fit of Drinking'. He, too, reminded Clare that it was foolish to love knaves and fools better than friends, family and fame. Were not his talents conferred on him by 'a wise Providence' and was it not 'a sin or profanation to trample upon the ruined wreck of God's image?'[30]

Clare again admitted that he was drinking too much and also taking 'a great mess of pills & physic'. If only he could get to London again and enjoy once more the company of learned men he would feel better. In Helpston he drank not for pleasure or conviviality but out of loneliness and frustration.

During those weeks of depression he had also been trying to correct the final proofs of *The Village Minstrel* and arguing with Taylor over some of the omissions, corrections and changes of words – such as *gulsh'd*, which Clare thought most expressive . . . 'it means tearing or thrusting up with great force'.[31]

The problem of his vocabulary was still an issue on which he and his publisher could not agree. Clare did not want to give any more ground. He felt that he was moving closer and more confidently towards the poet he had to be, not for his public but for himself. He wanted to move away from the stale traditions of rural poetry and those influences apparent in his earliest work. His language had to have more strength, not be diluted by words already thin with over-use and fashion. He knew too that he was writing about a world no one else could write about, that his words had to be different, had to come from – and be given back to – the place of his birth. The possibilities before him were great if only he could maintain his confidence and his independence to work. But not even his publisher understood this need. During the months of disagreements and differences the relationship between Taylor and Clare cooled. Clare began to believe that his publisher was already losing interest in him, that his new collection of poems would never appear. Mrs Emmerson, usually loyal to Taylor, began to express her own concern. On 5 June she wrote to Clare 'the procrastination is most shameful – every family of consequence who patronized your 1st volume will in another month be out of Town . . .'[32] She even sent her husband along to Fleet Street to find out from Taylor himself why there was such a delay, reminding him that London would be empty in July and August of people wanting to buy Clare's poetry. Drury also urged Clare to write Taylor a 'harsh, cool letter'.

But Taylor had other concerns on his mind. He and Hessey had recently bought up the *London Magazine* from Baldwin, Craddock and Joy for £500 and he was busy inviting work from new writers to fill its pages. He was also finding the task of editing Clare's poems increasingly tiresome and could not bring himself to completing the introduction he said he wanted to write for the new volume.

5

While Clare waited for the publication of *The Village Minstrel* Patty gave birth to their second child on 2 June 1821. But the infant – another daughter – died within a few days, leaving Clare with an ominous feeling of loss. He felt totally isolated. Helpston no longer had the same security, hope, or warmth. His neighbours grew more distant. His resentment and aloofness did not help. Since the success of a year ago he had become a stranger in his native place. Enclosure had finally put out of bounds some of his favourite walks. The men who frequented the Blue Bell ignored him. Visitors still came occasionally to see what he was like but he knew their interest now to be that only of curiosity.

When he eventually received a copy of *The Village Minstrel* in July – without Taylor's promised introduction – he showed hardly any interest at all. Matters were not helped when Taylor wrote to him on 7 August saying that he was about to apply himself once more to the task of completing his work but as the volume could not be brought out 'when the Town was in full Season it is of less consequence now whether it be this Day published or this Day month'.[33]

Octavius Gilchrist, also seeing Clare's depression, wrote to Taylor urging him to publish without further delay, otherwise he would kill his poet with intemperance. Taylor did not need telling. Clare admitted again – in a letter written in March – that he had made himself 'confoundedly drunk the last night I rolled to Drury's who can certainly say plenty to degrade me . . .'.

To make his despair even more acute, Clare had recently seen Mary Joyce again, and the occasion reminded him not only of his love for her but also of his loss. On 11 August he wrote to his publisher: 'I have not had dossity enough to answer your last till now – but you'll excuse me I have had the horrors agen upon me by once agen seeing devoted Mary & have written the last doggerel that shall ever sully her name & her rememberance any more 'tis reflection of the past & not of the present that torments me . . .'.[34] He enclosed the verses –

Where is the heart thou once hast won
Can cease to care about thee
Where is the eye thou'st smiled upon
Can look for joy without thee
Lorn is the lot one heart hath met
That's lost to thy caressing
Cold is the hope that loves thee yet
Now thou art past possessing
  Fare thee well

We met we loved we've met the last
The farewell word is spoken
O Mary canst thou feel the past
And keep thy heart unbroken
To think how warm we loved and how
Those hopes should blossom never
To think how we are parted now
And parted oh for ever
  Fare thee well

Thou wert the first my heart to win
Thou art the last to wear it
And though another claims a kin
Thou must be one to share it
Oh had we known when hopes were sweet
That hopes would once be thwarted
That we should part no more to meet
How sadly we had parted
Fare thee well[35]

But they were not to be the last verses he ever wrote to his Mary. Poems of passion, longing, love and regret, were to come from his tormented brain for the rest of his life. The more they were separated by time and distance, the more eloquent and moving grew the expressions of his love – a love confused, imagined, remembered and immortalized in the later ballads, and especially in his long poem 'Child Harold'.

He needed little more to make the summer of 1821 a miserable anticlimax to the excited optimism of a year earlier.

6

An illustration of Clare's unbreakable spirit came with an episode six months later, in January 1822. His friends, the Billings brothers, of Bachelors Hall, were in trouble and under threat of losing their old home. The house had been mortgaged for £200 during enclosure to a Jew – referred to by Clare as a second Iago – and the brothers now found themselves unable to pay off the instalments and interest. Clare was desperate to help them and asked Taylor to buy the copyright of all his poems for the next five years for the same amount of money. In doing so he could then take over the mortgage and save Bachelors Hall for his friends – and for himself, for he intended to rename it 'Poet's Hall'. Taylor would not hear of such an extravagant and ambitious scheme, and it was left to Lord Milton to pay off the arrears of £20 in interest and keep the Billings brothers as tenants for a few more years.

Having failed to become a property-owner, Clare went ahead with the poems he had planned to write, but his inspiration was erratic. He told Taylor, in a letter of 8 February 1822, 'the Muse is a fickle Hussey' who sometimes stilted him up to madness and then left him 'as a beggar by the wayside with no more than what's mortal'.

Clare took his struggle between being mortal and being a man worthy of immortality to the extremes of despair and hope. He was not, of course, the first or the last to do so. Sixty years later, Van Gogh was to write to his brother Theo: 'When I am at work, I feel an unlimited faith in art, and that I shall succeed, but in days of physical prostration, or when there are financial obstacles, I feel that faith diminishing and doubt overwhelms me'.[36]

15
Escapes to London

1

The Village Minstrel was eventually published in two volumes towards the end of September 1821. Each volume contained an engraved frontispiece – one of Hilton's portrait of the poet, and one of the cottage at Helpston. Two thousand copies were printed, with Taylor's long Introduction at last included, and reviews began appearing in the literary journals a few weeks later. Some were favourable, some reserved and a few very critical. The novelty of the peasant poet was no longer an excuse for imperfections or coarseness. If Clare wanted to be taken seriously as a poet he must be prepared to accept literary criticism at all levels. Certainly his new volumes came under a much closer scrutiny. An unsigned review in the *Monthly Review* for November 1821 began by questioning the worth of poetry from 'ploughmen, milkmaids, and other similar prodigies' and went on to say:

> Though the author of the poems before us is undeniably superior in correct observation, vigour of intellect, and native talent, to many others who have come before us with pretensions of a similar description, we do not consider him as forming an exception to the general tenor of the observation with which we have introduced our notice of his volumes. We do not conceive that occasional sweetness of expression or accurate delineations of mere exterior objects, can atone for a general deficiency of poetical language or the indulging in a style devoid of uniformity and consistency. *The Village Minstrel* is the principal poem in the collection and is evidently intended to afford a picture of the peculiar circumstances and early scenes of the author's life. To himself this topic is no doubt peculiarly interesting... To us, however, the writer's mention of himself appears, in general, too egotistical and querulous...[1]

The reviewer then complained of the poems' vulgarities, lack of shape, content and brief beauties, of the author's incapability of 'sustaining an equal flight' and of the bathos that frequently destroys the rare moments of sweetness. He concluded by saying 'when every allowance is made, sober judges will hardly be disposed to assign these poems, at the utmost, a place above mediocrity'.

Not all the reviewers were as harsh. The *European Magazine* said it 'could not for a moment hesitate in assisting and encouraging such an individual as John Clare'.[2] The *New Monthly Magazine* said of the new collection 'its poetical merits are quite sufficient to enable it to give pleasure to the reader, and it is calculated to excite in him feelings of sympathy and compassion'.[3] The *Eclectic Review* understood Clare's talent as much as anyone and found his new poems 'perfect in their kind like everything which Nature gives birth to... He may only be "as a hedge-row violet is to a Dutch tulip" but he was a true poet'.[4]

Inevitably, as Clare feared, his long poem was compared with James Beattie's 'Minstrel', but the likeness is a superficial one and can be seen now as a totally different work. It is true that not enough time or development was allowed between the publication of *Poems Descriptive of Rural Life and Scenery* and *The Village Minstrel*, but the new volumes did contain better poems alongside the repetitions and weaknesses of the earlier work. The success of that first volume was not, however, to be repeated. *The Village Minstrel* sold only eight hundred copies by the end of the year and Taylor shared Clare's fears that the bubble had already burst. In a letter to his publisher, dated 6 September 1821, Clare wrote: 'Let me wait another year or two & the peep show will be over & my vanity if I have any will end in its proper mortification to know that obscurity is happiness & that John Clare the thresher in the outset & neglected rhymer in the end are the only two comfortable periods of his life...'.[5]

John Taylor, who had been visiting relatives in the north of England during the October of that year, decided to call on Clare at his Helpston home. He published an account of their time together in the November issue of the *London Magazine*, in the hope that it would generate more interest in the Northamptonshire poet and his latest work:

> I believe we must go into low life to know how very much parents can be beloved by their children. Perhaps it may be that they do more for them, or that the affection of the child is concentrated on them the more, from having no other friend on who it can fall. I saw Clare's father in the garden: it was a fine day, and his rheumatism allowed him just to move about, but with the aid of two sticks, he could scarcely drag his feet along: he can neither kneel or stoop... The

father though so infirm, is only fifty-six years of age; the mother is seven years older. While I was talking to the old man, Clare had prepared some refreshment within and with the appetite of a thresher we went to our luncheon of bread and cheese, and capital beer from the Bell. In the midst of our operations, his little girl awoke, a fine lively pretty creature, with a forehead like her father's, of ample promise. She tottered along the floor, and as her father looked after her with the fondest affection, and with a careful twitch of his eye when she seemed in danger, the last verse of his Address to her came into my mind:

> Lord knows my heart, it loves thee much;
> And may my feelings, aches and such,
> The pains I meet in folly's clutch
> Be never thine . . .[6]

When their meal was over Clare showed his publisher the library that he had collected over the years. Taylor found it 'romantic' that so many fine volumes with their gold lettering should be housed in such a poor place for, 'except in cleanliness, it is no whit superior to the inhabitants of the poor peasantry'.[7] Clare walked with Taylor as far as Barnack, pointing out those local places that had inspired some of his poems, but the London publisher still confessed that one needed the imaginative eye of a poet to see beauty in what appeared to be very ordinary scenery indeed.

2

Taylor had seen for himself how necessary it was for Clare to get away again from Helpston, if only for a few weeks, and he agreed that he should come up to London in the spring of 1822.

Mrs Emmerson, who had now moved to her house in Stratford Place, certainly thought from the correspondence she had had with Clare during the winter that he needed a holiday and invited him to be her guest. James Hessey also shared her feelings and sent Clare £5 for his coach fare, suggesting that he should spend the first few days in Fleet Street with his publishers before staying with Mrs Emmerson.

Clare hoped that Octavius Gilchrist would again be able to travel with him but the Stamford literary grocer was too ill to leave home and told Clare that he must travel alone. Clare, eager to see his friends in London, could not wait. In the third week of May he joined the stage at the George, Stamford, and felt his spirit lighten as the Great North Road lengthened the miles between him and his village. It was not the most comfortable of journeys. The weather was bad and the roads in poor condition: 'We went 20 miles & upwards in the most dreadfull thunder-storm I ever witnessed & the rain was very heavy & lashing. . . .'[8] But he arrived safely and was soon caught up again in the excitement of the great city. It was a place where he could be extravagant, noisy, liberated and alive without his neighbours criticizing him. He could also enjoy himself without the responsibilities of his family inhibiting his sense of freedom. There was good company, exhilarating talk, always somewhere new to go, and something different to do. On this visit he was to stay for three weeks and meet again some of the outstanding literary figures of the day, recording excellent descriptions of them.

But one of the great wonders was still 'the continual stream of life passing up and down the principal streets all the day long & even the night'.[9] One of his most amusing pastimes was to sit by Taylor's window in Fleet Street and watch 'the constant successions throng this way & that' and he was reminded again of those tales told by the fireside years earlier of kidnappers and body-snatchers:

> When I used to go anywhere by myself especially Mrs E's I used to sit at night till very late because I was loathe to start not for the sake of leaving the company but for fear of meeting with supernatural agents even in the busy paths of London though I was a stubborn disbeliever of such things in the daytime yet at night their terrors came upon me tenfold & my head was as full of the terrible as a gossip thin death-like shadows & goblins with saucer eyes were continually shaping on the darkness from my haunted imagination & when I saw anyone of a spare figure in the dark passing or going on by my side my blood has curdled cold at the foolish apprehensions of his being a supernatural agent whose errand might be to carry me away at the first dark alley we came to[10]

All the fears that he had known as a child, afraid of passing Helpston churchyard, or of coming home in the twilight from Maxey flour-mill, were magnified in London. There were worse terrors than ghosts or Jack-o'-lanterns. Thieves, murderers and men-stealers hid in every doorway:

> I could not bear to go down the dark narrow street of Chancery Lane It was as bad as a haunted place to pass & one dark night I decided to venture the risk of being lost rather than go down . . .[11]

He did get lost and could not find his way back to Fleet Street where he was still staying. Each street he tried only increased his panic. He was in a labyrinth of shadowy thoroughfares that were all waiting to swallow him whole. At last he found a nightwatchman and offered him a shilling if he would show him the way. To begin with the nightwatchman declined, believing from the sight of this frightened visitor that he could earn more for himself than one shilling. How much? asked Clare. Nothing less than half-a-crown. Clare readily gave him the money and kept close to him as they moved through the darkness.

During the daytime, and with friends, it was different. He had met in London the painter Edward Rippingille, whose pictures he had first admired in Wisbech when he went for his interview with Mr Bellamy nearly twenty years ago. Rippingille introduced Clare to the Royal Academy and told the door-keeper that he was to let his friend in without a ticket any time he chose to appear. Clare took every opportunity of seeking refuge among the quiet galleries when the streets became too frightening, and in so doing learned to appreciate paintings.

When he went to London his family expected him to buy gifts to take back home for them. These shopping expeditions often caused him distress, especially when he thought his own dress would lead the shopkeeper to take advantage of him:

> I used to think that by going into the best looking shops in the most thoroughfare streets I should stand the least risk of being cheated so in I went & gave every farthing they set upon the article & fancied I had got a good bargain till experience turned out to the contrary when I first got up being rather spare of article of dress I went into a shop in Fleet Street & purchased as a first article a pair of stockings for which the man asked 3/6 & on my giving it without a word of contrariety he made a pause & when I asked him the price of another article he told me as he kept nothing but first class articles they were rather high in price & laying a ready made shirt on the counter he says that is 14 shillings I told him it was too high for me & with that he instantly pretended to reach me another which was the very same article agen this was 6/6 I paid it & found out afterwards that the fellows fine cloth was nothing but callico[12]

Patty was not slow in telling him when he eventually went home that he had been cheated by a city businessman who had taken him to be a fool.

Such unhappy experiences did not, however, spoil the overall excitement of being in London, especially when he could spent the time with Edward Rippingille. They shared many hours together in the ale-houses where the artist entertained the poet with his quick wit and skill at punning. Clare was to recall how they acted many of life's farces and cracked many jokes together and 'once spent a whole night at Offley's the Burton Ale house & sat till morning'.[13]

He had, by this time, moved from his lodgings in Fleet Street with Taylor and was now staying with Mrs Emmerson, with whom Rippingille was already friendly. In a letter of 30 June 1821 she had described him as 'a man of superior genius as an artist – but still more superior for his understanding and goodness of heart'.[14] She would usually give them a good dinner before they went out for their night's revelry and it was often in the early hours of morning before they returned home for bed. On one occasion Clare was locked out and had to sleep in a parked cab until Mrs Emmerson's servant-girl let him in.

Another attraction of London was the theatre, in all its forms. Most evenings he and Rippingille walked down Drury Lane and Tottenham Court Road to watch the actors and actresses arriving at the stage-doors. They particularly enjoyed going to the French Playhouse, though neither of them understood a word of French, because there was a very beautiful actress there who took their fancy.

After the performances they laughed and swaggered their way round the streets of London and tried to forget their thick heads in the morning.

While Rippingille was there to keep him company Clare was happy. But the artist was not always to be at his side. He had to return to Bristol where he had lecture engagements and Clare had to look after himself again. He went back to spending his days at Taylor's office where he could watch the world from the safety of the other side of a window.

3

He was to visit London on two more occasions[15] and, from his observations, left some vivid impressions of the men of letters he met and dined with:

> Hazlitt... sits a silent-picture of severity if you was to watch his face for a month you would not catch a smile there his eyes are always turned towards the ground except when one is turned up now & then with a sneer that cuts a bad pun or a young authors maiden table-talk to atoms... when he enters a room he comes stooping with his eyes in his hand as it were throwing under-gazes round at every corner as if he smelt a dun or thief ready to sieze him by the collar & demand his money or his life he is a middle-sized dark-looking man & his face is deeply lined with a satirical character his eyes are bright but they are rather buried under the brows...
>
> Then there is Charles Lamb a long remove from his friend Hazlitt in ways & manners he is very fond of snuff which seems to sharpen up his wit every time he dips his plentiful fingers into his large bronze-coloured box & then he sharpens up his head throws himself backwards on his chair & stammers at a joke or pun with an inward sort of utterance ere he can give it speech till his tongue becomes a sort of packman's strop turning it over & over till at last it comes out whetted

as keen as a razor ... but he is a good sort of fellow & if he offends it is innocently done ...

And there sits Cary the translator of Dante one of the most quiet amiable & unassuming of men he will look round the table in a peaceful silence on all the merry faces in all the vacant unconcernment imaginable & then he will brighten up & look smilingly on you ...

There was Coleridge [too] at one of the Parties ... he was a man with a venerable white head fluent of speech his words hung in their places at a quiet pace from the drawl in good set marching order so that you would suppose he had learnt what he intended to say ...[16]

With impeccable observation – and contradicting Martin's claim that Clare could not write prose[17] – he continued his descriptions of the writers in his company. There was Thomas De Quincey, 'the opium eater and abstruse thinker in logic', who was:

a little artless simple-seeming body something of a child overgrown in a blue coat & black neckerchief for his dress is singular with his hat in his hand he steals gently among the company with a smile turning timidly round the room ...

And there was J.H. Reynolds, who was always the life and soul of the party, equalling, if not surpassing, his fellow artist Rippingille:

He was the most good-natured fellow I ever met with his face was three-in-one of fun wit & punning personified he would punch you with his puns very keenly without ever hurting your feelings ... nothing could put him out of humour either with himself or others ... his teeth are always looking through a laugh that sits as easy on his puckered lips as if he were born laughing ...[18]

There were others, too, such as Allan Cunningham, who hated puns but was fond of Scottish border ballads 'and everything down no doubt to Scotch snuff', and T.G. Wainewright, the painter and forger who was a 'very comical sort of chap about 27 and wears a quizzing-glass and makes an excuse for the ornament by complaining of bad eyes'.[19]

But an event which left an even deeper impression on Clare's mind occurred during his third visit in 1824. This was the funeral cortège of Lord Byron as it passed through the city in July on its way to Nottinghamshire:

I saw his remains borne away out of the city on its last journey to that place where fame never comes His funeral was blazed in the papers with the usual parade that accompanies the death of great men I happened to see it by chance as I was wandering up Oxford Street on

> my way to Mrs Emmersons when my eye was suddenly arrested by straggling groups of the common people collected together & talking about a funeral I did as the rest did though I could not get hold of what funeral it could be but I knew it was not a common one by the curiosity that kept watch on every countenance By & by the group collected into a hundred or more when the train of a funeral suddenly appeared on which a young girl that stood beside me gave a deep sigh & uttered 'Poor Lord Byron' I looked up at the young girls face it was dark & beautiful & I could almost feel in love with her for the sigh she had uttered for the poet it was worth all the newspaper puffs & magazine mournings that ever were paraded after the death of a poet . . . the young girl that stood beside me had counted the carriages in her mind as they passed & she told me there were sixty three or four in all they were of all sorts & sizes & made up a motley show the gilt ones that led the procession were empty the hearse looked small & rather mean & the coach that followed carried his embers in an urn over which a pall was thrown[20]

Another spectator at that funeral was George Borrow who also stood in Oxford Street. He records his own impression in *Lavengro*[21] but not with the same simple awe as that felt by Clare. For Clare, Byron's greatness was beyond doubt. He shared the feelings of the common people who recognized his merits '& the common people of a country are the best feelings of a prophecy of futurity . . . they felt by a natural impulse that the mighty was fallen & they moved in saddened silence.'[22]

Byron's death was another loss to the world of poetry since Clare's first publication. Keats had died in 1821; Shelley was drowned in 1822; Bloomfield was to die soon after in 1823. In London Clare felt part of the weave of history and time; part of the important lives and events that others would only read about in years to come.

And what of Clare himself, in the eyes of others? How did they, the Londoners, see him? He was clearly not a silent, inarticulate observer making mental notes to write down later in the village of Helpston. He joined in the talk and was teased for his provincial sayings. Charles Lamb called him not only 'Princely Clare' but also 'Clarissimus'. Though they were often amused by his rustic manners, Clare was respected for the originality of his mind. His country dress was sometimes a disadvantage, as on the occasion when Thomas Hood took him out for supper in Soho. For a moment the door-keeper, thinking he was only the gentleman's servant, refused to let him in. But Hood introduced Clare as a famous poet and the door opened. H.F. Cary in his *Memoirs*[23] also recalled a time when Clare was staying with him at Chiswick. They had been to visit the grave of James Thomson, whose *Seasons* had inspired the young plough-boy. Later that evening they were joined by several friends, including Lamb:

> With the cheese had been placed on the table a jug of prime ale imported for the special use of Clare. As the servant was removing the glasses Clare followed him with his eye, let his own glass go without a sign of displeasure; but when the jug was about to follow, it was more than he could bear and he stretched out both his hands to stop it; the tankard was enough for him and he could dispense with the refinement of a glass.[24]

Thomas Hood was also to recall in his *Literary Reminiscences* that Clare was 'hardy, rough, and clumsy enough to look truly rustic [but] there was much about Clare for the Quaker to like; he was tender-hearted and averse to violence'. Hood also described Clare at those literary gatherings in his grass-green coat and yellow waistcoat, sitting among the 'grave-coloured suits of the literati' looking like a 'very cowslip'. John Hamilton Reynolds also caught a similar aspect of Clare when he referred to him as 'twinkling Clare'.

4

But London was not for ever and he always had to return home to the responsibilities of his family and the increasing indifference of his neighbours. Back once more in Helpston the drinking had to be alone, and often out of desperation. It was a weakness that worried Clare greatly. He wrote to James Hessey in January 1823, 'I shall & must do without drink next year let matters go as hard as they may its not only hurting myself but my family likewise.'[25]

That year, like the one which preceded it, was to be a miserable one for Clare. *The Village Minstrel* had not received the praise he had hoped for and Taylor was not showing much enthusiasm for a proposed new book of poems about the life of the countryside throughout the months of the year – to be called, eventually, *The Shepherd's Calendar*. The poems, too, were not coming as readily now as they did. Clare told Hessey, in the same letter about his drink problem, 'it is months now since I even scribbled a Sonnet'. His domestic pressures had been aggravated by recurring illnesses to his family. Patty had not fully recovered from the difficult birth of another child. This was another daughter, Eliza Louisa, born in June and named after Mrs Emmerson who was her godmother. Anna Maria was still a frail infant who became a victim of most epidemics that struck the village. That summer she had been very ill with measles and, as several children had died in the neighbourhood, Clare became terrified at the prospects of losing his own first, precious daughter. In a letter to Taylor, dated 31 July 1823, he said, 'my heart cannot forget aching tho this morning has found her so much better ... had I known the troubles that come with children in spite of the pleasures I would have had none.' He had neither the time nor the energy to give to all the poems he had to write. His nerves became more over-strung and uncontrollable. He could not eat or sleep and began vomiting and bleeding in the mornings. This lasted for three weeks until the local doctors were able to find a temporary remedy. His doubts about there ever having been a God of love and mercy grew. In an earlier letter of that year to Taylor he had said, 'doubts & unbeliefs perplex me continually & now I think seriously about an hereafter I am more troubled in my thoughts than I was before & I much fear that I shall never feel a sufficiency of faith to make me happy.'[26]

As the weeks passed Anna slowly recovered and Patty's health improved but Clare was to suffer the loss of a friend that diminished him greatly in spirit. Octavius Gilchrist died at the age of forty-four. Coming so soon after the death of Bloomfield, Gilchrist's death was a severe blow. It deprived Clare of one of the few people in the neighbourhood who understood him and still stood by him. Edward Drury had also left Stamford and returned to Lincoln. Clare felt the loneliness of Helpston becoming increasingly unbearable. Bloomfield's death brought with it another disappointment. The two poets had planned to meet later that year with the intention of talking about a biography that Clare wanted to write of Bloomfield. That, with many other schemes, seemed destined to fail before it even bore promise.

By the autumn Clare was more depressed than ever and suffering with the fen ague. There was no work, no writing. The over-crowded cottage frustrated him. When he was not 'windbound in my sooty corner' he was back in the Blue Bell, and hating every minute of it. He was in debt to the landlord. Earlier in the year he had confessed to Hessey that the sum of seven pounds 'grins at my Folly on the greasy manteltree at the Bell'.[27]

He had similarly confessed to Mrs Emmerson that he had fallen in love again, but with whom we cannot be sure. It was unlikely to have been Mary Joyce – though he did see her again in 1823 – and it could not have been a very happy or prolonged affair either. Mrs Emmerson referred to it in a letter of 6 May 1823:

> and so you have been love-sick of late! at varience with the world about a fickle woman! What says your dear Patty to this? But she need have no fears of your integrity of heart towards her – I honour your sentiments upon this point – and for all else she must be liberal towards you and remember that her husband is a poet and that he must have his idols of the mind as well as of the heart ... pray, do be content with

> one fair she – and leave all the rest of our sex to wander where they will except it be the loves of your imagination.[28]

The rest of that year was a critical one for Clare. His mind was again filled with doubts and fears about his health and his poetry. In a letter to Taylor, of 8 May, he said:

> I wrote to Hessey a long while back when in a very bad & restless state respecting coming up to London but he never so much as noticed ... doubts & unbelief perplex me continually & now I think seriously about an hereafter I am more troubled in my thoughts than I was before & much fear that I shall never feel a sufficiency of faith to make me happy ... I know one thing that is I am very anxious to get better because I know when a family looses its father the provider is gone.[29]

That family continued to grow and, ironically, the winter's one bright ray of happiness was the birth of his first son in January, who was named Frederick. Clare brightened for a while until he realized that it was one more mouth to feed and one more body to find room for in the cottage. His depressions returned and he longed to get away to London where he could receive more expert medical treatment as well as discuss his future with John Taylor. His publisher arranged for him to see Dr George Darling, the eminent Scottish physician who had cared for several of Taylor's authors, including Hazlitt and Keats.

It was late May before Clare could finally get away but he was to see Dr Darling within days of arriving in the city. The physician insisted that the poet should rest more, that he should not get too excited or involved in deep conversation, and that certainly his drinking should be kept to a minimum if not stopped altogether. Darling also attributed much of the trouble to the poet's own anxiety over his precarious position in the strange, competitive world of Letters. Clare was ambitious and wanted success. He wanted his work to be accepted and praised, his stature as a poet among poets to be confirmed. They were natural and understandable feelings but, from Clare's inauspicious beginnings, they were fires which demanded constant feeding. It was an intellectually and emotionally exhausting existence to compete in this way. Taylor had said of him, 'Clare has a great delight in trying to run races with other men.'[30] But his efforts and output always had to be double those of his contemporaries. Even the dinner-parties demanded more of him than they did of everyone else. To people like John Taylor, William Hazlitt, Charles Lamb and Edward Rippingille, prolonged and witty argument came naturally. They were experienced, eloquent men who could relax in their after-dinner conversations with confidence. Not Clare. He was always, so he thought, a man on trial. He enjoyed their company and could participate, but he was usually tense, watchful and, by the end of the evening, tired out – unless the drink had released him from his inhibitions, in which case he was paying the price that Dr Darling had warned him against. The doctor also urged Clare to stop worrying about his reputation as a poet. Fame and wealth were not only hungry, they were also elusive. His need for both was making him ill beyond cure. His feelings of inferiority, insecurity and despair would neither improve his health nor his work. Only a handful of writers knew ultimate success in their lifetime. Perhaps it was more than they should expect, having already received more than most. (As Dame Janet Baker was to write in 1979: 'When a piece of oneself is given to the world to be rejected from lack of understanding the suffering must be profound. But it is surely not the artist's business to be concerned with appreciation. He is only entitled to the work itself, not the fruits of it. . . .'[31])

Perhaps Clare was a man who might have been saved from the lunatic asylum if some of the material fruits had come to comfort him when all else seemed against him.

5

Having now met Clare several times on his previous visits to London, Mrs Emmerson was trying to be more understanding in her help towards his complex personality and knew him well enough to believe that the simple, country-girl in Patty could not fully satisfy all he desired of the fair sex. She knew that for Clare the Muse would always be personified in the body of a beautiful woman but did not help matters by believing that she could still play that rôle herself. During his third visit she sent him a note, saying, 'pray come to take your dinner with me tomorrow (Sunday), I shall be "Joan all alone" – my good man having started this morning for Bath. . . .'[32] Clare went, and stayed with her for several weeks. Whilst he was there she wrote to Patty assuring her that her husband's health was slowly improving and that he was in good hands. A few days later another letter was sent, which could not have pleased Patty when she knew of its contents: 'I am requested by your dear husband to beg of you to go to the *drawers upstairs* and get my *Portrait* in the red morocco case . . . you will then be so good as to let the Portrait be very carefully packed up in brown paper and get some friend to direct it to my address as below, as I am going to have it framed, by your husband's request, that it may hang-up in *your* cottage.'[33]

Towards the end of June, and perhaps as a peace-offering, she also sent to Helpston enough coloured muslin 'to make up four frocks – and a bit of striped white muslin for 2 more Sunday ones – also a little cambric muslin to make them 4 petticoats . . .'. She was also to send a 'couple of waist-coat pieces and the lining for them' begging Clare to wear them for her sake. Whatever the motive, Patty was practical enough to make use of everything she received, even if it did mean having the portrait of another woman on her cottage wall.

Mrs Emmerson's gifts, however, did little to make the next year and the next winter any more endurable. Inded, it was towards the end of 1825 that Clare expressed his growing irritation about her in a letter to Taylor of 19 December: 'Mrs E. is too intriguing in her friendships & dwells too much on show & effect to make me feel that it is not one of the first value neither do I admire her opinions & judgements. . . .'[34]

Throughout the months since his visit to London he had kept in touch with Dr Darling and was able to tell James Hessey, 'I am something better since I wrote Dr. Darling whose prescriptions I find now give me instant benefits in a far different & more direct manner than they did when in London for which I cannot account why. . . . I feel I owe [him] my present existence. . . .'[35]

Dr Darling was always of the opinion that the best place for Clare to be was back at home among the trees and meadows of his native landscape, where he might still find some peace and serenity. London appealed to the wrong side of his nature. As much as he needed intellectual company he needed to be more where he naturally belonged. Clare was certainly pleased to be home again, if only to be with his family, but he never felt quite so sure about Helpston. It was a different place now. The pattern of the streets and fields had changed, the population had grown, and he was often a stranger among strangers. Even his friends, the old neighbours and villagers who knew him as a boy, did not bother with him now. He was no longer certain of where he belonged.

16

'Th' Expense of Spirit'

1

The two friends on whom Clare relied greatly at this time were Edmund Tyrell Artis, the butler at Milton Hall, who was also an expert archeologist, and Mr T. Henderson, the head-gardener, who was a keen botanist. Clare had met both men in 1820 when he first visited Milton and had found them to be sympathetic, interesting companions. Artis was to make his name as the discoverer of Durobrivae – the once-important Roman town between Castor and Wansford – and he published several detailed maps and papers on his findings. His work was to establish that this area of the Nene Valley had once been a thriving Roman territory with potteries, warehouses, markets, barracks, wealthy houses and a road system, which can still be travelled today between Wansford, Southorpe, Upton, Barnack, Helpston, Market Deeping and Bourne.

Clare had mentioned Artis when writing to John Taylor in January 1822:

> I have been to Milton & spent 3 days with Mr Artis the Antiquary very pleasantly... he has discovered a multitude of fresh things & a fine roman bath is one of the latest discoverys the painted plaster on the walls was very fresh & fine when I saw it & the flues of the furnaces was proof without the least suposition [sic] of its being a bath he has also found the roman road that led to the river & the pavement is as firm as when first laid down[1]

If Artis's knowledge of archeology impressed Clare, Henderson's interest in botany did so equally and the two men compared notes for many years. The poet frequently questioned the gardener's conclusions and occasionally proved that there were more species of flower or fern than Henderson believed.

Clare said of these friends, 'I never met with a party of more happy & heartier fellows in my life there was Artis up to the neck in the old Roman coins & broken pots of the Romans & Henderson never wearied with hunting after the emporer butterfly & the hornet sphynx in the Hanglands Woods & the orchises on the Heath.'[2]

Through his visits to Milton Clare also came to know other members of the household staff. There was West, 'an upright honest man though his delight in reading extended little further than the prices that fat sheep & bullocks fetched'; and there was Roberts, 'who sang well and liked the poetry of Thomas Moore'; and 'Grill', the French cook, who 'possesd a fund of patient good humour & countenance unmatchable in England'.[3] (Frederick Martin, who in his *Life* of Clare described Grill's countenance 'like a full moon put into a dripping-pan and baked before a slow fire', also said that the cook – whose real name was Monsieur Grilliot – tried to teach Clare to speak French, with limited success.)[4]

In the depressing years which followed Clare's initial triumph the cook occasionally took food from Milton Hall over to the hungry Clares at Helpston. He always asked permission to do so but usually decided that an extra portion of game would not be missed. Game-shooting in the area had always been good and the two big estates of Milton and Burghley recorded some extravagant kills of over a thousand birds each shoot.[5] Monsieur Grilliot felt quite justified in making sure that a little of that meat reached the table of his poorer friend.

When Clare was not well enough to make the journey over to Milton Artis and Henderson would go to see him. Both men were well read and could talk about poetry for hours, if that was what Clare wanted; if not they would take long walks into the still-changing countryside around Helpston. In his journal for 16 September 1824 he wrote: 'Had a visit from my friend Henderson of Milton who brought *Don Juan* in his Pocket I was very ill & nursing my head in my hands but he revivd me & advised me to read *Don Juan* We talked about books & flowers & butterflys till noon & then he descanted on *Don Juan* which he admired very much I think a good deal of his opinion & shall read it when I am able'.[6] It was a work which was eventually to have a strange influence on him and provoke some of his most violent poetry.

Clare's reading seldom slackened, even when he was suffering with severe headaches and depression. During those years of 1820–25 he was reading Wordsworth, Burns, Shelley, Blake, Donne, Herbert, Milton, Shakespeare, and his perennial favourite – Isaak Walton's *The Compleat Angler*. He also read *The Vicar of Wakefield* every winter and browsed eagerly through all the book catalogues he received from London and Stamford. Lord Radstock kept him well supplied with newspapers and periodicals, sending as many as five or six a week.

In addition to these papers the Admiral was also making an assorted contribution to Clare's growing library. During that time he sent more than thirty books, including James Beattie's *The Minstrel*, William Cowper's *Poems*, Samuel Johnson's *Lives of the most eminent English Poets*, and a variety of obscure theological works intended for Clare's spiritual guidance.

Lord Radstock was constantly directing Clare's thoughts towards theology and had plans for improving the poet's external conduct to accord with his inner delicacy by getting him to visit a clergyman for instruction. The intention probably drove Clare into the Blue Bell, for he did not want to become another George Crabbe, even though some of his critics had suspected him of imitating the Suffolk poet. Clare had read *The Village*, *The Parish Register* and *The Borough*, but the two poets were worlds apart. Clare had made his views about Crabbe quite clear in a letter to Taylor as early as 1820: 'What's he know of the distresses of the poor musing over a snug coal fire in his parsonage box – if I had an enemy I could wish to torture I woud not wish him hung nor yet at the devil my worst wish shoud be a weeks confinement in some vicarage to hear an old parson & his wife lecture on the wants and wickedness of the poor'.[7]

Other contributors to his library – who had no such motives for turning Clare into a religious recluse – were Lord Milton, who gave several volumes, including the works of George Crabbe, John Dryden, Oliver Goldsmith, Alexander Pope, and a *History of Greece*; Mrs Emmerson and Mrs Marsh; and a number of Clare contemporaries who gave him inscribed copies of their publications. His library was eventually to contain over four hundred volumes and he also borrowed extensively from his friends.

Visitors to the Helpston cottage usually commented (as had John Taylor)[8] on their surprise at finding so many books in such a humble home, and this often led them to believe that Clare was in a much better position, financially, than he was. In addition to the books they would have seen 'some well engraved portraits, in gilt frames, with a neat drawing of Helpston church, and a sketch of Clare's head which Hilton copied in water-colours from the large painting and sent as a present to Clare's father'.[9]

2

Clare started keeping a journal in 1824 when he was thirty-one and for the next eighteen months left an almost daily account of his activities and feelings:

Tues. 7 Sept 1824 I have read Foxes *Book of Martyrs* & finished it today & the sum of my opinion is Tyranny & Cruelty appear to be the inseparable companions of Religious Power...
Thurs. 9th Sept 1824 Took a pleasant walk today in the fields but felt too weak to keep out long Tis the first day of shooting with the sportsmen & the poor hares partridges & pheasants were flying in all directions panic struck
Thurs. 23 Sept 1824 A wet day did nothing but nurse my illness coud not have walkd out had it been fine very disturbed in conscience about the troubles of being forced to endure life & dye by inches & the anguish of leaving my children & the dark porch of eternity whence none returns to tell of his reception
Friday. 22 Oct 1824 Read Hazlitt's Lectures on the Poets I admire his mention of the daisy as reminding him of his boyish days when he usd to try to jump over his shadow he is one of the very best prose-writers of the present day...
Wed. 10 Nov 1824 Read 'Macbeth' what a soul-thrilling power hovers about this tragedy I have read it over about 20 times & it chains my feelings still to its perusal like a new thing it is Shakespeares masterpiece...
Sat. Christmas Day Gatherd a handful of daiseys in full bloom... & a primrose root full of ripe flowers what a day this usd to be when I was a boy how eager I usd to attend church to see it stuck with evergreens (emblems of Eternity) & the cottage windows & the picture ballads on the wall all stuck with ivy holly Box & yew...
Sun. 23 Jan 1825 ... I am tired of writing[10]

Many of the other entries return to his own illness and the illnesses of his children, especially of his favourite child, Anna. But, despite these depressions and his weariness of writing, he continued to work on the long poems which were to make up *The Shepherd's Calendar*. In fact several of the journal entries can be found transposed into that work, as for instance, the above entry on Christmas Day which also appears in 'December':

Each house is swept the day before
And windows stuck wi evergreens
The snow is beesomd from the door
And comfort crowns the cottage scenes
Gilt holly wi its thorny pricks
And yew and box wi berrys small
These deck the unusd candlesticks
And pictures hanging by the wall[11]

As spontaneous and natural as much of Clare's verse reads, it is often contrived and *made* out of the material he had at hand. He preferred writing from impulse but could, after years of practice, also write to order. Poetry for him was a craft as well as an art and he could fashion the ordinary into the extraordinary, the commonplace into the unique with satisfying results.

The Shepherd's Calendar was to prove a perfect illustration of this gift. The work was difficult and often laboured, yet it contains some of his most vivid writing. The scenes were ones which he had described many times before and the characters had featured regularly in his earlier verses – the foddering boy, the ploughman, the giddy maids and brooding shepherds – but now they were being seen with a freshness of vision and a sharper focus, they were belonging to the poetry in a more natural way than before and also establishing their place in the history of rural England. Many of Clare's key words are in use again – 'melancholly', 'light', 'circle', 'little', 'childhood', and 'heaven'. We have the 'melancholly way', the 'melancholly sights' and the 'solitary crane' that:

> Swings lonly to unfrozen dykes again
> Cranking a jarring melancholly cry
> Thro the wild journey of the cheerless sky[12]

We have the lambs that 'at all hours/Come in the quaking blast like early flowers' and the frost that 'breathes upon the stiffening stream/And numbs it into ice again'.[13] We are taken back to the dusty barn where the boy-poet is flailing with his father:

> While oer his head shades thickly creep
> And hides the blinking owl asleep
> And bats in cobweb corners bred
> Sharing till night their murky bed
> The sunshine trickles on the floor
> Thro every crevice of the door[14]

We share too in the lament for all the old customs and traditions that are passing away, whether they are recipes for cures or beauty-treatment, courting rituals or seasonal games. Each month produces a poem of sustained interest and observation. The whole sequence presents us with a history and scenario of village life that has rarely been equalled. In *The Shepherd's Calendar* Clare's own descriptions of the seasons of the year reached a sureness of touch which confirmed his maturity as a poet:

> The village sleeps in mist from morn till noon
> And if the sun wades thro tis wi a face
> Beamless and pale and round as if the moon
> When done the journey of its nightly race

Had found him sleeping and supplyd his place
For days the shepherds in the fields may be
Nor mark a patch of sky – blindfold they trace
The plains that seem wi out a bush or tree
Whistling aloud by guess to flocks they cannot see[15]

3

Although Clare was now writing some of the best poetry of the age, *The Shepherd's Calendar* was not to restore his reputation or his prospects. Delays over its publication were to be even more protracted than those which accompanied *The Village Minstrel*, and in the spring of 1825 he had what he believed to be a premonition of how his latest work would be received. On Wednesday, 9 March, he wrote in his journal: 'I had a very odd dream last night & take it as an ill omen for I don't expect that the book will meet with a better fate I thought I had one of the proofs of the new poems from London & after looking at it awhile it shrank thro my hands like sand & crumbled into dust.'[16]

He received early proofs for correction three days later from James Hessey but they were incomplete and nothing like Clare had imagined. Taylor himself had become frustrated with the whole idea. He was tired too of editing and copying Clare's often erratic manuscripts and had engaged Harry Stoe Van Dyk – a young poet he had recently discovered – to help with the task of preparing fair copies of the poems. Van Dyk, like Clare, had also been taken up by Lord Radstock and Mrs Emmerson. He was a warm-hearted, gentle person, but soon regretted that he had become so involved in the unfortunate relationship that had developed between Taylor and Clare.

Clare did not know that Taylor had handed over his manuscripts to someone else until Van Dyk wrote to him in February. The 'editing' was to be severe, mainly at Taylor's suggestion. By the time *The Shepherd's Calendar* eventually appeared it was to have been reduced from 3,382 lines to 1,761, and Clare still had to write an alternative section on 'July' – which was nowhere as good as the original rejected by Taylor. Little wonder that he wrote in his journal on 30 April, 'if Doctors were as fond of amputation as they are of altering & correcting the world woud have nothing but cripples.'[17]

He had also written angrily to James Hessey about the treatment his new work was receiving, complaining that Van Dyk was still waiting to receive some of the poems from Taylor and that he himself was still waiting for further proofs which had been promised in three days three weeks ago: 'When delay is carried into a system its cause must grow a substitute for a worse name... I will just ask you to give a moments reflection to my situation & see how you would like it yourself.'[18]

It was Taylor who replied to that letter to Hessey. He told Clare that if he could find a publisher who could do a better job than he was trying to do then he would readily return the manuscripts.[19] Clare decided his battle was lost and let his publisher proceed at will. He began to believe that his dream would come true, that the poems would never appear in print.

His own patience and good intentions to live a sober life could hold out no longer. He started drinking again. He became so depressed that Patty took him over to Stamford to see Doctor Cooper. But Clare had little faith in him. There was no future and he doubted if he would live to see the year 1829. To darken his gloom even more his 'darling Anna' was taken ill and for several days came near to dying.

Clare then heard from some of his friends that all was not well with the firm of Taylor and Hessey and, in the summer of 1825, learned that their partnership had been dissolved. James Hessey decided to set up on his own as a publisher specializing in religious books. It was a venture which was to last only four years. In 1829 he became a print auctioneer and, failing at that, finally became a schoolmaster in 1833.

Taylor retained the right to handle Clare's work but delay continued to follow delay. In April Van Dyk left London for six weeks, without the poems in manuscript, and enquiries from Lord Radstock and Mrs Emmerson were seen as irritations and interruptions rather than concern. Taylor was equally dilatory over payments of the half-yearly dividends and Clare's income had now fallen to £30 a year.

The outlook could not have been bleaker. He gave up all hope of recovery and was relying now on the prescriptions he could get from Dr Darling for the pills he believed he had to take, for he was often alarmed with 'fresh symptoms of that numbness & stupidness in the head & tightness of the skull as if it was hooped round like a barrel'.[20] He could not sleep and was frequently up and walking the fields at three o'clock in the morning. Some days he vomited blood and could not eat. Nothing that Patty or his family tried to do helped. He was again reaching a desperation which took him near to suicide.

In the autumn of that year Taylor had also been taken ill and Lord Radstock died. Clare was especially grieved to get the news of the Admiral's death for he believed him to be a true friend. He had not always made life easy for Clare but his actions had usually been with the good intentions of helping the poet to order his life for the benefit of all. With Lord Radstock's death following so soon after that of Octavius Gilchrist, Clare realized that he had an ally less and that Taylor would be a more elusive man than ever. Mrs Emmerson was still in London but

Clare continued to have uneasy doubts about her and believed that without Lord Radstock she would have little influence in Fleet Street.

4

Clare's attitudes to Mrs Emmerson were often contradictory. In September 1825 she and her husband stayed at the New Inn, Market Deeping, and Clare was invited to be their guest. He stayed for three days and enjoyed being in their company. The lengthy correspondence was also renewed when Mrs Emmerson returned to London. But, in a letter to James Hessey, of 8 December, Clare spoke of her as a woman 'rather full of officiousness', and in a letter to Taylor, of 19 December, he repeated, 'Mrs E. is too intriguing in her friendship & dwells too much on show & effect to make me feel that it is not one of the first value neither do I admire her opinions & judgements.'[21]

It was an ungrateful, if not deceptive, attitude to take because at about the same time he must have been writing intimate, confessional letters to Mrs Emmerson. What he said we do not know but from her replies it is clear that he was very disturbed in his conscience about his recent behaviour. Writing to him on 22 December, she said:

> You have in your letter mentioned a subject in which I feel more than a common interest and anxiety – you promise in a 'few days to write more fully to me about it' – I shall wait with much solicitude your unreserved and free explanation of what may have taken place since I was at Deeping – half confidence will not on the present affair allow me to say more than to entreat you will not forget what is due to yourself and, need I add, to others who are deeply interwoven in all that can touch your honour and happiness . . . I beseech you, not to indulge during the Xmas in anything that may affect your Head – for it is on its strength alone you can rely – your poor Heart is alas! too yielding for your general good.[22]

Her reference to the 'present affair' and the comment that his heart was 'too yielding' show how used she was to hearing such troubled confessions about his waywardness and womanizing. But this time it was more serious. Assured of her understanding, Clare was persuaded to pour out the rest of his troubles soon after that unhappy Christmas.

On 11 January 1826, Mrs Emmerson replied:

> . . . you have been wandering from home, from yourself, and alas! from happiness: and much do I fear that my influence as your attached and true friend, will have little power to win you back to tranquillity and to domestic peace – and, above all, to your dear Children, for it

> is them I feel the most for, on the present occasion. I deeply regret 'the cause of your late out-breakings from propriety' – but why, my dear Clare, will you allow the temper or injudicious conduct of others to harry you away from your own reason, and induce you to do such things as can only bring upon you the loss of health, the expenditure of money, and that wretchedly disturbed mind of which you complain so forcibly, and with so much just reasoning ... I am not a 'prude' nor a 'moralist' but I would be enough of the philosopher and friend to prevail on you by every gentle, kind and reasonable entreaty to give up your acquaintance with * * * *; it is unworthy connexion, and can only bring you a train of miseries! I cannot enter further upon the subject than to thank you my dear Clare for the confidence you have reposed in me, and to beseech you, as you value my esteem and affectionate regard, that you will (having returned again to your home and family) call forth all your Social and parental feelings to induce you to be as happy as possible and to remain with your dear Children and your aged Parents; and I hope * * * * will do all in her power to make your mind more contented, and to enable you to pursue your literary labours ... I never wrote to you, my dear Clare, with such reluctant feelings as on the present occasion: I love to speak only in your praise – to extol your genius, to make others feel of your worth. How painful, then, is it to have the task of writing upon matters of weakness in a character where strength only should be found....[23]

Who this other woman could have been at the time is open to speculation. This 'unworthy connexion' could hardly have been Mary Joyce, who would not have been party to Clare's life at this level, nor is it likely to have been Elizabeth Newbon of Ashton, who was not to trouble him again. It might have been Betty Sell of Southorpe, the 'cyprian' Edward Drury had told Taylor about. There is a feeling about the whole affair that it was one of Clare's earlier girl-friends, not a casual pick-up in one of Stamford's seamier drinking-houses. Whoever it was, she caused him more remorse. He had been away from home, living a loose and extravagant life, over-spending and over-loving. He was fearful of his health, afraid that he might again have contracted a venereal infection, and was so stricken with guilt that life itself was not worth trying to save.

But what had driven him away from home? Had he quarrelled again with Patty because she had failed to understand him, or he her? He was, it seems, on the point of walking out on his family altogether, and not just because of a night or two of debauchery. There is more than a hint of passion in this affair. There is the real threat of someone taking Patty's place, and of Clare taking someone else's place. It is significant that at this time he began work on a verse-tragedy in which the subject was to be jealousy, or conscience.

The drama is incomplete. We can only fill that winter with further speculation. Clare returned to his wife and family and slowly began to restore a measure of harmony to their life in Helpston. By the June of 1826 Mrs Emmerson was able to write:

> I rejoice to hear other disagreeables are in the fair way of settling – but do not lose your firmness in this event of folly. Keep your own Station, and do not be hurried away by undue delicacy or fear in this unfortunate event... Without meaning to glorify errour or to espouse the frailtys of human nature, I should say the noblest way is to meet and to face our actions, and by a steady daring to conquer the weaknesses we have committed...[24]

5

Clare's way of meeting that challenge was, as usual, to set himself an immense schedule of work. Old manuscripts were taken out of the cupboards, new schemes were planned and poems had to be supplied to the literary magazines for what money he could earn. He composed several long poems in the style of earlier poets, particularly the Elizabethans; he began a series of Natural History Letters to James Hessey, wrote a number of essays on subjects such as 'Popularity', 'Landscape Painting', 'Criticism and Fashion', 'Money Catching or Common Honesty', and made notes for others on 'Industry', 'Mock Modesty and Morals', and 'False Appearances'. It was in his prose, he had told Taylor, that he hoped to 'expose the cant & humbug of the days fashion & opinions'.[25]

He returned, too, to the idea of writing fiction. The story which started out as notes from the *Memoirs of Uncle Barnaby & Family* became *The Bone & Cleaver Club*; and there are fragments of at least three other novels he wished to write – *The Two Soldiers*, *The Stage Coach*, and *The Parish Register*.

His poems were now appearing so regularly in the magazines – his 'imitations' in James Montgomery's *The Isis* and his sonnets in the *London Magazine* – that he was frequently forced to use the pseudonym 'Percy Green'.

But his main preoccupation was the publication of *The Shepherd's Calendar* which he had been discussing with his publishers now for over three years. James Hessey had urged Clare to try for something different back in 1823, but neither he nor Taylor could agree on what this difference should be. He had been told to write of 'Nature, the operations of the husbandman, the amusements, festivals, superstitions, customs &c., of the Country'.[26] But when the poems started to arrive in London Clare was told 'they abound too much in mere description & are deficient in Sentiment and Feeling and human interest'.[27] Taylor thought that the whole of the section on 'July' so banal that he had to ask for an alternative poem – 'instead of cutting out of the poem what is bad I am obliged to look earnestly to find anything that is good'.[28] Hardly the right tone to use on a poet of Clare's temperament and sensitivity, and hardly a fair dismissal of a poem which contained the lively workaday scenes, the 'feeling and human interest' advocated by James Hessey. Nevertheless, out went the lines:

Wi smutty song and story gay
They cart the withered smelling hay
Boys loading on the waggon stand
And man below wi sturdy hand
Heave up the shocks on lathy prong
While horse boys lead the team along
And maidens drag the rake behind
Wi light dress shaping to the wind
And trembling locks of curly hair
And snow-white bosoms nearly bare
That charms ones sight amid the hay
Like lingering blossoms of the may
From clowns rude jokes they often turn
And oft their cheeks wi blushes burn
From talk which to escape a sneer
They oft affect as not to hear

. . .

Along the roads in passing crowds
Followd by dust like smoaking clouds
Scotch droves[29] of beast a little breed
In swelterd weary mood proceed
A patient race from Scottish hills
To fatten by our pasture rills
Lean wi the wants of mountain soil
But short and stout for travels toil
Wi cockd up horns and curling crown
And dewlap bosom hanging down
Followd by slowly pacing swains
Wild to our rushy flats and plains

. . .

To witness men so oddly clad
In petticoats of bonded plad
Wi blankets oer their shoulders slung
To camp at night the fields among
When they for rest on commons stop
And blue cap like a stocking top
Cockt oer their faces summer brown
Wi scarlet tazzles on the crown . . .[30]

It is a poem full of life and social history and contains some of his best descriptive writing. Yet it had to wait over a hundred years to appear as Clare wrote it – as did many of his finest poems.

By the time he received proofs of the poems which were to appear in *The Shepherd's Calendar*, Clare heard rumours from the widow of Octavius Gilchrist that Taylor's name was in the bankrupts' lists and immediately wrote to Mrs Emmerson to find out if this was so. Although many booksellers were going out of business, Taylor was not one of them. Mrs Emmerson was able to reassure Clare that no whisper of the publisher's insolvency had reached her ears.

No sooner had this fear been dispelled, however, than he was faced with another problem – Edward Drury appeared on the scene again, this time with a letter dated 27 June 1826, claiming payment of £41. 9. 3d. 'for cash advanced to you whilst you were still writing the V—— M—— and for other expenses, viz. supplying you with Goods, procuring Medical advice for your Mother, Binding your Books and other particulars.'[31]

Clare slumped in his chair and wondered what he had done to deserve such misfortune. He did not have forty-one pounds nor did he believe Drury could demand that sum from him. He wrote immediately to John Taylor for advice. Taylor was not surprised. He had been in correspondence with Drury about some outstanding accounts and had asked for a payment of £100. 'Never mind Drury,' Taylor replied. 'He has made his Claim, and as far as it seems to be right we must allow it – I am sorry for his own sake that he should so far forget what is right as to urge his Claim with the threat of putting you to Trouble. He has Cause for Shame at having written such a letter. We are trying now to get the old Account settled, and when that is done I shall be glad to have no further Dealings with him.'[32]

Taylor also enclosed a cheque for £20, being the dividend money that was due from the shares and the half-yearly payments from Earl Spencer and the Marquis of Exeter. It was a cheque Clare desperately needed but it went little way towards easing the financial crisis or depressions.

6

The year of 1826 produced a very dry summer – with poor harvest and low wages. Clare took what labouring work he could but had to admit that 'the price of labour is so low here that it is little better than parish relief'.[33]

His own family continued to grow, however, despite such hardships. In June Patty had given birth to another son, who was christened John. Mrs Emmerson received the news with mixed feelings and wrote, 'Tell dear Patty she must not bestow any more dear little Johns upon you. . . .'[34] It was not Patty who needed such advice. Clare was to father three more children. Within a year Patty gave birth again, to a child which died before it was baptized.

His second daughter, Eliza, had, like Anna Maria, now started school, and Mrs Emmerson gave Patty a sum of money to cover the two girls' school expenses, promising that she would continue to be responsible for her god-daughter's education for as long as it could be continued. Whatever feelings Clare may have expressed about Mrs Emmerson, and however interfering she at times appeared to be, she was generous to his family in many practical ways, leaving him to get on with the task of writing.

He spent the rest of that year urging Taylor to publish *The Shepherd's Calendar* without further delay. But still publication was put back for one reason after another. In September he received a request from his publisher to write the preface to the new volume. In it, Taylor suggested, Clare would be able to 'account for the long delay in the coming out of the Volume on the score of ill health'.[35] As the publication had been advertised as long ago as January 1824, Clare felt this was hardly a fair excuse to put before the public, nor did he believe he should take all the blame. Nevertheless, he agreed to write the preface if only to avoid further delay. It was easier to swallow his pride now than to live with the sense of complete failure. It took him many days to address his reader but eventually he sent Taylor the following:

> Prefaces are such customary things, and so often repeated, that I think good ones cannot always be expected; and I am glad that they are so, for it gives me an opportunity of saying something which I am anxious to say, and at the same time leaves me the hope that I shall be pardoned for saying it so ill. I feel desirous to return thanks to my friends, who, I am happy to say, are too numerous to speak of here in any other than a general manner. To the Public, also, I return my hearty acknowledgements; and, however awkwardly I may write

them here, I feel them at heart as sincerely as any one can do; in fact, I ought, for I have met with a success that I never dare have hoped to realize, before I met it.

I leave the following Poems to speak for themselves – my hopes of success are as warm as ever, and I feel that confidence in my readers' former kindness to rest satisfied, that if the work is worthy the reward it is seeking, it will meet it; if not, it must share the fate of other broken ambitions, and fade away. I hope my low station in life will not be set off as a foil against my verses, ad I am sure I do not wish to bring it forward as an excuse for any imperfections that may be found in them. I cannot conclude without making an apology for the long delay in publishing these Poems, which, I am sure will be readily forgiven when it is known that severe illness was the cause.[36]

For a man who did not like uneasy compromises it must have been humiliating to write that last sentence. Only his hunger to get back on to the literary scene could have persuaded his conscience to take the blame for the long delay in publication. He did not want any more broken promises, thwarted ambitions, or patronizing attitudes. The poems had to stand as poems, not be accepted any more as the work of a peasant.

The work was now, almost, ready for publication and waiting only for the frontispiece which Peter De Wint had promised. This was finally completed in April 1827 and on 1 May Taylor wrote to Clare, 'Great and vexatious Delay took place in the plate, but now it is done I think you will like it, and agree with me that our Friend De Wint who had made the Drawing for nothing, out of Friendship for the Author, deserves a line or two of Thanks for his kindness.'[37]

The appearance that spring of *The Shepherd's Calendar* did little to change Clare's fortune. What public he thought he was addressing had melted into thin air. His 'numerous friends' could now be counted on the fingers of one hand. What was, in many ways, a major event in the literary world passed off as a whisper. The idea was not original. Other poets had written about the seasons, the months of the year, the yearly patterns of the village and country people, and the title did not appeal. There were favourable reviews. The *Literary Gazette* said it had 'a great deal of sweet poetry'[38] and the *Eclectic Review* recognized that 'The present volume, as compared with Clare's first efforts, exhibits very unequivocal signs of intellectual growth, an improved taste, and an enriched mind.'[39] But not all the critics agreed with that. The *London Weekly Review* took a very different view:

We happened to open this little book in so pleasant a mood that we almost felt our judgement might be somewhat improperly biased in

> the estimate of its intrinsic merits. We had not, however, perused many pages before we discovered that our self-suspicions were wholly groundless. Wretched taste, poverty of thought, and unintelligible phraseology, for some time appeared its only characteristics. There was nothing, perhaps, which more provoked our spleen than the want of a glossary; for without such an assistance, how could we perceive the fitness and beauty of such words as – *crizzling* – *sliveth* – *whinneys* – *greening* – *tootles* – *croodling* – *hings* – *progged* – *spindling* – *siling* – *struttles* – &c . . .[40]

Some months later, on 27 October 1827, the *Literary Chronicle* tried to restore the balance by claiming that the poems were 'pictures sketched with a masterhand, and possess the vivid colouring and peculiar freshness with which it is the province of genius to invest even the most exhausted subject'.[41]

But such praise was not enough. The new volume (which was a rushed and poor production by comparison with other publications of the day) sold even more badly than Taylor had feared. Only 425 copies were bought in the first two years and eventually the publisher was to offer the remaining stock at cost price to the poet in the hope that he could sell more locally. Against the advice of his friends Clare accepted the offer, but the experience was to be a bitter one. There were few people in and around Helpston who now wanted to buy his books, and days went by without a sale being made, even though he hawked his wares through the village streets where he was known.

Clare could not accept that his popularity was over, despite the fact that he had forecast its happening. *The Shepherd's Calendar* had drained him of much of his spirit. His desperation had driven him to pay a high price for a fame which eluded him. Nightmares and illness followed his exhaustion. There were days when he refused to go out of the house or even rise from his bed.

Of the few friends locally who continued to show an interest only Mrs Marsh, the bishop's wife, and Henderson, gave him the help he so badly needed. Edmund Artis had left the services of Milton Hall the previous year and Stamford had few attractions now. The generals, squires, magistrates and scholars who had invited him into their homes – or had visited him in Helpston – had long since forgotten he existed. The novelty was over. In the eyes of some of those early supporters Clare was arrogant and ungrateful. The ones who were still prepared to help did so not because of their own gain, or out of curiosity. They wanted to help Clare the man, as well as the poet.

Mrs Marsh was particularly kind at this time of his life. She frequently called at the cottage and occasionally asked Clare to dine with her at the

Palace in Peterborough. From a reference in one of Mrs Emmerson's letters in October 1827, it is clear that the Bishop himself also called to see Clare again, taking perhaps a further supply of port: 'The visit of the Bishop was very kind and his gift to you well suited I should think to your tastes – but it was certainly not a little "Malapropos" that you should not ask your noble visitor to enter your cottage, in consequence of the door being lock'd against you.'[42]

Was the cottage door really locked, in daytime, or was Clare too ashamed of his home to let the Bishop see what it was like? Hardly, for Patty was house-proud and always kept the place clean. Had she, more likely, locked him out after another quarrel? Possibly, for she could give as good as she took and frequently lost her temper with him. The Bishop may have been puzzled but he was not unforgiving and Clare continued to receive many kindnesses from the Marshes during the next four years when the poet's spirit was near to being completely broken.

He was now thirty-four. A very lonely and disillusioned man.

17
Time for Repentance

1

A visitor who was admitted to the cottage in 1827 was the sculptor Henry Behnes, who was to cast a fine bust of the poet in 1828. Behnes (who added the name Burlowe to his surname to avoid comparison with his brother, who was also a sculptor 'more gifted but degenerate'[1]) was shocked to see for himself Clare's poverty and lowness of spirit. He urged him to fight back, to visit London again, to reacquaint the world with his family's plight. When he returned home he wrote to Clare:

> Your Poetic Fame is abroad far and wide and riots on the Lip of Rank and Beauty. But yet Rank and Beauty, and in short the world as it goes, imagines that Poets live immediately upon the conjurations of their own wonder-working imaginations – you can and must undeceive it. Patty and the little ones say you must, they are eloquent and from their decision can even a genius appeal? The recluse must throw off his cowl for a season and his enquiry into the differences of the 'Bee and spider orchis' must be changed for the study of that wasp orchis man.[2]

The criticism here that Clare was not doing all he might for his family, that he attached too much importance to his own interests and pursuits, and that he had taken rejection too easily, spurred him for a time into another hectic period of writing. He also agreed with Behnes Burlowe that he should make immediate plans for a further visit to London. He wanted to see Dr Darling again, not only about the pains in his head but about a skin disease which had been worrying him during the autumn and winter. He had written to his London physician about the complaint but was told that it could not be treated without being seen. Clare, fearing the worst, began to see this mysterious illness as a punishment for his past conduct, especially the adultery about which he had confessed to Mrs Emmerson. His memory of the warnings he had learnt by heart from the Book of Job came back: 'They that plough iniquity and sow wickedness, reap the same. By the blast of God they perish and by the breath of his nostrils are they consumed.'

He wrote to James Hessey about these thoughts of damnation. Hessey replied:

> You ask for my advice as to what you should do to make your peace with God. Alas, my dear Clare, I am a poor Counsellor, but I will tell you what David did, when he, who was distinguished by so many marks of Divine favor, had been led by his evil passions into Commission of the double crime of Adultery and Murder – he said 'I have sinned against the Lord' – he humbled himself before the God of Purity, in whose sight he had polluted himself – and if you will read the 51st Psalm you will see in what Language he poured forth the agony of his Soul. You have sinned like him in the first instance, and in intention have been guilty of the second – but it pleased God to frustrate your rash design upon your own life and to afford time for Repentance.[3]

It was not the first time that Clare had gone through such moral and spiritual searching, nor was it the first time for him to turn to religion for guidance or comfort in time of stress. Three years earlier he had written to John Taylor about the thought of killing himself, but:

> from this change in my feelings I satisfactorily prove that Religious foundation is truth & that the Mystery that envelops it is a power above human nature to comprehend and thank God it is ... I agree with you that the religious hypocrite is the worst monster in human nature & some of these when they had grown so flagrant as to be discovered behind the mask they had taken to shelter their wickedness led me at first to think lightly of religion & sure enough some of the lower classes of dissenters about us are very decietful & in fact dangerous characters ... my opinion Taylor of true religion amounts to this if a man turns to God with real sincerity of heart not of canting & creeping to the eyes of the world but satisfying his own conscience so that it shall not upbraid him in the last hours of life ... that man in my opinion is as certain of heaven in the next world as he is death in this – because we cannot do wrong without being conscious of it[4]

This is an important statement of Clare's acceptance of the truth that exists between a mortal being and a God. It is more than a religious belief. It is a spiritual acceptance of the Mystery which envelops the truth, an awareness of the power in life that human nature cannot understand. Clare had been turned away from religion by the human frailty with the Church. The cant, hypocrisy, indulgence and self-interestedness had contradicted what he believed the scriptures taught. This longing to return to the Christian faith not only brought him some peace of mind, it also gave him a new impetus to fulfil his calling as a poet. He had written before about such a death and resurrection in 'To An Early Butterfly' and 'The Fountain of Hope':

> I rise above myself oer reasons shrine
> & feel my origin as love divine

Now God and Nature were more than one. They were each an expression of the other. In his long poem 'Child Harold' he was to write:

> ... he who studies natures volume through
> And reads it with a pure unselfish mind
> Will find God's power all round in every view
> As one bright vision of the Almighty mind.[5]

He could believe his 'origin as love divine' and accept the 'bright vision of the almighty mind' but where this new awareness of God's presence in the individual could be best expressed, in religious terms, remained a dilemma for many years and was never satisfactorily resolved for him within the acceptable thoughts of the day. There was still something restricting about the orthodox church which was class-structured and there was something not mysterious enough about the Revivalists who strove to break down class barriers – at least in their religious services. At one time Clare wanted to join the Ranters. He had told James Hessey about them in 1824:

> they are a set of simple & communing Christians with more zeal than knowledge earnest & happy in their devotions O that I coud feel as they do but I cannot their affection for each other their earnest tho simple extempore prayer puts my dark unsettled conscience to shame ... my feelings are so unstrung in their company that I can scarcely refrain from shedding tears & when I went to church I coud scarcely refrain from sleep – I thank God that he has opened my eyes[6]

As we saw earlier, Clare had expressed his interests in the Unitarians and the Quakers, but even with them there was something that did not measure up to his own creed. To act justly, to speak the truth, to love mercy, were actions to be held 'sacred in every country'[7] and an awareness of the divine in all that was human formed the basis of Clare's faith. Man was not alone, neither the beginning nor the end. Human nature debased the spiritual quest by its pettiness over sectarian religious attitudes. He wanted to find 'the Mystery that envelops' in a form that had dignity and awe. If it belonged anywhere it belonged in the fields and woods where he felt himself one with nature, a true child of Eden:

> There is a breath – indeed there is
> Of Eden left – I feel it now
> Of something more than earthly bliss
> That falls & cheers my sullen brow
> I gaze about upon the trees
> I view the sweep of distant hills
> More high than sources such as these
> Comes joy that in my heart distills
> I view the sky – away despair
> There falls the joy tis only there[8]

2

When the depressing year of 1827 was behind him Clare began to pursue his plans for another visit to London with greater determination. On 14 February 1828 Mrs Emmerson wrote begging him to stay with her: 'My dear Clare, let me, instead of listening to (or rather acting upon your melancholy forebodings) entreat you to cheer up, and in the course of another week make up a little bundle of clothes, and set yourself quietly inside the Deeping Coach for London. I will get your "sky chamber" ready to receive you.'[9]

Allan Cunningham also wrote asking him to come up to town without further delay. He could then see Dr Darling, discuss his literary affairs with John Taylor, and relax for a few weeks in pleasant company. Patty and his family were equally anxious for him to go if there was a chance of another stay in London improving his health and mood.

With his own mind made up Clare needed little further persuasion. He left Helpston on 24 February. But the capital had changed. The jovial dinner-parties and theatre visits were part of the past. Edward Rippingille had left town. Henry Van Dyk was seriously ill. Reynolds, De Quincey, Coleridge, had all gone their separate ways. Taylor was now busy publishing textbooks for the University of London and wanted nothing more to do with poetry.

Clare did see Taylor who suggested again that he should buy up the stock of his books at greatly reduced prices and hawk them around the villages at home. Once again Clare fell for the scheme and thought it would be a way of making some money out of his poetic ruins. But his friends were outraged at Taylor's suggestion and thought that no author should be subjected to such an indignity.

Clare spent a good deal of his time with H.F. Cary who took him on most days to the British Museum. He also met George Darley, Allan Cunningham and Behnes Burlowe. The visits to Dr Darling helped to calm his agitated state of mind and Mrs Emmerson made sure he had adequate food and rest.

After a couple of weeks she decided that Clare was well enough for a dinner-party and arranged an evening of celebration at 20 Stratford Place, at which most of the poet's friends were present, including William Hilton the artist and Behnes Burlowe. These men, like Clare, disliked such lionizing so the three of them chose to escape from the glitter and small-talk to a nearby public-house where they could dine on beer and cheese and enjoy their own conversation. They talked of art and fame, of poetry and immortality – wild and lovely dreams. The painter died in poverty. The sculptor perished alone in a hospital. And the poet spent the last twenty-three years of his life in a county lunatic asylum.

By the middle of March, Clare was homesick. On the twenty-first he wrote to his wife:

> My dear Patty – I am anxious to see you & the children & I sincerely hope that you are all well I have bought the dear little creatures four Books & Henry Behnes has promised to send Frederick a wagon & horses as a box of music is not to be had – the books I have bought them are *Puss in Boots Cinderella Little Rhymes* & *The Old Woman & Pig* tell them that the pictures are all colored & they must make up their minds to chuse which they like the best ere I come home – Mrs Emmerson desired to be kindly remembered to you and intends sending the children some Toys – I hope next Wednesday night at furthest will see me in my old corner again amongst you ... kiss the dear children for me all round give my remembrances to all and believe me my dear Patty
>
> Yours most affectionately[10]

His departure, however, was unexpected and sudden. Frederick Martin says that the sight of wild violets on his walk from Primrose Hill to Hampstead made him realize that London was not the answer, that the only cure he would ever find was in the familiar fields and hedgerows around Helpston. On the day that he wrote to Patty he also wrote to Allan Cunningham, 'I wholly intended to see you, but now I fear I cannot as my stay is grown so short so if I cannot, here is a "good bye" and God bless you, and as you are aware of my ignorance in travelling about your great Babel ... allow me to make up for the omission by a shake of the hand on paper as hearty as your imagination can feel it ...'.[11]

So eager was he to get away that he left most of his possessions, including his overcoat, at 20 Stratford Place and Mrs Emmerson had to parcel his 'goods and chattels' and despatch them by coach to the Bull Inn at Market Deeping.

3

But he was home again. And it was spring. The late March was warm, the countryside coming to life. His feelings for Patty, too, were as warm as they had ever been when he first courted her at Walkherd and Pickworth. To be with her now reminded him of those happier times recalled in his anniversary poem, 'To a Flower of the Desert':

> I found on thy bosom
> A treasure of spring
> A fairer & dearer
> Than summer could bring
>
> On the wild hills of Walkherd
> All withered & bare
> Had Eden existed
> I had thought it was there.[12]

Had Eden existed it belonged not only to Walkherd but also to Royce Woods, Emmonsail's Heath, the spinneys and lanes he had known as a boy in those pre-enclosure days. He had returned to them as well, to their quietness and healing:

> I seek for peace – I care not where tis found
> On this rude scene in briers & brambles drest
> If peace dwells here tis consecrated ground.[13]
>
> *
>
> Oh lead me anywhere but in the crowd
> on some lone island rather would I be
> Than in the world . . .[14]
>
> *
>
> Sweet solitude what joy to be alone
> In wild wood-shady dell to stay for hours[15]

On more than a hundred occasions Clare tells of this need to be alone with nature, to be alone on a natural cushion of a mole-hill by an old thorn bush or an hollow oak – 'There would I tenant be to Solitude. . . .'[16] 'Solitude and God are one to me. . . .'[17] All he wanted now was a mind 'oerflowing with excess/Of joys that spring from solitude.'[18] It was his constant plea:

> Oh take me from the busy crowd
> I cannot bear the noise

For nature's voice is never loud
I seek for quiet joys[19]

Although Clare loved solitude, one often feels he had another spirit walking with him, another soul with whom he wanted to share these quiet joys. So many of the poems are invitations to go with him, as in 'The Nightingale's Nest', already quoted – 'Hush, let the wood gate softly clap – for fear/The noise might drive her from her home of love. . . .'[20] He takes us for a walk through a sane, reliable world which silences the clatter and confusion of cities, a world certain of comfort in moments of distress, and of identity in moments of lostness. If we follow we find him pointing out some small detail we would have missed, until we too begin to see the insignificant and minute in total harmony with the universe; everything essential, beautiful, lasting and necessary – the daisy and the planet, the insect and the oak tree, all equal in a world that is part of a much greater creation. He was able to match his knowledge of the known with his vision of the unknown. More and more he sought for that healing silence after the clamouring world had let him down. His behaviour mellowed. His arrogance was tempered. His needs were different. He turned his vision inwards to see the world of nature mirrored more deeply in his soul. He was the artist now rather than the performer.

The poems of the next few years have not so much a sense of resignation, as of acceptance. There is a serenity about them, as in 'The Meadow Grass', 'The Woods', 'The Shepherd's Lodge', 'Fancys', 'On Visiting a Favourite Place', 'Walk in the Woods' and 'Sabbath Bells'. All have a sustained mood of gratitude and reconciliation with those ancient roots of Eden. Words like *calm* and *quiet* are used repeatedly. The rhythm and tone are now those of meditation rather than celebration:

There's something more to fill the mind
Then words can paint to ears & eyes
A calmness quiet loves to find
In these green summer reveries
A freshness giving youth to age
A health to pain & troubles drear
The world has nought but wars to wage
Peace comes & makes her dwelling here

I feel so calm I seem to find
A world I never felt before
& heaven fills my clouded mind
As though it would be dull no more
An endless sunshine glows around

A meadow like a waveless sea
Glows green in many a level ground
A very paradise to me[21]

This is Clare back on familiar ground, but with a difference. He is no longer the messenger bringing news from the fields, he is the message. No poet has ever gone so deeply into the silence of nature or given himself so completely to the spirit of solitude. Clare has now renounced ambition, fame and the theories of others. He has returned to the neglected shrines of his childhood to find that spiritual peace. In his poem 'On Visiting a Favourite Place' he goes back to the 'hills and hollows' near Barnack, that grassy, switch-back, miniature world of wild plants, rare orchids, birds and insects that had established its own kingdom in the pits and humps left from the excavations of the famous Barnack Rag – the stone which had been taken nine hundred years earlier to build the great abbeys at Peterborough, Thorney, Ely, Bury St Edmunds and several churches as far away as Norwich. Time had covered the scars of those ancient workings with grass and flowers. A different beauty had filled the holes left by man. Rare butterflies, forgotten flowers and sweet-smelling bushes had taken over. The poet had known the place since he was a boy. Now he returned to it for solace:

When last I roamed these bleachy swells
Of hills and hollows all was here
Oer which the heart in rapture dwells
Peace love & quiet everywhere
& nought is changed since last I came
Then can I help but be the same[22]

The skill with which Clare can now repeat a word-sequence or rhythmic-pattern is significant, gently impressing upon the reader the almost inexpressible mood of the moment: 'Peace love & quiet everywhere' – 'So calm so soft so smooth' – 'Uncropt unlooked for & unknown' – 'Unruffled quietness hath made/A peace in every place'. It is the sonorous language of poetry we usually associate with Tennyson's 'In Memoriam' but without his melancholy. It is a superb poem in which every word is carefully chosen, not only to harmonize with what goes before or after, but to vibrate with its own overtones of meaning. Clare was finding a deep, healing relief in the unruffled quietness. Later in the poem he says:

When last I paid a visit here
The book I brought for leisures way
Was useless for a volume dear
In crowds of pictures round me lay

The woods the heath the distant field
In strips of green & russet dye
Did such delicious pleasure yield
I shut & put the volume bye
The book at home was sweet indeed
But there I felt I could not read

. . .

Such scenes will make the mind divine
Earth grows a prophet to the eye
In such a mood God's love be mine
It were a pleasant thing to die
& when our thoughts that aid forgoes
O God how dull the journey grows[23]

The time of repentance was over. Clare knew for the next few years a truth which he had been searching for since childhood. Sadly its realization came too late to give his peace of mind any permanency.

4

Many of the poems being composed at that time were to be collected for a volume which Clare wanted to call *The Midsummer Cushion.* For a variety of reasons, this title and half of the poems had to wait over a hundred years for publication.

If his share of fame could have waited until 1828–32, when he was writing at the height of his power, his reputation would have been greatly different and the last years of his life probably spared the lunatic asylum. Equally, his life may have needed to survive those storms and disappointments in order to arrive at that stillness of mind which came before his eventual breakdown.

Whether through acceptance of his fate, or some new-found belief in a power beyond himself, Clare was now writing with a confidence and serenity he had not shown before:

Ive often on a sabbath day
Where pastoral quiet dwells
Lay down among the new-mown hay
To listen distant bells
That beautifully flung the sound
Upon the quiet wind
While beans in blossom breath'd around
A fragrance oer the mind

A fragrance & a joy beside
That never wears away
The very air seems deified
Upon a sabbath day
So beautiful the flitting wrack
Slow pausing from the eye
Earth's music seemed to call them back
Calm settled in the sky

& I have listened till I felt
A feeling not in words
A love that rudest moods would melt
When those sweet sounds was heard[24]

Again Clare was finding that there are some emotions for which language is inadequate and that the greatest poetry could not be expressed in words.

Just as his own peace of mind seemed more settled for a while, so too did his home life. The poems about his family radiate a similar happiness. We know from the letters and journal entries how fond Clare was of his children. They concerned him – their education, their well-being, their love of the countryside – all his life. He seldom went away without buying presents for them and he loved to have their company on some of his long walks. In the poem 'The Holiday Walk'[25] he records a happy day spent with Anna Maria, Eliza and Frederick. Throughout the poem we see how their attention is always being drawn to something they might otherwise miss. The words *Look!* and *See!* are used repeatedly. We get the feeling that Clare was actually writing the poem as he walked along. It also gives us a convincing picture of the poet as father, sharing his joy with them, away from the clamour of popularity or ambition:

See, theres a fine Butterflye sits on that leaf
Aye you may go creeping as still as a thief
It can hear you & see you – see there up it flies
With wings like a rainbow you've seen in the skies
Yes yes you may run there it crosses the stream
as far out of reach as a joy in a dream

. . .

Theres the cricket in brown & his cousin in green
The grasshopper dancing & oer them is seen
The ladybird dressed like a hunter in red

. . .

Do but look how the fields slope away from our eyes
Till the trees in the distance seem clouds in the skyes

The children are told to look at a hawk, at the sun, at boys swinging on a gate, at church-steeples, windmills, willow trees, a field-mouse, gnats, midges, partridges, 'showy corn-poppies shining like fox-hunters coats' and the gipsies who 'lie basking themselves at their ease'. It is another 'catalogue' poem, but deliberately and successfully so.

It was always this minute-by-minute involvement with everyday life that made Clare such an original, authoritative poet in writing about the countryside and village life. It also made him a poet without equal when writing of the moods of the seasons, not because he was a purely descriptive poet but because he was a reflective, meditative man giving his whole mind to the moment he was describing. The intensity of his concentration and involvement was like that of William Blake, or Van Gogh – ancient and new at the same time.

Clare saw not only the majesty of nature but also its frailty. The daisy-roots are traced back to Eden. There is as much wonder to be found in the egg of a bird as there is in a mountain. But the egg and the daisy survive, are reborn, protected, even though the foot of man can destroy the flower, even though the pettichap's eggs are so delicate that a 'green grasshopper's jump might break the shells'.[26] There is an immortality in the seasonal regeneration of nature that was a lesson to man. To follow Clare's eyes and thoughts throughout the year is to live almost as closely to nature as he did. Every month, practically every day, is a development of a season and a mood which reaches back into the past and also into the future. We can still see today a man ploughing and 'as the plough unbeds the worm' see 'the crows and magpies gather there'.[27] We can see too the black skies of winter pass and 'clouds like bright volcanoes slumber by', or notice how the crow will 'tumble up and down/At the first sight of spring/And in old trees around the town/Brush winter from its wing'.[28]

Summer was just as much a time for celebrations with its fairs, festivals, early harvest, fishing and long warm evenings with games on the village green. 'Summer Ballad', 'Summer Happiness', 'Summer Moods', 'Field Cricket', 'The Harvest Morning', these, and many more, tell their own joyous story of *belonging* to a place and a time. It was the season when the sun stayed longest in the sky, when it became the 'unfettered sun', the 'eternal ray', when it offered life and hope. It never lost its power or meaning for Clare. In those early days it rose in the east, round and simple and uncomplicated. It also rose over the village of Glinton and the home of Mary Joyce – 'in that hamlet lives my rising sun/Whose beams hath cheered me all my lorn life long'.[29] It had been a sun full of promise and at mid-day shone in triumph over Helpston. But the noon quickly turned to midnight. By the time Clare moved to Northborough in 1832 the sun would have spent most of its journey. He saw it then declining towards the western horizon, towards the end of the day where crimson shadows cast a pall over Royce Woods, Cowper Green, even Helpston itself.

Again, the significance of the sun in Clare's poetry is more than coincidental. We have it in all its moods and positions – 'sultry', 'glad', 'relentless', 'spoiling', 'creeping', 'faint', 'retiring'. The sun was the beginning of life, the magician of seed and flower, the last sentence. It was at times like God himself. Clare's relationship with it was an intensely personal and mystical one. It was his Maker and he its child.

5

If spring and summer provided him with plenty of subject-matter, so autumn and winter inspired him, perhaps even more so. He had once told James Hessey in 1820 that autumn was a busy time for poems 'the muses always pay their visits more frequent at that season'.[30] It was often a healing time – 'There's nothing calms the unquiet mind/Like to the soothing autumn wind'.[31]

It was the season in which the painter in him found an outlet, when 'the woods' tanned greenness beautifully burns/To russet, reds and yellows, where the eye/Revels in wild delights', when 'every leaf of bush and weed/Is tipt with autumn's pencil',[32] and where every object wears a changing hue. It anticipated the long winter weeks of writing, reading, sitting by the cottage fire, and the silence he enjoyed so much. Indeed, it is clear that Clare loved the winter as much as any time of the year, despite its hardships. He evokes every note and nuance out of its bleakness, its beauty, its solemnity and silence. In his day it was often far from being romantically 'pretty'. Before the drainage of the fens had been developed as efficiently as it is today winter flooding was common. Vast areas of the land to the east of Helpston could be under water for several weeks, isolating communities and depriving men of their work. In his journal entry of 2 December 1824, Clare had recorded that 'one of the largest floods ever known is out now' and that an old neighbour, Sam Sharp, was drowned when trying to get home from visiting his relatives at Deeping Gate.[33]

Wet or hard, winter was a lean time for most country families. Food supplies had to be eked out as the weeks went by. The gruel became thinner and the bread blacker. When Clare wrote 'Now the cutting winter's come' the word 'cutting' was loaded with meaning. A north-east wind coming in from the Wash and over the fens comes unhindered from the northern plains of Russia. It is full of ice. The local people call it a 'cutting wind' or a 'lazy wind that cuts right through you'. You hear it coming over the marshes, sharpening its edge on the brittle reed-stalks.

It strops itself on barbed-wire fences and naked thorns. It penetrates doors and window-panes. And, when it brings snow, the drifts can block roads and half bury cottages:

> What a night! The wind howls, hisses & but stops
> To howl more loud while the snow volley keeps
> Incessant batter at the window-pane[34]
>
> *
>
> The winter wind with strange & fearful gust
> Stirs the dark wood & in the lengthy night
> Howls in the chimney-top while fear's mistrust
> Listens the noise by the small glimmering light
> Of cottage hearth where warm a circle sits
> Of happy dwellers telling morts of tales[35]

And yet it was also a time of year Clare obviously enjoyed:

> To me more pleasing than a summer's morn
> Your scattered state appears – despoiled & bare,
> Stript of your clothing, naked & forlorn
> Yes, winter's havoc! Wretched as you shine,
> Dismal to others as your fate may seem
> Your fate is pleasing to this heart of mine
> Your wildest horrors I esteem[36]

At such a time he could sit by his fire and read, either to himself or to his family, and he could write for days without the fear of interruption. As with most of what we know about Clare's life, the evidence is to be found in the poetry, where so many ordinary, domestic moments were recorded:

> Tis winter & I love to read indoors
> When the moon hangs her crescent up on high
> While on the window shutters the wind roars
> And storms like furies pass remorselessly by.
> How pleasant on a feather-bed to lie
> Or, sitting by the fire, in fancy soar
> With Dante, or with Milton to regions high
> Or read fresh volumes we've not seen before
> Or o'er old Burton's *Melancholy* pore[37]

Those feelings were preserved and repeated over and over again. But the winter of his neglect, of his fading recognition, held no such comfort nor could it look forward to another spring. Part of him realized this, and part of him fought against it. As dejected as Clare was about the decline in the popularity of his poetry in London, he still believed that his poetry would one day find its place, and he continued to seek for consolation in the knowledge that he had returned to the true source of his poetry, that he had come back to be among the scenes and people from which had come the original core of his inspiration. He had changed, he had matured, he had learnt to live a more sober and resigned life in the only world that for him had any meaning or security. And, more than anything, he realized now that he could only be a true poet when he responded to that world, whether it brought fame or not. Only the poetry mattered. He believed that every moment and experience so far had been a preparation for the great work which was still to come. It was a belief he carried alone. And it was a belief still weighed down by poverty as well as neglect. If only he could have been given two or three years free of these worries, the rest of his story might have been very different.

18
The Last Years at Helpston

1

Although Clare's friends had advised him against buying up the unsold stocks of his poetry from John Taylor, he still believed it was an offer he could turn to his advantage and so he wrote to his publisher in April 1828, saying:

> Tho I have not as yet opened any prospect of success respecting my becoming a bookseller yet I still think there is some hopes of selling an odd set now & then & as you are so kind as to let me have them at that reduced rate when I do sell I shall make something worthwhile for a trifle which I thought so in my days of better dreams becomes something considerable now ... Will you be so kind as to send me the half dozen sets of my Poems as soon as you can with an extra half dozen of the Calendars & I shall take it as a great favour by your enclosing those little books as you promised me the Virgil & the Homer[1]

Having committed himself to becoming his own bookseller, he then placed an advertisement in *Drakard's Stamford News*, stating that copies of his publications could be purchased at his cottage in Helpston. Unfortunately his timing was not very good. Between his over-enthusiasm and Taylor's apathy, he had customers knocking at his door long before he had the books to sell. When the copies did arrive the impact of the advertisement had been lost and the impatience of his prospective buyers exhausted. He realized that the only thing he could do now was to hawk his wares around the neighbouring villages, becoming little better than a beggar.

To begin with he had some modest success, especially in the inns at Market Deeping where he was well known and where customers bought out of pity if not curiosity. But business in Stamford, Barnack, Glinton and Peterborough was less rewarding. Days went by without a single copy being sold. There were times when he walked more than twenty miles without taking a penny. His experience in Peterborough towards the end of the month was singularly disappointing. He had hoped that his work would sell better in the city. He had become a distinguished customer at the Angel Inn and the Red Lion, and was also looked upon as a celebrity in the Minster Precincts where he had been guest at the Bishop's Palace and had met several of the clergymen and their families. But no one was interested in buying poetry from the author. Some of the people he approached frowned on the very idea of the poet pleading with them to purchase his work and others politely closed their doors. After a long day trudging round the city streets he walked disconsolately home to Helpston, only to find that his wife was in labour and urgently needed a doctor. He dropped his bag of books on the table and hurried back to the city. By the time he returned with the doctor Patty had given birth to her third son, who was christened William Parker Clare on 4 May. The name of the mysterious, itinerant Scottish schoolmaster was perpetuated for another generation.

The Clares now had five surviving children to keep and the poet's ageing parents to support. Money was needed more than ever before. Days which would have been spent working on the land were used in vain attempts to sell his books. The summer passed without those hopes being realized and Clare became very depressed. Then, when he had almost given up, he was invited by Henry Brooke – the editor of the *Boston Gazette* – to be the guest speaker at the Mayor's annual dinner. Although he did not have much time for civic ceremonies, he agreed to go and walked the thirty-six miles to Boston, carrying a supply of books which he thought he might be able to sell in the town. This time he met with both success and adulation. The people of Boston had heard of him, wanted to buy his poetry and overwhelmed him with hospitality. On 15 October he was able to ask Taylor to 'send me 6 more sets of my Poems compleat & 6 of the Calendar as I have sold every one & not got a Vol left by me now'.[2] He was also able to tell his publisher of the reception he had enjoyed in that Lincolnshire port:

> the Mayor of the Town sent for me as soon as he heard I had come & treated me in a very hearty manner & wished me to procure him two copys of my whole poems & desired me to insert his name in every vol . . .[3] He was a very jolly companion & made me so welcome while a lady at the table talked so ladily of the Poets that I drank off my glass very often almost without knowing & he as quickly filled it but with no other intention then that of hospitality & I felt rather queer & got off almost directly after finding myself so but I was nothing like disordered yet it was wine & I was not used to the drink[4]

In fact Clare had not been used to any alcoholic drink during the year 1827–8. As he assured Taylor on 3 January 1829, 'I dont think I have drank a pint of ale together this two years in fact I can drink nothing strong now in any quantity & as to spirits I never touch & yet without them feel hearty & hale & have quite recovered from my last ailments . . . tho I dont think I am much qualified for an old man.'[5]

The temptations to indulge and fall back into his old drinking habits were certainly there at Boston. On the evening following the Mayor's banquet a group of young men took Clare off to another inn for supper, where they wanted him to make a speech especially for them. As soon as he realized this he declined their offer by assuring them that they would get little value for their money. As he told Taylor, 'this speechifying is a sore humbug & the sooner it is out of fashion the better.'[6]

Such reticence in becoming a public figure did not prevent other invitations to attend further dinner-parties and civic receptions at Hull, Grantham, Spalding and King's Lynn. But he refused to be drawn. He simply promised to sign and send the books he had been asked for as soon as he could get back to Helpston.

When he returned home he discovered that the young men of Boston had slipped £10 into his wallet and he was filled with regret that he had been so unwilling to do anything for such kindness.

With that gift, and the profits from the sale of books, Clare hoped that he would have enough money to see his family through the winter. But again, there were pressing debts to be settled and, with the approaching damp chills of the fens, all the family went down with a fen-fever which lasted for six weeks.

By 21 December 1828 he was forced to write bluntly to Taylor asking for some money 'for Christmas is nearly here & I want to get straight as near & as soon as I can'.[7] Taylor responded immediately by sending the annuity payment and an unexpected cheque from Lord Spencer.

Clare also heard from his friend Henry Behnes Burlowe who sent him 'two Bottles of the Best Blood of the Grape for Mrs Clare' and, for Clare himself, 'something in the shape of a bottle of kind Brandy, enough to make any Job modern or ancient bid defiance to – even his wife'.[8]

2

Whether Clare went back on his pledge and drank the brandy we cannot tell. Certainly his health improved quickly and during those winter months he was busy writing poems, many of which were published in such annuals as *Friendships Offering*, *The Amulet*, *The Anniversary*, *The Literary Souvenir*, *The Keepsake*, the *Book of Gems* and *Forget-Me-Not*. He did not like writing specifically for this often sentimental market but believed it to be the only way now to earn any money with his pen. One or two of the editors paid well, others forgot to pay him anything at all. The one annual which he did not mind contributing to was *The Anniversary*, edited by his friend Allan Cunningham. It also included the work of Robert Southey, James Montgomery and George Darley, and sold 6,000 copies before publication. But its success was brief and lasted for only two years. This may well have been because Cunningham was trying to pay his contributors a generous fee. Clare told him, 'I do not write as if I expected pay by the foot or page . . . you gave me too much for my last & I hope you will keep that in mind next year & not do so for I never feel the loss of independence worse then when I cannot serve a friend without knowing I receive a recompence in return for more than the labour is entitled. . . .'[9]

A new interest came in February when Clare received an invitation from George Baker to visit Northampton and collaborate with him on a history of the county he was writing. Baker died before this task was finished but his sister, Anne Elizabeth Baker, did become the author of a *Glossary of Northamptonshire Words and Phrases*, which was published in 1854, and Clare was to work with her for several years, contributing almost half the words which were eventually collected.

Such interests did not, however, solve Clare's financial problems and he thought the time had come to press Taylor again into presenting a statement of his royalties and other receipts. The accounts which his publisher produced were utterly confusing and, in a long letter of 15 November 1829, Clare suggested that there must be some mistake in some of the items:

> you must excuse my enquireys if I make them where none are necessary for my ignorance in such matters must be my innoscence of any impertinance that may appear so – as every wish in making enquiry is to be satisfied of things that I do not understand & not uttered with the intention to offend – so where I am right I feel convinced that you will allow it & where I am wrong I hope as strongly you will excuse me of any other intention then that of wishing to be right.[10]

Taylor tried to meet Clare's demands but did little to explain the complexities of the statements he had produced. The accounts were divided into five sections from A to E. Account A was a general record of the various sums paid between 1820 and 1829, showing the profits on sales and the dividends received. It was this account which claimed that Clare owed his publishers the sum of £140 – a figure he naturally disputed. Account B detailed the list of subscribers to the Fund started by Lord Radstock, and Account C covered the four editions of *Poems Descriptive of Rural Life and Scenery*. Although this volume had sold so successfully the accounts revealed, to Clare's surprise, that it made no profit at all for the poet. Taylor, Hessey and Drury had each received a share of the takings, with Taylor paying himself an extra five per cent for his work as editor. There was also that vexing question of the £20 which Drury said he had paid for the copyright of those early poems. Clare again wrote to Taylor about this matter, saying, 'I never received a farthing extra beyond the debt which he claimed of me & which you settled – the selling of the copyright was all fudge & pretence he persuaded me to agree that it ought to be so merely as he said to prevent you from hurting him in the end... it seems that instead of getting anything by the first edition I am the loser by £20....'[11] He also felt that Richard Woodhouse – Taylor's financial adviser – had been particularly hard with him on some of the charges for administrative and professional services. Account D was concerned with *The Village Minstrel*, which did show a profit of £58, half of which went to the publishers (including Drury) and half to Clare. Set against this, however, was the fee of fifteen guineas paid to William Hilton for painting Clare's portrait; an expense which was eventually accepted by Taylor. Account E told the sad story of *The Shepherd's Calendar* and showed that the poor sales-figures of 425 had failed to meet even the publication costs of £60, adding insult to injury, and leaving Clare with a depressed feeling of wasted hopes and exhausted talent.

From these accounts he also discovered that the £100 originally paid into the Subscription Fund by Taylor and Hessey had been paid back to the firm. Nothing appeared to be in his favour. Everyone else had profited from his work but financially his own efforts went unrewarded.

There were several other items which Clare had to ask Taylor about. One was the payment promised for poems printed in the *London Magazine* – 'You know I was to have twelve pounds a year while I wrote for it which was three years but if this be considered too much for the trifles inserted you may pay me by the article for I am not a bargain hunter – only pay me something.'[12]

Another query was about the £7 which James Hessey had received from a duchess who wished to help Clare. The money had never been sent to him nor was it shown in any of the accounts. These two items alone, Clare argued, meant that he was still owed £43. But Hessey had parted from Taylor and had since gone bankrupt. He could not, he claimed, be held responsible for the accounts of his ex-partner. Edward Drury also took another hard line when Clare appealed to him: 'I must now be excused for declining to take any interest in by-gone concerns which indeed afford me small reason for congratulation.'[13]

Clare looked at the figures and the excuses. They made a dismal picture of his ten years as a poet and he could not help telling Taylor that the publication of his poetry had been nothing but 'a damnable luxury'.[14] The accounts and the lack of interest in his work added up to a depressing sense of failure. The poetry had been more than a 'damnable luxury', it had also been a considerable expenditure of spirit and the cost was beginning to tell.

3

By the summer of 1830 changes were beginning to take place in Helpston which increased his feelings of sorrow and regret. His parents left their part of the cottage and went to live in another small house in the village, and Patty was again pregnant. Any hopes of independence and success were now shadows. The promises of 1820 were faint echoes somewhere beyond the fields he had praised. Nature, he felt, had turned her back on him. Plans to become a smallholder with his own piece of land had also failed. He was, as he had been ten years ago, no more than another day-labourer on someone else's farm. The struggle to rise above that humble position had been too demanding, his expectations too high. His chief solace now came from his books. He spent days reading and commenting on what he read. He returned to Shakespeare, Byron and William Cobbett, for whom he had a particular admiration:

> I look upon Cobbett as one of the most powerful prose writers of the day . . . a person may be very clever at detecting faults in composition & yet in the writing of it may be a mere cypher himself & one that can do nothing Such a one is Cobbett who has come forward & not only assailed the outworks of such a pedantic garrison but like a skilful general laid open its weakness to all [He] deserves more praise for the use of his labour than all the rest of the castle hunting grammarians put together for he plainly comes to this conclusion – that whatever is intelligible to others is grammar & whatever is commonsense is not far from correctness.[15]

Clare was equally stirred by Cobbett's exposure of the terrible conditions still being endured by the English peasantry whose homes were 'little better than pig-beds' and whose lives presented a picture of 'human wretchedness' to which he could find no equal 'not even amongst the free negroes in America'.[16]

The world beyond Helpston saw several other important events besides the publication of Cobbett's *Rural Rides*. The twenty-one-year-old Tennyson had appeared on the literary scene with his first volume, *Poems, Chiefly Lyrical*; Walter Savage Landor had published his two series of *Imaginary Conversations of Literary Men and Statesmen*; and, in the industrial world, the Manchester and Liverpool Railway was opened.

Such events concerned Clare now very little. He had returned to his own world and even that no longer had the security he once took for granted. With his growing family he needed a larger house and this meant he might be forced to leave the village of Helpston altogether.

Inevitably the worry about his future brought on some of his old illnesses, and he told Taylor in a letter of late September 1830:

> I have not been able untill now to write to you – for I have been dreadfully ill – & I can scarcely manage even now to muster courage sufficient to feel myself able to write a letter but you will excuse all – I have been bled blistered & cupped & have now a seaton[17] in my neck & tho much better I have many fears as to recovery but keep my mind as quiet as I can ... my fancys & feelings vary very often but I now feel a great numbness in my shoulder ... thank God my head is more relieved tho it stings now & then as if nettled[18]

In the same letter he told Taylor of the increase to his family of another daughter, named Sophia – after his sister Sophia who was now married and living at Newborough, three miles east of Glinton – and he also mentioned his plans for moving house: 'All I want is a cottage & a few acres of land but do you know I cannot get anything of the kind for love or money.'[19]

His 'quietness of mind' is confirmed in a letter a few weeks later to James Hessey:

> As to religion my mind is compleatly at rest in that matter my late deplorable situation proved to me that I had read the Bible successfully for it was an antidote to my deepest distresses & I had not the least doubt on my conviction of its truth ... I studied the Bible often & found it long before my illness – the one book that makes the carnallitys of life pallatable & the way to eternity pleasant – the one & only book that supplys soul & body with happiness – I also find in it the beautiful in poetry in perfection – I had read Homer but a greater than Homer is there – I found in it gems of the oldest excellence in sublimity which the great & oldest poets had borrowed to enrich their own lustre & what astonished me most was that I found beautys that I had never met with before tho I had read it over time after time when I was the happiest fellow in existance when I had no particular friends & no enemies at all – neither wanting the one or fearing the other[20]

He did have 'particular friends' at this time who were especially kind to him. The Reverend Mossop, vicar of Helpston, had become a loyal neighbour who was 'uncommonly kind' and he often sent his daughter with food and medicine to visit the Clares. Mrs Marianne Marsh also continued to be very helpful and considerate. Clare had become a frequent visitor to the Bishop's Palace during 1830 and Mrs Marsh had arranged for him to have the use of a room as a study, providing him with paper and ink, expecting in return only another poetic masterpiece. Clare did not settle down at all well to such an orderly, cold room, and would escape whenever he could to walk the streets to Peterborough. Sometimes he dined with the family and became especially friendly with one of the sons, George Marsh, who collected moths.

It was whilst he had been staying at the Palace in July that the Marsh family had taken him to see *The Merchant of Venice* at the local theatre (which stood where the General Post Office stands now) and where he displayed, perhaps for the first time in public, his emotional instability. Mrs Marsh was an enthusiastic supporter of the theatre at a time when there was a lot of feeling against it. When a troupe of actors arrived in the city to play Shakespeare she thought it would be an excellent treat for her guest. All went well for the first three acts but when Portia rose to deliver judgement, Clare became so involved in the action that he leapt from his seat in the Bishop's box and began cursing the villainous Shylock to the point of strangling him. Peterborough audiences were not used to such unscripted moments of drama and he was quickly escorted out of the theatre.

He returned home full of remorse and agitation. When the Reverend Mossop saw him the following day he was so alarmed at the poet's condition that he contacted Lord Fitzwilliam to see if immediate medical advice could be sought. Dr Skrimshire was asked to visit Clare straight-away, which led to the treatment already described in the letter to Taylor.

This outburst in Peterborough was the beginning of a long period of fear and melancholy, of violent pains in the head and stomach, of numbness in the lower parts of his body, and eruptions on the skin. Again his inner disquiet manifested itself physically and Clare believed himself to be ill beyond cure.

The news of his behaviour at the theatre soon became common knowledge, not only in the locality, but also in London. Behnes Burlowe and Mrs Emmerson both became immediately anxious about the poet's condition and wrote to him. Another person who had become a close friend was Frank Simpson, who had inherited Octavius Gilchrist's business in Stamford. He advised Clare to send an apology to Mrs Marsh without delay. Simpson's mother also wrote to him, saying, 'I have not the least doubt but that all your depression arises from a weak digestion and I recommend you very earnestly when you feel more uncomfortable than usual to take if it was even two or three times a day – or night if necessary – as much as would lay on a shilling of powdered Rhubarb and the same quantity of carbonate of soda mixed in a wine-glass of water.'[21] Well-meant, no doubt, but hardly likely to improve Clare's complicated, overwrought state.

But he did write to Mrs Marsh who, in her reply, readily forgave him for the embarrassment caused at the theatre: 'I must request you from us all that you will try to obliterate it from your Memory... I recommend you to eat a few of our grapes, which though not so sweet as in a more genial summer, are still very pleasant and I hope they will be beneficial to your health... eat them all *yourself* by degrees, and to make that the easier, I send some ginger-bread for the children.'[22]

No one could have been kinder and, for all his deprivations and troubles, Clare was extremely fortunate in having wealthy friends like Mrs Marsh to help him throughout most of his life. The social differences were, in most of his relationships, very well defined – whether with the Bishop's wife, Mrs Emmerson, Lord Radstock, or the Fitzwilliams – but they were easily overcome by a recognition of his uniqueness, both in his talent and his personality. To have been so highly favoured among the nobility and influential members of society inevitably separated Clare from his neighbours. He had always been detached from them but was more so now than ever. The thought of leaving Helpston was not such a dreadful possibility. But the thought of wrenching himself away from the scene of his happy past was one he could not yet accept.

4

Patty was, fortunately, physically strong and recovered from labour and illness very quickly to care for her husband, who recognized her qualities more than ever – 'she has been of much comfort to me both in illness & health & I always feel happy that I met with such a fortunate accident that brought us together for "an honest woman is the honour of her husband".'[23]

He was to need such a wife during the next few years and her efforts to protect him cannot be over-praised. Their love was not the idealized, romantic love of the imagination and, because she could not write, there is no written evidence of Patty's affection for Clare. But none is needed. Apart from the children she cared for Clare with a loyalty and tenderness when his behaviour deserved far less. She was a good mother, a good home-maker and a good wife. She may not have always understood her difficult husband but few would have done better.

Clare tried to share in the problems of his growing family by taking his children for walks, reading to them and being particularly concerned about their education. It was always his wish to make them 'all good common scholars' and to 'instill into all their minds the inestimable value & the upright integrity of common honesty'.[24]

Anna Maria and Eliza were already receiving an education, thanks mainly to Mrs Emmerson who paid their school fees, and now Mossop wrote to her to ask if she could help find a place for Clare's eldest son, Frederick, at Christ's Hospital. Both she and Behnes Burlowe tried but without success. Clare confessed to James Hessey that he would have found it very difficult to part with his son if he had to go away: 'The shock... will be so great that I never have had the courage to allude to it...'.[25]

Even in the asylum years which were to follow he was still to show this care over his children's education: 'I would advise you to study Mathematics, Astronomy, Languages & Botany' and 'don't forget your Latin & Greek & Hebrew... for in them you have Truth'.[26] In his confused state of those years he may have overloaded the syllabus, but he was still wise enough to tell his children, 'Learning is your only wealth'.[27]

5

Little news reached him now from London. He had been left to find out from the newspapers that William Hazlitt was dead and 'read it twice over' before he could believe it was the same man whom he had met and admired. That loss was another part of his own promising life fading away. Many of the illustrious names in whose company his own name had been mentioned, the men of genius with whom he had dined and talked, were now scattered, or dead, or forgotten. It would have been understandable if he, too, had decided to lay his pen aside and accept those memories with his own defeat. But he did not. He still continued to write, still made plans for a new volume of poems, still believed he could restore his reputation, and still believed in himself as a poet, whatever happened.

The early weeks of 1831 did not make it any easier to live with these intentions. His youngest son, William, was taken dangerously ill 'of an illness prevelant here',[28] an illness from which his sister Sophy's child had just died. With increasing anxiety his own maladies returned with severe pains in the head and stomach. In March he wrote to Taylor:

> I took a blue pill & on Monday morning I waked with a dreadful burning humour in my lisks & a contraction so as almost prevented me from making water... I awoke this morning with a burning heat in my fundament where the humour again made its appearance with prickly pains in my head arms & shoulders... I am so alarmed & so anxious to get better that if I cannot in no other way I will draw upon

> or sell out my fund money (if it can be done without extravagant loss) & take lodgings in an humble way as near Dr Darlings as I can[29]

He did not see Dr Darling again and, with the approach of summer, his health improved so much that he was prepared to take up an idea from John Taylor to compile an anthology of seventeenth-century minor poets. Taylor sent him several volumes to read but, despite his good intentions again, Clare was unable to finish the task. His comments on the poetry, however, suggest that he would have made a good editor. He liked the work of William Brown and Surrey's sonnets which he found 'tender & very poetical' but he was disappointed not to find more of 'the sublime or beautiful' and lamented the absence of Herrick or Suckling from the volumes which Taylor had sent, for he considered the lyrics of Sir John Suckling 'have never been surpassed & only equalled by Shakespeare'.[30]

He also had on loan from Taylor an edition of Chaucer which had once belonged to John Keats, and the association moved him deeply. Chaucer was among Clare's 'favourite Poems & Poets who went to nature for their images'[31] and he felt a close affinity with the early poet's love of wildflowers.

The relationship between Clare and Taylor was, nevertheless, becoming much more formal and their letters less frequent. Taylor was no longer interested in publishing any of Clare's poetry and told him he would be much wiser to think of earning a living from his old trade of working on the land. The half-yearly dividends had now fallen to £6. 17. 9d. and, although he still received the annuities from Lord Spencer and the Marquis of Exeter, it was nothing like enough to meet the demands of his family. Once again he found himself in debt and two years behind with his rent. He now needed £20 to quieten his landlord who was making it no secret in Helpston that the Clares owed money and could not be trusted. More than ever he was beginning to feel a stranger in his own village. When he did write to Taylor again in October that year, he told him of his certain plans to move home:

> I am going to leave here & commence cottage farming & therefore I shall want something to begin with & as I am rather unwilling to interfere with the fund money if I can help it I should like for you to use your interest for me & to do all you can . . . I shall have a good landlord & I am told the place is a good one & therefore it is all on my side further I shall have fewer regrets to leave this old corner where I now write this letter the place of all my hopes & ambitions[32]

The cottage he spoke of was in Northborough, a village three miles away. It was built by Lord Milton who had agreed to Clare being the first tenant at a rent of £15 a year, which included two acres of land and an orchard. Clare, who had even been consulted about its design, asked that the house stood with its back to the road with no front door, the only door being the one that led straight into his garden. In that way he hoped to escape from the unwelcome visitors whom he would be able to see from the three windows facing the street. The cottage would be thatched and have six rooms, which meant he would no longer have to use the kitchen as a study, and the children could have better sleeping space. The prospect of starting a new life in a new home quickly restored his confidence and optimism. This was the opportunity he had been waiting for, the answer which he had always believed would establish his independence and give him security. The boys would help him with the land. Patty, who had worked with pigs, sheep and cows as a girl on her father's smallholding at Walkherd, would be his 'estate manager', and he would be able to mix his life of poetry and farming to everyone's satisfaction. By the turn of the year he felt as 'happy at this moment as ever I did in my life'.[33]

But there were still problems. Even this modest small-holding needed capital to buy stock, seeds, tools and feeding-stuff. The cottage too would need more furniture than they possessed. This was where the fund money could have been used most effectively. Clare wrote to Taylor again but had no reply. Parson Mossop, who had been one of the instigators of the scheme for gaining some independence for the poet, wrote to Mrs Emmerson, who wrote to Taylor. Nothing could be done. Richard Woodhouse, who had originally drawn up the Deed of Trust, was now dying in Italy of consumption. Taylor had to wait for his return. But there was no return. Woodhouse, like Keats, died without ever seeing England again. Finally, Clare received the news from Mrs Emmerson that the fund could be used for no other purpose than to provide half-yearly payments during his lifetime. Hearing this, Clare now wondered whether he should move to Northborough after all. He began another plea to his publisher:

> all I wanted was to use my own means to sink or swim as good luck or bad luck might hereafter allow me – & to free myself from talking & writing kindnesses that hang like a millstone about my feelings – I thought one word from you would procure this[34]

This letter, like many others at that time, was not finished. The fears and uncertainties began to take over. Perhaps these difficulties were meant to prevent him from ever leaving Helpston. He now had grave doubts about tearing up his roots from those ancient fields from which he had drawn all his sustenance. In another unfinished letter to Taylor he spoke of the wrench it would be to leave 'the woods & heaths & favourite spots that have known me so long'. Every part of that country, he felt, knew he was going – 'the very molehills on the heath & the old trees in the hedges seem bidding me farewell'.[35]

Lord Milton inquired over the delay. The cottage was ready. Why didn't the man move? Patty was anxious to go as soon as possible. She had had enough of Helpston. She had left her own home for Clare twelve years ago. Home for her could now only be where there was peace and comfort for the family.

Once again Mrs Emmerson came to the rescue and raised a subscription. She and her husband gave £10 to buy a cow, which had to be called Blossom, Rose or May. Taylor contributed £5 to buy two pigs, and a further £5 was sent to help buy new tools. Mrs Emmerson, already referring to Clare as 'Farmer John', sent a bundle of clothes with a sum of money to pay the tailor for converting the garments into suits for the children. She also sent a further £10 to the Rev. Mossop to pay off all Clare's outstanding medical bills. Once again Clare knew that but for her constant generosity his life would have been so much harder.

6

The day for flitting was fixed. Clare took his last walk over the heath, on Cowper Green (now under the plough), through Hilly Wood and Royce Wood, and looked sadly upon Swordy Well and Round Oak Spring. Then he helped his family to stack their possessions on to a hand-cart. It was a warm, quiet morning in early June as the Clares moved slowly from the street, past the village cross and the church, away from the prying neighbours and the years of unreal memories. It was as if all the excitement of the little stir he had made in the world was no more than a dream. Even the happiness he had known in the fields and woods as a child seemed part of some sweet and half-forgotten sleep. He was now thirty-nine.

19
The Flitting

1

It was a good day to be moving house. The wet fields of winter would have dried out, the air would have smelt sweet with warm grass and blossom. The morning mist would have cleared, leaving the great sky of the fens brilliant above them – that 'gentle sky/Where not a cloud dares soil its heavenly light'.[1]

Early June usually shows the fen country at its best. The long low fields shimmer with the new green of crops answering the sun's call. Skylarks rise from every tuft and furrow 'winnowing the air' with such urgency as if their chains of song held the earth in orbit. Dark dyke-water suddenly glistens and comes to life with moorhens and kingfishers. Wild-flowers decorate the margins of the fields until the whole landscape becomes an illuminated manuscript.

As the Clares made their way along the field-path from Helpston to Etton and Northborough there would have been several different moods for the great sky to register. Patty was thankfully relieved to be going to a new house in another village, a house not only recently built but one far more spacious than the cramped cottage she had been forced to put up with for the past twelve years. At least she would be away from the village gossips and it would be *her* home. Maybe they would not be bothered so much now by those inquisitive strangers who still called from time to time to see her unusual husband. She had never known when someone would knock at the door wanting to meet 'the poet'. Being a poet was all very well while it lasted but it had brought more trouble than good fortune, and her husband should realize that the stir he had caused was over. Books might be very satisfying to people who could read and be sure of a good meal but there had been times when he had thought more about them than he had done about his family. He had even admitted lately that fame does little to feed your children and more often than not cheats you out of what you should rightfully own. He had made himself ill worrying about other people and success, and look where it had got him – he was back to being a farm-labourer, a worker on the land. Northborough would give them all a better chance. The change was for the best. The children would certainly be better there and perhaps their father would improve in both health and temper. There would be land to cultivate, stock to care for, an orchard to stroll in and food to eat. The new beginning could not happen quickly enough and Patty's step gained strength as she saw the manor house and the church of Northborough in the glowing distance.

Clare's enthusiasm, understandably, was unlikely to match that of his wife. It was not so much that he regretted leaving his native village and its people. His remarks about them had not always been very flattering and the place had changed so much with the arrival of new families and more houses. But he did regret leaving the past, that world in which all his joys and hopes had flourished. It was harder for him to tear himself away from those favourite scenes of his childhood. He was leaving more than a house. He was leaving the trees and bushes, the birds and flowers that knew him as much as he knew them. Nothing could ever compensate for that lost world. He was severing himself physically and spiritually from a place which had known all his secrets, dreams, triumphs and despair. Could any other landscape absorb him, listen to him, or comfort him as much as that gentle countryside around Helpston had done? He doubted it:

> There is no spot in the world that I shall like better [but] my affections now are fixd on other deeper interests & where my family are there will my home & my comfort be & they would make me a home every where & any where[2]

They were sincere sentiments. 'Home' was always to mean his wife and his children. Even when later he was thinking of Mary Joyce as his wife and of Patty as the bearer of his children, it was Northborough rather than Helpston to which he returned and he was to walk more than eighty miles to be with his family.

Even so, he must have stopped more than once on that early June morning to look back sadly at the dwindling landmarks of his old home – the church, the trees, the rooftops of a village to which the rich and the famous had once come to visit him when the future seemed to be full of promise and reward. Around him, too, were the fields and lanes where he had once walked with his childhood sweetheart, Mary Joyce. He could see now, only a mile away, the slender spire of Glinton church. Within its shadow she still lived, unmarried and within an arms's length of the new paths he would soon be walking. Was it too wrong to hope that he might see her again, meet her secretly by the lonely stile or hump-backed bridge which they had known as children? The move to Northborough reawakened in him that deep and early love until it became an obsession. It started that intense longing which both darkened and illumined his poetry for the next twenty years. From that moment his love for Mary grew so passionately in his imagination that every memory and vain hope of those earlier years became a reality – such a reality that within a very short time he began to believe that Mary was indeed his wife, that in some strange moment he had committed bigamy.

The day of his flitting was, in every sense, a momentous day, a day that was to change his life and work completely. Without Northborough there would not have been those intense love poems to Mary. Without Northborough there would not have been some of his most impressive poems, such as 'The Flitting', 'Badger', 'Decay', 'Remembrances', 'The Return', parts of 'Child Harold' and several realistic poems about the fens (quite different from the conventional nature poetry of the time), and many of his best sonnets.

Without the move to Northborough there may not have been the twenty-two and a half declining years in the lunatic asylum, or that final and tremendous effort to get the last ounce out of his creative genius. Without Northborough those early years at Helpston would have remained too much of an unfulfilled paradise, a safe dream-world in which to hide from the greater demands of a mature poet. The testing-fire was elsewhere, away from Eden.

The Northborough years, then, reveal Clare at the most crucial moment of his life, recognizing his true identity and stature as a poet, but finding it almost impossible to make his voice heard again in the world of letters where fashion had found other distractions. This silence from the other side caused him deep, gnawing anxiety. He knew that he had outgrown the role of the 'Northamptonshire Peasant Poet', that his work was now richer, more perceptive, stronger and more original than anyone was prepared to see. He was no longer in the same league as Thomson, Beattie and Bloomfield. He belonged now with Wordsworth and Byron.

But the discovery of Self has to be earned and the Northborough years sadly witnessed the man finally breaking under the constant strain of trying to give expression to his poetic vision alone. The demands had always been exacting, but he had once received encouragement and some recognition. Now, with so much to give, the doors were closed, the applause was inaudible. Greater faith than ever was needed to continue the increasing task of shaping the words indelibly on the page. But, already, his mind 'is dark & fathomless & wears/The hues of hopeless agony & hell. . . .'[3]

2

Had Clare been given the choice he might have preferred a cottage in Castor, Southorpe, Ashton, Barnack, or even Stamford – all places with which he had some connection and still on the western side of the limestone ridge dividing the uplands from the fens. But Northborough, as a place, was not unknown to him. Situated as it is between Glinton and Market Deeping he must have walked its lanes and paths since boyhood. Whether it was ever as beautiful as Frederick Martin's description is debatable – 'The noble earl had fixed upon Northborough as the residence of the poet on account of the thoroughly sylvan scenery all around, the little hamlet lying in a very sea of flowers, trees and evergreens. The spot indeed was beautiful enough. . . .'[4]

Perhaps, but it is unlikely that a fenland village in the nineteenth century could have lived up to such a claim. Even by Helpston standards Northborough was, in 1832, a small, unimportant place next to nowhere. It had a population of 230 against Helpston's 450, and it lacked the heaths and woodlands that Clare normally needed for his own solitude and comfort. It was also those few extra miles further away from the Great North Road which led to London. It increased his sense of isolation. What life and work he found there had to be of his own making.

The darker, brooding, lonelier landscape of those next few years was to be a fitting scene for his darker poems. It was to affect the tone and colour of his language. It was to provide the images that would mirror his own bleak moods. The soil was different. The air was different. The sun appeared in a different quarter of the sky. It was a world which, deprived of limestone, could not grow many of his favourite wild-flowers, especially the orchis he loved to study. There were fewer trees and fewer birds. The hedges were, he tells us, 'a deader green', the sun was like 'a homeless ranger'. Even the clouds and water lost their poetry, their deceptive innocence. Where once he had been able to sit by a stream 'thinking if I tumbled in/I should fall direct to heaven',[5] now he found

> The stream it is a naked stream
> Where we on Sundays used to ramble
> The sky hangs oer a broken dream
> The bramble dwindles to a bramble[6]

Northborough may have been only three miles away but it may as well have been thirty or three hundred:

> I walk adown the narrow lane
> The nightingale is singing now

But like to me she seems at loss
For Royce Wood and its shielding bough[7]

His time at Northborough has to be seen as the important link between the two greater halves of his life, responsible for what Alan Porter called 'the third Clare'.[8] From those five years we can look back to the extraordinary happenings in Helpston, and also forward to the tragic loneliness of the Northampton Lunatic Asylum. Home, childhood, innocence and love were already gone. The desperate longing for them was only just beginning. They were to haunt his mind for the rest of his life. He had been both blessed and cursed by the gift of poetry. His sadness was, in the end, the paradise glimpsed but cruelly lost:

Fame blazed upon me like a comet's glare
Fame waved and left me like a fallen star[9]

The strangeness of his new home gave him, to begin with, much time for reflection and within days of arriving he was at work on his poem 'The Flitting':

Ive left my own old home of homes
Green fields and every pleasant place
The summer like a stranger comes
I pause and hardly know her face
I miss the hazels happy green
The blue bells quiet hanging blooms
Where envy's sneer was never seen
Where staring malice never comes[10]

Already he had forgotten the many harsh things he had said about the people of Helpston where he had known plenty of envy and staring malice. But it is not only the cottage, or the village, that he mourns:

I miss the heath its yellow furze
Molehills and rabbit tracks that lead
Through beesom ling and teazel burrs
That spread a wilderness indeed

. . .

I sit me in my corner chair
That seems to feel itself from home
I hear bird music here and there
From awthorn hedge and orchard come
I hear but all is strange and new[11]

For more than two hundred lines Clare laments the world he has lost and clings desperately to those things he has managed to salvage – his memories, his books, his love for all of nature's simple pleasures, such as the daisies, birds' nests, and 'a love for every simple weed'.

He completed 'The Flitting' on 20 June 1832. It was to appear three years later in his last published collection *The Rural Muse* – a volume which was a travesty of his intentions. For several years he had been planning to publish another collection of poems at his own expense under the title *The Midsummer Cushion* and had publicly announced this in *The Athenaeum* during August 1832. He had also drafted his introduction and an explanation of the book's title:

> It is a very old custom among villagers in summer time to stick a piece of greensward full of field flowers & place it as an ornament in their cottages which ornaments are called Midsummer Cushions And as these trifles are field flowers of humble pretentions & of various hues I thought the above cottage custom gave me an oppertunity to select a title that was not inapplicable to the contents of the Volume[12]

But, again, many unforeseen troubles and delays prevented the publication of that volume. By the time that half of those poems were printed in 1835 another act of literary vandalism had taken place. Clare's original and imaginative title had been thrown out and the sentimental choice of Mrs Emmerson had been substituted. It must have been that lady who also changed the title of 'The Flitting' because when that poem appeared in *The Rural Muse* it was called 'On Leaving the Cottage of my Birth' – a most unClare-like title. Certainly on each of the manuscript versions of the poem it is called 'The Flitting', so either Mrs Emmerson did not like the word or did not understand its meaning.

By the time the volume was ready for the press Clare had become weary and ill over the worries it had caused him. The writing of the poetry was exhausting enough but the effort needed to get even some of it into the world was demanding to the point of destruction.

The manuscripts of 'The Flitting' in Peterborough Museum are interesting for another reason. One of them has some small sketches in the margin – one is of a group of people pushing a cart, presumably the Clare family on its way to Northborough, and another is the head and shoulders of a fair-haired young woman on a pedestal. Could it be anyone but Mary Joyce – or at least Clare's conscious longing for her, as he wrote his poem within a mile of where she still lived?

3

Any hopes of settling down quietly in Northborough, away from the affairs of the world and the pursuit of fame, were soon dispelled by a sequence of important events. The most upsetting trouble came from rumours appearing in the press. The August issue of *The Athenaeum* had published the story that the cottage at Northborough had been *given* to Clare by Lord Milton. The same story also appeared in the Stamford paper, *The Bee*. A worried and irate Clare wrote to the Reverend Mossop for advice:

> I wish to ask your advice respecting a paragraph copied from the Athenaeum into most of the local papers pretending to know of a matter of which I know nothing, viz. that Lord Milton has given me the cottage to live in &c &c. Not that I should take any notice of the folly of such gossip further than it troubles me and injures my feelings of a propinquity of independence for I came into the cottage with no such feelings or expectations . . . I expected to pay rent the same way as my neighbours . . . What is to be done should it be contradicted or should it be taken no notice of – I am very unwell & it troubles me[13]

He was advised to write to the editors of the papers refuting their stories. To the editor of *The Athenaeum* he began a letter, which he did not finish:

> Would you do me the favour to give my disapproval of these mistatements that are going the rounds of the papers in the shape of inflated pictures of my affairs – surely I have the same common right to come before the public as any other man & all I wish of the public is to judge of my productions as they please but I think no man can have the right to meddle with my affairs & make my poverty a peg to hand up his own prejudice & dictations as though he were a counsellor pleading a cause . . . I am poor but my independence is not at so low an ebb as these antipathies testify[14]

Clare's immediate anxiety was that Lord Milton would believe that he was responsible for the story, suggesting indirectly that the cottage should indeed have been a gift, but his efforts to put right one misunderstanding led to others even more harmful. In an attempt to contradict the reports of his new comforts and good fortune some of Clare's friends – including Allan Cunningham – went to the other extreme, stating that the poet's poverty was the result of being cheated out of profits he should have received from his published volumes. Because of this injustice he was now expected to keep himself and a large family on an income of £15 a year. His publishers and patrons had forsaken him and, while they prospered, he had been left to starve. Whilst it was true that some people had made money out of Clare, such ill-considered remarks were not likely to help him now. Clare was very angry over this further distortion of the truth and knew he would be seen as the ungrateful upstart his enemies often thought him. Nor did he want this unfavourable publicity at a time when he was appealing to the public to subscribe to his new volume of poems which he was soon to put before them. He wanted more than anything that these new poems should have a chance and be judged for what they were – the best he had yet produced. Again he had to remind the meddlers, 'I am not seeking charity but independence.'[15]

But the damage was done and John Taylor for one was so incensed when he read the articles that he threatened legal action against all concerned. Clare was beside himself with agitation and fear. It took months for the storm to die down and interrupted an important period of his creative work. To make matters worse, the Northborough small-holding was far from flourishing, mainly because of the shortage of cash. Clare had told Taylor only two months before that he still had 'neither cow nor pigs nor anything else' and was now 'worse off than before I entered on the place'.[16] Once again he found himself in debt and too ill to work at anything. The bleak winter landscape of the fens did little to console or inspire. The days were very different now from those early summer days when he had first arrived. The empty grey silence left him longing for the world he had known:

Ah could I see a spinney nigh
A puddock riding in the sky
Above the oaks with easy sail
On stilly wing and forked tail
Or meet a heath of furze in flower
I might enjoy a quiet hour
Sit down at rest and walk at ease
And find a many things to please
But here my fancys mood admire
The naked levels till they tire
Nor een a molehill cushion meet
To rest on when I want a seat[17]

It was a familiar picture of a land that had still not been efficiently cultivated and which surrendered easily to the fogs and frosts, the floods and blizzards of winter. Clare no longer went for walks but sat brooding in his corner, his hopes and determination almost exhausted. In a letter to H.F. Cary he had written, 'I sit sometimes and wonder over the little noise I have made in the world until I think I have written nothing as yet to deserve any praise at all.'[18] Even so, he still hoped he would do something better before he died and so 'in spite of myself I rhyme on'. But even that flickering ambition began to fade and his nights were again disturbed by vivid dreams of failure and neglect.

Dreams were always an important factor in Clare's self-analysis and they were frequently to become the subjects of his poems. Some, like 'The

Dream' and 'The Nightmare', have an apocalyptic imagination as their strength, dreams in which he sees his own judgement-day, where faces 'with wings of dragons and fangs of flame' writhed in 'agonies of wild despair':

> And days misspent with friends and fellow man
> And sins committed – all were with me then[19]

On 13 October 1832 he had dreamt that a 'Guardian Spirit in the shape of a soul stirring beauty' again appeared to him with 'the very same countenance in which she appeared many years ago . . . I cannot doubt her existence'.[20] In the dream he found himself in a strange place among a host of people who paid him much kindness and attention. But he was terribly depressed until this guardian spirit – 'a young woman with dark & rather disordered hair & eyes that spoke more beauty than earth inherits' – came up to him and, in a 'witching voice', whispered sentences which he could not remember on waking. But of this he was sure, she had previously appeared to him on several occasions. The first dream in which she came to him was in those early years before he had even written a line of poetry:

> I thought she suddenly came to my old house led me out in a hurried manner – into the field called Maple Hill & there placed me on the top where I could see an immense crowd all around me in the north west quarter of the field towards Hilly Wood and Swordy Well[21]

There he saw soldiers on horseback moving in 'evolutions of exercise' and crowds of people of various description 'as at a great fair' but the finest lady out of them all was the beautiful girl at his side:

> I felt shamed into insignificance at the sight & seemed to ask her from my thoughts why I had been so suddenly brought into such immense company when my only life & care was being alone & to myself – you are only one of the crowd now she said & hurried me back & the scene turned to a city where she led me to what appeared to be a booksellers shop where I reluctantly followed her she said something to the owner of the place who stood behind a counter when he smiled & at his back on a shelf among a vast crowd of books were three vols lettered with my own name – I see them now I was very astonished & turning to look in her face I was awake in a moment but the impression never left me I see her still she is my good genius & I believe in her ideally almost as fresh as reality[22]

He had written of this guardian presence in another notebook where he said:

I feel a beautiful providence ever about me as my attendant deity she casts her mantle about me when I am in trouble to shield me from it She attends me like a nurse when I am in sickness puts her gentle hand under my head to lift it out of pains way . . . she places herself in the shadow that I may enjoy to my service the sunshine & when my faith is sinking into despondency she opens her mind as a teacher to show me truth & give me wisdom[23]

The two poems which came out of those experiences are full of 'troubled seas', 'dread immensities', 'wild confusions', 'memory's shadows', and the frailty of hope. 'Millions of hopes hung on a spider's tie/'Tween time's suspense and fate's eternity.'[24] These poems are also full of that 'beautiful providence' ever about him. There are times when one feels an unconscious search in this dream figure for his twin sister who died at birth – 'The strongest fled and left the weak to die . . . But recollections of her earthly name/Were lost, if e'er she had a claim to one.'[25] Soon the identity of the figure moves towards Mary Joyce 'with flowing robes, blue eyes, and face divine'. Later, in 'The Nightmare', he names 'That lovely shadow which had been my guide':

'Twas Mary's voice that hung in her farewell,
The sound that moment on my memory fell –
A sound that held the music of the past,
But she was blest and I alone was cast . . .

Sometimes the dreams do not even come out of the memories of the past but appear to project themselves into the events that are yet to be – 'A feeble picture of the dread to come'. In a note to the poems he affirms that they were about 'actual dreams' though he also wished to 'acknowledge that whatsoever merits [they] may be thought to possess they owe it in part to the *English Opium Eater* as they were written after the perusal of that singular and interesting production'.[26] De Quincey's *Confessions of an English Opium Eater* had first appeared in the October and November issues of the *London Magazine* in 1821, and were published in book form in 1822 and 1823. Clare read his contemporaries diligently and found De Quincey's work particularly fascinating.

Clare did not forget his dreams and he greatly needed his guardian spirit to come to his aid during that miserable winter of 1832–3. In one of his prose fragments he recalled the particular dream he had written about in his poem 'The Nightmare', where he went with his fellow villagers to witness their day of judgement:

I instantly followed with the rest feeling great depressions & rather uneasiness of mind The crowd went on to the church-yard & then into the church as soon as I entered the gates I heard a loud humming as

> of the undertones of an organ & felt so affraid that before I got opposite to the school door I shrunk back & felt a wish to return to my reccolections of home & at that moment something of a delightful impulse took me by the arm & led me forward – I see the yellow gravestones which I stood opposite when she came to my side just at the school door – I looked sideways for hope & fear – she was in white garments beautifully disordered but sorrowful in her countenance yet I instantly knew her face again – when we got into the church a light streamed in one corner of the chancel & from that light appeared to come the final decisions of man's actions in life I felt awfully afraid tho not terrified & in a moment my name was called from the north-west corner of the chancel when my conductress smiled in exstacy & uttered something as prophetic of happiness I knew all was right & she led me again into the open air when I imperceivably awoke to the sound of soft music[27]

These dreams of 'a beautiful presence of a woman deity' were again experienced at Northborough (as they were to be several times during his years in the asylum) and, despite all his hardships and disappointments, Clare believed that some power was still looking after him. His trust in that power gave him strength. It was something much more positive than resignation, passivity or fatalism. He had been entrusted with a gift and his 'guardian genius' alone promised him that one day he would be happy and free. The trials of a mere mortal would be easy to bear for that share of immortality which he believed he would eventually inherit. It was another aspect of Clare's innocent, almost primitive and unshakable belief in a divine selection, as old as the Greek gods themselves and as binding. He had to go on writing in order to survive, even into madness. His role as husband, father, lover, man, ended during the Northborough years and soon after the death of Mary Joyce. Another Clare takes over. He is already a traveller beyond place and time.

4

Whatever faith he had in immortality his mortal problems were by no means getting less. During the first week of January 1833, Patty gave birth to their last child, another son, who was christened Charles. The event filled Clare with remorse. He went out, says Frederick Martin, and 'wept bitterly'.[28] When he did not return in time for his evening meal Anna Maria, his eldest daughter, now thirteen, went out to look for him. She found him lying semi-conscious on the embankment between Northborough and Etton. 'He looked deadly pale and, being quite insensible, had to be carried home on the shoulders of some labourers... and for nearly a month he was unable to leave his bed.'[29] The parish doctor was called, assumed that Clare only had a touch of ague, and prescribed some medicine which the patient stubbornly refused to take.

When the spring arrived with its warmer weather and the poet's strength slowly began to return he would not, to the surprise of his family, go from the house. Occasionally he would stroll into his garden but within minutes would be back in his favourite chimney-corner where he spent hours reading, mainly works of a theological nature. Any writing at this time was his attempts to put into verse certain passages of scripture, especially from the Book of Job, Proverbs, and the Psalms. He briefly lost interest in his own poetry and in the preparation of *The Midsummer Cushion*, and he refused to see any visitors. He withdrew even deeper into his 'land of shadows', speaking as little as possible to his wife and family. His children, whom he had once happily taken on his walks, were now puzzled that their father did not want to go out with them or hear them reading from the books he had bought for them. Patty was at her wits' end trying to cope with the smallholding, with the family and her new baby. A detached, silent, unhelpful husband was the last trial and she frequently lost her temper.

Beyond this bleak and depressing world a few of Clare's friends were still trying to keep his name alive. Some new poems appeared in the literary magazines such as the *New Monthly* and the *Literary Magnet*, and several were printed in anthologies such as *The Pious Minstrel*, *Living Poets of Great Britain* (which was published in Paris) and the *Naturalist's Poetical Companion*. His proposals for publishing *The Midsummer Cushion* had been in circulation since the summer of 1832 and had already brought in over two hundred subscriptions. On the face of it there still appeared to be good reason to hope that his true reputation as a poet would be established before long. But when the Peterborough printer, who had agreed to publish the volume, said he wanted a hundred pounds for the steel engravings Clare had to have second thoughts. He did not have that amount of money to spend on anything, certainly not on publishing his poetry. For a time it looked as if his last efforts were to be thwarted even worse than before. Then, after several months of enquiries, a relative of the Peterborough printer, a man by the name of J. How, agreed to take over the publication. How worked for the London firm of Whitakers (better known for its publication of the *Almanack*) and he accepted the responsibility for getting the poems copied and printed. Once again Mrs Emmerson and her husband became active on Clare's behalf and offered to edit and arrange the poems for the press. They even managed to persuade John Taylor to proof-read the selection for them. They then advised Clare to sell the copyright of his new volume for an immediate sum rather than to wait months for uncertain royalties. In this way he would have money in hand with which to pay some of his debts, which now stood at £35. Reluctantly, Clare agreed, and the copyright was sold to Whitakers for the sum of £40. His hopes of seeing *The Midsummer Cushion* published in its entirety and under that title, however, were soon shattered. He discovered that less than half of the poems he had submitted were to be included and most of those had been selected by Mrs Emmerson, who had her own individualistic, romantic and unsound taste in his poetry. All the best poems were excluded and his own, original title was discarded to make way for the more prosaic, unimaginative and trite title given by Mrs Emmerson, *The Rural Muse*. It is ironic that the lady who had helped him so much should fail to appreciate his true quality and, in the end, spoil his chances of any resurgence.

5

When *The Rural Muse* was published in July 1835 it met with favourable reviews in the *Athenaeum*, the *Literary Gazette* and especially in *Blackwood's Edinburgh Magazine*, whose critic, Professor John Wilson, in a long and detailed appraisal expressed his pleasure in finding that Clare's 'fine sensibilities have suffered no abatement' and that the new volume was 'worth ten times over what you will have to give for it'.[30] The *New Monthly Magazine* also said that the reader would be 'pleased to observe a far superior finish and a much greater command over the resources of language and metre' in the longer poems but thought less highly of the sonnets.[31] The *Druid Monthly*, noting that 'the poetry of John Clare is entirely distinguishable from all others', urged its readers to buy: ' "*The Rural Muse*" is worthy of many editions. Oblige yourselves by taking copies of it; shew that you have the true respect and admiration of Genius . . .'[32]

This was the reviewer who had visited Clare at Northborough three years earlier and he recalled the occasion:

> Clare's cottage at Northborough is large and commodious; it is situated in a nice flower-garden with an orchard attached to it, the view given in the frontispiece to *The Rural Muse* is correct. We found Clare and his 'Patty' surrounded by their family . . . The first glance at Clare would convince you that he was no common man; he has a forehead of a highly intellectual character; the reflective faculties being exceedingly well-developed; but the most striking feature is his eye, light-blue and flashing with the fire of genius . . . He walked with us round his garden and orchard. Rubbing the perfume from the blackcurrant

leaves ... he pointed out to us a spot in the hedge of his orchard where a nightingale had built her nest, which some rude hand had removed, and he expressed his sorrow at the spoilation, and his indignation at the offender, in no measured terms. There is in Clare a simplicity of heart and manner which endears him to you with the first knowledge of him ... his manner and his conversation are most enchanting and delightful. We look upon the few hours we spent at his cottage at Northborough as among the happiest of our life[33]

The reviewer had gone with the editor of the Stamford paper, *The Bee*, to visit Clare, and his account of that meeting at least shows there were calmer and brighter days for the poet at his Northborough home. One moment of that day is recalled by Clare in his poem 'Home Happiness':

I walk round the orchard on sweet summer eves
And rub the perfume from the blackcurrant leaves
Which, like the geranium, when touched leave a smell
That lad's-love & sweetbrier can hardly excel

His sense of smell was, like his sense of sound and sight, highly developed. We find it illustrated again in his sonnet, 'Beans In Blossom', where 'luscious comes the scent of blossomed bean/As oer the path in rich disorder lean/Its stalks....' The word *luscious* is one which he can hardly leave alone when wanting to convey an almost sensual pleasure in nature. He uses it many times, even when writing of 'the luscious sky'. Smells especially brought back moments of other days and gave him a feeling of continuity with those pleasant places he had lost.

The Rural Muse, despite its mutilations, contains those qualities which distinguished Clare from all others. Nevertheless, the loyalty and praise of the reviewers had little impact. Apart from the initial subscribers the volume sold very slowly on the open market and, a year later, had fallen far short of exhausting the first edition. The degree to which the poet's popularity had declined was confirmed by Spencer T. Hall, who was to say in his essay on Clare and Bloomfield (in 1866) that in 1849 he could have bought any number of uncut copies of *The Rural Muse* at a bookseller's shop in Stamford for one-and-sixpence.

Clare's disappointment at the book's failure to re-establish his reputation in the literary world was extreme. He had warm letters of appreciation from some of his old friends – James Montgomery, Edward Rippingille, Alaric Watts and Captain Sherwill. John Taylor also praised the work as a major achievement. But Clare realized that it had not achieved what he most wanted – confirmation of his place in the world of poetry along with those whose positions were already assured.

Although the new publication did not, and could not, become another sensational event in his life, a few visitors did start arriving at his cottage again, some wanting to meet the poet and get his signature on their copies of the book, others – just like the ones who had turned up at Helpston – curious, idle name-droppers more interested in the poet's family and circumstances than his genius. Clare could see them from his window, approaching along Church Street, and would quickly slip out of the only door on the other side of the house to hide in the orchard, leaving Patty to answer the questions, make the excuses, give explanations and occasionally sell a copy of his poems.

But he was walking away from more than just a few inquisitive visitors. He behaved at times as if he wished to disown all that he had produced – the poems, the brief success, his family and the many hopes. All that mattered now were the unwritten poems and the image of Mary Joyce, just a mile away in the village of Glinton. The guardian spirit of his dreams still beckoned and, like a sleep-walker, he was powerless to resist.

20

Removal to High Beach[1]

1

The summer of 1835 was very hot and, to get away from the house, Clare regained his old habit of going for long walks. Frequently he would stay away from home all day, contemplating the two ambitious works he was then wanting to write – 'Child Harold' and 'Don Juan' – not direct imitations of Byron's two poems but often influenced by them.

The mastery which Clare had achieved by this time shows that he was now technically capable of such sustained writing, but whether his mind was strong enough to control that power was already in doubt. The delays in getting his poems published at the right time, the failure of most people to recognize the importance of encouraging his poetic growth, meant that his own major efforts came too late. The energy needed for such a creative task had been debilitated by the day-to-day anxieties over survival.

But he never gave up hope and, for a time, it looked as if it might just be possible for him to recover. He was able to enjoy that summer without too many fears over money. He had received his half-yearly payment from John Taylor; the £40 had arrived from Whitakers for the copyright of *The Rural Muse* and, through How (who had by this time left the firm), an application had been made to the independent Literary Fund for financial assistance. The committee agreed that Clare should be given £50. All his debts were paid, the orchard and land at Northborough were responding to the long summer's warmth, and his Muse was once again filling his brain with new poems. All appeared to be well and could have been even better had it not been for Clare's state of mind. Beneath this surface of well-being and comfort, the dark fears of failure and the deepening distress about his health still continued. In August 1835 he wrote to Taylor:

> I am scarcely able to do anything I feel anxious to get up to London & think I should get better how would you advise me to come I dare not come up by myself do you think one of my children would do to come with me write me as soon as you can . . . Thank God my wife & family are all well[2]

Two months later he was writing a long, detailed letter to Dr Darling asking him for advice and treatment:

> I am very unwell & though I cannot describe my feelings well I will tell you as well as I can – sounds affect me very much & things evil as well as good thoughts are continually rising in my mind I cannot sleep for I am asleep as it were with my eyes open & feel chills come over me & a great sort of night mare awake . . . I cannot keep my mind right as it were for I wish to read & cannot – there is a sort of numbing through my private parts which I cannot describe & when I was so indisposed last winter I felt as if I had inflamation in the blood & at times as if it went round me & at other times such a sinking as if I was going to sink through my bed[3]

He went on to plead with his physician to help him in some way before he grew worse. But he was not invited to London again. John Taylor had other guests and could not accommodate Clare. Mrs Emmerson, herself now unwell, was going to rest for a few months in 'a sweet enchanting country retreat' near Bath. And Dr Darling could only suggest that his patient would find all the help he needed from a careful reading of the twenty-third, twenty-fourth and thirty-sixth Psalms.

Struggling as he was with the responsibility of his few rented acres, Clare might have found it difficult to take comfort from 'Put thou thy trust in the Lord and be doing good: dwell in the land and verily thou shalt be fed . . .', or, 'I have been young and now am old; and yet saw I never the righteous forsaken, nor his seed begging for bread. . . . Hope thou in the Lord and keep his way and he shall promote thee, that thou shalt possess the land.'[4] Clare had hoped patiently for a long time and, despite his renewed search for a deeper understanding of God's ways, he could no longer believe that the meek would inherit the earth. Even John Taylor, in proof-reading *The Rural Muse*, had written to correct his theology by changing the phrase 'Death's long happy sleep' to 'Heaven's eternal Peace!' believing it better to have 'bad Divinity' rather than 'good Atheism'.[5] Taylor's only other piece of consolation that year had been of others' misfortunes and that, by comparison, Clare was lucky: 'Poor Charles Lamb is dead – perhaps you had not heard it before – He fell down and cut his face against the gravel on the Turnpike Road, which brought on erisypelas, and in a few days carried him off . . .'[6]

With London taking so little interest in him now, Clare turned for help to the Peterborough physician, Dr Smith, who was taking a growing interest in the poet's work. He had encouraged people to subscribe to *The Rural Muse* and would sometimes listen to Clare reading aloud a new poem which had just been written. On one of these occasions the doctor found his patient in a much happier mood and when asked why, Clare told him to hear some recent verses which he had composed to his first love Mary Joyce. Clare said he had seen her only the day before, passing his window. (Frederick Martin claimed that this could not have happened as Mary was already dead, but he was wrong. Mary did not die until July 1838 – three years later – and it is more than likely that Clare saw her in Northborough as well as Glinton. Certainly the verses he read to Dr Smith that day sound newly-inspired. They have an immediacy and passion about them that allow something of his excitement and memories to shine through, even in their sadness.) The doctor listened as the poet's soft, rich voice brought back his hopes:

First love will with the heart remain
When all its hopes are bye
As frail rose blossoms still retain
Their fragrance till they die
And joys first dreams will haunt the mind
With shades from whence they sprung
As summer leaves the stems behind
On which springs blossoms hung

Mary I dare not call thee dear
Ive lost that right so long
Yet once again I vex thine ear
With memorys idle song
Had time & change not blotted out
The love of former days
Thou wert the last that I should doubt
Of pleasing with my praise

When honied tokens from each tongue
Told with what truth we loved
How rapturous to thy lips I clung
Whilst nought but smiles reproved
But now methinks if one kind word
Were whispered in thine ear
Thoudst startle like an untamed bird
And blush with wilder fear

I felt a pride to name thy name
But now that pride hath flown
My words een seem to blush for shame
That own I love thee on
I felt I then thy heart did share
Nor urged a binding vow
But much I doubt if thou couldst spare
One word of kindness now

And what is now my name to thee
Though once nought seemed so dear
Perhaps a jest in hours of glee
To please some idle ear
And yet like counterfeits with me
Impressions linger on
Though all the gilded finery
That passed for Truth is gone[7]

Such deep and tender feelings for her could not have been expressed in poetry like that when he most wanted to impress her; the nearness which joined them and the distance which separated them produced a new poignancy. A later poem, 'With Garments Flowing', also confirms that he saw Mary again, that he had deliberately gone to look for her on one of their favourite walks of years ago:

I guessed thy face without the knowing
Was beautiful as e'er was seen
I thought so by thy garments flowing
And gait as airy as a queen
Thy shape thy size could not deceive me
Beauty seemed hid in every limb
And then thy face when seen believe me
Made every former fancy dim

. . .

Thy face that held no sort of scorning
Thy careless jump to reach the may
That bush – I saw it many a morning
And hoped to meet thee many a day
Till winter came & stripped the bushes
The thistle withered on the moors
Hopes sighed like winds along the rushes –
I could not meet thee out of doors
But winters gone & spring is going
And by thy own fireside Ive been

And told thee dear with garments flowing
I met thee when the spring was green
. . .

And on that long-remembered morning
When first I lost this heart of mine
Fame all I'd hoped for turned to scorning
And love & hope live wholly thine
I told thee & with rapture glowing
I heard thee more than once declare
That down the lane with garments flowing
Thou with the spring wouldst wander there[8]

Many of the songs and ballads that were to find their way into 'Child Harold' came from those desperate attempts at Northborough to make himself Mary's lover again. He had lost her once through his own naiveté and weakness for a woman's attention. He had been impatient and clumsy. It was only now that he discovered just how deeply he really loved her – she who had been far more faithful. Now to her gentle beauty was added purity. She was above women – spiritual and physical.

The half-mile lane (which is now North Fen Road) that separated the bottom of Clare's garden from Glinton must have been walked a thousand times as he went in search of her along a path 'Where the speed-well knots grew & the Kingcups were shining like flame':

She sees the wild flower in the dells
That in my rambles shine
The sky that oer her homestead dwells
Looks sunny over mine

The cloud that passes where she dwells
In less than half an hour
Darkens around these orchard dells
Or melts a sudden shower

The wind that leaves the sunny south
And fans the orchard tree
Might steal the kisses from her mouth
And waft her voice to me[9]

The small stone bridge, arched modestly over the narrow stream, could well have been their trysting place and was certainly a spot from where Clare would have looked longingly towards the needle spire of Glinton Church and Mary's village. Not much has changed since then. The water in the dyke still reflects the sky. In summer it mirrors the 'tender watching sky' and its green banks are decorated with wildflowers. In winter it returns a cold look to the sky and the sleeping grass buries its memories. But whatever the season, it is not difficult to feel Clare walking there, heavy of heart and longing for other days. Just as the move to Northborough brought him many deeper experiences and so realized the summit of his intellectual powers, so too did it intensify within his crumbling world of reality the memory of his love for Mary Joyce until that obsession became the only thing that mattered. Unreality became reality. Northborough had brought them closer together than ever before. It had reawakened within him all that was pure and innocent in their childhood affection, and he believed that they could return to that state of grace offered to them as children. Now, more than twenty years later, she was more beautiful. Her shape, her size, her every limb, her smile, her hair, the colour of her eyes and the sound of her voice, all came back with an unbearable weight of regret that they had not been allowed to share their very special lives together.

But how much did that regret, and Clare's sense of failure, distort the truth? How much thought had he given to her during those twenty years when he had made love to other women and had been happy with his wife, Patty? Had the hours of debauchery been only his self-debasing protests against the fates who had deprived him of someone like Mary? Was this late love for her born out of the illness, or the illness born out of the love? Whichever, from that day when he saw her again from his window, she became the sole purpose for living – she *was* his poetry. He would pursue her to the farthest horizon and through the longest nights until his passion was spent. Eden, enclosure, nature, all took second place and were used only to express her virtues and her loss. She became not only his guardian spirit and White Goddess, she became also his wife. Paradise was almost regained – if only Mary had been real and there to meet him.

The despair, guilt, confusion and longing aggravated his anxiety to days of violence or total withdrawal. Winter cut him off from Mary's world completely:

> I can't expect to meet thee now
> The winter floods begin
> The wind sighs through the naked bough
> Sad as my heart within
>
> . . .
>
> Though winter's scenes are dull & drear
> A colder lot I prove
> No home had I through all the year
> But Marys honest love[10]

2

By the winter of 1835–6 Clare felt doubly rejected and neglected by London and Northborough. His mental state, according to Frederick Martin, 'became alarming. His ordinarily quiet behaviour gave way at times to fits of excitement, during which he would talk in a violent manner to those around him.'[11]

To worsen matters his mother died on 18 December 1835, at the age of seventy-eight, and was buried in Helpston churchyard. Clare was deeply upset. The finer qualities of her country nature had always impressed him and he had received her encouragement long before the world had ever heard his name. She had walked miles on poetry's errands and had protected him as much as possible from the harsh realities surrounding his childhood. She had planned and worked so hard to give him a better life and, even when he had decided to go his own way, she had supported him. That he had, in the end, been able to do so little for her, saddened him greatly and his Christmas was made miserable by her loss.

Parker Clare, now totally crippled and in need of care, left Helpston and went to live with his son at Northborough, thereby adding another burden to the already overworked Patty. Whether Parker ever considered spending any of his time with his daughter it is hard to say. It is most unlikely as Sophy now had her own family at Newborough, a fenland village three miles further east, and such distance created its own problems. It is also more likely that Parker would have preferred to be with the Clare grandchildren, and the cottage at Northborough could still find room for him. As it was he stayed long enough to see his son committed to the Northampton General Lunatic Asylum in December 1841. Parker died three years later in 1846 at the age of eighty-two and his body was taken back to Helpston to lie alongside his wife, Ann.

3

A year after the death of Clare's mother, John Taylor chose to stay in Stamford for the night on his way back from Retford to London. Although it was a bitterly cold December he made up his mind the following morning to ride over to Northborough and visit Clare. Having heard of the poet's poor health and increasingly strange behaviour he also thought it wise to take a local doctor with him. They found Clare sitting in his favourite chimney corner and thought he looked just as usual. He talked sensibly in reply to Taylor's questions and still seemed to know all the people they spoke about. He smiled too when his former publisher reminded him of those earlier days and the happier events in London. But, after a while, Taylor realized that Clare was not listening and could see that the poet's mind was already 'sadly enfeebled'. He recalled also that Clare was constantly talking to himself and that some phrases were 'pronounced a great many times over with great rapidity – "God bless them all", "Keep them from evil", "Doctors!" – but who it was of whom he spoke,' commented Taylor, 'I could not tell – whether his children, or doctors, or everybody... I think the latter.'[12]

Taylor would have been more accurate to say the children, for Clare had constant anxieties over them and was continually concerned about their future. Earlier letters have proved this and those letters still to be written from the asylum were to confirm that the most lasting and lucid thread of thought was for his family.

Taylor remembered the children who were 'seven in number... a very fine family, strongly resembling [their father]: the youngest, a boy of three or four years old; the eldest, a girl, sixteen. There are 3 boys and four girls' and, said Taylor, their mother was a 'very clever, active woman who keeps them all very respectable and comfortable, but she cannot manage to control her husband at times; he is very violent I dare say occasionally.'[13]

The doctor's opinion was that Clare should go to an asylum. After their visit he and Taylor went to see the Reverend Mossop to ask if an approach to the Earl Fitzwilliam could be made to help them find a suitable place where Clare could be looked after. Lunatic asylums were still generally appalling places for anyone to spend the rest of their lives and Clare's friends hoped that they might be able to find a private home where he could receive specialized medical care. He needed a refuge and a rest from the world which had left him bereft.

Clare would not have agreed with them. His only refuge was still in the poetry that came almost daily to his troubled mind. During these years he continued to create his vivid sequence of rural portraits which retain their freshness and authenticity one hundred and fifty years or so later. No one would be surprised to see these characters in the village today – the local gossip 'who hastens out and scarcely pin her clothes/To hear the news and tell the news she knows'[14]; the braggart who teases the girls and, when rebuffed, 'nettles deep his pomp and pride... Bumptious and vain and proud he shoulders up/And would be something if he knew but how'.[15] The local soldier returns from his campaigns 'full of battles and renown' but grateful to find the old place he knew as a boy is still the same. The packman breaks his journey and spends a night in the village. The mole-catcher and the plough-boy go out and come back from the daily tasks. The school-boy 'with slate and bag at back and full of books' saunters off to school[16] – perhaps one of Clare's own sons. The gipsies arrive and set up their usual camp. Daybreak comes over the flats of the unwooded fen. The village street slowly comes to life between the winding river and 'the open church tower and its little bells'.[17] The Morris dancers arrive to entertain the villagers in the evening and the tramp starts looking for a 'hovel at the close of day' in which to sleep and the poet returns home to his chimney corner to immortalize their little lives. Days pass. Seasons change, and not a moment is missed or left unrecorded. When the mist creeps in over the fens 'the shepherds almost wonder where they dwell ... the ploughman goes unseen behind his plough/And seems to lose his horses half the day' and then the mist closes in upon them so completely that 'the place we occupy seems all the world'.[18]

When Clare wrote about one of his own walks he did so with a quiet conversational ease that speaks for any walker afraid of trespassing:

> I dreaded walking where there was no path
> And prest with cautious tread the meadow swath
> And always turned to look with wary eye
> And always feared the farmer coming by
> Yet everything about where I had gone
> Appeared so beautiful I ventured on
> And when I gained the road where all are free
> I fancied every stranger frowned at me
> And every kinder look appeared to say
> 'You've been on trespass in your walk today.'
> I've often thought the day appeared so fine
> How beautiful if such a place were mine –
> But having naught I ever feel alone
> And cannot use anothers as my own[19]

Again, that poem has the weaknesses (which he never conquered) of carelessly repeating words in the same poem without adding to their strength – in this case he uses *appeared* three times in six lines – but there is something so magical and honest about it that such weaknesses can be overlooked. The control, confidence and poetic certainty to speak as he feels are beyond doubt. It anticipates the style of Robert Frost and breaks so freely from the stale rigidity of most nineteenth-century nature poetry.

As we have already seen, the tone of Clare's poetry changed with the change of landscape; the artist's eye in him mixed more sombre colours. The greater depths of space around Northborough helped his growth towards identity and maturity. In response to this uncompromising world he became even more of a realist than a romantic. His imagery was always original and ahead of his time. Now it gained a sharper edge. Had his health lasted he could have used that landscape to even greater effect.

But, at the time when he was more aware than ever of what he *could* do, he lacked the energy to concentrate. After years of pouring out too many poems to please others he was nearing creative exhaustion. He could no longer meet the challenge of his surroundings or ideas. More and more he took comfort in the memories of childhood and that dream-world of which Mary Joyce was the most important being. He would, however, walk that lane to her village but a few more times. 1837 was the last real year of freedom he was to know in his own country.

4

The new age which 1837 brought in with the coronation of Queen Victoria did not bother Clare now. Wars, empires, reputations, fame – what did they all mean? He had written about them once. Now the only world that mattered was the world within:

Summers pleasures they are gone like to visions every one
And the cloudy days of autumn and of winter cometh on
I tried to call them back but unbidden they are gone
Far away from heart and eye and for ever far away
Dear heart and can it be that such raptures meet decay
I thought them all eternal when by Langley Bush I lay
I thought them joys eternal when I used to shout and play
On its banks at clink and bandy chock and taw and ducking stone
Where silence sitteth now on the wild heath as her own
Like the ruin of the past all alone

When I used to lye and sing by Eastwells boiling spring
When I used to tie the willow bough together for a swing
And fish with crooked pins and thread and never catch a thing
With heart just like a feather – now as heavy as a stone
When beneath old lea close oak I the bottom branches broke
To make our harvest cart like so many working folk
And then to cut a straw at the brook to have a soak
O I never dreamed of parting or that trouble had a sting
Or that pleasures like a flock of birds would ever take to wing
Leaving nothing but a little naked spring

. . .

O I never thought that joys would run away from boys
Or that boys should change their minds and forsake midsummer joys
But alack I never dreamed that the world had other toys
To petrify first feelings like the fable into stone
Till I found the pleasure past and a winter come at last

Then the fields were sudden bare and the sky got overcast
And boyhoods pleasing haunts like a blossom in the blast
Was shrivelled to a withered weed and trampled down and done
Till vanished was the morning spring and set the summer sun
And winter fought her battle strife and won ...[20]

To accept the loss of that childhood, the loss of Mary Joyce and the opportunity of happiness with her, to accept the loss of recognition and the elusive status of poet, were all too much. The struggle for acceptance, his ill-health, poverty and overwork had all slowly contributed to the breakdown which had decided his few friends to seek immediate medical advice on his behalf.

A few months later, in June 1837, a stranger arrived at the cottage with a message from John Taylor. Clare was to prepare himself for a journey: 'The bearer will bring you up to town and take care of you on the way ... the medical aid provided near this place will cure you effectually....'[21]

Patty pleaded for more time, believing that she could still nurse her husband back to good health. But it was too late. The arrangements had all been made. Clare was to leave the following morning. With a glorious fenland summer at its height he was taken from Northborough to Dr Matthew Allen's private asylum at High Beach, on the south-western boundary of Epping Forest. The dream was broken.

But, even in this terrible separation from his family and countryside, Clare's guardian angel had not completely forsaken him. Of all the asylums to which he could have been taken he was fortunate to have been put under the care of Dr Allen – a strange but much enlightened man in the treatment of mental illnesses, at a time when severe and often cruel discipline was considered necessary to tame patients who were labelled lunatics.

Matthew Allen was a pioneer in the more humane treatment of those people suffering from some disturbance of the mind and he had clear views on how they might be cured. Before opening his own private asylum at High Beach in 1825 he had worked with Dr Lang at York Asylum for five years where he was commended by the governors for his 'constant and successful efforts in establishing and perfecting the mild system of treatment there'. His superior, Dr Lang, had already introduced some mild forms of treatment in 1814 when most other asylums still believed in restraining their inmates by blood-lettings, ice-cold baths, chains and frequent beatings. Asylums were even more effective than workhouses at dehumanizing people. A wrong choice would have destroyed Clare completely. As it was, he was sent to a man who practised the revolutionary ideas of allowing his patients freedom within the grounds, the chance to work and play, with plenty of fresh air and good food. Patients should also be encouraged to take part in healthy amusements, in occupation for mind and body, and persuasion must always take priority over physical punishment. Successful treatment would come in the gradual trust and confidence the patient gained in the person trying to help. The deeper this relationship developed, the better chance there would be of a return to self-control and self-respect. Patients should be encouraged to graduate, like students, through degrees of instruction until they were ready to live as a member of the doctor's family and, if successful, eventually return to their own homes. By the time Clare became a patient Dr Allen had already published *Cases of Insanity* (1831) and *Essay on the Classification of the Insane* (1837). He was also running three houses in High Beach as his hospital – Fairmead House (where Allen and his family lived), Leppits Hill Lodge, and Springfield. There was a double thorn-hedge walk between Fairmead House and Leppits Hill Lodge which enabled the patients to have both privacy and security as they passed from one to the other. There was another house nearby called Fairmead Cottage and this too had a short double thorn-hedge linking it to Fairmead House. Although there is no reference to this in the previous accounts of Clare's years at High Beach, it is more than likely that Dr Allen also used this cottage for some of his special patients, or – as he preferred to call them – residents. From this cottage could be seen the small private chapel to which Clare referred in 'Child Harold':

> Here is the chappel yard enclosed with pales
> & oak trees nearly top its little bell
> Here is the little bridge with guiding rail
> That leads me on to many a pleasant dell

and again:

> How beautiful this hill of fern swells on
> So beautiful the chappel peeps between
> The hornbeams – with its simple bell – Alone
> I wander here hid in a palace green

It was a scene that was to remind him so often of the walks he had taken with Mary Joyce by the stream near Glinton.

It is clear that Clare became one of Allen's special residents and would have been accommodated for some of the time in the secluded cottage rather than in one of the larger houses. At Fairmead Cottage he would have been nearer to his favourite walks which were to inspire many of the cantos of 'Child Harold' and later lyrics. Evidence of his stay in the cottage comes too from his descriptions of the lake with its water-lilies. The only lake in Dr Allen's houses was in the garden at Fairmead Cottage. The only other lake in the village was in the grounds of the house where the Tennysons lived and it is unlikely that Clare would have seen that. Behind the cottage was a large field and a path leading to the Owl, the public-house used by Clare on a number of occasions and where he was on sufficiently good terms with the landlord's wife, Mrs King, to lend her some of his books, including his copy of Byron's works.

The whole area around the houses used by Dr Allen would have appealed to Clare's sense of the grandeur in nature, with its vast hornbeam forest, its tall beeches, its oaks, elms, birches and chestnuts. In a short letter to his wife on 23 November 1837, he wrote, 'the place here is beautiful & I meet with great kindness the country is the finest I have seen....'[22]

But the beauties of nature were not enough to ease or satisfy Clare's mind. In a letter he was to draft to Mary Joyce in 1841 (three years after her death in Glinton) he said, 'nature to me seems dead & her very pulse seems frozen to an icicle in the summer sun.'[23]

In such surroundings, however, Clare's few friends – and especially Dr Allen – believed he could be nursed back to a complete recovery. Writing of the poet's admission to his asylum, Allen said,

> He was then exceedingly miserable, every instant bemoaning his poverty, and his mind did not appear so much lost and deranged as suspended in its movements by the oppressive and permanent state of anxiety, and fear, and vexation, produced by the excitement of excessive flattery at one time, and neglect at another, his extreme poverty and over-exertion of body and mind, and no wonder that his feeble bodily frame, with his wonderful active powers of mind, was overcome.[24]

Allen went on to say that if a small pension could be obtained for Clare, to give him security, he would recover quickly and remain well for the rest of his life. Relieved of all material anxieties, and disciplined in the use of his energies, Clare could have returned to his family within a fairly short time. He was, then, no raving madman at this stage, or ever. Had he still been young enough, and had there still been a war, he might have enlisted into the army for a couple of years (as he had tried to do several times earlier in his life), letting someone else solve his problems and sublimating his anxieties in other, more active fears. Considering he had spent years complaining of the symptoms which Dr Allen now diagnosed, it was unfortunate that his publishers, patrons and friends could not have found someone like Matthew Allen sooner. But, having found him, they were at least prepared to pay for the poet's treatment at High

Beach. John Taylor had suddenly taken charge again and started appealing to Clare's friends for support. Clare's removal to the asylum, however, had been so swiftly and secretly organized by Taylor that few of his friends knew where the poet was. Mrs Emmerson had heard that Clare had been taken away but she believed that it was to York Asylum. Early in 1838 she wrote to Patty asking that one of the children should write and tell her exactly what had happened. She received a reply from Clare's eldest son, Frederick, and in April wrote back to Patty, saying, 'It is a great comfort to hear that your dear Husband enjoys a more tranquil state of mind – and, that his general health is so much improved by the change of air and kind treatment of Dr Allen . . . I have recently paid "five pounds" into the care of Mr Taylor, as my portion of the "subscription" which is to pay Dr Allen's charge for the medical and kind care of our dear Clare.'[25]

With that last gesture of concern and practical help Mrs Emmerson disappears from Clare's history, and with her disappeared the hundreds of letters he wrote to her during their seventeen-year relationship. Without them it is impossible to know exactly what Clare's feelings for her were, but he was at least able to say of her that she 'was one of the best friends I ever had'.[26] She died, without further correspondence or mention, in 1847.

The removal to High Beach separated Clare from nearly all that was past. The next twenty-five years were to introduce new acquaintances, new places and interests, but nothing could restore what had been or bring back that which was lost.

21
Land of Shadows

1

After an initial period of depression and sadness at being taken so suddenly from his home, Clare appears to have responded to the treatment he then received at High Beach. By December 1839 Dr Allen was able to report that his patient was in good spirits, 'stout and rosy in appearance' and never troublesome.[1] He still believed that if Clare could be relieved of his anxieties he could return to a normal life. With this in mind he decided that a new appeal for funds should be made and went so far as to express the hope that £500 could be raised for Clare and his family.

A similar attempt had been made by a few friends two years before but it met with little success. Allan Cunningham had written of the poet's needs in an article published in *The Anniversary* (1837), and S.C. Hall had printed his account in the 1838 edition of *The Book of Gems*, when he referred to Clare as 'short, thick, but not ungraceful ... plain, but agreeable ... a manner so dreamy as to have appeared sullen ... and his forehead so broad and high as to have bordered on deformity'. But, he recalled, 'Clare had a peculiarly winning smile' which transformed him.[2] Hall's melodramatic plea for someone to help Clare out of his poverty may well have antagonized some readers when he said, 'It is not yet too late for a hand to reach him: a very envied celebrity may be obtained by some wealthy and good Samaritan....' Would Clare have been embarrassed by the nature of this perpetual begging, or was he now beyond caring? Had the proud independent spirit of the earlier years now completely surrendered to the reliance on other people to help him out of each financial crisis? Was it now charity at any price? Clare's attitudes on this matter were often confused. There were times when he felt it the duty of those with wealth to rescue him from his poverty. And there were occasions when he appeared to be something of a sponger who did not mind where the money came from as long as some of it came to him. He expected people to give when he needed. He frequently sought favours and could be cynical about the favours he received, as shown in his attitude to Mrs Emmerson. But the countryman's pride in him was always wounded when his begging was made so public.

The only notable person to reply to S.C. Hall's appeal was the Marquis of Northampton, who felt that he had some responsibility towards 'the county poet', though he had to confess that he was not 'one of his exceeding admirers and should by no means be disposed to place him in the same rank with Hogg or even with Bloomfield and Crockford. Still, he is a great credit to our county, and it would, I think, be a great disgrace to it if Clare was left in that state in which you mention him to be. . . .'[3] The Marquis suggested another publication by subscription and said that Clare should ask the Queen if she would allow him to dedicate his next book to her 'as that would be a considerable advantage'.

Clare was in no fit state to think about royal dedications or patronage. After the terribly disappointing sales of *The Rural Muse* he was not even worried about writing for an audience any more. He had tried to please the public before but it had repaid him with polite coolness, if not indifference. Freed of those false allegiances and expectations, he was to write some of his most successful work during the next few years.

But, as if neglect had not done enough to extinguish the name of John Clare from publishers' lists and booksellers' windows, an announcement appeared in 1840 that he was dead. The news was first given in the *Halifax Express* in May, claiming that the poet had died in York Asylum. It was then reprinted in *The Times* on 17 June 1840. Dr Allen wrote immediately to the London paper to correct the story. His contradiction of the facts, with his own account of his patient's health, was printed in the paper on 23 June:

> He is at present in excellent health and looks very well, and is in mind, though full of many strange delusions, in a much more comfortable and happy state than he was when he first came . . . the moment he gets pen or pencil in hand he begins to write most beautiful poetic effusions. Yet he has never been able to maintain in conversation, nor even in writing prose, the appearance of sanity for two minutes or two lines together, and yet there is no indication of insanity in any of his poetry . . .

So Clare lived, though not as happily as Dr Allen might have suggested. He had indeed entered a 'land of shadows'[4] and only the poetry appeared unchanged and undying. For most of the time it still came to him as lucid and as fresh as it had always done, and some of his finest lyrics were to be written during the next four years. But there were signs of his deteriorating condition. The darkness was encroaching and the mental turbulence can be felt in the strange and angry poem he was then trying to write – 'Don Juan':

> My Mind Is dark And Fathomless And Wears
> The Hues Of Hopeless Agony And Hell
> No Plummet Ever Sounds The Souls Affairs
> There Death Eternal Never Sounds The Knell
> There Love Imprisoned Sighs The Long Farewell
> And Still May Sigh In Thoughts No Heart Hath Penned
> Alone In Loneliness Where Sorrows Dwell
> And Hopeless Hope Hopes On And Meets No End
> Wastes Without Springs And Homes Without A Friend[5]

2

Dr Allen's suggestion that a new appeal should be made on Clare's behalf was taken up by Cyrus Redding, the editor of the *New Monthly Magazine* and founder-editor of the *English Journal*. He became very interested in Clare and was to visit him on three occasions during the poet's stay at High Beach and later in Northampton. Redding announced the new appeal in the *English Journal* on 15 May 1841, repeating it in the issue for 29 May. His plea did not go unheeded. The Queen Dowager gave £50; Lord Fitzwilliam again made a contribution and the Marquis of Northampton promised £5 a year. Several smaller donations were received but the total fell far short of the £500 which Matthew Allen wanted. Allen was not a particularly unscrupulous man but he often had ideas for using other people's money and made no secret of the fact that most of the donations he received would go towards the cost of keeping Clare at his asylum.

But no amount of money could save Clare now. His needs could not be met by anything that charity or pity could provide. Help always came too late. His dream was beyond mending. The sickness had been there longer than anyone realized. It was a poverty of the heart now and he was sick for home and Mary Joyce. The cantos of 'Child Harold' written at High Beach show how intense this loneliness and longing were:

> In this cold world without a home
> Disconsolate I go
> The summer looks as cold to me
> As winters frost and snow
> Though winters scenes are dull and drear
> A colder lot I prove

No home had I through all the year
But Marys honest love

. . .

My love was ne'er so blest as when
It mingled with her own
Told often to be told agen
And every feeling known
But now loves hopes are all bereft
A lonely man I roam
And abscent Mary long hath left
My heart without a home

The whole of 'Child Harold' encompasses Clare's two worlds – the past and the present; his home and what he now saw as his prison; the landscape around Northborough and Glinton, and the unfamiliar scenery around High Beach. It is clear to follow the two main themes of this most autobiographical of poems from the places of their inspiration. From Glinton we have:

Heres where Mary loved to be
And here are flowers she planted
Here are books she loved to see
And here the kiss she granted

Here on the wall with smiling brow
Her picture used to cheer me
Both walls and rooms are naked now
No Marys nigh to hear me

The church spire still attracts my eye
And leaves me broken-hearted
Though grief hath worn their channels dry
I sigh o'er days departed

And from High Beach we have:

Mary is abscent – but the forest queen
Nature is with me – morning noon and gloaming
I write my poems in these paths unseen
And when among these brakes and beeches roaming
I sigh for truth and home and love and woman

Back in Northborough he was able to feel closer to Mary even though she was lost forever:

I love thee nature in my inmost heart
Go where I will thy truth seems from above

Go where I will thy landscape forms a part
Of heaven – e'en these fens where wood nor grove
Are seen – their very nakedness I love
For one dwells nigh that secret hopes prefer
Above the race of women ...
.... I bear
Life's burthen happily – these fenny dells
Seem Eden in this Sabbath rest from care
My heart with love's first early memory swells
To hear the music of those village bells

For in that hamlet lives my rising sun
Whose beams hath cheered me all my lorn life long

But, away from the security and familiarity of his native landscape and the scenes he shared with Mary, Clare was, as always, lost and confused:

I have had many loves – and seek no more
These solitudes my last delight shall be
The leaf hid forest and the lonely shore
Seem to my mind like beings that are free

. . .

Wrecked of all hopes save one to be alone
Where solitude becomes my wedded mate
Sweet Forest with rich beauties overgrown
Where solitude is queen and reigns in state
Hid in green trees I hear the clapping gate
And voices calling to the rambling cows

And then, slowly, the two worlds became one, a new world that no one could share. Just as he had walked toward the horizon as a child to find what existed at the world's end, so now he looked out again beyond the boundaries of Dr Allen's gardens, beyond the forest's edge and the distant hills towards that world where he felt he alone belonged. One day, perhaps, when no one was looking, he would go. He would make the long journey towards that discovery. In the meantime he had to content himself with hoeing the garden, planting flowers and meeting people who wanted to see for themselves what he was like, to see if he matched up to Matthew Allen's description of him when he said he was 'improved and improving – in appearance wonderfully – stout and rosy' even to the extent of saying that Clare's lot now was 'all life and fun'.[6] It was hardly that, and Clare was never less than homesick and often silent for days with pining for his family.

3

Dr Allen tried to make sure that most of the visitors were sympathetic and not likely to over-excite his patient. Among them was Cyrus Redding, who wrote: 'I found Clare in a field cutting up thistles, a small man and slender rather than stout. He was pleased to see me. We entered at once upon the subject of poetry. He was in his conversation as simple as in his verse. He had nothing of the clown about him but his dress. He leaned upon the tool he was using, and spoke of Byron and his poetry in perfect good taste.'[7]

Two years later, Redding was to comment on the physical change he found in Clare.

> We were surprised to see how much the poet was changed in personal appearance, having gained flesh and being no longer, as he was, formerly, attenuated and pale of complexion. We found a little man of muscular frame and firmly set, his complexion fresh and forehead high, a nose somewhat aquiline and long full chin. The expression of his countenance was more pleasing but somewhat less intellectual than that in the engraved portrait prefixed to his works in the edition of *The Village Minstrel* published in 1821 ... He made some remarks illustrative of the difference between the aspect of the country at High Beach and that in the fens from whence he had come – alluded to Northborough and Peterborough – and spoke of the loneliness away from his wife, expressing a great desire to go home, and to have the society of women.[8]

It was not only his wife Patty he wished to have but also Mary Joyce and, by this time, Clare was not even sure to which one he was married. In one of his notebooks he wrote:

> God Almighty bless Mary Joyce Clare and her
> family now and forever – Amen
>
> God Almighty bless Martha Turner Clare and
> her family now and forever – Amen

He was also writing long letters to them both, as his wife, and it worried him deeply that he had been allowed to commit bigamy, that he was already married to Mary Joyce when he had to marry Patty; that Patty came into his life solely to bear his children when he was not really free to wed her:

> They took me from my wife and to save trouble
> I wed again and made the error double[9]

And yet there were times when he could also see them both as equals:

> Mary and Martha once my daily guests
> And still as mine both needed loved and blest[10]

Whatever confusion he may have had over who was his wife, he did know that he had children and his wish to be with his family is clearly shown in his letter to Patty, dated 17 March 1841:

> My Dear Patty
>
> It Makes Me More Than Happy To Hear That You & My Dear Family Are All Well – And You Will Be As Well Pleased To Hear That I Have Been So Long In Good Health & Spirits As To Have Forgotten That I Ever Was Any Otherwise – My Situation Here Has Been Ever From The Beginning More Than Irksome But I Shake Hands With Misfortune & Wear Through The Storm – The Spring Smiles & So Shall I – But Not While I Am Here – I Am Very Happy To Hear My Dear Boy Mention His 'Brothers & Sisters' So Kindly As I Feel Assured That They Love One Another As They Ever Have Done – It Was My Lot To Seem As Living Without Friends Untill I Met With You & Though We Are Now Parted My Affection Is Unaltered – & We Shall Meet Again I Would Sooner Wear The Trouble's Of Life Away Single Handed Than Share Them With Others – As Soon As I Get Relieved On Duty Here I Shall Be In Northamptonshire – Though Essex Is A Very Pleasant County – Yet To Me 'There Is No Place Like Home' – As My Children Are All Well – To Keep Them So Be Sure & Keep Them In Good Company & Then They Will Be Not Only Well But Happy – For What Reason They Keep Me Here I Cannot Tell For I Have Been No Otherwise Than Well A Couple Of Year's At The Least & Never Was Very Ill Only Harrassed By Perpetual Bother – & It Would Seem By Keeping Me Here One Year After Another That I Was Destined For The Same Fate Agen & I Would Sooner Be Packed On A Slave Ship For Africa Than Belong To The Destiny Of Mock Friends & Real Enemies – Honest Men & Modest Women Are My Friends
>
> Give My Best Love To My Dear Children & Kiss the Little Ones For Me Good Bye & God Be With You All For Ever. . . . I Hope The Time Is Not Long Ere I Shall See You All By Your Own Fireside Though Every Day In Abscence Seem's To Me Longer Than Year's
>
> I Am My Dear Wife Your Affectionate Husband
>
> JOHN CLARE

This eccentric use of capitals became a feature of Clare's writing at that time, both in his letters and in the poems, and seemed to operate in accordance with his changing moods. At about the same time he was drafting a letter to Mary Joyce (who had died in 1838) where his writing was normal:

> My Dear Wife Mary
> I might have said my first wife first love & first everything but I shall never forget my second wife & second love for I loved her once as dearly as yourself & almost do so now so I determined to keep you both for ever – & when I write to you I am writing to her at the same time & in the same letter God bless you both for ever & both your families also I still keep writing though you do not write to me for if a man has a wife & I have two – but I tell it in a couplet with variations as my poetry has been the world's Hornbook for many years –
> *For if a husband will not let us know*
> *That he's alive – he's dead – or maybe so*
> No one knows how sick I am of this confinement possessing two wives that ought to be my own & cannot see either one or the other If I was in prison for felony I could not be served worse than I am Wives ought to be allowed to see their husbands...
> My dear Mary take all the good wishes from me as heart can feel for your own husband & kiss all your dear family for their abscent father & Pattys childern also & tell Patty that her husband is the same man as he was when she married him 20 years ago in heart & good intentions God bless you both... the love I have for you my dear Mary was never altered by time but was always increased by abscence
> I am my dear Mary
> Your affectionate husband
> JOHN CLARE

As well as his confusion over his wife, Clare was becoming equally confused about himself. His admiration for Byron led him increasingly to identify with that poet and his work. Clare was, at this time, still engaged on his long poem 'Child Harold' and also trying to shape 'Don Juan' into a similar work, but with less success.

Amongst his manuscripts of that period were draft advertisements in which he announced his intentions to publish:

> A New Vol of Poems by Lord Byron
> Not Yet Collected in his Works
> Containing: Songs New Cantos of Child Harold
> And Scripture Paraphrases additional Hebrew Melodies
> Letters etc Fragments etc.,[11]

The words 'Scripture Paraphrases' and 'Letters' were later crossed out.

Another draft advertisement spoke of 'The Sale of Old Wigs and Sundries – A Poem by Lord Byron' to be 'Speedily Published' and his linking of Byron with prize-fighting can be seen in his entry:

Boxer Byron
made of Iron, alias
Boxiron
At Springfield.[12]

His close identification with Byron was but one of the many illusions experienced by Clare during the High Beach years, and later at Northampton. He also saw himself as Shakespeare, Lord Nelson, Robert Burns and Jack Randall the boxer. He had always shown an interest in boxing – a love he inherited from his father, who was a well-known wrestler, and also from his visits to London when he went to the ringside at Five Courts with Edward Rippingille. In the notebooks from High Beach we find:

Jack Randalls Challenge To All The World
Jack Randall The Champion Of The Prize Ring Begs Leave
To Inform The Sporting World That He Is Ready To Meet
Any Customer In The Ring Or On The Stage To Fight For
The Sum of £500 or £1000 Aside A Fair Stand Up Fight
Half Minute Time Win Or Loose He Is Not
Particular As To Weight Colour Or Country All
He Wishes Is To Meet With a Customer Who Has
Pluck Enough To Come Up To Scratch[13]

His identity with Nelson was to intrigue J.F. Nisbet a few years later when writing of Clare's year in the County Lunatic Asylum. Nisbet recalled in his study *The Insanity of Genius* (1891) that the poet 'seemed to assimilate everything that he read or heard, picturing events so vividly in his mind that he related them afterwards as if he had seen or taken part in them... and he was accustomed to tell most graphically his pretended experiences of the battle of the Nile and the death of Nelson.'[14] Earlier, Clare himself had written, 'John Clare/Fell On the Deck of the Belerophon/Where his brains were knocked out/With a Crowbar by the Crew.'[15]

4

Although Clare had visitors to see him at High Beach, there was one visitor to Dr Allen's asylum who poses something of a mystery – a strange coincidence of which neither Clare nor the other poet from Lincolnshire seemed to be aware – or, if they did, made no mention of it. Living less than a quarter of a mile away at Beech Hill House, overlooking Fern

Hill, was the twenty-eight-year-old Alfred Tennyson, who had recently moved down to Essex with his family from the Somersby parsonage. He was still unmarried and still slowly establishing his own reputation as a poet. He had already published *Poems Chiefly Lyrical* in 1830; had been part of a revolutionary expedition to Spain; had come down from Cambridge without obtaining a degree; had fallen in love with Emily Sellwood – who was *eventually* to become his wife; he had been on tour to the Rhineland with his dear friend Arthur Hallam; and was already at work on 'In Memoriam' following Hallam's death in 1833.

Tennyson was in very different circumstances, and his poetry was to make him an extremely wealthy, influential man who would win the praise and patronage of Queen Victoria. In many ways no writer could be more different from Clare – and yet they have their similarities. Tennyson also responded to his native landscape, to that Lincolnshire countryside of wolds and sand-flats which influenced his sense of sound, colour, space, and even speech cadences:

> Stretched wide and wild the waste enormous marsh
> Where from the frequent bridge
> Like emblems of infinity
> The trenched waters run from sky to sky[16]

Tennyson came to know the Allens very well. He sought the doctor's advice on the depressions and fears of breakdown he was then suffering, and later dined with the family on several occasions. He was, wrote James Spedding, 'delighted with mad people whom he reports most agreeable and the most reasonable persons he had met with'.[17] But did he, among all those mad people, meet John Clare? It seems highly probable that Matthew Allen would have introduced the two poets at some time and yet there is no record of their meeting even though the younger poet left High Beach before Clare.

Tennyson's association with Allen was, in the end, to have disastrous results for both men. In 1841 Allen persuaded him to invest £3,000 of his family's money in a scheme for machine wood-carving. Unfortunately for everyone, the enterprise failed and Allen was declared bankrupt in 1843. The loss to Tennyson was doubly great as it coincided with the breaking-off of his engagement to Emily Sellwood. Her father now saw no prospect for his daughter in marrying an impecunious poet. Tennyson became disillusioned and bitter, and afterwards was to write of Allen:

> He is fled – I wish him dead –
> He that wrought my ruin –
> O the flattery and the craft
> Which were my undoing[18]

But Tennyson was not to remain penniless for long. After the publication of 'In Memoriam' (and, in 1845, a Civil List pension of £200), he was allowed to marry Emily Sellwood in 1850. Within a short time he was both famous and rich. He even managed to reap some benefit from a life insurance policy which Allen had taken out as a security against the failure of his investment.

Allen did not fare as well. Misfortune and calumny hastened his end and he died in 1845, a bankrupt and defeated man. After his death, his wife tried to run the asylum with the help of a Dr Foster, but it was not a success. One by one the houses were closed, and Fairmead was demolished in 1860.

5

The four years at High Beach have to be seen as the last desperate effort to keep alive Clare's creative spirit. There were to be odd moments of astonishing creativity during the later asylum years but 1837–41 were the years of culmination as far as his conscious mind was concerned. The two long poems from this period – 'Child Harold' and 'Don Juan' – demonstrate the disintegrating ability of the poet to control his creative energy. In them he reached previously untouched heights of beauty and also sank to a coarser despair. The wealth of truly haunting and memorable stanzas to be found in 'Child Harold' places Clare as an equal with any lyricist in the English language. The whole poem is one of the most remarkable achievements of Clare's life. It is like Beethoven crying out from his deafness, or Van Gogh conveying the fatal intensity of his vision on to canvas. It is the last exalted and ecstatic surrender to the purpose of one's life. In 'Child Harold' the ink is never dry. This is not Clare the miniaturist, or the nature-poet, or the peasant-poet. This is Clare the complete poet, touching greatness before the collapse of his powers. His reading of Wordsworth, Blake and Shakespeare echoes through the lines:

> Dull must that being live who sees unmoved
> The scenes and objects that his childhood knew
>
> . . .
>
> Where is the orphan child without a friend
> That knows no fathers care or mothers love ...
> Growing to cares & sorrow manifold
> Bud of the waste a lamb without a fold

and 'The sailor rocking on the giddy mast ...'.

But what shines out from this poem, from the man who complained that while in a madhouse 'stagnant grows my too refined clay', are those love lyrics which only Clare could have written:

> No single hour can stand for nought
> No moment hand can move
> But calendars an aching thought
> Of my first lonely love
>
> Where silence doth the loudest call
> My secrets to betray
> As moonlight holds the night in thrall
> As suns reveal the day
>
> I hide it in the silent shades
> Till silence finds a tongue
> I make its grave where time invades
> Till Time becomes a song
>
> I bid my foolish heart be still
> But hopes will not be chid
> My heart will beat – & burn – & chill
> First love will not be hid

The dramatic change which was to divide his personality between 'Child Harold' and 'Don Juan' is already evident in the former:

> My life hath been one love – no blot it out
> My life hath been one chain of contradictions
> Madhouses Prisons Wh–reshops . . .

but the final savagery and coarseness of the other poem still come as a shock:

> 'Poets are born' – and so are whores – the trade is
> Grown Universal . . . .
> I wish young married dames were not so frisky
> Nor hide the ring to make believe they're single
> I wish small beer was half as good as whiskey
> And married dames with buggers would not mingle

After an attack on Prince Albert he then turns his attention to the Queen, to Wellington and Melbourne:

> These batch of toadstools on this rotten tree
> Shall be the cabinet of any queen
> Though not such coblers as her servants be
> They're of God's making – that is plainly seen
> Nor red nor green nor orange – they are free

To thrive and flourish as the Whigs have been
But come tomorrow – like the Whigs forgotten
You'll find them withered stinking dead and rotten

Clare was never a good satirist. He lacked the subtlety and elegance to give his lines an edge. 'Don Juan' is a crude piece of writing and not typical of him. It does, however, show that he still took an interest in the nation's affairs, still read the newspapers and could still get angry over what he saw as wrongs and injustices.

Just how much of these two poems was written at High Beach or Northborough it is difficult to say. As Robinson and Summerfield explained in their introduction to *The Later Poems of John Clare* (1964):

> Clare intermingled all sorts of material on the pages. The poems of *Child Harold* and *Don Juan*, closely related in subject matter, are woven in with each other on the pages, together with a long series of scripture paraphrases, notes, letters, and the journal of his escape from High Beach... What we have before us in Clare's manuscripts is a mass of material conditioned by a dominant mood or emotion, further complicated by Clare's need to use every scrap of paper in the book...[19]

One thing is clear from all Clare's writing during these four years and that is his longing to be always at home with his family and the places he knew. Wherever the bulk of 'Child Harold' was written, the landscape and memories of Glinton, Helpston and Northborough predominate.

6

At Northborough Patty occasionally received reminders of her husband's earlier popularity. Letters arrived from friends and well-wishers, among them Charles Clark – farmer, pamphleteer, printer and eccentric author, who published under such pseudonyms as Malthus Merryfellow, Doggerel Drydog, Quintin Queerfellow and Thomas Hood the Younger. Clark lived at Great Totham Hall, near Witham, in Essex. In addition to publishing his own compositions, he liked collecting manuscripts from other authors. He had written a flattering letter to Clare in October 1832, asking to be listed as a subscriber to the new publication – *The Midsummer Cushion* (*The Rural Muse*) – and he also approached Matthew Allen about the possibility of publishing, at his own expense, a volume of Clare's latest poems. Clark wrote to Patty on 2 January 1841:

> My Dear Mrs Clare – Having lately made several unsuccessful attempts to obtain a copy of a little volume of Poems by your poor husband, on whose fate altogether it is really quite meloncholy to

reflect, I write to say, that I shall be most particularly obliged by your informing me, at your earliest convenience, where I could satisfy my said desire ... Your unfortunate husband's productions are such favourites of mine, that, I assure you, I have already taken a very great deal of trouble about the said volume, but have quite failed in my endeavours after all. Possibly you may have already heard of my name, for such interest do I feel for the welfare of you and your family, that I have actually offered to print and bring out at my own expense, for the benefit of the same, a selection from your poor husband's lately written, and other unpublished pieces, as originally suggested by Dr Allen of High Beach, in his letter published in 'The Times' in June last... In all probability, too, I should have been able to have brought out the little volume by this time but for the extraordinary neglect (if it is not something worse!) of the said Dr Allen. The fact is, I have lately actually written three or four letters to him on the subject – the last about three weeks since – without obtaining an answer from him whatever!... By the bye Mrs C. if you possess any little *poetical* or other scrap in *your husband's handwriting*, that you would not mind parting with, I should be highly gratified by your enclosing the same with the above named work of his, as I take a peculiar pleasure in collecting such little curiosities of men of genius. I should certainly prefer some little specimen *in poetry*, but any mere scrap in 'humble prose' I should prize – the *older* the same, too, I beg to say, the more acceptable, as it is always the more interesting to trace the progress of genius at the *commencement* of its career....[20]

Clark went on to ask Patty about the origins of some of the poems, including 'The Rose-bud in Humble Life' and 'Familiar Epistle to a Friend', the manuscript of which he wanted to borrow, presumably for a piece of literary piracy, of which he was not without guilt. He had already printed in *Three Very Interesting Letters* (1837) a letter he had obtained, which Clare had written in 1824 to Thomas Inskip, the friend of Robert Bloomfield.

Whether Patty received this long and demanding letter, or just ignored it, we cannot say. The impatient Clark was writing again on 3 February, saying:

My Dear Mrs Clare – A whole fortnight having now elapsed without my hearing from you in reply to my letter I am fearful it did not reach you ... If it did, pray let me hear from you in the course of a day or two, that I may proceed in ascertaining the cause of Dr Allen's extraordinary conduct in with-holding your poor husband's poetical compositions from those who are really anxious to befriend his family... I beg to say, that if I do not hear from you after posting this,

I shall conclude that neither of my letters reached you and shall immediately take some other method to ascertain where you are to be found . . .[21]

Perhaps Patty wisely asked one of the children to reply to the determined gentleman, if only to keep him from turning up at Northborough. His intrusion is brief but of interest because of the light it sheds on Dr Allen's indifference to enquiries, and his neglect in doing more to get Clare's new poems published.

Clare, himself, was not only homesick to the point of distraction, but getting equally tired of being Allen's patient. His medical progress was at a standstill and the monotony of the grounds becoming frustrating to a man accustomed to wide open spaces:

Yclep'd old All–n – mad brained ladies curing
Some p–x–d like Flora and but seldom clean
The new road oer the forest is the right one
To see red hell and further on the white one[22]

The road through the forest, the road home, was too great a temptation. Clare decided there was only one thing to do – escape!

22
A Broken-down Haymaker

1

July 24th 1841 – Returned home out of Essex & found no Mary – her & her family are as nothing to me now though she herself was once the dearest of all – & how can I forget[1]

Clare's account of his journey home from Essex to find Mary Joyce is a most moving piece of autobiographical writing. For courage and endurance, for tragedy and pathos, it has few equals of any time. The loneliness and despair of this sick, deluded man walking more than eighty miles in search of someone already dead gain dignity in the simple narrative he uses. It is a stark and unforgettable story of a man's unhappiness.

It was not an impulsive act to walk out of Dr Allen's home and take to the road. He had planned it for some time. One Sunday, while walking in the forest, he got into conversation with some gipsies who offered to hide him in their camp and help him escape. But they wanted money and Clare could only promise that he would pay them one day. When he went back to join them a few days later they had gone. All that was left behind on their camp site was an old hat which Clare put in his pocket.

The gipsies had at least told him which way to go and so, with nothing more than 'honest courage' and a little tobacco, he set out for the dark lands of the fen-country, for Northborough and Glinton. But, not having made a map of the gipsies' directions, he took the wrong turning, lost his way, and found that he was travelling south instead of north. When he came to a public house called the Labour in Vain he asked one of the customers who was just leaving if he could show him the way to Enfield:

> I walked down the lane gently & was soon in Enfield Town & bye & bye on the great York Road where it was all plain sailing & stearing

> ahead meeting no enemy & fearing none I reached Stevenage where being Night I got over a gate crossed over a corner of a green paddock where seeing a pond or hollow in the corner I forced to stay off a respectable distance to keep from falling into it for my legs were nearly knocked up & began to stagger I scaled some old rotten paleings into the yard & then had higher pailings to clamber over to get into the shed or hovel which I did with difficulty being rather weak to my good luck I found some trusses of clover piled up about 6 or more feet square which I gladly mounted & slept on ... I slept soundly but had a very uneasy dream I thought my first wife lay on my left arm & somebody took her away from my side which made me wake up rather unhappy I thought as I awoke somebody said 'Mary' but nobody was near – I lay down with my head towards the north to show myself the steering point in the morning ...

When daylight came he left his night's 'lodging' and made his way back to the Great North Road. He saw other impoverished travellers sleeping under a hedge. A man on horseback passed him and said, 'Here's another of the broken-down haymakers' and threw him a penny with which to buy half a pint of beer. When Clare reached a pub near Baldock – called the Plough – he went in to spend a ha'penny and to escape a heavy shower. Later he met two drovers and asked them if they had any money to spare, but the were 'saucy' and laughed at him, so he begged no more of anybody. He walked on, passing some well-built houses and another village, then called at a house in the village of Potten to get a light for his pipe. An old woman and a young girl were busy making Bedfordshire lace 'on a cushion as round as a globe'. They were very civil to him and talked for a while. He continued his journey and eventually met up with a 'kind talking country man' who was able to tell him that the parson and the overseer both lived a good way off, too far from them to help:

> so I went on hopping with a crippled foot for the gravel had got into my old shoes one of which had now nearly lost the sole had I found the overseers house at hand or the Parsons I should have gave my name & begged for a shilling to carry me home but I was forced to brush on pennyless & be thankfull I had a leg to move on ...

He then asked another countryman if he could direct him to a safe farmyard where he could rest and was told to look for a place near the Ram public-house. But when he came to a heap of stones he sat down and went to sleep by the side of a shed under some elm trees:

> but the wind came in between them so cold that I lay till I quaked like the ague & quitted the lodging for a better at The Ram which I could

hardly hope to find – It now began to grow dark apace & the odd houses on the road began to light up & show the inside tennants lots very comfortable & my outside lot very uncomfortable & wretched – still I hobbled forward as well as I could & at last came to the Ram the shutters were not closed & the lighted window looked very cheering but I had no money & did not like to go in there was a sort of shed or gighouse at the end but I did not like to lie there as the people were up – so I still travelled on the road was very lonely and dark in places being overshaded with trees...

And as darkness deepened be became fearful of being lost. He came to a place where the road branched off into two turnpikes, one to the right and the other straight ahead. Further on was a milestone which he first passed and then went back to read to find out where the other road might lead. He found it led to London. Perhaps there was a sigh, or perhaps he closed his mind to the memories. He said no more than to admit that for a moment he forgot which was north or south and, when he continued, went on 'mile after mile' convinced that he was going in the wrong direction:

> yet I could not sit down or give up but shuffled along until I saw a lamp shining as bright as the moon which on nearing I found was suspended over a Tollgate before I got through the man came out with a candle & eyed me narrowly but having no fear I stopt to ask him wether I was going northward & he said when you get through the gate you are; so I thanked him kindly & went through on the other side & gathered my old strengths as my doubts vanished... I at length fell in with an odd house all alone near a wood... there was a large porch over the door & being weary I crept in & glad enough I was to find I could lye with my legs straight the inmates were all gone to roost for I could hear them turn over in bed as I lay at full length on the stones of the porch – I slept here till day-light & felt very much refreshed as I got up...
>
> I have but a slight reccolection of my journey between here & Stilton for I was knocked up & noticed little or nothing – one night I lay in a dyke bottom from the wind & went sleep half an hour when I suddenly awake & found one side wet through from the sock in the dyke bottom so I got out & went on... the road very often looked as stupid as myself & I was very often half asleep as I went on the third day I satisfied my hunger by eating the grass by the road side which seemed to taste something like bread I was hungry & eat heartily till I was satisfied & in fact the meal seemed to do me good the next and last day I reccolected that I had some tobacco & my box of lucifers being exhausted I could not light my pipe so I took to chewing

Tobacco all day & eat the quids when I had done & I was never hungry afterwards...

As tired as he was, he remembered passing through Buckden and arriving in Stilton where he was 'compleatly foot-foundered & broken down'. He lay down in the road and half slept. A young woman came out of a house and said, 'Poor creature,' but another more elderly woman said, 'O, he shams.' When Clare got up and hobbled away he heard her saying, 'O no, he don't.' When he reached the inn at Norman Cross he asked if the road to the right led to Peterborough and was told that it did:

So as soon as ever I was on it I felt myself in homes way & went on rather more cheerfull though I was forced to rest oftener than usual before I got to Peterborough a man & woman passed me in a cart & on hailing me as they passed I found they were neighbours from Helpstone where I used to live – I told them I was knocked up which they could easily see & that I had neither eat or drank anything since I left Essex when I told my story they clubbed together & threw me fivepence out of the cart I picked it up & called at a small public house near the bridge w[h]ere I had two half pints of ale & twopenn'rth of bread & cheese when I had done I started quite refreshed only my feet was more crippled then ever & I could scarcely make a walk of it over the stones & being half ashamed to sit down in the street I forced to keep on the move & got through Peterborough better than I expected... bye & bye I passed Walton & soon reached Werrington & was making for the Beehive as fast as I could when a cart met me with a man & woman & boy in it when nearing me the woman jumped out & caught fast hold of my hands & wished me to get into the cart but I refused & thought her either drunk or mad but when I was told it was my second wife Patty I got in & was soon at Northborough but Mary was not there neither could I get any information about her further than the old story of her being dead six years ago which might be taken from a bran new old Newspaper printed a dozen years ago but I took no notice of the blarney having seen her myself about a twelve month ago alive & well & as young as ever – so here I am homeless at home & half gratified to feel that I can be happy anywhere...

Three days later, on 27 July 1841, he wrote a letter to Mary Joyce – whom he now addressed as Mary Clare:

My dear Wife,

I have written an account of my journey or rather escape from Essex for your amusement & hope it may divert your leisure hours – I would have told you before now that I got here to Northborough last friday night but not being able to see you or to hear where you was I soon began to feel homeless at home & shall bye & bye feel nearly hopeless but not so lonely as I did in Essex – for here I can see Glinton church & feeling that Mary is safe if not happy & I am gratified though my home is no home to me my hopes are not entirely hopeless while even the memory of Mary lives so near me God bless you My Dear Mary Give my love to your dear & beautiful family & to your Mother – & believe me as I ever have been & ever shall be

My dearest Mary
Your affectionate husband
John Clare

That Patty should have met her husband at Werrington was surely no coincidence. Had Clare's Helpston neighbours given more thought to the state of their village poet and gone first to Northborough to tell Patty of his condition and return? And had Patty set off to look for him? If so, a sad reunion for her when all her demented husband wanted was to see Mary Joyce.

A few days later, after the completion of his journal from High Beach, Clare was writing to Dr Allen:

My Dear Sir

Having left the Forest in a hurry & not time to take my leave of you & your family but I intended to write & that before now but dullness & disappointment prevented me for I found your words true on my return here having neither friends nor home left but as it is called the 'Poet's Cottage'[2] I claimed a lodging in it where I now am – one of my fancys I found here with her family & all well – they met me on this side Werrington with a horse & cart & found me all but knocked up . . . where my poetical fancy is I cannot say for the people in the neighbour-hood tell me that the one called Mary has been dead these eight years but I can be miserably happy in any situation & in any place & could have staid in yours in the Forest if any of my friends had noticed me or come to see me but the greatest annoyance in such places as yours are those servants and stupid keepers who often assumed as much authority over me as if I had been their prisoner & not liking to quarrel I put up with it till I was weary of the place altogether so I heard the voice of freedom & started . . .

I had eleven books sent to me from How & Parsons Booksellers some lent & some given me – out of the Eleven I only brought 5 vols back as I dont want any part of Essex in Northamptonshire agen I wish you would have the kindness to send a servant to get them for me I should be very thankfull not that I care about the books altogether only it may be an excuse to see me & get me into company that I do not want to be acquainted with – one of your labourers Pratts wife borrowed Childe Harold – & Mrs Fishers daughter has two or three more all Lord Byron poems – Mrs King late of the Owl Public house at Leppits Hill & now of Enfield Highway has two or three all Lord Byrons Poems & 'The Hours of Idleness'[3]

Clare had clearly not been without female company, even admirers, whilst at High Beach. But now he wanted to be independent again, even at home, paying for his board and lodging:

I look upon myself as a widow or bachelor I dont know which – I care nothing about the women now for they are faithless & deceitfull & the first woman where there was no man but her husband found out means to cucold him by the aid & assistance of the Devil but women being more righteous now & men more plentiful they have found out a more godly way to do it without the Devil's assistance & a man who possesses a woman possesses loss without gain the worst is the road to ruin & the best is nothing like a good cow – man I never did like much & woman has long sickened me I should like to be to myself a few years & lead the life of a hermit – but even there I should wish for one whom I am always thinking of & almost every song I write has some sighs or wishes in Ink about Mary If I have not made your head weary by reading this I have tired my own by writing it so I will bid you goodbye[4]

Dr Allen replied on 18 November saying that he was sorry to hear of Clare's painful journey home but was relieved to hear that he found no greater happiness now in Northborough than he did in High Beach. If he had not been happy there it was his own fault and not his doctor's. But he was still welcome to return if he wished and could live a hermit's life there if that's what he wanted and did nothing to make himself 'unpleasant'. Allen also wrote to John Taylor, enclosing his account for Clare's treatment and expenses, saying that he had tried to persuade Mrs Clare to send her husband back but 'she thought him so much better that she wished to try him for a while'.[5]

Allen never saw Clare again. Within four years his business venture was a disaster and he was bankrupt and dead. His treatment of Clare had helped, even if circumstances had prevented it from being wholly successful. He, also, had arrived too late upon the scene and was, in the end, even more pathetic than his patient.

2

In his calmer, more rational moments Clare was able to accept that

Mary was lost forever, that the news he had received of her death was true and final:

> I cant expect to meet thee now
> The winter floods begun
> The wind sighs thro' the naked bough
> Sad as my heart within[6]
>
> . . .
>
> Thou soul within a soul thou life of life
> Thou Essence of my hopes and fears and joys
> M—y my dear first love and early wife
> And still the flower my inmost soul enjoys
> Thy love's the bloom no canker worm destroys[7]

With Mary dead all hope was dead and life had no meaning – 'Summer is Winters desert and the Spring/Is like a ruined city.' The final effort to find happiness had failed.

During his five-month stay at home Clare wrote further stanzas for 'Child Harold' and made his own fair copy of the whole poem, excluding some of the verses scribbled into his notebooks at High Beach. Some of those verses were written in the margins of the daily newspapers and even on the pages of a catalogue that Patty had received of an auction sale to be held near Crowland, a few miles away.

For a man who, within weeks, was to be taken away from home as a lunatic to spend the rest of his life in an asylum, there is an impressive serenity in the lines he wrote during these last days at Northborough:

> Sweet solitude thou partner of my life
> Thou balm of hope and every pressing care
> Thou soothing silence oer the noise of strife
> These meadow flats and trees – the autumn air
> Mellows my heart to harmony – these fenny dells
> Seem Eden in this sabbath rest from care
> My heart with loves first early memory swells
> To hear the music of those village bells

'Child Harold' is not a poem of defeat, even though we read, 'Time cannot clear the ruined mass away', even though 'Life is to me a dream that never wakes' and 'Night finds me on this lengthening road alone'. Clare may tell us that 'Friends cold neglects have froze my heart to stone/And wrecked the voyage of a quiet mind' but he is also able to confirm that 'Love is the eternal calm of strife' and that, even in prison, he will find freedom in remembering the native soil where he once walked in love:

I'll cling to the spot where my first love was cherished
Where my heart nay my soul unto Mary I gave
And when my last hope and existence is perished
Her memory will shine like a sun on my grave

It is, despite all things, a poem of triumph. The triumph of love to endure and to survive death, the triumph of poetry to survive and ennoble life, and the triumph of the human heart over despair. Spring is reborn out of winter. Eden is glimpsed again from the windows of insanity and, out of the darkness, the daisy strikes again its claim to eternity with 'Its little golden blossom frilled with snow':

As once in Eden under heavens breath
So now on blighted earth & on the lap of death
It smiles forever

Whatever might happen in the affairs of men, life and poetry, poetry and love, would be 'never altered by time'.

3

The last weeks of autumn drifted quietly into the first grey days of winter. The fields were black, empty and wet. The water rose in the dykes and threatening clouds built up on the horizon. Clare could no longer walk far from home. The narrow lane to Glinton already felt like a road to a foreign country. The few hours of daylight allowed him to look out from his window at a desolate village. People still passed to and fro on their errands but were wrapped against the cold winds and were silent. By tea-time darkness closed in, the lamps were lit and Clare sat in his chimney-corner quietly reading or mumbling softly to himself. His family gathered round him and tried to interest him in their own activities, but it was not easy. There was a distance now between his children and himself, even to the point of losing patience with their chattering or their enthusiasm for books.

December arrived and with it the first fall of snow. The neglected garden and the empty orchard bore their fruitless blossom. There would be weeks of waiting, wondering, hoping for a change of fortune and the promise of a better spring. The children talked excitedly of Christmas. They fetched holly and other evergreens to decorate the cottage as they had always been encouraged to do. Keep the traditions and customs alive, their father had always urged. Put the sprigs of berries round the pictures on the wall, place a Christmas candle in the window, bake a plum cake and remember all the happy memories of Christmases long ago. They tried. They filled the room with all the symbols of those joyous times. They sang and recited the seasonal stories. Christmas Day approached and the men looked forward to a day with their families, to a day's holiday away from the naked fields or draughty barns.

But for Clare no amount of planning or well-wishing could now bring back the joys he had known in his childhood. All the efforts of his family to restore the customary cheer to his home failed dismally. They even seemed to mock his memories and the darker hauntings of his depression. The future promised by those earlier years had brought only despair, defeat and sadness. After thirty years of hoping and dreaming, he was now a disillusioned, forgotten, unsuccessful poet who could not achieve recognition and who could no longer find happiness. It was as if most of his life had been wasted, misdirected, even ridiculed by those who had deceived him for their own ends. He was bitter and frustrated. Not even Christmas could raise his spirit now and the well-meant endeavours of his wife and children only made it worse. He flew into a violent temper. Weeks of brooding and strange behaviour had alerted Patty to the storm which she knew would break. She had told the doctors of the seriousness of her husband's condition. For a month or more they had wanted to put him away in an asylum again but she had pleaded with them to leave him at home where she felt there was still a chance of recovery if only she could nurse him through the winter. If she could succeed in that then she felt certain that the brighter days of spring would restore him to better health. But the deterioration had been worse than she ever feared. She was afraid now of what might happen next, afraid for her children. She had to send for the doctors. Doctor Fenwick Skrimshire and Doctor William Page arrived from Peterborough. Their examination confirmed one thing in their minds – John Clare was insane and should be committed to the county asylum. So certain were they that this would be the outcome that arrangements had already been made for the poet to become a patient at the Northampton General Lunatic Asylum. Their certificate of application for Clare's admission makes sad reading. The poet's usual employment was given as 'Gardening'. The supposed cause of insanity was claimed to be 'Hereditary'. And the reason for his final breakdown was 'years addicted to poetical prosings'.[8]

Although he was to be admitted as a pauper patient, he was to be treated as a gentleman, and Lord Fitzwilliam again agreed to help by offering to pay eleven shillings a week towards Clare's maintenance for as long as needed. Proposals for Clare's removal to Northampton had, in fact, been made to his Lordship eighteen months before the poet had walked out of Dr Allen's care and certainly before any plans had been made by the Peterborough doctors. On 29 March 1840 Dr Thomas Prichard, the new superintendent of the Northampton Asylum, had written:

> I would beg also to remind your Lordship that poor Clare the Poet has been some years at a private asylum near London, he could certainly be taken care of here at as small, if not at a less expense than that which is now incurred, and I should think it would be a source of pleasure to his friends that he should be within easy access by them which is not now the case. Mr Baker the Antiquary and County Historian is very anxious on this subject & I believe has mentioned it more than once to the Hon'ble Capt: Spencer. Perhaps as your Lordship resides more immediately on the spot your interest in this matter would be more effective . . .[9]

Dr Prichard then went on to thank Lord Fitzwilliam for his 'liberality' towards the new institution and for becoming one of its founders.

As 1841 ended Clare at last came under Prichard's care. On 29 December he was again removed from his wife and family and taken away, this time for good. No one could have foreseen how many years he was to be kept as a patient in the asylum, or how important those years were to be seen by future readers of his work. Whatever else might happen Clare remained 'a poet and a lover still', and was to be so for another twenty-three years.

Although Patty realized that her husband could only be cared for in this way, she wept bitterly when he was taken struggling from their home. Clare himself wept and cried out to be left alone. But the Northborough cottage had seen the last of him. The carriage moved away and hurried through the main street where a few villagers whispered and shook their heads.

But the cottage had not seen the last of the sorrows that were to be associated with the poet and his family. Four of his children, and also his father, were to die in his own lifetime. Patty was to know more than twenty years of loneliness and hard work there. Nevertheless, she faced the new year of 1842 with determination and courage. The house and the land still needed looking after. The children and Parker Clare still needed caring for, and there would be little help from outside. Patty's own parents were dead. Some of the neighbours were quietly relieved that her husband had been 'put away'. It would be better for her in the end. There was nothing you could do for someone whose mind had gone. He was best out of the way. He wouldn't know. Within a few years Patty even became known as 'Widow Clare', so sure were the local gossips that her husband was 'put away' for good and would never be seen again. She was then to become well-liked among the villagers, helping those who needed help, baking and mending for those who could no longer do such tasks for themselves, and always carrying a supply of home-made sweets in her pocket to give to the children she met on her rounds. Practical, down-to-earth Patty still believed that life had to be lived and got on with it with the same resolution she had always shown.

Fifty miles away a bemused and frightened Clare wondered what this strange, new institutional world had in store for him. For all that it mattered he could be dead. He saw himself 'in the land of Sodom where all the peoples brains are turned the wrong way'[10] and withdrew deeper into himself. He was an exile now in that very county with which his name was to be irrevocably linked.

In the asylum records his name appears under the initials 'J.C.' in the *List of Private Patients, whose Payment for Maintenance are in the lowest remunerative rate of payment viz. 21s. per week, shewing the Amount of Benefit derived from the Funds of the Institution.*[11] The asylum therefore paid ten shillings a week on Clare's behalf from its general funds which, together with Lord Fitzwilliam's contribution, allowed him to have the comfort and status of a gentleman with a small room to himself and, to begin with, considerable freedom. Whatever other deprivations and sadnesses he had to endure, he was no longer a broken-down haymaker. No more would he have to eat grass or sleep in a water-filled dyke. For the next twenty-three years he was to have the protection of a spacious house built specially for lunatics. He now had a new identification.

23
The Asylum

1

The Northampton General Lunatic Hospital and Asylum, as it was then called, was built in 1836–7 and opened for the reception of patients on 1 August 1838. It was enlarged in 1843 and the total cost, including twenty-four acres of land, amounted to £35,000. When Clare became a patient there in 1841 it was, therefore, a new building with new staff, new ideas and a degree of comfort far removed from the older mental asylums. The *Northamptonshire Directory* of 1849 was to say of it:

> This invaluable institution stands on an elevated situation, about one mile east of Northampton on the Billing Road, commanding a varied and interesting prospect, embracing the park and woods of Delapre, the picturesque vale through which flows the silvery Nen, Queen Eleanor's Cross, and Hunsbury Hill. It represents nearly a complete quadrangle, is built of the beautiful white Kingsthorpe stone, faced with Bath stone; its decorations are neat and tastefully executed, and its architectural designs, like its external arrangements, are simple and domestic. The galleries, which are fourteen feet in width by sixty in length, afford an excellent promenade in wet weather, whilst the day or sitting rooms are furnished after the model of ordinary rooms, with fire-places and other requisites. There is a constant supply of hot water accessible to all parts of the house. Baths, – hot and cold, and showers, have their appropriate places. The laundry is upon the latest and most approved principle. This healthy and agreeable site, with its large and diversified grounds, affords recreation and amusement to the patients, furnishing a variety of occupations to those who can thus be captivated . . .[1]

For anyone who had to be 'captivated' and who would not be conscious of their losses, the asylum must have offered the best retreat possible from the harsh lack of understanding that would have existed elsewhere. It was clearly a comfortable, well-appointed establishment and the staff was engaged to pursue the new policies of treating the insane like normal sick human-beings in need of care, peace and rest. The idea from the beginning was to dispense with all sombre thoughts of melancholy and secrecy.

The superintendant at the asylum when Clare was admitted was Dr Thomas Prichard, a man ably equipped to carry out the good intentions of this doctrine, and a man who allowed his patients a considerable degree of freedom. During the first ten years Clare was encouraged to explore the grounds and walk into town as often as he wished. His favourite spot was to become the portico of All Saints' Church, where he frequently talked with local people and occasionally wrote a verse or two for them in exchange for a pipe of tobacco. In 1848 the local artist George Maine was to draw Clare sitting there, looking well-dressed, well-fed, and with notebook and pencil in hand. Maine died two years later at the age of forty-nine.

Clare received a number of visitors at the asylum, and one of the first was Spencer T. Hall, who recalled the event in his *Biographical Sketches of Remarkable People* (1873). He found the poet now 'rather burly, florid, with light hair and somewhat shaggy eyebrows, and dressed as a plain but respectable farmer, in drab or stone-coloured coat and smalls, with gaiters, and altogether as clean and neat as if he had just been fresh brushed up for market or fair. . . .' Hall remembers that Clare talked at great length about being prepared for a prize fight. He asked him if he was not more proud of his fame as a poet than his prowess as a boxer. 'Oh poetry,' replied Clare, 'ah, I know, I once had something to do with poetry, a long while ago; but it was no good.'

Other visitors included Cyrus Redding (who had visited Clare at High Beach), William and Mary Howitt, J.H. Wiffen, Eliza Cook, John Dalby and Claridge Druce, the author of *The Flora of Northamptonshire*. Three of Clare's children also made the difficult journey to Northampton to see their father – John, William and Eliza each went at least once, and John possibly on other occasions. That Patty herself did not go can be easily explained and it is certainly unfair to accuse her of neglect or indifference. When her husband was placed in the asylum in 1841 it would have meant Patty travelling from Northborough to Thrapston by hired gig and there catching the Cambridge to Oxford coach which would take her to Northampton at a cost of £4. When the railways came to the county in 1845 the journey would have been both easier and cheaper, costing little more than seven shillings. But, by then, Clare's recognition of her as his wife was so much in doubt that the visit could well have been a sad and painful experience. And, as with his stay at High Beach, Patty still had the responsibility of running the house and working the land, of looking after her children and father-in-law. Two days away was more than she could afford. There were to be other reasons too why Clare did not receive as many visits from his family as some critics think he should. His eldest son Frederick died in 1843 at the age of nineteen. Anna Maria, his first child who had married Samuel Sefton, died in 1844 at the age of twenty-four. Parker Clare died in 1846, aged eighty-two. And, in 1850, Patty herself was taken seriously ill and the family was threatened with eviction because of unpaid rent. William, who was a landworker, could not find employment because of the agricultural depression and seldom worked more than one day in a fortnight for a wage of one-and-sixpence. The only member of the family who tried to hold their affairs together was the youngest son, Charles, who had recently become articled to a solicitor in Market Deeping for a salary of £4 a year. But Charles, too, was to die in 1852 at the age of nineteen and so Clare was to lose half of his family during his own lifetime. His daughter Eliza Louisa married Anna's widower – Samuel Sefton – but was confined to her house through very poor health. William and John later left the district and 'Widow Clare' was left to make what she could of the remnants of her life until her husband died in 1864. With such a background of misery and misfortune, and with Clare's obsession with Mary Joyce as his wife, it is not surprising that Patty did not make the effort to visit her sick husband in Northampton.

John Taylor made a brief visit to the asylum to see his one-time protégé and in 1844 Clare's portrait was painted by another local artist, Thomas Grimshawe. A frequent visitor throughout these years was G.J. De Wilde, who was editor of the *Northampton Mercury*. He also met Clare in the town and they went for walks together. On one occasion he recalled how Clare quoted from Shakespeare and Byron and claimed the lines as his own. When De Wilde corrected him, he said, 'It's all the same. I'm John Clare now. I was Byron and Shakespeare formerly.' It was De Wilde who was to give Frederick Martin a first-hand account of those asylum years. In a letter of 25 February 1865 he wrote:

> I saw Clare frequently during his residence at the Asylum here. At first he was allowed to come into the Town (the Asylum is a mile out of it) unattended, and his favourite resort was beneath the portico of All Saints Church where in summer time he would sit for hours together. He was moody and taciturn and rather avoided society. He would talk rationally enough at times, about poetry especially, but on one occasion in the midst of conversation in which he betrayed no signs of insanity, he suddenly quoted passages from Don Juan as his own . . .

'I'm the same man' he said, 'but sometimes they called me Shakespeare and sometimes Byron and sometimes Clare'...
In his youth he must have been a handsome man, with a countenance beaming with sensitive intelligence. Hilton's Portrait was no doubt thoroughly faithful. When I first knew him you were struck with the likeness, though he had even then that peculiar heaviness of brow which increased with his years and seemed to overweight his brain and prevent its free action... As he advanced in years the eye was almost lost beneath a heavy pent-house of brow... He usually had one hand in his breeches pocket and the other in the breast of his waistcoat. He chewed tobacco and no present was so acceptable to him as a screw of the weed.[2]

By 1845, although his mind was failing noticeably, Clare gained a good friend in W.F. Knight who had just been appointed as House Steward at a salary of £60 a year. For the next five years Knight was to encourage and help Clare to write those last poems which were to add a new dimension to the already complex talent of the asylum's most distinguished patient.

2

We shall return to that relationship later. In the meantime it is necessary to stay with Clare's first few years in the asylum to show that it was not always a painful experience. His mind was, to begin with, much calmer at Northampton than it had been at High Beach or Northborough. He was no longer working on such demanding poems as 'Child Harold' and apparently now had no desire to escape, even though there was every opportunity for him to do so. De Wilde tells of an escape plot by other patients, who wanted Clare to go with them, but he refused and told them that they would be fools to try. That he was homesick is beyond doubt. His letters to his family are proof of his aching need of their presence and love. In his most rational moments he could not understand why he was not allowed to be with them but, for the most part, they were, he seemed to realize, part of a previous existence, like Mary Joyce and his few years of fame. For days he was content to walk around the attractive gardens of the asylum or go into town where he would amuse himself looking at the shop-windows or writing in the portico of All Saints. Sometimes, said De Wilde, he would sit for a long time just staring up at the sky as if in a trance.

In 1845 Dr Pritchard left the Asylum and his place was taken by Dr P.R. Nesbitt, who was criticized by some of Clare's earlier supporters for imposing a stricter discipline on his patient. This was not altogether fair as Clare's behaviour by this time was already making Dr Prichard think twice before allowing him out of the grounds. Clare could appear very balanced and normal for days, and then quite suddenly become a strange, violent person again, who would not have been safe in town. Dr Nesbitt certainly allowed him as much freedom until his behaviour made it necessary to restrict his movements. In a letter which W.F. Knight wrote to Joseph Stenson on 3 March 1846, he said, 'You will be sorry to hear that poor John Clare is not allowed to go out of the walls of this place – for on Saturday last he went into town and someone made him intoxicated – for this he is incarcerated.'[3]

Whether this was but a temporary punishment or for good is not clear. Clare may have been allowed into town again under supervision and to be 'incarcerated with the walls' of the asylum was not so severe as it sounds. In his annual report for 1846 the new superintendent reaffirmed the avowed intentions of the managers and staff to help the patients live as full a life as their conditions allowed:

> To diversify the routine of life, and to sweeten existence even in an Asylum, various amusements are in request, from active games of play in the grounds, or excursions of three or four miles into the country in summer, to the more passive occupations of bagatelle, chess, or dominoes in winter. Occasional musical parties in the centre of the house take place – the violin and piano, with the sweetest of all music, the human voice, diffusing their gladdening harmony around. Sometimes the scene of action is transferred to the female gallery, for the entertainment of a larger section of the community, who enter into all the vivacity of a country dance. The pleasure which these harmless hilarities afford have more than a transient interest; there is a tincture of the past, present, and future – in the anticipation, in the reality, and in the recollection . . .[4]

It is important to consider this report not only because it gives a detailed impression of life in the Asylum, but also because it reveals what a sensitive person Dr Nesbitt must have been and how fortunate Clare was to still be under the care of someone who could appreciate the past and the present, the recollection and the reality. When the superintendent could also see how well Clare and Knight worked together, he was equally wise in keeping in the background until some disciplinary action might be needed. If he kept Clare confined to the grounds, he did so for good reason and was not being any harsher than his predecessor.

Nesbitt remained at Northampton until 1858 and later wrote his assessment of Clare's condition during those years:

> I was always led to believe that his mental affliction had its origin in

dissipation. It was characterized by obsessional ideas and hallucinations. For instance he may be said to have lost his own personal identity as with all the gravity of truth he would maintain that he had written the works of Byron, and Sir Walter Scott, that he was Nelson and Wellington, that he had fought and won the battle of Waterloo, that he had had his head shot off at this battle, whilst he was totally unable to explain the process by which it had been again affixed to his body. He was generally docile and tranquil, but would brook no interference – anything approaching to this last would excite his ire in a torrent of ejaculations of no ordinary violence in which imprecations were conspicuous: but this was an exceptional state of things. Seated on a bench and with his constant friend a quid of Tobacco, he would remain silent for hours. He was a passionate lover of the beauties of Nature – wild flowers being especially objects of interest to him. He was once asked how he had contrived to write his pretty poetry – his reply was that it came to him whilst walking in the fields – that he kicked it out of the clods. On another occasion he presented me with the following scrap

Where flowers are, God is, and I am free.

... If there was one subject more than another that he had an aversion to it was biography – he designated it as a parcel of lies – but the beauties of poetry he could always appreciate, and was never more at home and at his ease than when the production of one of the time-honoured Bards was placed in his hands.

He was essentially a kind-hearted, good-feeling man with an unusually large cerebral development, possessing great breadth and altitude of forehead, such as we are in the habit of associating with men of the highest Intellect.[5]

During both Dr Prichard's and Dr Nesbitt's time Clare was looked after most sympathetically. Physically he had seldom been better. Visitors were often surprised, as Spencer Hall had been, to find such a robust character. He would have received regular meals, frequent exercise and nightly sleep. All his physical wants were cared for and he no longer had the responsibility of providing for his family. His time was his own now to read and write. But he needed more than such comforts or benefits. However considerate his superiors might have been, and however accommodating the asylum was, Clare could only see himself as a helpless captive. As his mind became more tortured, the more he inwardly raged against such an institution. On 15 June 1847 he wrote to his youngest son, Charles:

My Dear Boy

I am very happy to have a letter from you in your own handwriting

> & to see you write so well I am also glad that your Brothers & Sisters are all in good health & your Mother also be sure to give my love to her but I am very sorry to hear the News about your Grandfather but we must all die – & I must say That Frederick & John had better not come unless they wish to do so for its a bad place & I have fears that they may get trapped as prisoners as I hear some have been. I may not see them nor ever hear they have been here I only tell them & leave them to do as they like best – its called the Bastille by some & not without reasons – how does the flowers get on I often wish to see them – & are the young children at home I understand there are some I have not seen kiss them & give them my love to them & to your Mother[6]

He was to write again in February 1848, warning his children against Pride and showy dress, and advising them to pay more attention to 'Mathematics, Astronomy, Languages & Botany'. At the end of the letter he asked after his father, forgetting that he had died a year earlier. Eight months later Charles received another letter in which Clare's longing to be with his family is more hopefully expressed:

> I think I shall not be long now before I see you & as I have so particularly enquired after each & all of you so lately in my last I shall only say God bless you all now & forever – live happy & comfortable together in your old house at home for go where we will & be as we may always remember 'there is no place like Home' – be good children & be kind to your Mother & always obey her wishes & you will never go wrong I always found it so myself & never got into error when I did it[7]

Again he urged his children to keep at their studies, adding to their subjects Latin, Greek and Hebrew – though it is unlikely that they ever extended their interests to such extremes. He also said he wanted to get home 'to see after the garden & hunt in the woods for yellow hyacinths . . . and blue Primroses'. In a letter to Patty, written in the July of that year, he said, 'I am very weary of being here You might come & fetch me away for I think I have been here long enough.'[8]

In many of the asylum letters he was to ask about friends and neighbours, both in Northborough and Helpston, many of them already dead. He asked after William and John Close, John Cobbler, John and Mary Brown and their daughter Lucy, John Woodward and his wife, Old John Nottingham and his wife Sally, James Bains, Tom and Sam Ward and a dozen others, including Mrs Bullimore who had been his first teacher at the little school in Helpston in 1797–8. And always, the plea to be allowed home.

But neither Patty nor anyone could even consider this possibility.

Clare's mind was now too bemused and the separation from reality too long. And yet, during these years, his creative spirit refused to die or give in. He may have ceased to exist as husband, father, lover or normal human-being, but he was still a poet. Between 1841 and 1860 he wrote nearly eight hundred and fifty poems as well as the scores of verses which he scribbled down in exchange for a quid of tobacco. G.J. De Wilde recalled that there were vast quantities of Clare's ballad-scraps current among the townspeople of Northampton. Many of the poems which W.F. Knight helped to transcribe were far below Clare's usual standard but there were many moving poems coming from the quieter moments of Clare's mind, poems such as 'The Pale Sun', 'The Tell-Tale Flowers', 'Clock-a-Clay', 'The Dying Child', 'Childhood' and those tender love poems, including 'Love Lies Beyond the Tomb' and 'Oh, Wert Thou In The Storm':

Oh wert thou in the Storm
  How would I shield thee
To keep thee dry and warm
  A camp I would build thee

Though the clouds poured again
  Not a drop should harm thee
The music of the wind and rain
  Rather should charm thee

Oh wert thou in the storm
  A shed I would build for thee
To keep thee dry and warm
  How would I shield thee

The rain should not wet thee
  Nor thunderclap harm thee
By thy side I would set me
  To comfort and warm thee

I would sit by thy side, love
  While the dread storm was over
And the wings of an angel
  My charmer would cover

The finest poem he ever wrote to Patty was written in the asylum 'To My Wife – a Valentine' (which W.F. Knight called 'Clare to His Wife'):

Oh once I had a true love
  As blest as I could be
Young Patty was my turtle-dove
  And Patty she loved me.

We walked the fields together
By wild roses and woodbine,
In summer's sunshine weather,
And Patty she was mine.

. . .

We loved one summer quite away
And when another came,
The cowslip close and sunny day,
It found us much the same.
We both looked on the selfsame thing,
Till both became as one;
The birds did in the hedges sing
And happy time went on . . .

There were still more poems for Mary Joyce, more poems about the seasons, poems of memory and recollection, poems in a variety of verse-forms – for Clare was always experimenting with his craft – and poems in which his individuality (and belief in the individual) still shines through:

The world is all lost in commotion,
The blind lead the blind into strife;
Come hither, thou wreck of life's ocean,
Let solitude warm thee to life.
Be the pilgrim of love and the joy of its sorrow,
Be anything but the world's man:
The dark of today brings the sun of tomorrow,
Be proud that your joy here began.
Poor shipwreck of life, journey hither,
And we'll talk of life's troubles together.[9]

Released now, as he was, from all allegiances, expectations and critics, his poetic imagination reached new heights of simple purity:

I lost earth's joys but felt the glow
Of heaven's flame abound in me
Till loveliness and I did grow
The bard of immortality.

I loved but woman fell away
I hid me from her faded flame,
I snatched the sun's eternal ray
And wrote till earth was but a name.[10]

There was even one last hope that another volume of poetry would be published. Cyrus Redding, Thomas Inskip and W.F. Knight had discussed this as the only way of gaining for Clare some rightful recognition of his talent before he died. But the hope faded. Inskip was now an old man and died in 1849. Knight left Northampton in 1850 for a new appointment in Birmingham. Dr Nesbitt also left the asylum and the new superintendent – Dr Edwin Wing – did not have the same interest in this strange and ageing patient. Clare was thrown back into his own dark world, a world of shadows and silence. Sometimes he was persuaded to write a poem, and when he did he drew from his vision and talent verses which suggest little of his disturbed experiences of mind. More and more he went back to those days at Helpston, to the memories of childhood, in poems such as 'The Green Lane', 'My Schoolboy Days', 'Invite to Eternity', 'Pear Tree Lane' and 'The Daisy'.

In 1860 he gave a copy of that poem to Agnes Strickland, the documentary historian, and, in reply to some of her questions, left a startling description of his condition:

> they have cut off my head and picked out all the letters of the alphabet – all the vowels and consonants – and brought them out through my ears; and then they want me to write poetry! I can't do it[11]

When asked which he liked best, 'literature or your former vocation?' he replied: 'I liked hard work best, I was happy then. Literature has destroyed my head and brought me here.'[12]

3

Another visitor during those last four or five years was John Plummer, a Kettering journalist. He was able to confirm that Clare at least enjoyed a degree of comfort in his old age that he might not have known had he been anywhere but Northampton: 'Passing through several of the wards we were ushered into what we first deemed to be a gentleman's private sitting-room, but which was the ordinary sitting chamber of the better class of patients; and which appeared very cosy and comfortable with its mahogany chairs, table and couch, warm soft carpets, and cheerful fire . . .'[13] Clare was waiting to receive his guests and Plummer was struck by the 'mild benevolent-looking features' of the poet.

Almost to the end of his days Clare retained the dignity and noble bearing that had puzzled his acquaintances throughout his life. In old age he looked to some like King Lear himself, and to others like a lion with a white mane. Although nearly bald on the top of his head, Clare had for a number of years worn his grey hair down to his shoulders, perhaps a last, subconscious effort on his part to still play the role of the artist, just as the olive-green coat had been forty years ago when he was still only a lime-burner. Someone who caught a likeness of the poet then was the Bristol artist George Duval Berry, himself an inmate of the asylum from 1854–64. He drew Clare six months before the poet's death.

In many ways now those forty years were all a dream and Clare could not distinguish the reality from the unreality. Time had no meaning for him. The world had no purpose. There had only been one world and he was its only inhabitant. He could no longer reach out and touch what once belonged to him. There was only a blurred image of how things used to be.

Laurens Van Der Post, in his book *Jung and the Story of Our Time*, recalls Jung saying to him once, 'The hell of the mad is that not only has time suddenly ceased to exist for them but some memory of what it and its seasons once meant to them remains to remind them of the fact that it is no longer there.'[14]

Occasionally, on warm autumn days, Clare was wheeled out into the garden so that he could admire again the flowers and the sound of birds. But these meant little to him now. Often he became noisy, excited, and would 'often swear most coarsely'.[15] He was then taken back to his room and locked in. The man who thought he was Byron, Shakespeare, Nelson and the country's champion fighter was now an enfeebled geriatric, his mind and body both gone.

There was one final, defiant gesture in the early spring of 1864 when he wrote his last poem, 'Birds Nests':

> 'Tis spring, warm glows the south,
> Chaffinch carries the moss in his mouth
> To filbert hedges all day long,
> And charms the poet with his beautiful song;
> The wind blows bleak o'er the sedgy fen,
> But warm the sun shines by the little wood,
> Where the old cow at her leisure chews the cud.

But the true creative power had gone, the vision faded. April had always been a favourite month. It was a time for birth, not death. That year the weather was exceptionally warm, though the sun could no longer stir the heart of the poet into further song. In his poem 'The Dying Child' he had asked:

> How can an infant die
> When butterflies are on the wing
> Green grass and such a sky,
> How can they die at spring

It was to be Clare's last spring. Throughout 1863 he had suffered several apoplectic seizures which became more and more severe. His legs failed him and he was confined to bed. On 10 May 1864 he had a particularly serious attack and the superintendent notified Patty of her husband's worsening condition. Ten days later, on 20 May, he died quietly in the late afternoon, a few minutes before the clocks chimed five.

4

It had always been Clare's wish that he should be buried in his native village of Helpston, next to his parents and where the sun shines longest. He had even expressed his wishes for the inscription he wanted on his tombstone – 'Here rest the Hopes and Ashes of John Clare'. He wanted nothing else, no date, no quotations. 'I wish it to live or die with my poems.'[16] Instead the description of him as the Northamptonshire Peasant Poet was perpetuated and he received Virgil's claim that 'A Poet is Born Not Made'.

The family of Bellairs, and Mr Spencer, who now lived at Woodcroft Castle, heard the news and immediately made arrangements for the poet's body to be brought back home. It arrived, by train, the following Tuesday in a coffin made of the best oak with brass handles and a brass plate bearing his name. It was the only rail journey Clare ever made and he would have hated the thought of travelling along those tracks which he once feared would spoil his countryside.

As it happened, his body arrived too late for burial on 24 May and so the coffin was placed on trestles in the bar of the Exeter Arms, which was just as well, for Patty and her family had not been informed of the funeral arrangements. A letter addressed to her from the asylum had gone to Helpston instead of Northborough. She did not get it until late that Tuesday afternoon when Clare should have been buried.

During that afternoon a curious rumour had gone round the village claiming that it was not John Clare in the coffin at all, that the asylum could have sent any old lunatic's body to be buried in Helpston. So the lid of the coffin was removed and the villagers filed by to witness for themselves the corpse of their local poet. Some said it was, some said it wasn't, the face had changed so much. Rumour bred rumour. These were also the days of the Resurrectionists, the body-snatchers of grisly repute, and word went round the village that a famous London surgeon had hired two unscrupulous men to pay a midnight visit to Helpston where they were to cut out the brain of John Clare so that it could be examined to see how a madman could write such fine poetry. The villagers agreed to keep watch over the body all night. Whatever feelings they may have had about Clare in the past, or now, they were not going to let him suffer that final indignity.

On Wednesday, 25 May 1864, the sun rose slowly over Glinton and by mid-day was high above Helpston. By early afternoon the church-bell began to toll, the coffin was brought from the Exeter Arms and carried into the church. The mourners included Patty, her sons William and John, her daughter Eliza and Clare's sister Sophy. The Reverend Charles Mossop was also there and 'all the inhabitants of the village were present in the church and churchyard during the ceremony'.[17] The burial service was read by the Reverend Edward Pengelley of Glinton and as he uttered the words 'ashes to ashes and dust to dust' the air trembled with the silent sadness of the day.

After the funeral Patty and the rest of her family returned to Northborough, not to forget but to remember. A correspondent to the *Stamford Mercury* on 3 June wrote of an interview he had recently been given with the poet's widow: 'Mrs Clare wept as she spoke of the many good qualities of her dear departed husband and of the ardent love he had always shown for her ere he was so mentally afflicted...'

There were other visitors too, including a representative of Whitakers, the publishers who had brought out *The Rural Muse* in 1835. He now promised to pay Patty £10 a year for the rest of her life if she would let his firm have all the manuscripts she still had in her possession. Reluctantly, and not even knowing their true value, she agreed.

Spencer T. Hall also visited her, as did Frederick Martin, and she was at least aware that the memory of her remarkable husband would live on beyond the parish boundaries of Northborough and Helpston.

For a few years she continued to go about the village trying to help anyone in need, but gradually her own health began to fail and the long wet winters began to take their toll. Her daughter Sophia had gone to live in Spalding and, whilst staying in that Lincolnshire town with her during February 1871, Patty was taken ill. She never recovered and died there at the age of 72. Her body was brought home, not to Helpston to lie near her husband, but to Northborough where she was buried next to her four children and other members of the family.

The row of gravestones for the Clares and the Seftons in the cold eastern corner of Northborough churchyard makes a sad reminder of a family which gave so much, and suffered so many misfortunes, all in the name of poetry. It is where the family story ends. All the main characters in the life of John Clare had now gone with him on 'the dark journey/ That leaves no returning'.[18] Four of his children were dead. Mary Joyce was dead. Mrs Emmerson and Lord Radstock had died some years before, and, within six weeks of Clare's own death, John Taylor died on 5 July at the age of eighty-three. All that remained were the thousands of poems which were one day to travel the world and recreate for other generations a glimpse of that paradise he had known as a boy – a world of innocence, hope, joy and celebration, which does not have to be limited to a particular county or century. Clare celebrated Creation and left an account of Man's quest for its perfection.

> Amidst the wreck of perishable leaves
> How fresh and fine appears the evergreen.[19]

5

Clare was essentially a poet of the spirit. To share his vision is an enrichment of one's own experience. To ignore him is to close dark curtains on a bright day. In his poems he still walks the world he created, still watches with 'unwearied eye' the daily goings-on in life. As H.J. Massingham wrote of him in *The Athenaeum* (January 1921), 'Clare possessed a greater knowledge of earth and natural life than any other poet whose appeal is one of literature. Both as man and creator he was, I think, primarily a spiritual type.'

The texts and meanings of Clare's poems may be analysed and argued over, but the spirit of the man is there for all who seek, to find and respect. He is, indeed, more alive now than ever. With all the odds against him he has proved that there is in human nature a will to triumph and to survive. For such a life there can be no ordinary end.

Appendix

The question will always be asked, 'How mad was Clare?' With all the advances in medical science and psychological study we still cannot be sure. As Mrs Anne Tibble reminded us in her introduction to the *Selected Poems* (Dent 1965), 'Almost all the medical evidence upon which could be built any full analysis of the kind of madness from which Clare suffered was burnt by a fire,' and much of what has been written since has had to rely on conjecture. Dr Thomas Tennant, a later superintendent at the asylum, wrote of Clare's illness in *The Journal of Mental Science* (January 1953): 'there are conflicting views regarding his type of illness. In my opinion this was a cyclothymic disorder [caused by extreme alternations between high and low spirits], and not a schizophrenic one as suggested by one of his recent biographers. Apart from the actual symptomatology, the excellence of much of his poetry written in hospital, and the slow development of deterioration support this diagnosis. . . .' The term used by the Tibbles in their *Life* . . . was *manic-depressive*: 'Clare was most likely of a manic-depressive temperament. His bursts of creative work were followed by periods of exhaustion, and these were often prolonged by pecuniary worry and under-nourishment.'

Clare was ill, there can be no doubt about it, but whether it was necessary for him to spend a quarter of a century in asylums is doubtful, even for those times. 'By the standards of the day,' wrote James Reeves in his introduction to *Selected Poems* (Heinemann 1954), 'he was a madman [but] if he could have commanded the skilled devotion of a loving and loved companion, there would have been no need for Northampton Asylum.'

Could Mary Joyce have given him that 'skilled devotion' and prevented his breakdown? Did the illness grow out of loneliness and despair, out of a lifetime's longing and disappointment? Clare was certainly a disappointed man and his feelings of failure added to those anxieties referred to by the Tibbles. But I do not think Mary Joyce was the answer, any more than Patty was. The major problem was in the demands of the creative spirit to survive and reach new heights of achievement. Whatever mental weaknesses Clare may have inherited from either his absent Scottish grandfather, or any other member of his family, they were aggravated by the responsibility placed upon Clare to become *somebody*. There was a conflict, and he could do little about it other than obey the demands of his spirit. As Vincent Van Gogh wrote to his brother Theo in August 1883: 'There is no anguish greater than the soul's struggle between duty and love, both in their highest meaning. When I tell you I choose my duty, you will understand everything.'

The Romantic idea that genius and madness go hand in hand cannot be entirely dismissed. It is too much of a coincidence to consider the lives of Van Gogh, Hölderlin, Schumann, or the eccentric behaviour of Blake, Beethoven and Balzac, without admitting that there is a pattern of mental disturbance among some men and women who have to live with a creative gift, and who have a longing for artistic perfection. They are always searching, both for themselves and for their ideal. As Keats said in a letter to Richard Woodhouse (October 1818), 'A Poet is the most unpoetical of any thing in existence, because he has no Identity . . . he has no self.' Each poem, painting, or piece of music is a search from darkness into light. The result usually falls short of the expectation. The frustration and sense of failure can be hard to bear. The cost is high, as it was for Clare, and the rewards can never be measured because they usually come too late.

Writers and artists do not *choose* to become what they are. They accept the task they have been given. Many would often rather be carpenters or bakers, for, as Clare said, 'I liked hard work best, I was happy then. Literature has destroyed my head and brought me here.' But the asylum brought 'a soothing silence o're the noise of strife' and as Clare lost touch with his search for identity he still continued to write poems, for to cease that activity would be to cease life altogether. It was a compulsion which drove him to distraction back in 1820 at the age of twenty-seven. Edward Drury had expressed his fears then about Clare staying sane for long if he pushed himself so hard. Those demands were to last for another forty years. With little but his natural gift to sustain him, Clare was bound to suffer. His mental instability, his weakness for a life of dissipation – whether women or drink – and the complex duality of his personality, the problems of earning enough money to support his family and his unsuccessful attempts to be seen as an equal with Wordsworth or Byron during his own lifetime, all went towards the illness which drove him into a life of bleak isolation and eventual imprisonment.

Dr Russell Brain in *Some Reflections of Genius* (1960) compared Clare's mental illnes with those of Smart, Cowper, Newton, Goethe and Samuel

Johnson. It was a disorder, he said, 'to which men of broad general views coupled with a sensitive imagination are naturally exposed.' Clare's moods fluctuated between periods of ecstatic happiness and profound despair, between love and anger, violence and passivity, between periods of intense hard work and weeks of idleness. His depressions made him angry because they deprived him of his greatest happiness – the writing of the poems which liberated him from all life's problems and disadvantages and made him a man apart.

It is certain that had Clare been a twentieth-century poet he would have had the benefits of the progress which has been made in treating mental illness. He would not have been forced to spend more than twenty-five years away from his family. He might still have been ill but he would have received different treatment. But that would then have given us a very different story.

Notes

Full details of abbreviations used in the text:

BOOKS	
The Poems	*The Poems*. Edited by J.W. and Anne Tibble. Dent, 1935
The Letters	*The Letters of John Clare*. Edited by J.W. and Anne Tibble. Routledge & Kegan Paul, 1951
The Prose	*The Prose of John Clare*. Edited by J.W. and Anne Tibble. Routledge & Kegan Paul, 1951
Selected Poems and Prose	*Clare: Selected Poems and Prose*. Edited by Eric Robinson and Geoffrey Summerfield. Oxford University Press, 1966 and 1967
Midsummer Cushion	*John Clare: The Midsummer Cushion*. Edited by Anne Tibble and R.K.R. Thornton. MidNAG/Carcanet Press, 1978
The Sheperd's Calendar	*The Sheperd's Calendar*. Edited by Eric Robinson and Geoffrey Summerfield. Oxford University Press, 1964
Sketches in the Life of John Clare	*Sketches in the Life of John Clare by Himself*. Edited by Edmund Blunden. Cobden-Sanderson, 1931
Poems Descriptive	*Poems Descriptive of Rural Life and Scenery*. Printed for Taylor and Hessey, and E. Drury, 1820
Martin's *Life*	Frederick Martin. *The Life of John Clare*. Macmillan, 1865. New edition by Eric Robinson and Geoffery Summerfield. Cass, 1964
Tibbles' *Life*	J.W. and Anne Tibble. *John Clare: a Life*. Michael Joseph, 1972
MANUSCRIPTS	
NMS	Northampton Manuscripts in Northampton Public Library
PMS	Peterborough Manuscripts in Peterborough Museum
BM Egerton	British Museum, Egerton Folios

Introduction

1 'The Eternity of Nature': *Midsummer Cushion.*
2 H.J. Massingham. *The Athenaeum* (January 1921).
3 'Memory': *Midsummer Cushion.*

1 The Claim

1 Helpston is now in the county of Cambridgeshire.
2 'A Vision': *The Poems.*
3 See Clare's reference to this in his letter to Taylor, March 1831.
4 *The Letters*: 2 April 1820.
5 Drury's correspondence with Taylor: NMS 43.
6 'The Nightingale's Nest': *Midsummer Cushion.*
7 'The Badger': *Selected Poems and Prose.*
8 'The Fox': *ibid.*
9 Robert Graves. *The Crowning Privilege* (1955).
10 J. Middleton Murry. *John Clare and Other Studies* (1950).
11 'The Flight of Birds': *John Clare: Selected Poems*. Edited by Anne Tibble (1965).
12 'The Nightingale's Nest': *Midsummer Cushion.*
13 'I Am': *John Clare: Selected Poems*. Edited by Anne Tibble.
14 'Walk in the Woods': *Midsummer Cushion.*
15 'The Meadow Grass': *ibid.*
16 'The Progress of Rhyme': *ibid.*

2 The Place

1 Edmund Blunden. *Nature in English Literature* (1929).
2 Geoffrey Grigson. Introduction to *Selected Poems of John Clare* (1950).
3 Octavius Gilchrist. The *London Magazine* (January 1820).
4 'Winter in the Fens': *The Poems.*
5 Edward Storey: see *Portrait of the Fen Country* (1970) and *The Solitary Landscape* (1975).
6 Durobrivae: the Roman settlement in the Nene Valley between Castor and Waternewton.
7 See 'Langley Bush': *John Clare: Selected Poems*. Edited by Anne Tibble.
8 Mrs Bessie Garfoot Gardner. *Clare's Village* (privately printed, no date). Also J.E.B. Glover, Mawer and Stenton. *The Place-names of Northamptonshire* (1933).
9 *Ibid.*
10 Daniel Crowson. *Rambles with John Clare* (1978).
11 *Ibid.*
12 Dorothy Marshall. *English People in the Eighteenth Century* (1956).
13 *The Shepherd's Calendar.*

3 The Family

1 Martin's *Life.*
2 *The Prose.*
3 Lawrence Stone. *The Family, Sex and Marriage in England 1500–1800* (1977).
4 *Sketches in the Life of John Clare.*
5 *Ibid.*
6 Drury's letters to John Taylor: NMS 43.
7 County Records Office, Delapre Abbey, Northampton.
8 *Sketches in the Life of John Clare.*
9 *Selected Poems and Prose.*
10 'The Eternity of Nature': *Midsummer Cushion.*

4 Childhood

1 *The Prose.*
2 'Decay': *Selected Poems and Prose.*
3 *The Prose.*
4 *Ibid.*
5 Martin's *Life.*
6 *Sketches in the Life of John Clare.*
7 See illustration in David Powell, *Catalogue of the John Clare Collection in Northampton.*
8 *The Prose.*
9 *Sketches in the Life of John Clare.*
10 *Ibid.*
11 Dorothy Marshall. *English People in the Eighteenth Century* (1956).
12 *The Prose.*
13 *Selected Poems and Prose.*
14 'Childhood': *Midsummer Cushion.*
15 *Ibid.*
16 *The Prose.*
17 'The Ant'. *The Poems.*
18 'Recollections After a Ramble': *ibid.*
19 See Margaret Grainger, *Peterborough Catalogue of Manuscripts.*
20 *The Prose.*
21 *The Shepherd's Calendar*: 'July'. Original version printed in the 1964 edition.
22 *The Prose.*
23 'The Village Minstrel' (1821).
24 *The Prose.*
25 'Childhood': *Midsummer Cushion.*

5 Starting Work

1 *The Prose.*
2 *Ibid.*
3 *Ibid.*
4 *The Letters:* Autumn 1817.
5 *Ibid*: March 1821.
6 *The Prose.*
7 *Ibid.*
8 *Ibid.*
9 *Ibid.*
10 '*The Village Minstrel*' (1821).
11 'Will O' Wisp': *The Poems.*
12 *The Prose.*
13 '*The Village Minstrel*'.
14 *Ibid.*
15 *Ibid.*
16 *Ibid.*
17 *Sketches in the Life of John Clare.*
18 *Ibid.*
19 *Ibid.*
20 'The Progress of Rhyme': *Midsummer Cushion.*

21 *Ibid.*
22 *Sketches in the Life of John Clare.*
23 *Ibid.*
24 *The Prose.*
25 *Sketches in the Life of John Clare.*
26 *The Prose.*
27 *Ibid.*

6 Leaving Home

1 *The Prose.*
2 *Ibid.*
3 *Sketches in the Life of John Clare.*
4 *Ibid.*
5 *Ibid.*
6 See Margiad Evans, *A Ray of Darkness* (1978).
7 *The Prose.*
8 *Ibid.*
9 *Ibid.*
10 *Ibid.*
11 'Childish Recollections': *The Poems.*
12 Laurens van der Post. *Jung and the Story of Our Time* (1976).
13 'Sighing for Retirement': *The Poems.*
14 *The Prose.*
15 *Ibid.*
16 *Ibid.*
17 *Ibid.*
18 *Ibid.*
19 *Ibid.*
20 'The Gipsey's Camp': *The Poems.*

7 Mary Joyce

1 'To Mary' (II): *The Poems.*
2 'The Enthusiast: A Daydream in Summer': *Midsummer Cushion.*
3 *Ibid.*
4 'Nutting': *Midsummer Cushion.*
5 See both Martin's and the Tibbles' *Life.*
6 'The Progress of Rhyme': *Midsummer Cushion.*
7 *The Prose.*
8 Drury's letters to John Taylor: NMS 43.
9 'The Village Minstrel' (1821).
10 'The Progress of Rhyme': *Midsummer Cushion.*
11 'The Rural Muse': *John Clare: Selected Poems.* Edited by Anne Tibble (1965).
12 *Sketches in the Life of John Clare.*
13 *The Prose.*
14 'Ballad' ('Where is the heart ...'): *Midsummer Cushion.*
15 'First Love's Recollection': *ibid.*
16 'Ballad' ('Tis Spring returns'): *ibid.*
17 *Ibid.*

18 *The Prose.*
19 *Ibid.*
20 'Remembrances': *Midsummer Cushion.*

8 Enclosure

1 W.G. Hoskins. *The Making of the English Landscape* (1955).
2 'The Village Minstrel' (1821).
3 'The Parish': *John Clare: Selected Poems.* Edited by Anne Tibble (1965).
4 W.G. Hoskins, *op. cit.*
5 'The Village Minstrel'.
6 *Ibid.*
7 Edward Storey. *Portrait of the Fen Country* (1970).
8 'A Favourite Nook Destroyed': *The Poems.*
9 W.G. Hoskins, *op. cit.*
10 John Barrell. *The Idea of Landscape and Sense of Place in the Poetry of John Clare* (1972).
11 'The Mole-catcher' ('When melted snow leaves bare ...'): *The Poems.*
12 Martin's *Life.*
13 Copy of letter loaned by George Dixon, Honorary Librarian, Peterborough Museum Society.
14 Hawthorn hedges.
15 *The Prose.*
16 'The Mores': *Selected Poems and Prose.*
17 Clare was writing some years before Waterloo but Professor Hoskins's point is an important one.
18 'The Progress of Rhyme': *Midsummer Cushion.*
19 *The Prose.*
20 'The Progress of Rhyme': *Midsummer Cushion.*
21 *Ibid.*
22 *Ibid.*
23 'The Parish': *John Clare: Selected Poems.* Edited by Anne Tibble.
24 *Ibid.*
25 *Ibid.*
26 *Ibid.*
27 *Ibid.*
28 'On a Lost Greyhound': *The Poems.*
29 'To the Rural Muse': *Midsummer Cushion.*
30 *Ibid.*
31 *Selected Poems and Prose.*

9 Expectations

1 'Solitude': *The Poems.*
2 'Dawnings of Genius': *The Poems.*
3 *Poems Descriptive.*
4 'Wild Bees': *The Poems.*
5 'Summer Evening': *ibid.*
6 'Reflections on Autumn': *ibid.*
7 'The Last of Autumn': *ibid.*

8 See 'My Mary' – his parody on Cowper's poem; 'To the Snipe' – a syllabic poem; 'Winter' ('From huddling night's embrace') – for internal rhyme; and 'The Flitting' and 'The Meadow Grass' – for greater control.
9 *The Prose.*
10 Octavius Gilchrist. The *London Magazine* (January 1820).
11 Several of these poems were ultimately omitted from the new hymn-book of 1982.
12 *The Prose.*
13 *Ibid.*
14 'The Instinct of Hope': *The Poems.*
15 'The Stranger': *ibid.*
16 'The Progress of Rhyme': *Midsummer Cushion.*
17 *The Prose.*
18 *Ibid.*
19 *Ibid.*

10 Martha (Patty) Turner

1 Martin's *Life.*
2 Spencer T. Hall. 'Bloomfield and Clare' from *Biographical Sketches of Remarkable People* (1873).
3 Taylor's Introduction to *The Village Minstrel* (1821).
4 From the original Clare manuscripts at Oundle School.
5 *Sketches in the Life of John Clare.*
6 *The Prose.*
7 'Song' ('Of all the days in memory's list'): *The Poems.*
8 *Ibid.*
9 'To Patty' ('Fair was thy bloom ...'): *Midsummer Cushion.*
10 'To Patty' ('Thou lovely bud ...'): *The Poems.*
11 *The Prose.*
12 'Clare to His Wife' (Knight's title): *Selected Poems.* Edited by Anne Tibble (1965).
13 *The Letters*: March 1821.
14 'Elegy on the Ruins of Pickworth': *The Poems.*
15 'Virtue Lives on': *ibid.*
16 'The Rural Muse': *Midsummer Cushion.*
17 'What is Life?': *Selected Poems and Prose.*
18 Mark Storey. *Clare: The Critical Heritage* (1973).

11 Towards Publication

1 *The Prose.*
2 Note from Clare to Henson: PMS.
3 *The Prose.*
4 Martin's *Life.*
5 *Ibid.*
6 *The Prose.*
7 Drury's letters to Taylor: NMS 43.
8 *The Prose.*
9 *Ibid.*
10 *Sketches in the Life of John Clare.*
11 *Ibid.*

12 *Ibid.*
13 *Ibid.*
14 Edmund Blunden. *Keats's Publisher* (1936).
15 Taylor's correspondence: NMS 43.
16 *Ibid.*
17 *Ibid.*
18 *Ibid.*
19 *Ibid.*
20 *The Prose.*
21 *The Letters*: 1819.
22 Octavius Gilchrist: The *London Magazine* (January 1820).
23 Taylor's Introduction to *Poems Descriptive.*
24 Drury's letters to Taylor: NMS 43.
25 Taylor's Introduction to *Poems Descriptive.*

12 'Wearing into the Sunshine'

1 Martin's *Life.*
2 Drury's letters to Taylor: NMS 43.
3 *Ibid.*
4 For complete review see Mark Storey, *Clare: The Critical Heritage* (1973).
5 *The Prose.*
6 Tibbles' *Life.*
7 *The Prose.*
8 *Ibid.*
9 *Ibid.*
10 *Ibid.*
11 *Ibid.*
12 *Ibid.*
13 Drury's letters to Taylor: NMS 43.
14 *The Letters*: May 20 1820.
15 *Ibid.*: 16 July 1820.
16 *John Clare: Selected Poems.* Edited by Anne Tibble (1965).
17 Clare correspondence: BM Egerton 2245–48.
18 *The Letters*: March 1821.
19 *Ibid.*
20 Martin's *Life.*
21 *The Prose.*
22 *Ibid.*
23 *The Letters*: May 1820.
24 *The Prose.*
25 *Ibid.*
26 *Ibid.*

13 Fame

1 *The Prose.*
2 *Ibid.*
3 See Trevor Hold, 'The Composer's Debt to John Clare', *The John Clare Society Journal* (July 1982).

4 *The Prose.*
5 *Ibid.*
6 *Ibid.*
7 Clare correspondence: BM Egerton 2245–48.
8 *The Prose.*
9 Clare correspondence: BM Egerton 2245–48.
10 *The Letters*: March 1820.
11 Mark Storey. *Clare: The Critical Heritage* (1973).
12 *Ibid.*
13 *The Prose.*
14 *Ibid.*
15 *Ibid.*
16 *Ibid.*
17 *Ibid.*
18 *Ibid.*
19 Clare correspondence: BM Egerton 2245–48.
20 *Poems Descriptive*. First edition.
21 Clare correspondence: BM Egerton 2245–48.
22 *Poems Descriptive.*
23 PMS.
24 Clare correspondence: BM Egerton 2245–48.
25 *Ibid.*
26 *The Letters*: 16 May 1820.
27 Taylor to Clare: May 1820. NMS.
28 *The Letters:* July 1820.
29 Clare correspondence: BM Egerton 2245–48.
30 *Ibid.*
31 *Ibid.*
32 'The Poet's Wish': *The Poems*

14 Agreements and Disagreements

1 The death of Richard Woodhouse in Rome greatly aggravated the delay over the settlement of Clare's accounts but Taylor must share the blame.
2 *The Letters*: June 1820.
3 *Ibid.*: February 1820.
4 *Ibid.*: 19 March 1820.
5 *Ibid.*: April 1820.
6 *Ibid.* See also letter of 15 November 1829.
7 *The Prose.*
8 Taylor's correspondence: NMS.
9 Clare correspondence: BM Egerton 2245–48.
10 *Ibid.*
11 *Ibid.*
12 *Ibid.*
13 *Ibid.*
14 *Ibid.*
15 *Ibid.*
16 *The Letters*: 19 April 1820.
17 *John Clare: Selected Poems*. Edited by Anne Tibble (1965).
18 *The Letters*: 31 August 1820.

19 *Ibid.*
20 Clare correspondence: BM Egerton 2245–48.
21 *Ibid.*
22 *The Prose.*
23 'To one who has been long in city pent ...': *Keats's Collected Poems.*
24 From 'A Rhapsody': *The Poems.*
25 *The Letters*: March/April 1820.
26 *Ibid.*: 23 January 1821.
27 *Ibid.*: March 1821.
28 *The Village Minstrel.*
29 *The Letters*: March 1821.
30 Clare correspondence. BM Egerton 2245–48.
31 *The Letters*: March 1821
32 Clare correspondence: BM Egerton 2245–48.
33 *Ibid.*
34 *The Letters*: 11 August 1821.
35 'Ballad': *Midsummer Cushion.*
36 *The Letters of Van Gogh.* Edited by Mark Roskill (1927).

15 Escapes to London

1 Mark Storey. *Clare: The Critical Heritage* (1973).
2 *Ibid.*
3 *Ibid.*
4 *Ibid.*
5 *The Letters*: 6 September 1821.
6 Mark Storey, *op. cit.*
7 *Ibid.*
8 *The Letters*: May 1822.
9 *The Prose.*
10 *Ibid.*
11 *Ibid.*
12 *Ibid.*
13 *Ibid.*
14 Clare correspondence: BM Egerton 2245–48.
15 Clare's third visit was in 1824; his fourth in 1828.
16 *The Prose.*
17 Martin's *Life*. Second edition, pp. 122, 192.
18 *The Prose.*
19 *Ibid.*
20 *Ibid.*
21 George Borrow. *Lavengro*, ch. 39.
22 *The Prose.*
23 See Bibliography.
24 H.F. Cary. *Memoirs.*
25 *The Letters*: January 1823.
26 *Ibid.*: May 1823.
27 *Ibid.*: June 1823.
28 Clare correspondence: BM Egerton 2245–48.
29 *The Letters*: 8 May 1823.
30 Taylor's Introduction to *Poems Descriptive* (1820).

31 Dame Janet Baker in *The Sunday Telegraph*, Colour Supplement No. 127.
32 Clare correspondence: BM Egerton 2245–48.
33 *Ibid.*
34 *The Letters*: 19 December 1825.
35 *Ibid.*: 8 December 1825.

16 'Th' Expense of Spirit'

1 *The Letters*: 24 January 1822.
2 *The Prose.*
3 *Ibid.*
4 Martin's *Life*, p. 195.
5 *The Stamford Mercury* reported in 1832, for instance, '1,100 heads of game lying in heaps at Burghley House Park'.
6 *The Prose.*
7 *The Letters*: 1820.
8 Mark Storey. *Clare: The Critical Heritage* (1973).
9 *Ibid.*
10 All Journal extracts taken from *The Prose.*
11 *The Shepherd's Calendar.*
12 *Ibid.*: 'March'.
13 *Ibid.*: 'February'.
14 *Ibid.*: 'May'.
15 *Ibid.*: 'November'.
16 *The Prose.*
17 See Introduction to *The Shepherd's Calendar.*
18 *The Letters*: 17 April 1825.
19 Clare correspondence: BM Egerton 2245–48.
20 *The Letters*: 15 September 1825.
21 *Ibid.*: 8 December 1825.
22 Clare correspondence: BM Egerton 2245–48.
23 *Ibid.*
24 *Ibid.*
25 *The Letters*: 19 December 1825.
26 Mark Storey, *op cit.*
27 *Ibid.*
28 *Ibid.*
29 Scottish drovers brought their cattle as far as Huntingdon before handing them over to local drovers who took them into London.
30 See original version in *The Shepherd's Calendar.*
31 Clare correspondence: BM Egerton 2245–48.
32 *Ibid.*
33 *The Letters*: 15 July 1826.
34 Clare correspondence: BM Egerton 2245–48.
35 Mark Storey, *op. cit.*
36 *Ibid.*
37 Clare correspondence: BM Egerton 2245–48.
38 Mark Storey, *op. cit.*
39 *Ibid.*
40 *Ibid.*
41 *Ibid.*
42 Clare correspondence: BM Egerton 2245–48.

17 Time for Repentance

1 Tibbles' *Life*.
2 Clare correspondence: BM Egerton 2245–48.
3 *Ibid.*
4 *The Letters*: August 1824.
5 *The Later Poems of John Clare*. Edited by Robinson and Summerfield (1964).
6 *The Letters*: 20 August 1824.
7 *The Prose*.
8 'On Visiting a Favourite Place': *Midsummer Cushion*.
9 Clare correspondence: BM Egerton 2245–48.
10 *The Letters*: 21 March 1824.
11 *Ibid.*
12 'The Anniversary': *Midsummer Cushion*.
13 'Peace': *The Poems*.
14 'Pastoral Liberty': *ibid.*
15 From 'A Rhapsody': *ibid.*
16 'Pastoral Fancies': *ibid.*
17 'Universal Goodness': *ibid.*
18 'On Visiting a Favourite Place': *Midsummer Cushion*.
19 'Sighing for Retirement': *The Poems*.
20 'The Nightingale's Nest': *Midsummer Cushion*.
21 'The Meadow Grass': *ibid.*
22 'On Visiting a Favourite Place': *ibid.*
23 *Ibid.*
24 'Sabbath Bells': *ibid.*
25 'The Holiday Walk': *ibid.*
26 'The Pettichap's Nest': *ibid.*
27 'The Last of March': *ibid.*
28 'Crows in Spring': *The Poems*.
29 'Child Harold': *The Later Poems*. Edited by Robinson and Summerfield.
30 *The Letters*: 29 June 1820.
31 'The Autumn Wind': *The Poems*.
32 'Autumn Landscape': *ibid.*
33 *The Prose*.
34 'Snowstorm' (I): *The Poems*.
35 'Happiness of Evening': *Midsummer Cushion*.
36 'A Winter Scene' (Hail scene of desolation . . .'): *The Poems*.
37 'The Winter's Come': *ibid.*

18 The Last Years at Helpston

1 *The Letters*: April 1828. (See also note in Tibbles' edition.)
2 *Ibid.*: 15 October 1828.
3 *Ibid.*: 15 October 1828.
4 *Ibid.*: 3 January 1829.
5 *Ibid.*: 3 January 1829.
6 *Ibid.*: 3 January 1829.
7 *Ibid.*: 21 December 1828.
8 Clare correspondence: BM Egerton 2245–48.

9 Quoted in June Wilson, *Green Shadows* (1951).
10 *The Letters*: 15 November 1829.
11 *Ibid.*
12 *Ibid.*
13 Clare correspondence: BM Egerton 2245–48.
14 Taylor's correspondence: NMS.
15 *The Prose.*
16 William Cobbett. *Rural Rides.*
17 *Seaton*: horse hairs or thread twisted and drawn through the skin to keep open a wound or infected tissue; part of Dr Darling's prescribed treatment, together with the use of leeches and poultices.
18 *The Letters*: September 1830.
19 *Ibid.*: September 1830.
20 *Ibid.*: October 1830.
21 Clare correspondence: BM Egerton 2245–48.
22 *Ibid.*
23 *The Letters*: October 1830.
24 *The Prose.* See also letters from the Asylum.
25 *The Letters*: October 1830.
26 *Ibid.* See also Asylum letters to Clare's son, Charles: 1848–9.
27 *Ibid.* See also Asylum letters to Charles.
28 *Ibid.*: 15 January 1831.
29 *Ibid.*: 7 March 1831.
30 *The Letters*: October 1831.
31 *The Prose.*
32 *The Letters*: October 1831.
33 *Ibid.*: January 1832.
34 *Ibid.*
35 *Ibid.*

19 The Flitting

1 'Pastoral Fancies': *The Poems.*
2 PMS: A fragment of a letter.
3 'Child Harold': *The Later Poems of John Clare.* Edited by Robinson and Summerfield (1964).
4 Martin's *Life.*
5 'Recollections after a Ramble': *The Poems.*
6 'Decay': *Midsummer Cushion.*
7 'The Flitting': *ibid.*
8 Mark Storey. *Clare: The Critical Heritage.* (1973).
9 'Child Harold': *The Later Poems.* Edited by Robinson and Summerfield.
10 'The Flitting': *Midsummer Cushion.*
11 *Ibid.*
12 See introductory note in *Midsummer Cushion.*
13 *The Letters*: 1 August 1832.
14 *Ibid.*: Autumn 1832.
15 *Ibid.*
16 *Ibid.*: 6 September 1832.
17 'The Fens': *The Poems.*
18 *The Letters*: August 1832.

19 'The Dream': *The Poems.*
20 *The Prose.*
21 *Ibid.*
22 *Ibid.*
23 *Ibid.*
24 'The Nightmare': *The Poems.*
25 *Ibid.*
26 See Clare's own footnote to 'The Nightmare' and 'The Dream': *The Poems.*
27 *The Prose.*
28 Martin's *Life.*
29 *Ibid.*
30 Mark Storey, *op. cit.*
31 *Ibid.*
32 *Ibid.*
33 *Ibid.*

20 Removal to High Beach

1 Throughout this chapter, and following chapters, I have reverted to the original spelling of High *Beach* – meaning *bank* and not *tree*. This spelling was used in the Chapman and Andre Map of 1777 and was also in regular use by local people up to the early part of this century. Several of Clare's correspondents used it and Mr Sydney Lawrence Young – who was born at Fairmead Cottage, High Beach – confirms that this is the correct spelling.
2 *The Letters*: 27 August 1835.
3 *Ibid.*
4 Clare correspondence: BM Egerton 2245–48.
5 *Ibid.*
6 *Ibid.* See also Clare's letter to Taylor, 15 January 1835.
7 'First Love's Recollections': *Midsummer Cushion.*
8 'With Garments Flowing': *Selected Poems.* Edited by Anne Tibble (1965).
9 'Child Harold': *The Later Poems of John Clare.* Edited by Robinson and Summerfield (1964).
10 *Ibid.*
11 Martin's *Life.*
12 Quoted in June Wilson, *Green Shadows* (1951).
13 *Ibid.*
14 'Scandal': *The Poems.*
15 'Braggart': *ibid.*
16 'The Schoolboy': *The Poems.*
17 'River Scene' ('Now came the river sweeping round'): *ibid.*
18 'November': *ibid.*
19 'Trespass': *ibid.*
20 'Remembrances': *Midsummer Cushion.*
21 Clare correspondence: BM Egerton 2245–48.
22 *The Letters*: 23 November 1837.
23 *Ibid.* See Asylum letters 1841.
24 Quoted in June Wilson, *op. cit.*
25 Clare correspondence: BM Egerton 2245–48.
26 *The Prose.*

21 Land of Shadows

1 Though provided for John Taylor's benefit, Allen wrote to Taylor's new partner – Walton.
2 S.C. Hall. *Book of Gems* (1838 and 1844).
3 *Ibid.*
4 'An Invite to Eternity': *Selected Poems and Prose.*
5 'Don Juan': *The Later Poems of John Clare.* Edited by Robinson and Summerfield (1964).
6 Allen's letter to Taylor. Quoted in Tibbles' *Life.*
7 Cyrus Redding. *Fifty Years' Recollections* and *Past Celebrities I Have Known* (1858).
8 *Ibid.*
9 'Child Harold': *The Later Poems.* Edited by Robinson and Summerfield.
10 *Ibid.*
11 NMS.
12 *Ibid.*
13 *Ibid.*
14 See J.F. Nisbet, *The Insanity of Genius* (1900).
15 NMS.
16 Tennyson's 'Ode to Memory': *Collected Works.*
17 Spedding's letter, quoted in *Epping Forest: Its Literary and Historical Associations* (1945).
18 Tennyson's 'Ode to Memory'.
19 See Introduction to *The Later Poems.* Edited by Robinson and Summerfield.
20 Copies of these letters made available by Peterborough Museum Society.
21 *Ibid.*
22 'Don Juan': *The Later Poems.* Edited by Robinson and Summerfield.

22 A Broken-down Haymaker

1 *Clare: The Journals, Essays and the Journey from Essex.* Edited by Anne Tibble (1980).
2 The Northborough cottage was always known as 'The Poet's Cottage' up to 1950.
3 *The Letters*: August 1841.
4 *Ibid.*
5 Quoted in Tibbles' *Life.*
6 'Child Harold': *The Later Poems.* Edited by Robinson and Summerfield (1964).
7 *Ibid.*
8 Martin's *Life.* See also editors' note on p. 00.
9 Copy of letter kindly loaned by Delapre Abbey Records Office, Northampton.
10 *The Letters*: July 1848.
11 *Northamptonshire Past and Present*, vol. III, no. 5 (1964).

23 The Asylum

1 Whellan's *Northamptonshire Directory.* First edition (1849).
2 *Sketches in the Life of John Clare.* Letters quoted by Edmund Blunden.
3 W.F. Knight. Quoted in *Northamptonshire Past and Present*, vol. III, no. 5 (1964).
4 Dr Nesbitt's *Annual Report of the Northampton General Lunatic Asylum for 1846.*
5 Quoted in Blunden's Introduction to *Sketches in the Life.*
6 *The Letters.* See Asylum letters 1847–9.
7 *Ibid.*

8 *Ibid.*
9 'Come Hither': *John Clare: Selected Poems*. Edited by Anne Tibble (1965).
10 'A Vision': *ibid.*
11 Quoted in Tibbles' *Life*.
12 *Ibid.*
13 Mark Storey. *Clare: The Critical Heritage* (1973).
14 Laurens van der Post. *Jung and the Story of Our Time* (1976).
15 Northampton General Lunatic Asylum Casebooks.
16 Quoted in Tibbles' *Life*.
17 *The Stamford Mercury* (June 1864).
18 'Love and Memory': *Midsummer Cushion*.
19 'The Last of Autumn': *The Poems*.

Bibliography

Works of John Clare, Published in his Lifetime

Poems Descriptive of Rural Life and Scenery. Printed for Taylor & Hessey, and E. Drury. London 1820. 2nd and 3rd editions 1820; 4th edition 1821.

The Village Minstrel and Other Poems. Printed for Taylor & Hessey, and E. Drury. London 1821. 2nd issue 1823.

The Shepherd's Calendar; with Village Stories and Other Poems. Published for John Taylor by James Duncan. London 1827.

The Rural Muse. Published by Whitaker & Co., London 1835.

Editions of Clare's Poetry and Prose, Published after his Death

The Life and Remains of John Clare. J.L. Cherry. Warne and Co., London 1873.

Poems by John Clare. Selected and Introduced by Norman Gale. G.E. Over, Rugby 1901.

Poems by John Clare. Selected with an Introduction by Arthur Symons. Henry Frowde, London 1908.

John Clare: Poems Chiefly from Manuscript. Edited by Edmund Blunden. Cobden-Sanderson, London 1920.

Madrigals and Chronicles. Edited by Edmund Blunden. The Beaumont Press, London 1924.

Sketches in the Life of John Clare by Himself. With an Introduction by Edmund Blunden. Cobden-Sanderson, London 1931.

The Poems of John Clare (2 vols). Edited by J.W. and Anne Tibble. Dent, London 1935.

Poems of John Clare's Madness. Edited by Geoffrey Grigson. Routledge & Kegan Paul, London 1949.

Selected Poems of John Clare. Edited by Geoffrey Grigson. Routledge & Kegan Paul, London 1950.

The Letters of John Clare. Edited by J.W. and Anne Tibble. Routledge & Kegan Paul, London 1951.

The Prose of John Clare. Edited by J.W. and Anne Tibble. Routledge & Kegan Paul, London 1951.

Selected Poems of John Clare. Edited with an Introduction by James Reeves. Heinemann, London 1954.

The Later Poems of John Clare. Edited with an Introduction by Eric Robinson and Geoffrey Summerfield. Manchester University Press 1964.

The Shepherd's Calendar. Edited with an Introduction by Eric Robinson and Geoffrey Summerfield. Manchester University Press 1964.

Selected Poems of John Clare. Chosen by Leonard Clark, with Introduction by Anne Tibble. Arnolds, Leeds 1964.

John Clare: Selection of his Poetry. Edited by J.H. Walsh. Chatto and Windus, 1967.

Clare: Selected Poems and Prose. Edited by Eric Robinson and Geoffrey Summerfield. Oxford University Press 1966 and 1967.

John Clare: Selected Poems. Selected, with Introduction, by Anne Tibble. Dent/Everyman Library 1965 and 1967.

John Clare: Selected Poems. Selected with an Introduction by Elaine Feinstein. University Tutorial Press, London 1968.

Poèmes et Proses de la Folie de John Clare. Edited by Pierre Leyris. Including *Le Psychose de John Clare* by Jean Fanchette. Mercure de France 1969.

Birds Nest: Poems by John Clare. Edited by Anne Tibble. Including 'Clare the Bird Watcher' by James Kirkup. MidNAG, Northumberland 1973.

John Clare: The Midsummer Cushion. Edited by Anne Tibble and R.K.R. Thornton, with Introduction. MidNAG/Carcanet Press, Manchester 1978.

John Clare: The Journals, Essays, and the Journey from Essex. Edited by Anne Tibble. Carcanet New Press, Manchester 1980.

John Clare: The Rural Muse (second edition). Edited by R.K.R. Thornton. MidNAG/Carcanet, Manchester 1982.

Biographies

The Life of John Clare. Frederick Martin. Macmillan 1865. Reissued with Introduction by Eric Robinson and Geoffrey Summerfield. Cass, London 1964.

The Life and Remains of John Clare. J.L. Cherry. Warne and Co., 1873.

John Clare: a Life. J.W. and Anne Tibble. Cobden-Sanderson 1932.
Green Shadows: a Life of John Clare. June Wilson. Hodder & Stoughton 1951.
John Clare: his Life and Poetry. J.W. and Anne Tibble. Heinemann 1956.
John Clare: A Life. J.W. and Anne Tibble. Michael Joseph 1972.

Catalogues of Manuscripts

The John Clare Collection in Northampton Public Library. Edited by David Powell. Northampton 1964. Supplement added in 1971.
A Descriptive Catalogue of the John Clare Collection in Peterborough Museum and Art Gallery. Margaret Grainger. Peterborough, 1973.

The Manuscripts

See above catalogues for the two major collections.
British Museum MSS. Egerton 2245–50. Six volumes of letters to Clare, from John Taylor, Mrs Emmerson, Lord Radstock, Octavius Gilchrist, the Bishop of Peterborough and others.

Reference Volumes

Baker, A.E. *Glossary of Northamptonshire Words and Phrases* (2 vols). John Russell Smith, London; Abel and Sons, Northampton 1854.
Barrell, J.D. *The Idea of Landscape and Sense of Place in the Poetry of John Clare*. Cambridge University Press 1972.
Blunden, Edmund. *A Selection of Poetry and Prose*. Edited by Kenneth Hopkins. Rupert Hart-Davis, London 1950.
——. *Keats's Publisher*. Jonathan Cape, London 1936.
Cary, H. *Memoir of H.F. Cary*. Moxon 1847.
De Quincey, T. *Works: London Reminiscences*. Edited by D. Masson. A. and C. Black 1890.
De Wilde, G.J. *Rambles Round About*. Dicey, Northampton 1872.
Fisher, James. *The Birds of John Clare*. Kettering 1956.
Gosse, Edmund. *Silhouettes*. Heinemann 1925.
Grainger, Margaret. *John Clare Collector of Ballads*. Peterborough 1964.
Graves, Robert. *The Crowning Privilege*. Cassell 1955.
Grigson, Geoffrey. *Poets in their Pride*. Phoenix House 1962.
Gittings, Robert. *John Keats*. Heinemann 1968.
Hall, S.C. *The Book of Gems*. 1838 and 1844.
Hall, S.T. *Biographical Sketches of Remarkable People*. 1873.
Harrison, Thomas. *Birds in the Poetry of John Clare*. Peterborough Museum Society 1957.
Hood, E.P. *The Literature of Labour*. Partridge, 1851.

Hood, E.P. *The Peerage of Poverty*. Judd and Glass 1859–61.
Hoskins, W.G. *The Making of the English Landscape*. Hodder & Stoughton 1955.
Lewis, C. Day. *The Poetic Image*. Jonathan Cape 1947/48/49.
——. *The Lyric Impulse*. Chatto and Windus 1965.
Marshall, Dorothy. *English People in the Eighteenth Century*. Longmans 1956.
Mitford, M.R. *Recollections of a Literary Life*. 1854.
Murry, J. Middleton. *John Clare and Other Studies*. Neville, London 1950.
Nisbet, J.F. *The Insanity of Genius*. Richards 1900.
Pemberton, Jean Paira. *Poèsie et Folie chez John Clare*. University of Strasbourg 1979.
Redding, Cyrus. *Fifty Years' Recollections*. London 1858.
Richmond, Kenneth. *Poetry and the People*. Routledge and Kegan Paul 1947.
Storey, Mark. *Clare: The Critical Heritage*. Routledge and Kegan Paul 1973.
——. *The Poetry of John Clare: A Critical Introduction*. Macmillan 1974.
Thomas, Dylan. *The Early Prose Writings*. Dent 1971.
Thomas, Edward. *Feminine Influence on the Poets*. Secker 1910.
Williams, Raymond. *The Country and the City*. Chatto and Windus 1973.

Index

WORKS OF JOHN CLARE

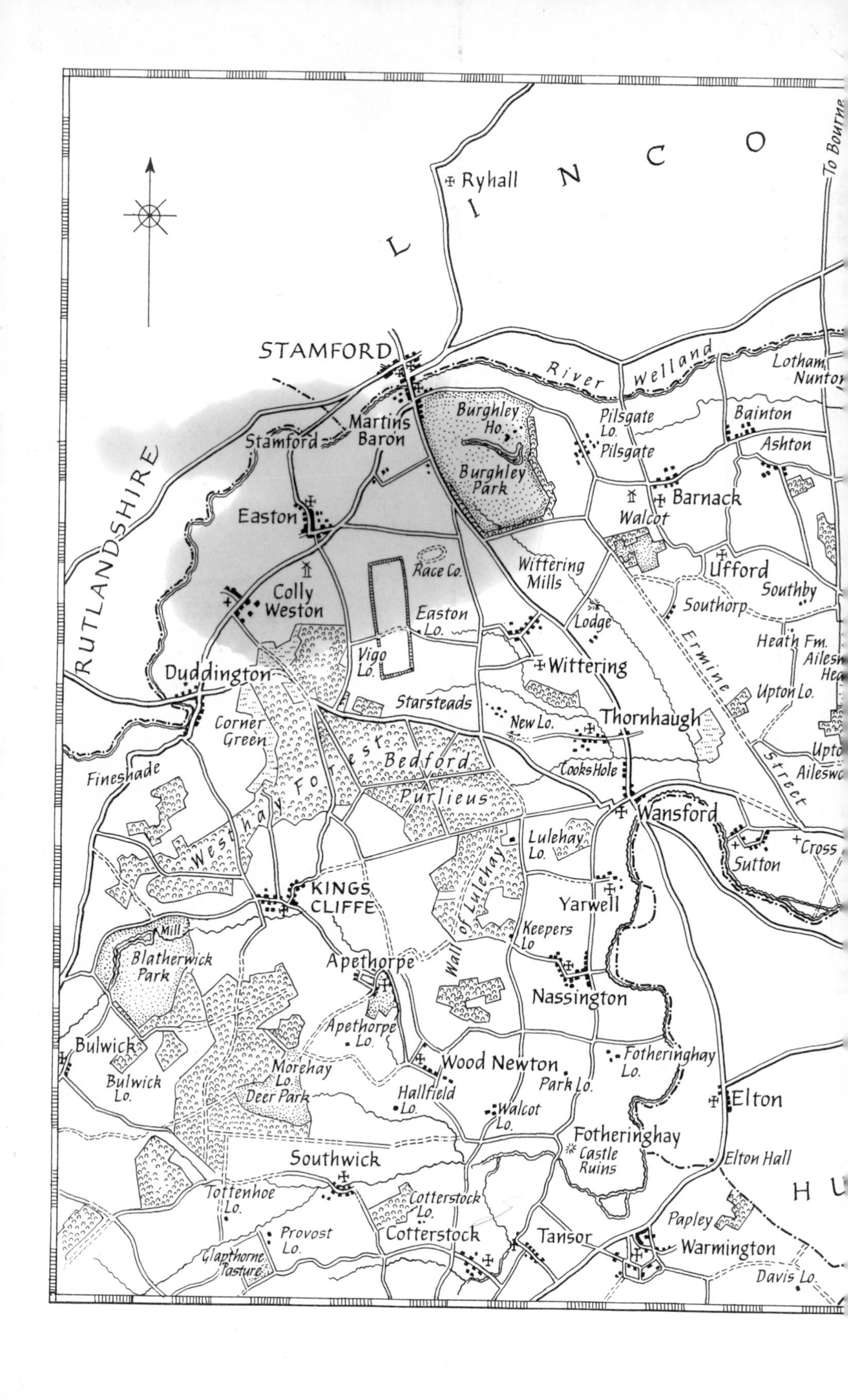

Ryhall
L I N C O
To Bourne
STAMFORD
River Welland
Lotham
Nunton
Burghley Ho.
Burghley Park
Martins Baron
Stamford
Pilsgate Lo.
Pilsgate
Bainton
Ashton
RUTLANDSHIRE
Easton
Barnack
Walcot
Race Co.
Wittering Mills
Ufford
Southby
Colly Weston
Southorp
Easton Lo.
Lodge
Heath Fm.
Vigo Lo.
Wittering
Duddington
Ermine Street
Upton Lo.
Starsteads
Corner Green
New Lo.
Thornhaugh
Bedford Purlieus
Westhay Forest
Fineshade
Cooks Hole
Wansford
Sutton
Cross
Lulehay Lo.
Wall of Lulehay
KINGS CLIFFE
Yarwell
Keepers Lo
Mill
Blatherwick Park
Apethorpe
Nassington
Apethorpe Lo.
Bulwick
Bulwick Lo.
Morehay Lo.
Deer Park
Wood Newton
Fotheringhay Lo.
Hallfield Lo.
Park Lo.
Walcot Lo.
Elton
Fotheringhay
Castle Ruins
Elton Hall
Southwick
Tottenhoe Lo.
Cotterstock Lo.
H U
Papley
Provost Lo.
Cotterstock
Tansor
Warmington
Glapthorne Pasture
Davis Lo.